FIRST HARVEST

FIRST HARVEST

JEWISH WRITING IN ST. LOUIS, 1991-1997

Edited by Howard Schwartz and Barbara Raznick

**Missouri Center
for the Book**

**Missouri Authors
Collection**

The Brodsky Library Press
St. Louis
1997

This book was brought to publication with generous assistance from the
Edith and Lawrence Sagarin Memorial Publication Fund, the Lubin Green
Foundation a supporting foundation of the Jewish Federation of St. Louis,
Rabbi James L. and Lori B. Sagarin, Charles Sandelman, Nathan S. Cohen,
Barbara and Michael Shuman, Mr. and Mrs. Ben Feldman, Edward M.
Londe, Marylou Ruhe, Marcia and Carl Moskowitz, Alice and Irv Sudin,
Sylvia Ray Persow Friedman, Sylvia Cherrick, Janet. B. Eigner, Dr. and
Mrs. Isaac Boniuk and Rose K. Scharff.

First Harvest
Jewish Writing in St. Louis 1991-1997
The Best of the Sagarin Review

ISBN 0-965788-0-8

The Saul Brodsky Jewish Community Library and the Central Agency for
Jewish Education are supported by the Jewish Federation of St. Louis.

With love, we dedicate this anthology to
Ethan Ron Erlich, our new godson.

Lori, Jim and Eliana Sagarin

Contents   i
Foreword   vi
Introduction   vii

I. POETRY

Marc Bregman   3   The Sabbath Bride
Louis Daniel Brodsky   4   Masada in My Pocket
                         5   For the Time Being
Michael Castro   6   For Moise Gadol
                         8   Poem for Grandma
Amy Cohen   11   Shalom Alechem
Ira Cohen   12   Crowned in St. Louis
                        13   The Butterfly Bush
Janet B. Eigner   14   Jewish Quarter, Chania
                        15   How Words Become Unholy
Larry Eigner   16   Remember Sabbath Days
                        16   The Closed System
Ben Feldman   18   What Does My Soul Do?
                        19   Kaddish
Donald Finkel   21   Finders Keepers
                        21   Lame Angel
                        22   Lilith
Rachel Friedlander   24   Recollections of the Night
                               You Got Engaged
Allison Funk   25   Forms of Conversion
Diane Garden   27   Kindness, in his Own Way
Julie Heifetz-Klueh   28   Ezekiel's Wife
                        29   The Messiah's Kitchen
                        30   Poppy Smoked a Cigar When
                               He Did the Backfloat
Betty Harris Ibur   32   Fifty-six Hundred
Jane Ellen Ibur   33   God on Noah
                        33   Grandmother and Me
Malka Z. Kornblatt   35   The Immune System
Staci D. Kramer   36   Yom Hashoah
                        37   A Good Rainbow Is Hard to Find
Rachel Kubie   38   The Early Widow, Ruth
Lynn E. Levin   39   A Stranger Visits Our Seder
Rabbi Bernard Lipnick 41   Limerick
Susan Litwack   42   Inscape
                        42   Two Rivers

Edward M. Londe	45	A Tapestry of Prayers
	46	The Celestial Yeshivah
Jerred Metz	47	Angels in the House
Bert Minkin	48	For Sarah Cohen
	48	The Oral Tradition
	48	The Ketubah
Howard Nemerov	49	To Joy Our Student, Bidding Adieu
Sherry K. Park	50	Lot's Wife Speaks in the Tradition of Lilith
Vicki E. Pickle	51	Sabbath Windows
	52	Her Grandfather's Desk
	53	The Photograph
Rachel Popelka	54	Viva/Vitro
Miriam Raskin	56	Isaac
	56	Sam, Graveside
Dana Robbins Regenbogen	58	The Miracle Within
	58	Still Alive
Lilia Rissman	59	Shabbat
Michele Klevens Ritterman	61	Dad
	61	I Asked the Carpenter
Daphna Rodin	62	Taste
Bronia Rosen	63	Remembering
Lisa Rosen	65	Havdalah
	65	Solitary
Karen Beth Sachs	66	My Grandpa
Jane Schapiro	68	Postpartum
	69	The Beating of Butterfly Wings on a Hot July Day
Andrew Schreiber	71	Queen Esther
Steven Schreiner	72	The Expulsion
	73	In the First Place
Howard Schwartz	76	A Wall Rubbing
	76	The Last Sunset
	77	The Tribe of the Jewelers
	78	The Ghost in the Steam Bath
Shira Schwartz	80	Borrowed Paradise
	81	Sunday Morning in Jerusalem
Laya Firestone Seghi	82	Jewish New Year's Alphabet
	83	Before Memory
Barbara Langsam Shuman	84	L'Chaim
Jean Simon	85	A Calling
	86	Rachel Speaking

Jason Sommer	87	Lifting the Stone
	89	My Ancient Fathers
Judith Saul Stix	90	Noah's Bride
	91	Pilgrimage
Phil Sultz	92	From the Beginning
Wendy Surinsky	93	Lunar Eclipse
Michah Turner	95	In the Beginning
Constance Urdang	96	Mexican Afternoons
	97	Ways of Returning
Shlomo Vinner	98	Training on the Shore
	98	Directing the Traffic
Jane O. Wayne	100	The Family Album
	100	In a Closed Car
	101	From a Half-Filled Cup

II. MODERN MIDRASHIM

Rabbi James M. Bennett	105	Listening to the Angel
Rabbi Tsvi Blanchard	107	The Tale of the Ram
	107	The Tale of the House
Marc Bregman	109	The Third Tablet of the Covenant
	110	The Death of Moses
Rabbi Helen T. Cohn	112	Ruth Packs Her Bags
Lorraine Eason	113	The Tower of Babel
Rabbi Miriam Tirzah Firestone	115	Tirzah's Lament
Julie Heifetz-Klueh	119	Why the Butterfly Is Never Mentioned in the Bible
Jerred Metz	120	Angel Rolling the Heavens Together
Bert Minkin	121	Feet First
Rabbi James L. Sagarin	122	Why God Created the Rainbow
	123	Who's the Best?
Hal Schmerer	125	How the Kaddish Was Discovered
Howard Schwartz	127	Adam's Soul
	127	The Yoke of Moses
	128	The Fiery Serpents
	129	The Dream of Isaac
Laya Firestone Seghi	131	Rivka on Mount Moriah
Rabbi Susan Talve	134	A Midrash on the Moon
	135	And Abraham Rose Early in the Morning

III. JEWISH FOLK TALES

Rabbi Maurice Lyons	139	Missing the Mark

Howard Schwartz	141	Jewish Tales of Illusion
	142	The Enchanted Inn
	145	The Underground Forest
	150	The Tale of the Kugel

IV. LIFE STORIES

Diann Joy Bank	157	Grandma Annie's Gourmet Delights
Gloria Shur Bilchik	159	The Ark and the Poet
Irving H. Breslauer	162	The Tenth Man
Rabbi Helen T. Cohn	165	Esther's Place
Robert A. Cohn	169	Note in a Bottle
Shelly R. Fredman	173	Between Two Worlds: Leah's Story
Gloria Rudman Goldblatt	176	Tricking the Angel
	177	From the Shtetl to St. Louis in 1912
Rabbi James Stone Goodman	180	In Israel They Speak Hebrew
	182	How Reb Shlomo Gave Me My Name
Felicia Graber	187	Metamorphosis
Julie Heifetz-Klueh	190	The Blue Parakeet
Rabbi Robert P. Jacobs	192	Stephen Wise Takes Command
Cissy Lacks	194	Miriam's Way
	206	Dos Iz Mishuga
Edward M. Londe	207	Half a Dream
Marcia Moskowitz	209	Charlie and the Angel of Death
	216	Sheldon
Vicki E. Pickle	221	Schulman's Market
Seymour V. Pollack	222	My Mother and Macy's
Miriam Raskin	229	Forgetting and Remembering
Barbara Raznick	233	A.K.A. Zelda
Marylou Ruhe	235	The Storyteller
Rabbi James L. Sagarin	237	When Our Baby Died: One Father's Story
Joan Schultz	248	A Candlestick Blessing
Howard Schwartz	249	How I Became a Writer
Maury L. Schwartz	258	My Father Read to Me
	260	My Mother Fed Me
Barbara Langsam Shuman	266	The Rainbow Covenant
Rabbi Lane Steinger	269	Mutter
Daniel Suffian	271	Kaddish
Rabbi Susan Talve	273	Sarika's Story

V. FICTION

Rabbi Tsvi Blanchard	279	The Tale of the Garden

Irving H. Breslauer   281   Pincus Edelman
Stanley Elkin   286   Criers and Kibitzers, Kibitzers and Criers
Shelly R. Fredman   316   One Up in the Sky
                                323   Love Like Coriander
Robert Friedman   339   The Legend of Zeml the Wise
Naama Goldstein   341   The Follower
Rabbi James Stone Goodman   349   Basketball with the Ancestors
Gene Holtzman   352   The Professor's Work
Irving Litvag   356   Commodore Levy
Edward M. Londe   361   The Legend of the Gypsy Cantor
                                362   If the Suit Fits, Wear It
                                364   The Tallis Weaver
                                365   The Teffilin that Cried
Rabbi James L. Sagarin   369   Avrom's Light
Beverly Schneider   370   The Four Leaf Clover Story
Henry Schvey   378   The Funeral
Charles Schwartz   383   A Tale of Two Antique Dealers
Howard Schwartz   396   The Book of Vessels
Laya Firestone Seghi   406   Going to the Mikveh
Pamela Singer   426   The Real Revenge of Lilith
Morrie Warshawski   430   Moishe's Dream

VI. ESSAYS
Marc Bregman   437   The Four Who Entered Paradise
Robert A. Cohn   443   The Shared Journey of Philip Roth
                                and Woody Allen Re-visited
Walter Ehrlich   457   The Jewish Community of St. Louis:
                                the First Hundred Years, 1807-1907
Pinhas Giller   462   The Deluge Continues
                                464   Desolation
Rabbi Zvi Magence   466   Generosity
Marc Saperstein   468   The Simpleton's Prayer
Howard Schwartz   480   Spirit Possession in Judaism
Rabbi Susan Talve   486   Creating New Jewish Rituals

Glossary   490
Notes on Contributors   496

Foreword

About 2,200 years ago, the Jewish sage Yose ben Yoezer taught: "Let your home be a meeting place for wise men; become dusty with the dust of their feet; and drink their words as a thirsty person drinks water."

We are living in an age of tension and stress. Our culture gives out mixed signals of conflicting norms. There are times when things are serene and tranquil and other times when things are jittery and fretful. In such times we need to call upon the wisdom of Jewish tradition to help us find our way through.

During the past six years, The Sagarin Review has given St. Louis Jewish authors an opportunity to share their insights and viewpoints. Their individual styles, temperaments and interpretations of the human condition have shed light on what might otherwise be a confusing and contradictory world. We are indebted to them for their artistry and have produced this anthology of their finest writings for wider dissemination.

Our sincere appreciation is extended to each and every contributor to this volume. Particular acknowledgment, however, goes out to Professor Howard Schwartz of the University of Missouri, St. Louis, and his co-editor, Barbara Raznick of the Saul Brodsky Jewish Community Library, for their guidance of this publication from its very inception. Their hard work and dedication have helped ensure a work of the highest standing. Thanks also to Rabbi James and Lori Sagarin for their support of this endeavor over the years. I consider it a privilege to have been part of this cooperative creative effort.

May this able literary work be well-read and well-received.

Rabbi Howard M. Graber, Ph.D.
St. Louis College of Jewish Studies

Introduction

There is an unusually rich literary tradition linked to St. Louis, where writers as diverse as Marianne Moore, Tennessee Williams, T.S. Eliot and Williams Burroughs once made their homes. Among the writers of St. Louis are many Jewish authors. They range from those with national reputations, like the late Stanley Elkin and the poet Donald Finkel, to those first discovering their calling as writers.

This anthology grew out of an unusual community journal, *The Sagarin Review: The St. Louis Jewish Literary Journal. The Sagarin Review* has been published annually since 1991, and this anthology has drawn upon a good portion of the first five issues, plus an issue's worth of new material. Our intention in editing *First Harvest: Jewish Writing in St. Louis: 1991-1997* has been to bring together the best writings by Jewish writers born in or living in St. Louis. It is the first comprehensive anthology of this kind.

The existence of *The Sagarin Review* is due to the support and inspiration of Rabbi James L. Sagarin. From the first, the journal has been published by the Saul Brodsky Jewish Community Library, under the auspices of the Central Agency of Jewish Education. To date, St. Louis is the only city to support such a community Jewish literary journal. In addition, the staff of *The Sagarin Review* has sponsored an annual reading from the contributors of each issue, which has become one of the literary highlights of the year.

In editing this anthology, the editors have embraced a wide variety of types of Jewish writing, from poetry and fiction, to life stories (our most popular category) to specifically Jewish forms, such as modern midrashim, which reimagine legends of biblical and rabbinic origin. We have also included sections on Jewish folklore and essays.

We are grateful to our contributors, who have offered us their best work, and to our readers, who have made the publication of this anthology possible.

We would like to acknowledge a debt of gratitude to Carol Wolf Solomon for her precise proof reading and other invaluable assistance in preparing this volume. Special thanks also go to June Kravin, Gladys Reichenbach, Phyllis Horowitz and Maurice Eichler for their help.

Howard Schwartz
Barbara Raznick

I.
POETRY

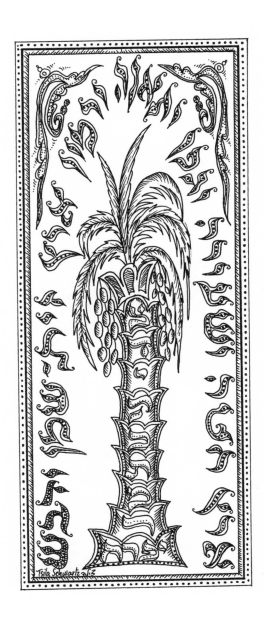

Marc Bregman
The Sabbath Bride

Again I peer expectantly into the darkness
bound on three sides
by the walls of the week.
For six days I have not dared to look beyond,
to gaze above or below or behind the lines and letters.
But now, as the sun sets, I see again—
Slowly her form begins to take shape before my eyes.

As always
she is veiled from head to toe.
Black turns to white in a swirl of light.

As always
I begin the song:

Lekha dodi, likrat kallah
Penai Shabbat neqabbalah

Come on, my friend, to greet the Bride
With Sabbath Queen let us abide

Our song swells.
By the glow of the lights
kindled in her honor
the veil unfolds.
Slowly it unravels
thread by thread

Boldly she steps again into our midst.
We clasp her in our arms.
She rests her head on our shoulder.
She closes her eyes.
We sleep.

Louis Daniel Brodsky
Masada in My Pocket

For the last five days,
I've carried around with me in my pants pocket
Three dolomite rocks
I picked up off the 114-degree floor
Of that flat-topped dome
1300 feet above the northern end of the Dead Sea
Everyone for the past 1900 years,
No matter in which tongue they've stitched memory,
Has called Masada.
Maybe they're mere souvenirs
Or talismans calculated to ward off forgetting;
More likely, they're tokens of pride in my religion
That, with every step, press against my thigh
With just enough bite to remind me
That travail, anguish, fright, even suicide,
Are sacrifices Jews have made for their monotheism.

Despite having been home two days now,
Perhaps the reason I've saved these rocks
Is that I'm a Zealot, one of a band of believers
Refusing to submit to the enemy
Or abnegate my right to pray to *Elohim,*
A survivor transported to this era
Almost two millennia later
To repudiate atheism and paganism.
Ah, but what need have I to keep relics
Such as these three stones from that Herodian fortress
I pocketed five days ago?
Better I surrender them to potential friends
Than throw them at foes
So they might share with me the ecstasy I sense
Realizing dying defying infidels
May not be faith's best way to Paradise.

For the Time Being

For Harry James Cargas

My fifteen–year–old daughter and I
sit outdoors on the porch,
Side by side on an old depot bench,
Quietly reading,
She *The Diary of Anne Frank,*
I *Death of a Salesman.*
Blinded to night's arrival,
We gain insight into signifiers
That have unexpectedly connected us
In a functional oneness
Souls occasionally experience
When least suspecting grace
Will express unspoken intimacies
They've unknowingly shared
Since long before either was born.

Just like this evening,
While grieving independently
Over gratuitous afflictions of literary others,
We've simultaneously intuited
Our kinship with Anne and Willy
And theirs with each other
Through forebears relating me with my daughter,
Her with her dad,
The two of us, Jewish waifs,
Cocooned in affluence,
Sitting side by side on a bench
On history's front stoop,
Quietly reading,
Safe from the past and the future,
For the time being.

Michael Castro
For Moise Gadol

(editor & publisher of *La America*, the first Judeo–Spanish
language newspaper in the United States, 1910–1925)

Warrior for truth,
armed only with pen,
press, & knowledge
that language is power
the powerless don't know
they possess. *La America,*
your organ, vital
beat of a community body
politic, split into clans—
Salonika, Rhodes, Monastir, Constantinople,
Kastoria, Adrianople, Janina, Corfu, the Lower
East Side, Harlem—*La America*
feeds all branches, nurtures
common root, transplants
ancient strength of language tree
to immigrant sidewalks,
dreams. Moses
of the ghetto, tablets
in your pockets, your jobs
are countless, hours endless;
poverty is timeless.

In the beginning
was the Word, Moise. & in *La America*
you/we begin again. Touch
each new arrival, every
neighborhood group. Watch
your watch, pause, think, drink
coffee, eat okra at a cheap cafe;

plot, scheme
how to pay the bills; write notes:
this lunch is research, remember
to mention the need for better food in these
    Turkish corner joints
in the next edition (if you can get it out).
Then off to the next meeting, the next
argument, battle. Abuse & ridicule
your thanks. Bulgarians talk funny
they say. No matter.
Sephardim (believe you/me)
    are clannish, proud
people, with good reason—say
    ignorance, provinciality
the enemy—poverty (a state
of mind)—ego, selfishness,
stages, overcome, stress,
through Unity. *Unidad. La*
America, your organ, plays this song's vital beat
over & over & over:
Unity is Power.
    Language is consciousness: the media
    the message.

(Write on,
Ghetto Moe. Don't mince
words. Remind us
of Babel. Demand
respect, reject
charity, speak out
eccentrically, know God
is one, too; in exile,
too.)

Dead in 1941,
Hitler stalking kin,
broke, half-nuts, buried
by your rival, who could not arrange
a grave site next to your wife's, or
even among our people.
Unity is Power. Is
anyone listening? reading?
praying?

You are remembered, Moise,
by a few, with wry smiles,
as that original—*loco-meshugge*—
who claimed Christobal Colon was
one of us, hustling,
not knuckling under, discovering
yet another home, opening
La America.

Poem for Grandma

The room was dark & full of musty furniture,
plush, velvety, worn armchairs, a velour couch
draped with the lacy yellowing doilies she embroidered,
bowls filled with sucking candies on every surface,
a sense of the grave closing in, the sun banished
for some unseen offense.
Somewhere in the Bronx, circa 1950.
The radio abuzz with guys, like my father, named Joe—
DiMaggio, McCarthy, G.I. (& only last week,
I met a Cheyenne Indian who said, "My name's Joe,
but call me Angel. Too many 'Joes' in this world,
not enough 'Angels'"). She came from Ios, the island
where Homer was born, or so the story goes, as Rebecca tells it.
    She was a Romaniot,

who Grandpa had to teach Ladino.
Got out of Salonika
before the Great Fire set by the British
destroyed the Jewish quarter, before the Turkish bombings, before
World War I, before
the Holocaust, before
all her children.

From that clear Greek birthlight
to smoky steerage, Harlem, another
language (she'd teach him), another walkup
cave on another island, another
beginning to manage: *brisses* & weddings,
the complexities of lives
    never fully here;
    & the burial arrangements, remembering...
    the passage...
of time, each moment a gravestone
knocked over, a piece of candy offered
to sweeten the conversation,
    the accented word
exhaled into the traffic's exhaust,
a stitch in the tapestry, steady
gnarling hands
barely moving in the dimness,
slipping the needle in
& out, & later, lighting
yahrzeit candles, dark-eyed wrinkles
turning back, & squinting, to see
the pattern.
    Dusk
in the worn plush Bronx, alone,
toothless, still squinting

(outliving the others),
in this oppressive shade. Lucky
to be an immigrant smile slowly woven
through New York's patchwork bustle.
　　A fixed jaw. A crack
　　in the drawn curtains of the twentieth century.
A patch of light on the drab dusty rug.
An imperious, stubborn strength beaming down
on her little grandchild.
Michael

Amy Cohen

Shalom Alechem

A mere few hours old he sits among
The rows of babies bundled up to rest.
His cry is like a song that's yet unsung —
We wonder if he knows how much he's blessed
His family that stays fixed and mesmerized
Outside the wall of glass which separates.
"And though he has no name," I realized,
"He represents the good that yet awaits."
He carries in his fist a love Divine
To catalyze recovery from birth.
His newly-granted presence is a sign
Of G-d's persistent hope for us on earth.
And thankfully, he will deliver bliss
When he becomes a Jew at next week's *bris*.

Ira Cohen

Crowned in St. Louis

Rosh Hashanah 5756

My name is boundless
I am hidden even from
myself
No one can understand me
but they know that I exist
What I am becoming
is already here
A thread of light illuminates
the vessel of understanding
The shattered glass which
lies on the museum floor
is a reminder from the grim
past
to wait for what will come
to meet you at the gate of
nothingness
Your secret being will emerge
on the point of a needle
raising sparks which stammer
in the night
The scattered light seeks the
source
Let us sing in unison
all our selves together
with ourselves,
all creatures of the light,
all creatures in the light.

The Butterfly Bush

It happened by chance
that on a mulching expedition
with Michael Castro and Adelia
I discovered that Light was buried
in a Jewish cemetery here in St. Louis
not too far from Kidder.
Of course everyone was there,
Cohens all over the place
& Bravermans, Rothmans—
Schwartz and Ginsberg too.
As if to prove the poem we went
among the gravestones in search
of Light
where I photographed my friends
together in the green
I have seen Light in the graveyard before,
even at night, but something made me
beware of Kidder.
I think it was there I lost my glasses
Nothing can reach me now
unless I find my true heart's vision—
walk straight into the sunlight
Hello, Sam—Hello, Minnie
Coming from the desert we bring you stones.

Janet B. Eigner
Jewish Quarter, Chania

> *Now to lime I entrust/ My true Laws.*
> *Olysseus Elytis The Axion Esti*

You too could miss it,
as you hike to the Cretan shore,
follow Ida's curving pencil lines
to the synagogue at Chania,
on tiny dead-end Kondylaki lane,
white stucco crumbling in sunny chiaroscuro,
where comets of redolent jasmine roof courtyards,
and squat widows in black
vine laundry through rouge bouganvilla.

You too could miss it,
charmed by the laze of calico cats,
the soothe of gray fieldstone at your feet,
until your eye follows the outdoor canary's song,
and, head up, you notice two large hemispheres,
windows like dark, half-open eyes in a scarred stone face,
filigree of iron for lashes,
Stars of David for pupils,
rusted above granite half-nude of its clay cover,

and if you doubt *Der Fuhrer's* smirch,
push the padlock on the rough planked door,
gaze through the inch of space your effort gains
at the dusty courtyard
empty of all but the strutting randy cock
who courts his hens.

How Words Become Unholy

When the ceremonial moment arrives
to mouth aloud or in silence a word or phrase,
held by centuries of men in the palm of communal awe,
your jaws stiffen, your gut tangles.

You are alone as when in his company you first might have adored him,
might first have trusted him as though he were a god,
before his slow harrow
raked your soul of its shield,

before he wrapped *Shema* in false holiness,
Shema which no longer meant blessed,
cast a pious cape over his shame,
spit at your hope,

while at the temple
without ever owning his deed,
nor begging your forgiveness,
he displayed
the good daughters who answered his prayers,
Master, Lord, Our Father,
and you stood next to him, half his height,
heard him say with a tremble too familiar
Adonoi, excluding safety, compassion,
those resonant words,

though now you can,
alone on the whisper of feet,
walk the Indwelling Sky with ground, raven, *Shekhinah.*

Larry Eigner

Remember Sabbath Days

Remember
Sabbath days to
keep time still
how multiple clothe
the past it's
not bare but
it takes time
to look eat
and prepare darkness
among the stars.

The Closed System

The closed system
Of earth
Of the Ark

Love
Mercy

shut him up carefully
in it like involved self the
wandering spot with
the man family beasts

the needs after predictions of
your own acts

rise up go forth
on the water beyond
the walls that
can be made

creation
and the floods
the more there is the more
begins

a kind of chain
firecrackers or
burning woods
having defined a thing
and called it Evil
in all proportion
the outsized Men

Ben Feldman

What Does My Soul Do?

Under an umbrella of stars
pulsing their light

I sleep. What is it
my soul does in sleep

when dreams overflow,
washing the walls

of my mind?
Under the moon

does my soul lift its hands
trying to cup the moon glow

splashing from the urn
of the moon's dark chamber?

In the vortex of night,
beside the bed of sleep

I utter the *Shema*
with a heart poised in prayer.

For if my soul fails to return
to my body's home

when the fire of morning beats its breast
to the annunciation of day

and the spider moves
from the eye of her web

God will know
I never forgot the *Shema*,

Never.

Kaddish

From dust God breathed man
into life.

An act of holy breath
surpassing any illusion

a magician knows.
But God is no magician

and man was not made
from immortal dust.

When the light
of the heart darkens

like the crow's black coat
behind the back

of a dying sun
we fall onto the earth

our bed of bones
and speak no more.

But the dead listen
in the earth's cool chamber

to the blessings

of the *Yahrzeit* flames

in the rooms of our memory
while the heart

murmurs the *Kaddish*
sanctifying God

in the palm
of our dearest

loss.

Donald Finkel
Finders Keepers

In that tribe the priests are chosen
for memory alone
they have forgotten nothing
can give the gods their testimony
twelve nights running
chanting to each of the four winds in turn
that none be insulted

whereas the poets have memories
so frail
rising they remember neither
the nightmare nor the night before
wake without history
forebears
crying
ma ma
a lamb on a stone

each day
they construct anew
not merely their own
truncated lives
but the language of the tribe

Lame Angel

Lame Angel slumps at his desk
his basket is empty
but his hand
clasps and unclasps the indifferent air
like an embryo practicing its grip

like an embryo
he practices everything
swimming creeping chinning himself on the cord
even flying in place

under his shirt his downy shoulderblades
throb like a deer's first horns
he scrapes them against his chair

sometimes in high places
he goes to use them
as a one-legged man might run from a burning house
he'll die before they sprout

clenched in his teeth perhaps
a morsel of wind
a worm rehearsing perpetually the life of a butterfly
but a worm to the end

Lilith

She hissed in my ear
What can you lose?
she wasn't bad
but for the nose
that battle axe
long loose black hair
black arrogant eyes
generous mouth
great creamy boobs
on the frame of a boy
she laid for dwarves
and garbage men
fucked like a snake

beak like a hawk
held open house
in her round bed
without a foot
without a head

where is she now
slithering across what
littered moonscape
stirring with that
irreverent snoot
the dreams of virgins
dry gritty
snatches of spinsters
night lizard
demon of lonely sleepers
while we tumble and turn
in our four square bed
between us a field
a flock a house
two grumbling boys
twenty years
of sweat and bread
and everything to lose

Rachel Friedlander

Recollections of the Night You Got Engaged

For Sheryl and David

Motion underlay the air the night you got engaged:
words to hands to arms to fingers, all the cities
of the heart electrifyingly connected by the colored lines
of moving head and heartlights. I confess that
I was watching through that early winter darkness
—thick grey woolly blanket of December evening—
waiting for your shining solid cylinder of light,
steadfast predecessor, gleaming cone thrown
over hillcrests, pulling all travellers hand-over-hand
heartwards, homewards. When you turned together,
beaming pair, irresistibly illumining us all,
something fell straight into place the way
a child at the front door knows to call "they're here!"
So swing me up in your big bright spotlight,
spin me round like a favorite uncle, leave me dancing
gleaming with the fiercest happiness of knowing
you now pledged for all your journeys, ribbon-threaded
highways linking words to hands, all strands of love,
your own and ours, bystanding; enter with your dazzling news
and fill our living room with light and O my belly solid full of joy.

Allison Funk
Forms of Conversion

Measured in miles or kilometers,
the distance we travel is the same.
A man is so many stone;
pounds do not increase him.

and the beggar who trades rubles
for dollars is still a poor soul.
Yet there are forms of conversion
we regard as miracles: coal, water and air

by some process she does not understand
become the nylons a woman removes
as carefully as a fisherman
loosens a fish from his hook.

And a man who trades one wife
for another sincerely believes
he increases his chances
for love. True—

a stereoscope can synthesize two images
of a London street, giving a viewer the illusion
of entering a foreign place. But bread
remembers its ancestors: wheat and yeast.

Copernicus did not invent our poles
of joy and grief when he found the world
was a guest in the galaxy
circulating shyly around an impressive host.

What does it take to change a person's blood
from say A to O; banish one's parents

to the last seats in a theater: separate
for all time milk from the meat?

The rabbis were rightly suspicious
when I entered the mikvah. They knew
the last breath I took before immersion
would be the air I would choke on again when I surfaced.

Diane Garden
Kindness, in his Own Way

This man a stranger to most
of our family comes every day
to sit *shivah* for my father.
Somehow he's found our house.
At the funeral he kept
on asking, *Is this the place
where they'll bury Mr. Garden?*
While the mourners huddle
humming stories about
my father that fill the rooms,
he just sits by himself,
drinking coke after coke,
upsetting my mother when
he spills them on her floor.
He's completely silent,
but for blurting out
Are you doing this tomorrow?
He doesn't understand
this ancient Jewish ritual.
He only knows my father's
still here for him, that he's
given him a place to come
where he finds comfort in
the presence of so many people.

Julie Heifetz-Klueh
Ezekiel's Wife

I should be used to it by now,
the startle, the pale, sudden intake
of breath over everyday phenomena.
Ants that are not ants
but proud ones going up
with myrtle boughs to the Holy One,
clouds that are not clouds
but breasts of the Shechina
heavy with kindness.
To you the ground speaks back.
And now this latest vision
a massive cloud with lightning
at its center,
a chariot with topaz wheels
that moved but did not move,
wings, four faces, four eyes.

It was a butterfly, Ezekiel.
A small orange butterfly
with eyespots on each wing
looking for marigolds by the Keber
caught in a strong north wind,
pure electric motion.
To you it was God's chariot,
the secret of creation.
And when it passed,
with the usual frantic search for a pen
you disappeared.

I know what comes next,
the absent expression,
my questions unanswered,

in the middle of the night
your side of the bed, empty
breakfast cold on the plate
left as though something has you
by the throat and won't let go
until you're done with it.

Then you'll say it wasn't you,
nothing to do with you,
the ending wrote itself.
And you'll call yourself
an ordinary man, a secretary
who merely takes it down
the way that it's been given.

The Messiah's Kitchen

When the Messiah comes,
She'll have my Grandmother's hands.
We'll find Her in the kitchen on Francis Place
among the jonquils, cookie tins of buttons,
one green Buddha.
There will be an honest brisket in the oven,
the promise of nutmeg and cinnamon.

Most likely She'll be wearing Her baker's apron,
sitting at the table in Her stocking feet
to give Her bunions a rest, while She mends Pop's pants,
rereads the history of Charlemagne, or 101 Famous poems,
humming a family tune.
Startled by the footsteps on the stairs, She'll gather
the strands of rebel silver back into Her sturdy bun,
take out the last of the Rosenthal China:
Tea and schnecken for all Her darling children.

Her lilac eyes,
hungry to hear what the world has taught us in Her absence,
ready to teach the truth about the Angels.
When we hear Her sweet soprano laugh
that never knew a stranger
and sit and listen to the warm
in the muslin afternoon
all that is patient and wise and golden
will put an end to silence,
and each of us will know "She loves me best."

Poppy Smoked a Cigar When He Did the Backfloat

Poppy never talked about God or Heaven.
He told me stories about the Indians in Broken Bow.
Yiddish, Choctaw, what's the difference?

We played Canasta for pennies.
"Take a chance," he'd say. "Columbus took a chance."
He was Lucky Joe at cards. In the morning
he made us 4 fried eggs—bad for his diabetes—
but hot water with lemons for digestion.

In the summer on Sundays we went swimming.
Poppy smoked a cigar when he did the backfloat.
"There's no such thing as too much sun
or too much chocolate," he'd say, paddling by.
March, last time I saw him, I was 20.
I wore red shoes to the hospital. He never moaned
when I showed him a picture
of my Gentile boyfriend, "Take your time,
Dooliebug," he winked. "You can have
the King of Siam if you want him. Me,
next year I'm gonna buy a red convertible."

He said I was his penicillin, better than
chicken soup. Two days later he died.

At the cemetery his coffin looked too small
to hold him. Birds were singing, unexpectedly
the day turned warm. Still, when I feel
like dancing, or throwing aces back to back,
whenever the cherry tree's in bloom, it's Lucky Joe.

Betty Harris Ibur
Fifty-six Hundred

The halls are grey and long
With railings on the side
And many rooms in which we hide our dreams

In wheelchair prisons we are strapped
Like infants we once were
Trapped in a fog

We wait for you to come and touch our hand
And heart so that we understand
We are alive.

Jane Ellen Ibur
God on Noah

Was I completely misunderstood?
He's packing two cans of tuna fish,
chicken wings, oxtails,
pickled pigs feet, turkey necks,
pork chops, frozen shrimp, canned salmon,
jars of herring, chicken backs, turkey tails

Was I that unclear?
Sardines in mustard sauce,
Mrs. Paul's breaded fish sticks,
sides of beef, hog snouts,
rump roasts, chicken breasts,
bacon, hamburger, crabmeat

Was my choice of men so wrong?
Legs of lamb, veal cutlets,
ham steaks, tongue, ham hocks,
turkey tails, jello, buffalo fish slabs,
pork butts, ham shanks, beef ribs,
pork ribs, gizzards, whole turkeys

I'm stunned. Everything is packed
in two's. I shake my head, drop
it into my hands. And now the rain.

Grandmother and Me

poker to her mah jong
scotch to creme soda
wild hair to her hair net
hamburger to coffee cake
purple to her navy blue

I'm skinned knees to stockinged legs
smoke to perfume
horseradish to her plums
mahogany to pine
basement dark to open windows

raunchy to respectability
rough to her smooth
loose to her tight
rubber band to her ribbon
loud to her soft

sweat to her powder
night to her day
peanut butter to her jelly
cowboy hat to hair net
boots to her heels

horse to her taxi
anger to her acceptance
baseball to canasta
wood to her china
outrageous to her calm

denim to her lace
woman to her lady
granddaughter to her grandmother

Malka Z. Kornblatt

The Immune System

Dedicated to Dr. Michael Karl

In the beginning, God created healing.
Then, came pain.
God saw that the healing was good.
God called the healing, Time.

Staci D. Kramer

Yom Hashoah

pieces of blackened flesh
    burn into my mind,
        I remember...

cries of dying children
    haunt me in my sleep,
        I remember...

vultures wearing swastikas
    fly above my head,
        I remember...

Candles shining brightly
    in a ghetto where all is dark,
        I remember...

To the strains of the death waltz
    they danced away their lives,
        I remember...

Even if I wanted to
I could not forget

A Good Rainbow Is Hard to Find

I stepped on a rainbow today
bursting, spinning it disappeared
but I didn't stop to watch
or even look
while it slid across the street

when you break a rainbow
a second rainbow's hard to find
or maybe once you see how fast
they disappear
it's harder to look for that
second rainbow

never mind the pot of gold

Rachel Kubie

The Early Widow, Ruth

On a fool's blue night she's left
to slap at strangers' fence-posts
and kick up tufts of weed.
She feels a fool and lost again,
with one cool orange in her pocket
(and a slow yellow moon lifting,
catching up the day's last veil,
softening earth's face to start
her march, her slow procession,
night). Why! She could punch
herself, but there are windows lit.
Strangers are awake. The sunburnt grass
warms her feet and she is tired.
She will stop here; she will sleep
on a bench or in a shed somewhere.
She is alone and cold and hidden
in the dark. Perhaps, she thinks,
she will find the others
in the morning. Maybe she was right,
and this is on the way. Her ring
is loose; it slips from her finger
and she holds it in her fist.
She is growing thin.

Lynn E. Levin
A Stranger Visits Our Seder

Each year, we've joked nervously of this,
and now the moment's come—
Sam opens the door as the fourth cup's poured
and, behold, a stranger's there.
Wrapped in a torn blanket, a leather belt,
topped with matted hair,
stinking to high heaven, he bellows,
"Good news! Good news!"
and limps, spring mud on his weary shoes,
into the home we've scrubbed and polished for Passover.
Silence falls upon us like an April snow.
We halt as in a fresco of a feast:
cousins in mid laugh;
Mom as she leans to kiss Joel;
Joel, his eyes round as the hard-boiled eggs;
Sarah, her mouth wide open
as her grape juice spills upon her plate.
"Be fruitful and multiply!" he commands and shambles near.
Lunatic, I think. Dangerous fanatic.
I can see it now, the family falling before his wrath
like so many bottles of wine upon the white tablecloth.
He flails a haggadah and smiles a wild smile,
"Justice, justice shall ye pursue!
Study for justice. Study for the trial."
The hungry lions of his eyes roam
from face to face, seeking whatever it is madmen seek—
weakness or wisdom, converts, enemies,
dreamers of the same dreams.
"What a spread!" he says eyeing the place.
He lifts a piece of matzoh.
"This is the bread of affliction!

This is the bread our forefathers ate in the land of Egypt!
Bring on the serving plates!"
He takes the prophet's chair,
drains the silver cup in one gulp.
"Nu? I haven't eaten since yesterday."
We pass brisket, kugel, tsimmes.
"Let all who are hungry come and eat!" he cries with an upraised fork.
"Let all who are in need come and celebrate the Passover."
To Joel and Sarah, pale as potatoes, he sighs,
"Ah, the kinder. The world rests upon the breath of children."
Then his eyes dart around the room, he spies
a Lladro on the coffee table, jumps up,
smashes it, and cries,
"Idols, Idols and chatchkes! False dolls!
How could you? You...you...Jezebel!" he shrieks at me
as I try to call the police.
That's when Sam and Morris collar him
and throw him out into the street.

Rabbi Bernard Lipnick
Limerick
Based on Gen. 17:17; 18:12

There was once an old man named Abe
Whose wife was promised a babe
Though they laughed at the thought
To them little Isaac was brought
By a celestial midwife called Gabe.

Susan Litwack
Inscape

When a woman cannot open her heart
she cannot breathe.
When she opens it
strange things fly in:
demons and angels
without wings
snow falling
homeless whisperings
calling
from a world
without words.

When a woman opens the heart
she is praying for her soul.

Two Rivers

I was born where two rivers meet.

My parents wanted me. They only had my brother.
With me, they replaced themselves.

Lions guarded the entrance to the city.
The street was umbrellaed with trees,
Summers, we sat on the porch, swatting mosquitoes,
sucking on ice
Winters, snow cushioned the metal seats,
sending the gossip inside.

There was the house where no one came or went
the dog with the big belly
Mrs. Rowden who could only make boys

and Ilene's father who did Playboy pinups with oils.
There was the boy who punched me in the gut
out of some crazy passion,
after twenty years, said he was sure sorry
he was bringing home big money
now but had no wife.

I bopped the avenue but caught a generous whacking
and my brother was commissioned
to take my hand, pull on my gummy boots
and ruin my chances of being someone on the playground.

I never had a room of my own.
I slept with my brother, his incessant banging on the blue radio.
Slept with my grandmother in her bed but she never
rolled over on me she was too careful and too old.
Slept with my younger sister in the pink beds, pulled apart
then pushed together depending on whether we were speaking.

I was alone only when my eyes closed.
I kept my dolls stuffed in drawers.
I told my sister I hated her in my sleep
and flat denied it in the morning.

I saw my parents struggling to provide happiness
for the aunts and cousins upstairs
but it never worked.
The first cousin died, but not before
we went to see Gypsy Rose Lee.
The second took his own life, which it is bad luck to confess.
The third made millions happen too quickly.
He made handsome sons and one beautiful daughter.
He ate cigars like candy. His wife was a hometown beauty.

There were disappointments.

The dog spilling his guts on the doorstep
and not telling anybody,
the pain of his empty cage, his uneaten food, his heavy chain
attached to the house like an umbilicus.

The doctor who kept saying I'd get taller
and broader and the boys who hemmed and hawed
and puffed themselves up like toads.
Many became fat forever. Others shrank to almost nothing
having wasted themselves pumping gasoline
and drinking Boone's Farm wine until morning.

I grew up all told on Amherst Avenue.
I fell in love with a blonde boy who loved Jesus.
The day my grandmother died I stopped eating animals.
I saw the Cardinals take the pennant by surprise.
I saw the Gateway Arch give my city respect.
I heard the President die on the radio
as I bumped home on the school bus.
I didn't know the difference between South and North.
I saw older boys refuse to fight for any country.

I left home three times
before I finally left for good.

I felt strong currents thinking of the Mississippi
spread out like long fingers, reaching beyond Missouri.

Edward M. Londe
A Tapestry of Prayers

On a plain surrounded by mountains
whose majestic heights
are haven to angels,
a tapestry of prayers woven by *Tzaddiks* in Safed
ascends at dawn each day.

A cello, its baritone voice
can be heard echoing through the canyons;
a beautiful note held eternally.
Its colors are as tides on a pristine beach
on an undiscovered island.

Listening we can hear their hymns of praise
to our Father.
The sunrays frolic upon the peaks
as young mountain goats in spring,
then kiss each peak
as a mother kisses her children
when they sleep.

When we die, we become stars in the sky.

The Celestial Yeshivah

For all who have lost a child

The first breath and last breath are one.
We shatter the shackles of time
to take an angel's path
to that celestial yeshivah
where all young men go
when they die.
So fathers, mothers, your sons
are in the company of *Tzaddiks.*
Shed tears as you must, but be joyous
to know the company
they now keep.

Jerred Metz

Angels in the House

Their wings beat the floor,
stirring the dust.
The hook in the fireplace
trembles and food spills
on the flame.

The dining room rings with their chewing,
their gluttonous cries, their
rumbling bellies. Plates rattle on the table;
the human guests cannot enjoy the meal.

In all the bed chambers
angels cluster about
the dead. Fiercely breathing the
thick air, they lay eggs on the turning flesh.

Books scattered about the floor,
ladders climbing the walls,
the walls themselves full of books,
golden letters stamped on each spine,
the room is filled with words.
In each corner an angel writes and
as it writes it sings of each room in turn
praising each room's name.

Bert Minkin

For Sarah Cohen
(1892-1969)

My grandmother
tucked a shiny sugar cube
between her teeth
to sweeten the hot tea
she stirred with a silver spoon
and sipped from a glass.

Kissing a handful of damp grass
to sprinkle, respectfully, on her grave
I recall her tea–moist lips
anointing my face with sweetness.

The Oral Tradition
For Howard Schwartz

Whenever I tell a story
I see my grandmother's lips moving
as she read to herself
every evening in the kitchen
and pray that the English I speak
resonates with her Yiddish wisdom.

The Ketubah

Long after the vows are heard
and the wedding is over
the written marriage contract
endures and endures.

Memories of passionate embraces, kisses, promises
may be warm and exciting
but, like flesh, they are fleeting.
You'd better get it in writing.

Howard Nemerov

To Joy Our Student, Bidding Adieu

In Memory of Joy Ezra

Your friends, dear woman whom I never knew
But by the delighted kindness of your smile,
Impersonal but kindness and delight
Received and like a blessing on the day,
Had got accustomed to the thought of death
As age and preparation and farewell,
With things to settle, time to settle things
Before we left; now you've surprised us
As you had scarce the time to be surprised,
Leaving the company and the lighted room
With the wine and warmth and amiable talk
To go home in darkness, on the rainy roads,
To cross the avenue none gets across—

But suddenly, my dear, struck off the books,
Gone missing in the middle of the way
For time's remainder, such as it may be.
Remembering your smile, I wish that I
Had learned it better, and got it down by heart,
That no more lights the narrow hall of day
With all your troubled kindness, your delight.

Sherry K. Park
Lot's Wife Speaks in the Tradition of Lilith

I disagree
with a God
willing to destroy
his reflection
in Sodom and Gommorrah.
Self-hatred.

My plump red heart
floats in scentless salt,
frozen in milky curved clouds,
and love speaks to me from
the world's materials:
the half-shell of a
hatched robin's egg,
the dried brown rose petal.

I would rather
be Lot's salty wife,
and look homeward
to brimstone scorched
instinctual flesh
than go forth
cynical in a flawed
God's work.

So I am
sown with salt,
frozen
in the powerful
sterility of my
good backward gaze.

Vicki E. Pickle
Sabbath Windows

A musty taste hits a parched tongue.
Stained curtains hang to the sides
of an old bedroom window
where a bee buzzes over a sunflower.
A white spread
is thrown carelessly
over unmatched sheets and baubled pillows.
Chenille dots like poppies in a peasant field.

I lay sideways on the bed
playing solitaire.
The smell of kasha
lingers down the narrow hallway
from Grandma's Sabbath kitchen.
She moves between the kitchen
and me. Playing an ace.
Cooking kasha.
I listen as she tells me
where to place the next card,
always hoping to win.
I leave my imprint
on the soft, yielding mattress.
The sun fades.
I tuck away Friday's games.

By the kitchen window
Grandma drapes white lace
over coarse, black hair.
In silence, I watch
her arms circle over candles
in graceful motion. Her eyes covered
she recites the ancient blessings,

carrying on the traditions
of her grandmothers before her.

Her Grandfather's Desk

Her Grandfather's desk sits unpretentiously
in the corner of his den.
It is filled with a lifetime
of memories. Yellowed photos tucked away
under unpaid bills. Losses unspoken.

On a chair carved with horses
the language of his youth
enters her heart. Her legs
swing over his knee. Stories
stream in Russian and Yiddish.
The words of ancestors.
An immigrant's life.

The top drawer is filled with trinkets.
A special piece of gum,
just for her. A deck of cards
breezes by her nose
as he pretends to bite it off.
A poker hand lays unplayed.
The floor lamp casts a shadow
over diamonds, over clubs.

Echoes of laughter
sail out patio doors.
Birds gather to eat
their daily portion
of this grocer's bread.
His philosophy becomes hers.
She lays her head against his chest,
leaning on Grandpa and the cherry walnut desk.

The Photograph

He rubs the worn edges
of the photograph
like the fringes
of a cherished *tallit,*
kissing each solemn face.

Mother, Father,
sisters, brothers.

Like the gentle heart
of a wounded soldier,
he keeps the images
in a safe place
undisturbed, immortalized,

the secret hiding
only appropriate
considering his losses.
He loosens the board
in the drawer of newspaper
clippings and bills,
part of the ritual.

Circling the tear-stained
photograph, he touches each soul
with the words of a mourner,
Yit ga dal ve yit ka dash
she mei ra ba.
The echos surround him.

Leaving the photograph,
he lives another day
of life.

Rachel Popelka
Viva/Vitro

A *minyan* of silica,
Following the rhythms of *klezmer.*
The spaces between these dancing forms,
No more than the starry holes in between
The branches of the Sukkah.

Each letting the divine
Weave a web of
Vitreous elements
That entwine the sacred vessels
Into a central Torah.

Each one a piece of the other.
Singing in joy, they
Bind the dark lines of the *tallis*
With the ancient
Crowned calligraphy.

The tied *tzitzit*
Entwine not only cord
And commandments,
But tie the ends
Of the Diaspora.

Shake the *etrog,*
The *lulav,*
Reach to all corners
North, south, east, west–
To the heavens and earth

To come full circle
Sidelocks curling

The spiral scrolls
of the tree-ringed Law.

Inspired by a glass sculpture at the St. Louis Art Museum entitled:
"Hoshanos (Special Prayers)" by Gianni Toso.

Miriam Raskin
Isaac

Resuffering the past,
presuffering the future,
allows me no rest.
Night after night I close my eyes,
my head down on the ground again,
and somehow see it all again:
myself high on Moriah again,
on top of that wood again,
knife at my throat again,
ready to breathe my last again,
and I tremble again,
exceedingly tremble again,
and I am saved again.
Why am I saved again?
Save the others, I say,
save the six million, I say,
and he says No again,
and I must wake again
and wonder why.

Sam, Graveside

At the side of the grave he stands and waits,
ready to confront for the first time the real thing,
real death, not the Saturday morning TV variety
that takes life from creatures that never had any.
I watch this little blue-eyed guy with freckles—
reddish hair half hidden under a blue *kippa*—
and am awed by his cool. He is almost nine,
and sure, already, of who he is, or soon will be.
I see how the mix of genes that made him—
sturdy ones that, between them, survived

potato famines in Ireland and pogroms
all over Europe—gave him the right stuff.

It pleases me that he is here, somber and straight,
every bit as interested in death as he is in life.
Have you been to a funeral before? I ask.
"No," he says, unsmiling, "but I know all
about death. I've read about it in books."
Ah, Sam. I've read about it in books, too
and am not half so confident, so tough.
He watches carefully, then lifts the spade
to drop some clods of dirt upon the coffin.
Inside, I think my aunt is also proud.

Dana Robbins Regenbogen
The Miracle Within

From the den
I can see the light
emitted
from the menorah.
The candles,
small as they are,
radiate a brilliant light
that illuminates the room.
Perhaps I can ignite
the light
within myself,
thus illuminating
my world.

Still Alive

The hands that used to beguile us
with your magic tricks
now lay curled at your side.

The legs that hoisted us
on pretend circus rides
now struggle with every step.

Even your lips betray
the words
you wish to speak.

But your eyes
so much alive—
dance with joy as they
gaze upon your great-grandchildren.

They cannot hide

Lilia Rissman
Shabbat

We leaned weakly on our front door
and fell in as our step-mom
pulled it open.
We dumped our lives
on the floor of the hall—
our saxophones and flutes,
shoes and coats,
books and backpacks,
and the occasional latch hook.
Oh no, take all of your junk to your rooms!"
We followed orders
and strolled into the dining room
where dinner was already laid out.
It was a relatively short service
we sang candle and wine blessings
(the long version!)
and bread blessings.
During the prayers my aunt was the only one
who didn't even attempt to be in tune.
With Judaism, the Sabbath
is supposed to be a time of rest,
but with loads of homework
and full-time jobs,
soccer games, community service
friends, and (omigod, like, social lives?)
It's easier to be American than it is to be Jewish,
so Shabbat never really happens.

But after a hearty dinner
the words and melodies of our songs and blessings
are sweet and familiar
and I feel real joy in singing them.

Some might look at our daily lives
and think we're just as much Gentiles as Jews,
but on out Shabbat,
no matter how different,
I feel just as Jewish as anybody else.

Michele Klevens Ritterman

Dad

In memory of Morris Brandeis Klevens

Dad,
what are you doing
around here,
spying on me
from behind the newspaper stand
like a jealous lover.

How young you are!
and handsome,
with that European style.

Now that you're gone,
you're everywhere.

I Asked the Carpenter

I asked the carpenter
to ease the edges
of the wooden fence posts.
I felt the loss
of my father
too sharply
in the corners roughly cut,
as if they might easily
cause fresh harm.

"So, ease the edges,
please," I said.

This the builder could
and did.

Daphna Rodin
Taste

I have a pretty Arab friend
We speak Hebrew together
When I eat
She wishes me a good appetite
She simmers beef in olive oil and green spices
The smell warms the kitchen we share
I breathe her dinner and eat tomatoes with cheese
Our smiles to each other are warm as the kitchen
She giggles with her friends
They are all so pretty
They give me tastes of their food
It smells more exotic than it tastes
I thank them
Smiling into their flushed faces

Today a policeman followed my friends
Threatening and shouting
"It is because we are Arabs" one girl tells me
My friend cries angrily
She babbles about the Jews
And the underprivileged
I watch her
I comfort her as I can
She touches my knee to tell me more
I want to say "see I am a Jew"
"They thought we were terrorists"
She cries
She will not be consoled
I stare at her wet cheeks
I don't speak
Her pimple scars blink
Like red lights
We are
Each other's bad guy

Bronia Rosen

Remembering

Remember, remember, child of mine,
how it was in the ghetto,
remember, remember your life,
how it passed by.

Grits and wheat flour,
black bread and black coffee,
that's the only thing we have here,
that's like prison life.

The king of the ghetto is old Chaim Rumkovski,
he takes care of everybody,
and he thinks to be famous someday.

We got our own police force,
We got our own post office,
We got our own commissary,
but it's all a dream,
because the Germans can come and destroy
it all in a minute.

The commissary is pretty busy,
they give out all the food,
the food is not so good,
but at least our stomachs don't growl.

It's better for the government workers,
they get not only grits,
but meat and butter and cheese,
they eat that and are all happy.

The best is for the smugglers,

they're not afraid of the guards,
they jump over the fences,
and give good things to us.

Even Chaim is really mad,
but the smugglers don't worry about that,
they lay down their own lives,
and they get rich by themselves.

The country and the government,
that's only a dream,
everything can be destroyed in a minute
by the German soldiers.

Lisa Rosen

Havdalah

The Rabbi's children speak three languages.
English for their country;
the language of Shakespeare and computers,
science, business and Hollywood.

Yiddish is spoken to family,
the bittersweet humor of the *Shtetl,*
years of exile,
a world unto ourselves.

Hebrew is reserved for prayer,
the language of God and Commandments
chiseled in stone.

Solitary

Late night, a crack of light outlines the door.
The furniture staggers and thumps in William's room.
In the *Old Testament* Jacob lay down to sleep in the desert
but wrestled instead all night with an angel.
William struggles alone with heavy furniture:
a dresser, a bookcase, a desk, a bed.

Karen Beth Sachs
My Grandpa

Bouncing belly
swaying side to side,
you *daven*
the *Amidah*
Back and forth.
Down and up. Never
missing a beat. Every
Shabbas morning in a seat
assigned to no one but
you.
        I watch
as you remove your *tallis.* Old and
ragged it makes do.
Any *kippa* will please.
On your head it stays
glued.
        You taught me
the Torah. Prepared me
for my day. You too
chanted, you led us all,
your mumbled voice
harder to understand
harder. Amazed
I watch and smile.
Say with nothing but
pride, this
is My Grandpa. I
love you,
My Grandpa.
        I watch
as you
lie on that

hard cot, tubes
stick everywhere.
Your shaking chest
rises and falls.
I *daven* now. Tears in
my eyes. I want to turn my
tears away. But I
stay. You will be safe. Hold
my hand.
    I love
you my
Grandpa.
I love
you.

Jane Schapiro
Postpartum

> *"To her that flies in rooms of darkness—pass quickly, quickly, Lilith."*
> *(Hebrew inscription to Lilith, the demoness who strangles newborns.)*

Lilith. It's you isn't it,
casting your shadow across my lawn,
your nails scraping against my window screen?
You're watching me, I can see
the black coins of your eyes.
Come in, come in, she's waking,
any minute her scream.
Down the hallway, second room on the left,
you'll find the door's unlocked,
I've been waiting for you.

Don't worry.
She's alone.
Do what you do,
but tell me,
I'm not the only one am I?
There must be others like me who
in the early hours
empty their breasts and swear
this is the last,
not another drop more.

How many confessions
have you heard in unlit rooms?
The mother who keeps dreaming
the same dream, her daughter face down
on the ocean's floor and herself
sleeping soundly
oh so soundly on the warm sand.

Perhaps you've seen me
bending over the crib,
my spine arched like a readied bow,
my fingers, feet braced.
We're all the same aren't we?
We come so close, to the almost,
the nearly,
and then that cry. It breaks
through like a cold brick
and before we know it
we're swaying again,
hoisting the warmth into our arms,
rocking, patting, pressing,
humming. Inside worn-out tunes

your name, Lilith, Lilith,
keeps turning up,
a charm spewed from the sea,
a new moon reminding
it's possible, a woman can fly off
like the night heron
in any direction.

The Beating of Butterfly Wings on a Hot July Day

On our way home in the middle of traffic
my nephew leans forward from the backseat and asks
if God is watching,
listening to us this very minute.
Puddles spot the sidewalk.
A willow sways inside a breeze.
Two butterflies descend on a roadside weed.
He waits for my answer.
I concentrate on each word, each pause, aware
of myself moving into focus. For a second

I emerge, become
the gust of wind.
Later we'll talk of other things,
he'll leave, I'll dissolve
into the background,
a detail,
essential, like the puddle,
the breeze,
the breeze on the willow,
butterfly wings
on a hot July day,
but slight,
so slight
nothing matters, not
the question nor the answer.
Only the asking marks a difference,
the coalescing,
the beating of butterfly wings on a hot July day.

Andrew Schreiber
Queen Esther

The old chair didn't lend much support.
As I sat with a blank expression,
the table was a barrier between us.
Her tremulous voice echoed through my head.
"Open the book."
My eyes scrambled over the page
looking for a familiar pattern,
a place to start.
I stumbled
through verses,
Every so often looking for reassurance
and getting a slow nod,
the light catching in her silvery crown.
Finally, after struggling
I let out a sigh of relief.
She looked at me with a smile
"Not bad," she said, her eyes twinkling.
I gratefully took my reward, bubble gum
and a seven day rest.

Steven Schreiner

The Expulsion

After the painting by Thomas Cole

Anger carved a deep river,
a river of anger carved deep
and buried in the still stone.

Point your staff that way, over there;
prop his arms up men
if you want to win this fight.
Even so,
I will not forget
your first act: to name,
nor your second, disobedience.

They ran, hiding their bodies,
clutching at breast and crotch
caught by bushes
hooked with thorns, flesh
jagged rocks tore,
the heat departing.

That was the hour God chose to walk there.

How long did they have
to leave the garden;
the lambs confused, the birds aware
of commotion and species,
predatory darkness, the easy kill?

They were walking a long time
when the sword's light dimmed
behind the first curve.

It would be slow centuries
before they would know the earth again.

They walked, changing before their own eyes
into each other's need.
Denial drove them.

That night
they feared the dark
but cherished each other more

And dreamt long marches
following their bodies
long columns, trees burning,
moving to a flow unseen
the angry river.

In the First Place

1.
I don't think I ever understood
my mother's pain. The birth
after forty, the words I overheard

on the school ground. Janet
looked different, and all babies
are ugly, but at a month or two

when I said something
I was told to be quiet. Mother
went back to teaching Special Ed.

2.
This morning I read of
a tall, awkward boy named David

taught by a retired teacher

to tell time and to read.
One day he shouted
"It's a quarter past four"

to strangers, giving them his gift.
When he learned to read
"The cat runs up the tree"

his mother wept. In his prayers
at night he spoke
to God: "You are so good to me."

3.
I never saw my mother weep.
Each time I think of Janet
running up the street

to meet me home from school,
leaning and tottering
and nearly losing balance,

I think of how happy she was
to recognize my face,
to know the meaning

of home. All the way down the hill
her small hand, permanent
and warm, drew me toward our house.

When the brief witness of her mind
let go, my mother said simply,
"The hospital called."

4.
Under her pine tree
Janet's bronze plaque tells time.
My mother may own the plot next to hers

near her late husband, and there
she may choose to lay down
the burden she kept unborn.

My mother taught me not to weep
for the joy Janet felt
or the chance to see her again

where there are no books
and there is no time, where we began
to believe she came from in the first place.

Howard Schwartz
A Wall Rubbing

    For Yitzhak Greenfield

Late at night
When no one else was nearby
We reached the Wall
There
While you stood guard
I held this page against a stone
And began to rub.

Soon
Dark letters began to emerge
That slowly formed themselves
Into words
I tried to decipher them
But there was not enough light.

When the rubbing was finished
We hurried home
To read what was written there
But the words
Like tears
Were mute
And all we could discover
In the outline of that ancient stone
Was a long silence.

The Last Sunset

    In memory of Gabriel Preil

Surely Gabriel knew
That he might be returning to Jerusalem
To take his leave

Of this world.
But how
Could he have known it would come
On a Friday night
In the arms of the Sabbath Queen?

The collector of autumns
And sunsets
Has himself been gathered
In the holy land
In the city
Where his soul resided
Even when his body
Was far away.

If only
He could tell us
What the last sunset
Was like.

The Tribe of the Jewelers

A glowing jewel
Like a lodestar
Still guides them through the desert.

While others see a landscape
Of rocks and sand
Stretching before them
They perceive the jewel
Concealed in every rock
Like a hidden sun.

In their hands
The layers of the past peel away

Like the skin of an orange
Revealing the precious core
Within.

The secrets of the jewelers
Are passed down
From father to son:
How to distinguish what is precious
From what is not;
How to cut away what is not needed;
How to set free
All of the hidden
Faces.

This is my tribe.
I can still see my father
Bent over a table
Peering into the eye of the jewel
Searching for the mysteries
Inside.

As I bend over this page
And whisper
The silent prayer of the jewelers,
I hear my father
Whispering my name.

The Ghost in the Steam Bath

Some days
You took me with you
To the steam bath
And now
Whenever I come back
I find your ghost

As palpable as the swirls of steam
Rising up
All around me.

Even though the old bath house
Has been torn down
I can still see you
Surrounded by friends
Sharing tales
Or sitting together
In silence
There
Above all
You were at home.

Dad
If there is anywhere
You can be found
It is here
Even when the steam rises up
Thick as a cloud
I know you are there
On the other side of the room
Curled up on a bench
At rest.

Shira Schwartz
Borrowed Paradise

The opal glistens in the black ocean,
Between blue and black.
Words form, extinguished
By your fiery kiss on my quiet lips.
Unspoken language, questioning itself,
Mystifying the unexplainable, refusing to answer,
Afraid, of the ultimate
Truth.
Passionate lovers hold one another
In moonlight.
Cast between the raw umber of the trees,
On the dewy blanket which dissipates on my body,
Our eyes fixed, staring, through the hard exterior of a once
Painful moment.
And you somehow flew back to this world,
Leaving my borrowed paradise.

A rock placed between sky and sea,
Engraining, engraving, my once soothed soul.
Owls laugh as they close their eyes.
Tears become a waterfall, endless.
Green eyes watch the world in anger,
Red, bloody anger.
A revolution, churned, until
The acid burns my eyes.
Threads, once woven together, are now
Separated
And ripped apart one by one.
I mourn for the lake that flooded,
Or dried out, which was it?
I can't breathe, neither can he

In the blackness of the cold night,
Where my open eyes burn,
Before my tears.

Sunday Morning in Jerusalem

Fallen wombs in a dark pool
Welling up, the blood washes away my tears
Hardened like an egg, ready to crack
Big Bang, lifted up to Heaven, not creation, destruction
Lives taken by a stranger power, suicide.
Attacked, destroyed, abused, stretched to the limits
A bomb on bus 18 on Sunday morning
Number eighteen
Chai, Life .... but it's only death
Terrorists creating terror, terrorizing Jews
Terror, Jihad, suicide, Hamas, sabotage
The gates to heaven are flooding, while one enters the doors of Hell.
Innocent passengers, soldiers, children and teenagers
Cut off from life, cut off from Chai
Prayers rise from the white stone
Like the fog that has settled on Jerusalem
A cry rises from Jerusalem, to be lost forever in God's tears.

(Shira Schwartz was a member of the NFTY/EIE high school program in
Jerusalem in the winter of 1996. She wrote this poem after the second bus
bombing in Jerusalem.)

Laya Firestone Seghi
Jewish New Year's Alphabet

Apples and honey
Brighten the solemn season's
Consideration, introducing
Delight in a New Year:
Elemental winter,
Fundamental spring,
Greening again to
Harvest
In traditional
Jewish time.
Kernels of
Light
Methodically sown,
Nightly, in
Open furrows
Planted with
Quintessential
Religious
Sensibility and
Touching
Ultimately beyond mundane
Vicissitudes to
Wield an
Xceptional
Yearly homecoming, a spiritual
Zenith.

Before Memory

You remember everything
And I remember too
I simply don't remember
that I remember.

The language you speak
comes with difficulty for me
but in your words
I hear my mother tongue speak.

Once, even before memory,
we spoke without translation.
Of what were we speaking
So earnestly?

I recall only
The halting rhythm,
Something hidden,
Something revealed.

Barbara Langsam Shuman
L'Chaim

Gramma Flora lifts high her glass
To just above her head
And with that regal gesture,
So simple and so grand
She proclaims: *"L'Chaim!"*
To life!
To the 96 years she has lived
To the life she prays is ahead for her
And to the long life she wishes for all of us.
My heart captures that moment
So full of grace and meaning.

She has toasted *"L'Chaim!"* on hundreds of occasions
Celebrating rites of passage, milestones, love and joy.
Today she toasts at a small family gathering
And celebrates the blessing of being there.
So many tastes have passed her lips and pleased her palate
From mother's milk to lemonade to wine.
Today her drink of choice is plain water
And she savors the cool clear liquid
As if it were honeyed nectar
Smooth and soothing on her tongue.
Two months later she is gone
And now I replay that sweet, true moment
In my heart and in my mind.
Gramma Flora lifts her glass and proclaims *"L'Chaim!"*
I can see her, hear her now.

Jean Simon

A Calling

Israel is calling me, brashly,
wind whipping
through persimmons and figs,
pine nuts and olives.
I answer her,
flirting with her vendors,
hawking at their corners.
She holds out a frothed hem,
twirling garlands
of rock round her ankles,
each stone a scab.
String-quartet trees bend,
screeching old legends.
She has been trounced
and bounced back,
wounds closed,
with brilliant petals,
memory,
sea-sure grins.

Rachel Speaking

You and I used to sit by the fire and sip looks
till the moon dropped slowly in our blood.
Our people were at war: who heard of a moon and
a star at war, and of sand sipping blood?

We used to lie by the embers
and sip looks till the stars twinkled in our blood.
We sat hidden: I would not show myself to your moon-
on-the-flag lapping up a six pointed star.
Who heard of a moon and a star at war?

You and I used to sway by the fire
while the moon floated on its back in our veins.

It is again war. Brown skin, gold sand, purple blood,
drained moon. We fire.

Jason Sommer
Lifting the Stone

Not when I call them do the pictures come:
I intend to sleep, and a landscape I never knew
I noted reels by as if seen from a car—
tufted grass backed by a stand of trees,
or a cityscape of grey apartment houses
remembered for no reason that I know of,
not backdrop for events, just incidental
music played between the acts, a scene
to watch as scenes change, till a blurry image
of a wooden shack in New York state somewhere,
equally random seeming at first, clarifies
as one of the oddly assorted places
my father pointed out for its resemblance
to the hut that he was born in.

I'm nowhere then,
abstracting his story out of its settings,
wanting to think of it as a large stone,
a boulder under which are things I need.
The straw-roofed Czech village, and the camps
with the strung wire through which the dark eyes plead
like droning whole notes on a musical staff,
a diagram of sorrow, are a stone
which I, a Theseus, putting off majority,
can't lift.

And even imagining I can
take the forms of my anxious dreaming.
I struggle from room to room in some cold warren
and the class has moved, or Zeyde's deathbed
is in thirty-four, a stern attendant says
as if I should know. So these are the Chinese boxes.

The shrinking gift sequentially deferred,
the expectant rise defeated over and over
by another box. The earth conceals its bulk
until the stone is dug out, hugged up,
and below the stone is another, and under that
again a stone, on down into rooty dirt.
Inside the hole I have not properly pictured
in my mind but which in logic must be there,
I finally come to sword and sandals but
they are tiny—baby shoes, a toy sword.

My Ancient Fathers

My ancient fathers
in Schechem and Jerusalem
took grave affront at a mere
tug upon the ringlets of the dark
patriarchal beard,
and the accidental hands
that brushed the Lord's high ark
were a dead man's.

My grandfathers in the ghettoes
of Muncach, Vilna and Prague,
suffered not the razor's touch
upon the temple side-locks,
and as a sign upon their arm,
tight against the skin,
they wrapped the leather thong
of tefillin.

My fathers in the towns
of Belsen and Dachau with shorn heads burned
in shame—and still they teach
what they have learned:
to take the altars in
out of the world, beyond the reach
of men.

Judith Saul Stix
Noah's Bride

Smelling oncoming rain,
surging with courage,
each thing made
assured of welcome
enters the ark,
enters the womb
to be reborn.

The rising waters merge
my own small sea of tears
with ferment of the air,
with fumes of origin. Treetops
bend to my hand.
Jaybirds' plaintive cries
and crows' canopy
the raw ghettoes of fish.
A year of solitude,
a year of rocking.

Beyond my flotsam soul
home earth emerges from the mist
like island knolls,
streams of fragrance
coasting down the swells
like swans.
Storms, gratitude,

bright skies. Dove's
sweet entreaty to his mate
brooding upon the waters
hatches the egg of the new

world, the soaking fields
springing irises,
an arch of light.

Through the fertile mud
Noah strides
onwards, limping
to his rendezvous
with fatherhood,
with arks of wine.

I drown.

Pilgrimage

The soil of Palestine is sand and potsherds;
its punctuating stones are sometimes sheep.
This is the land of heroes, miracles,
and monuments, crushed ancient layers, opened
gates, one Old Man's eagle vision. Land
of remembrances, rocks that remember,
of lovely, laughing, dark-eyed young girls,
of black coats, ear-curls, narrowing gates.
Villages sparkle more completely and more
abundantly than stars under the holy
rooftop of this sky. Life lives intensely
in the Land of Israel. Oranges drop
as if from heaven; blanketing scent-clouds
blossom the lawns at night. We sniff a spring-tide
moon, its full and dark. Luck falls to travelers
who're lacking amulets—or had we them?
Hearken to David's music heard in dreams,
but waken to our Babylonian time.

Phil Sultz
From the Beginning

Every Morning
the old man climbs
the hill where he
sees everything
from the beginning.

It snowed all day
and the next
morning either
in Southern France
or in Northern
Spain. There was
also an avalanche
somewhere. Also
there was something
in Rome.

It was Sunday morning
in Rome. As if time
had stopped, the silence
became very apparent
to my friend and I.
My friend told me he
wears a thirty eight
regular.

He decided he would
be a portrait, so he went
to the museum and stood
against the wall.

Wendy Surinsky
Lunar Eclipse

For Lorraine Glass-Harris

turn like the moon
is what the moon said
on the night of the lunar eclipse
while itself only a sliver of light turning
from the shadow cast by the earth
turning
in a night singing the song of separation,
of two spheres revolving, rotating,
steadily away from each other
a night whose mouth lies full with
a wondrous silence of awe
broken with the cry
my god, my god, oh my god
released from the deepest center of an ever-widening,
ever-growing opening
that pushes two beings apart and into separate spaces
which had been waiting through all of time
dark, calm, expectant

and their separation, when complete, is still defined, in part,
by what lies between them
a world of its own
through which flow unseen forces
strong enough to elicit the tides,
keeping the waters constantly breaking,
always asking—are you ready to be born?
without summoning the seas upward in exodus

patiently turning
the moon's brightness emerges

its every pore bristled and scoured by a steel wool shadow
turning until it appears as a wholeness

turn like the moon
naming itself and its mother
like two pregnant women embracing
whose round, full bellies keep them apart
for the shape of these worlds
they say their name
sung by the woman in pleasure
hummed by the woman in labor
like some celestial onomatopoeia
simply
o

August 16, 1989

Michah Turner
In the Beginning

In the beginning time was without form,
a past without substance
a future without shape.

Then a garden was planted in time
And time was given boundaries,
boundaries that separated
holy from profane.

All souls were placed within the garden
So that the memory of the garden
Would forever be placed within all souls.
and since then...

Each morning our souls are returned to us
We are released into the wilderness of time,
to relocate the boundaries
to reclaim the garden
to take root in eternity.

Constance Urdang
Mexican Afternoons

It is as difficult to disentangle the train from the landscape
Which it bisects, a particolored string
Threading its way between groundswells of patterned desert,
As to follow the argument
In the book on my knees. Everything is a distraction:
A thousand butterflies above the millefleur field,
A filament of music drifting up
From the town's deep center, as the slow afternoon
Meanders toward uncertain consummations.
Now the train vanishes, pulled into the hillside
By its invisible string. The pages of the book
Flutter *adios, adios,* and in the pale sky
A sickle moon signals the darkness coming.

What am I doing here? This is not my country.
Even the sky is foreign, at home there is nothing
So unfathomable and at the same time opaque;
It is easy to get lost in it, or on one of
The many little roads that look, from here,
As if they might lead to the water.
Don't think it is a simple matter of translation—
Yesterday in the restaurant a friendly tourist
Boasted that he had come back
After twenty-five years, and found nothing changed.
Nobody contradicted him, not even
The three naughty little boys who ran barefooted past the tables
Shouting "goodbye, goodbye," meaning, "hello, hello."

The gardener does not know the name
Of that flower like a spear thrust up
Bright as arterial blood, out of a leafy scabbard;
And when he tells me this plant

Is called virgin's tears
I do not believe him.
Even when he clasps my hand
In greeting or goodbye, the distance between us
Is greater than the spaces between the stars.
Nothing bridges it. From my house
I can see his house, the birds in cages,
But even when he tells me how to find it
The streets are without names, and I lose my way.

Ways of Returning

Returning through the back streets, through alleys so narrow
The walls of the houses part like grass,
Leaning backward, their patience demonstrated
By scarred plaster, worm-eaten sills, and
Thrust through a chalk-blue door,
A clenched brass fist, everything the same
As it was, the sun, boys shooting marbles the same,
The same flies buzzing minarets of garbage, the same fists;
Or skating across the enormous mirrored spaces
Of an airport, in St. Louis or anywhere,
Passing the snack bars, the Budget Rent-a-Car, electronic games,
Seeing the men and women queued up to telephone
To say to someone, to anyone
At the end of the line, Hello, it's me,
I'm back; or, after driving all day long
To come into town at nightfall, the avenues
Festooned with lights, every block so familiar
You catch a glimpse of yourself coming down the street,
Yourself, in a coat you wore then, carrying something
You carried then, or maybe are carrying still.

Shlomo Vinner
Training on the Shore

Children
they teach to walk,
soldiers
to crawl.
And between one lesson and another
they are shown the sand
God showed Abraham
when He made him a nation
wandering like sand.
They are shown the moon-struck sea,
grass sprouting from the hearts of stones
that once were the wall of a temple.

And at midnight dew rises
from the beloved land,
the blessings of stars bring forth the grass,
the blessings of the grass,
the stars.
Children
they teach to walk,
soldiers
to fall.

Directing the Traffic

A young policewoman directs traffic
in the heart
of Tel Aviv,
in the heart
of the afternoon,
at two o'clock
on a hot day.

Her movements
replace electrical circuits
that replace
ancient motions.
Her hips
dance among irises
of smoke and fume.
Her clothes
cling to her body,
sweat
on her breasts
like drops of sea
on a goddess
rising from the foam.
Petrifying monsters
obey her,
kneel at her feet,
then go on.
No time for thought
I watch
from the sidelines
as noise intensifies
and smoke.
She does
what's needed:
directs the traffic.

Translated from the Hebrew by
Laya Firestone Seghi and Howard Schwartz

Jane O. Wayne
The Family Album

The spine creaks when you open it;
the thick pages flap
like black wings between your hands.
You don't stop
until you notice one of her,
sitting on a wall, a girl your age
in braids, a school uniform—
white middy-blouse, dark tie,
dark stockings on her dangling legs.

You must be studying the mouth
they say you have,
the grandmother you never knew.
You even rub your hand
slowly over the shiny girl
the way I do a window
when I can't tell which side
the dust is on—
before you let the cover drop.

In A Closed Car

As a child it always came over me
in the closed car on the way to visit
my father's mother at the nursing home:
that sudden sinking
in a bag of kittens, and the rock
weighing me down—motion itself
pulling me under.
The whole ride there
against that forced embrace—fumes
of gasoline, of cigarettes, of dread
rising in my nostrils, nausea
bulging in my throat—I closed my eyes.

When I opened the tight collar
of my Sunday coat, some other passenger
sighed in me. That sigh
still surfaces through a haze of smoke.
In the back seat with the windows up,
I can hear a hollow tapping
against the metal tray, the same hand
flicking off the ashes, flicking
petals from a rose.
When the sun glares at a certain angle,
I can't see where I'm going.

From a Half-Filled Cup

When he left last night
as quickly as he kissed me on the cheek
some numbness settled over me,
like a cover on a drowsy child,
until this morning
when I cleared the dishes from the dinner table.
His half-filled cup must have
brought the evening back, must have held him,
like some spirit in a magic lamp,
so when I touched the rim, my finger circling
the way a child rubs a crystal glasss
to bring the hidden music out,
I thought about his lips, his saliva
in the milky dregs,
and before I carried it to the sink to pour it out —
for a moment, only for a moment —
I thought of drinking
those cold dregs, of drinking more
than what he hadn't,
and of the odd desire
to take that fluid's darkness on my tongue —
a kind of kiss, but colder.

II.
Modern
Midrashim

Rabbi James M. Bennett
Listening to the Angel

He awakes with a start, shaking and drenched in sweat. Confused and still half asleep, he looks around the tent, trying to find the source of the new voice he is sure he has heard. There beside him lies Sarah, sound asleep. "It couldn't have been her," he thinks to himself. "But who then?" He softly arises and peers out into the cloudless night. Nothing stirs.

Finally, he closes his eyes and tries to sleep, but he cannot rid his head of the echoing words, *"Abraham, Abraham. Listen to me. Do not do it."*

The night wears on, and finally he drifts into a fitful sleep. In his dreams he hears the fateful commandment, this time from a voice he knows, the voice of his God: "Abraham, I want you to take your son, your beloved, your only son, Isaac, and go to the place that I will show to you..." He trembles, but through the veil of sleep he knows that it must be done. *(The other voice calls out again, gently, "Abraham, Abraham." There is no response.)*

Early the next morning he awakens, quietly so as not to awaken Sarah, and gathers his things. He packs the bags and loads them onto the ass, taking the fire and wood and the knife that he will need. Calling softly to Issac and the servants, he sets off on the long journey. The ass stumbles a bit, and turns aside from the trail as they leave the camp. His ears perk up at the sound of the voices, mostly familiar, but one unknown calls out, unheeded. *("Abraham, stop, do you know what you are doing?")*

The long, mysterious journey continues through the desert. The voice becomes more desperate, more concerned with each passing moment. *("Abraham, why don't you listen? What are you doing?")* Abraham points out the serene beauty of the desert to the boys, but does not speak to his beloved son, Isaac, who rides on in silence. No one hears the voice.

At the foot of Mount Moriah they stop. *("Abraham, what will it take to make you hear me? Think of what you are about to do.")* Unloading the wood and the fire and the rope and the knife, Abraham is startled, and looks upwards towards the mountain, as if he has heard a strange and unfamiliar sound. The servants query, "What is it?" "Nothing, it must have been the wind," comes the response. Isaac stares blank-faced at his father, confused and yet in awe.

The ascent begins. They walk together in silence, Isaac bowed under the weight of the wood tied to his back, Abraham carrying only the knife and the fire. Tearfully, sobbing comes the voice. *("Oh Abraham, Abraham, how can you do this? He is your son.")* Suddenly Abraham stops and turns, startled by the sound he thinks he has heard from a few feet behind. "What is it, my son?"

Isaac looks up. "Nothing, father. I did not say a word." *("It was me, not him. Oh please, please listen." Frantically, the voice rises in pitch, in desperation, in agony. "What will it take to get you to hear me?")* A moment later, "But father?" "Yes, my son, here I am." "Father, I am confused. Here is the wood, and there are the knife and the fire. Where is the lamb for the sacrifice?"

"God will provide the lamb, my son." Silence. Only the wind, and the sound of their climbing, as a few pebbles trickle down the hillside. *(The tears turn to sighs, and then anger. "Are you unfeeling? How can you subject your son to this? Do you truly intend to do this thing? Will you hear me once the knife has pierced his throat?")*

Abraham takes the logs from Isaac's sweating back, places them on the altar, and binds his frightened son to the place where he will offer a sacrifice. *("Abraham! Abraham! Listen now! You must hear my voice. This is your last chance! Do not do this thing! Abraham!")* Abraham prays for release, even as he dutifully raises the knife above his head. His hand quivers; he watches the gleaming blade as it moves downward, almost with a life of its own, toward the taut neck of his son, his only son, his beloved, Isaac ... Suddenly, blessedly, finally, he hears the voice of the angel. *"Stop! Abraham, do not harm your son ... !"* Abraham drops the knife, his hand and heart shaking. At the moment of truth, when there is no chance of error, with all he loves at stake, he finally hears the voice. Abraham crumbles to the ground, sobbing, exhausted, and gives thanks. The only sounds are his sobs, Isaac's cries of fear and anger, and the voice of the angel.

Rabbi Tsvi Blanchard
The Tale of the Ram

Reb Zvi said: "All the hidden things in the universe are hidden together in one small back section of Heaven. There the Messiah waits for the time when he is to come. There also live all of the other great hidden things. There lived the ram which was sacrificed in place of Isaac. And when you are together in eternity, what you are at your deepest begins to show. And the ram, in a fit of rage at being locked up in a room for so long, gored the Messiah.

"When he came before the Heavenly Court, the Holy One, blessed be He, said: 'Ordinarily, the first time an animal gores it is considered as if it were an accident. But you are a ram with knowledge and wisdom. You are a ram who is like a person, and a person is always considered responsible for the damage that he does. You have gored the Messiah. This shall be your punishment: you shall be put to death, and it shall occur as soon as possible.' With that the ram was transported to the next sacrifice to be made on the face of the earth. He found himself on Mount Moriah, replacing the boy whose father was no longer going to sacrifice him."

Reb Hayim Elya asked: "How badly wounded was the Messiah?" Reb Zvi replied: "So badly that he will come only when his wound is healed."

The Tale of the House

Reb Zvi said: "Someone once asked: 'How is it possible that there can be so many Jewish *Neshamahs*, Jewish souls, and only one Torah for all of them?' This is the story.

"A man once built a house. And he wanted the house to be a home not only for his family and himself, but for all of his children and his children's children. But he knew that there is really no way to build a house big enough to fit not only those who were there then, but everyone who would come afterwards.

"So he decided to solve the problem in a strange way. He demanded of God and received permission to bring all of the souls who would ever be in his family together at the same time, and they would decide which kind of house suited them best. And for a while he was pleased. But when all the souls had gathered together, he wasn't pleased at all. For if they had had an eternity, they could not have found a house that would satisfy them all.

"Finally, in desperation, he said, 'How will I do it? If I do not hear from one soul present how a house can be built that all of you souls will be happy in, I won't build a house at all.' And he thought they would have to compromise, but they could not compromise.

"And just at the moment he was about to give up, one soul, the soul of the youngest, the last of his line, said, 'I will tell you how to build the house, but it will take a great sacrifice. You should build the house that you want to build. And then you should give it a very special property: everyone will see in the house what they need to see.

'... But although they will always feel that they are seeing what they need to see, the reality will always be just a little bit different. And they will always want to find out what the true house is really like. So the house will be perfect for every generation that lives in it. But at the same time, they will be aware that there is also another house, and they will want to find that house, and they will thirst after finding it, some more than others. And because of the effort required to find that house, those that do will be even more satisfied with the real house than they were with the one they thought satisfied them to begin with, from the effort required to discover it.'

"This compromise was agreed upon with one condition: that the house for the last child should be identical to the house that the first man built. And when the last child agreed that yes, he wanted to live in the real house, then the man was able to go ahead and build it."

Marc Bregman
The Third Tablet of the Covenant

We learn that Moses remained on the summit of Mount Sinai neither eating nor drinking for forty days and for forty nights. During the day he was instructed in the Written Torah, and during the night he learned the Oral Torah from the mouth of the Holy One Himself. Each day from sunrise to sunset Moses, like one who is called to read from the sacred scroll, stood in awe and read as the Written Torah was revealed, word by word written by the Finger of God upon the two tablets of sapphire glowing with a supernal light even in the midday sun. And the writing rose up before Moses like fire, black as a raven upon white fire pure as snow, curling up as the locks of hair upon the head of the Ancient of Days. And each lock was made of innumerable hairs and each hair was as radiant as the golden glow of the sun. But as the sun set each day, Moses sat as well, and swaying gently to and fro began to learn the Oral Torah from the Mouth of the Holy One Himself.

Now, it is said that the Oral Torah contained not only all the seventy interpretations of each and every letter and word of the Written Torah, but also every question and its answer that every student of the wise would raise in all the coming generations. And even Moses, the greatest of the prophets and the wisest of the sages, could not retain the limitlessness of this teaching. So on the last day, Moses rose before the Holy One and said: "Master of the Universe, I know that it is Thy will that not all of Thy words be written. But the mystery of Thy unwritten word is too great for me to bear. May it be Thy will that these words be written as well." And the Holy One answered: "The words of My Mouth are not to be written as the writing of My Hand, but you are permitted to record the heads of the sections of the words of My Mouth, as a disciple may record the words of his master, so that none of My words shall be forgotten, but may be handed down from you to your disciples and from them to their disciples in every generation." So Moses fashioned a tablet of stone and took up a flint to scratch with his own hands what he learned at night from the Mouth of the Holy One, blessed be He. But as he touched flint to stone, he saw within the tablet the words forming themselves, and each new facet revealed and contained boundless depths, glittering with the distant light of Torah.

Now at the end of the forty days and nights, Moses arose and took up the two sapphire tablets, one in each arm. But the stone tablet of the Oral Law he placed within his *Tallit,* next to his heart, and girded his outer garment to begin the descent. But when he approached the camp and saw the Calf and the people rising up to laugh, he was seized with a towering rage, and cast the tablets from his hands. Immediately they crashed to the earth; the burning letters of the Written Torah flew up to heaven and the glowing sapphire was dimmed. Then all was silent, as Moses stood glaring down at the people. But then was heard a distant rumble, and from the heavens a great angel with the head of a bird appeared. And plummeting down with outstretched talons, it plucked the Oral Torah from Moses' heart and slowly ascended back into the heavens.

The Death of Moses

One day Reb Pinhas of Koretz assembled his closest disciples. For a long while they sat in silence. Then Reb Pinhas told them that after much soul searching he had decided to reveal to them one of the most deep and dangerous secrets of the Torah—the secret of the *Torah Kadmonit*—the Primal Torah.

Reb Pinhas began: "The Torah was originally created as an incoherent jumble of letters. Only when a certain event occurs in the world, only then do the letters combine to form the words telling of that event. This has been true from the very beginning of time. For only when the World was actually created did the Hebrew letters making up the words: *Bereshit bara Elokim*—In the beginning God created ... actually form themselves into words."★

Before Reb Pinhas could continue, the youngest of the Hasidim arose, as if in a trance. Moshe ben Itzhaq bowed ever so slightly in the direction of Reb Pinhas and said: "With your permission, Rabbi, may I be allowed to elaborate on your words?" A look of deep sadness crossed the face of Reb Pinhas for a fleeting moment as he gazed at his young disciple. But then, silently, he nodded his assent.

Moshe ben Yitzhaq began: "This is how we die. When the time has come for each of us to pass away, the necessary letters are summoned out of the incoherent jumble of what is still to be revealed of our Holy Torah. And then, slowly, they begin to assemble themselves—but in reverse order. First the man's name: *Hey - Shin - Mem*.★★ Then the announcement of his death: *Tav - Vav - Mem - Yod*. Spelling out *YaMot Moshe*—Moses shall die. Then finally, the *Vav* is seen approaching from a very great distance. It descends slowly but relentlessly like a black dagger from above, finally falling into position at the beginning of the first word—changing the future into the past: *Va Yamot Moshe*—And Moses died. And this is how we all die." Moshe ben Yitzhaq raised his eyes to heaven as if peering far off into the distance and ceased to speak.★★

The Hasidim sat stunned. They turned to the Rebbe for some sign of what to do. Finally Reb Pinhas broke the silence: *"Va Yamot Moshe al pi HaShem*—And Moses died by the Word of God."★★★

★See G. Scholem, *On the Kabbalah and its Symbolism* (New York, 1965), pp. 76-77
★★Note that spelled out in the normal order this forms the Hebrew word *HaShem*—the epithet used by pious Jews for the name of God [M.B]
★★★See Deut. 34:5

Rabbi Helen T. Cohn
Ruth Packs Her Bags

All week the women have said, "Don't go. The road is long and dangerous. How can three women alone..."

They are right, of course. Soon the grain will be ripe; she should help her parents with the harvest, be first among the women in the fields.

"Don't go," they say. "Here you have a home; there you will always be a stranger." She folds her clothes carefully then looks around the familiar room. A pull stronger than blood draws her to follow the woman who awaits her.

"You are so brave," they say. "We could never bring ourselves..."

This is not courage, she thinks, this is not bravery. A woman stands at the doorway casting a long shadow. I must follow her. This is not courage; this is simply my life.

Lorraine Eason
The Tower of Babel

Oh. You understand me? Good. Then listen.

I was one of the people who worked on that tower. It was my job to shape the bricks. Others, they brought the clay, the straw, the water. Endless trips they made. Hauling, gathering, pouring.

I squatted near the coals lifting the warm mixture and patting it down into shape. I liked the way it felt in my hands—warm, pliable, gritty. This mixture of the earth. I knew I had a part in the alchemy. I squatted in my smooth spot day after day shaping this mixture of earth and water baked over fire to be built into the air. I liked my part.

At the time when dusk arrived, we stopped to get water. Only then did I look up into the sky. Only then did I see the new heights to which my bricks had ascended. Each day it was a little higher. I liked to save this looking up until my work was over. I liked the slow and steady ascent.

All of us, the girls who made bricks, at the same task. It was quiet. Each of us taking part in the alchemy. Combining the elements God had created. Each of us in silent unison.

One day after dusk, I went home just like any other day. There, my mother squatted over the fire making a meal of grains and herbs. She watched my face. She studied it, though she knew it well.

"What do you see?" I asked her.

"Youth. And the absence of thought." Her reply did not move me.

It was the same day after day. The tower grew until it was difficult for the workers to haul the bricks so high. Still, I saved my looking up until the time at dusk. Still, I liked the feel of the warm clay in my hands.

My mother began to question me. "For what do you do this work? Who will it benefit? What reason do you have to be pleased?" These were her questions now when she studied my lineless face.

I had no answers. But her questions began to echo in my head as I formed the bricks in quiet unison with the young women at the base of the tower. One day, I became so distracted by doubting questions that my hands forgot the task. The clay stuck to my palms and the straw punctured my skin. I went home.

"Mother, why do you question me so?"

"You have lost the will to question yourself?" A question answered my question.

I went back to work.

That day a cloud surrounded the tower. It was thick and dark and threatened to fill the village. I looked up without pleasure. A transient hush, like the abrupt intake of air, overtook us all. It was then that it happened. As we tried to speak to one another—to question the origin of this darkness—we could not make any sense of our words. We turned from side to side and looked above and behind, but there was no one among us who seemed coherent. Sounds came—incomprehensible, frightening sounds, in every tone and pitch—sounds, but no meaning. Some of my friends fell on their knees and began to pound at the dirt. Others stood rigidly motionless looking up into the darkness. Many had begun to flee from the site of the tower. I ran as quickly as I could home to my mother.

She looked at me without alarm. For a moment, I understood her. "You must go from this place." I felt as if I was being torn from the very flesh that sustained me. Would the light not return again from beneath the clouds?

I clung at her skirts as Mother hurriedly continued. "Find your way to a new place where your work can be useful, where you... by your words and actions... Know that *Adonai* did not intend for us to live and work without purpose, day after day the same...."

She said more; I am sure. But I only watched her lips move and heard nothing more than babel.

Rabbi Miriam Tirzah Firestone
Tirzah's Lament

My name is Tirzah and my life is with a wandering people. It is said that we were not always wanderers but this is all I have known in my fourteen years. This tent and our animals and, of course, my people. Soon, very soon it is said, we will stop wandering and cross the Yarden River to our homeland. For this we have all waited. As for me, I am not sure. There is much that changes in these days. With my sisters I have done a daughter's duty. Some even say it has made us leaders. I know only this: in the last moon my lovesong has turned into a lamentation. I will tell you my story.

I was well beloved by my father, now dead. I have never known my mother. But my father, well honoured in our tribe of M'nasheh, loved me. If you will tend my secret well, it was I he loved best, the youngest of his five. Never did my father begrudge me my life though he lost his wife in my delivery. Rather he would swear her rare beauty had come into me at my birth. I think he loved me as he had loved her.

Neither did he despise us for not coming as boy children. Though you can be certain he was derided in plenty by his brothers and uncles. Five girls, you see, would only lose their staff its prosperity. Father would only smile. He would answer calmly that five strong ewes were better than twenty lame rams any day. Then they would all laugh, for a time.

But their chiding was hardest upon our second sister, Milcah. She seemed to take it as a blow upon her own heart. You see, she is not good to look at. She is a strong girl and acts much like a young man, going out to do the work of the men, the hauling and saddling, the shearing in springtime. For her it seems to be a bitter lot to have been born a female. She and I are very different. I am certain that the idea to approach Moshe and the Elders came first from her.

For when my sisters called me to the tent now six full moons ago they were as one. Fire feeding on fire. Not even Noah, the quiet one, stood back. Their eyes glowed like eight embers before me and I grew excited before even knowing of their plan. How could I have known the mixed end it would bring? It was a way to pay honour to Father. And to ourselves as well. And to all women, daughters of the staff, that we be counted as rightful heirs to our fathers. There have been other daughters before us. Not under the staff of M'nasheh but in the tribes of Asher and Naftali. Two families of girls with no sons to inherit the father's name.

But when their fathers passed to the ancestors, the daughters remained silent and their legacy passed to the sons of the tribe. This would not be our lot. And now it will not be the lot of any of our women again.

But listen to me. How valiantly I speak for the plight of women. When I myself am left like a kid with its hoof stuck in a hole, unable to move as its twin skips ahead. You see, I am young. And not known for thinking ahead. When Moshe returned with the answer from *Adonai,* we were wild with joy. *Ken Dovrot B'not Zlafchod!* (Num. 27:7) Those words marked our victory. *Adonai* itself had spoken that we were in the right, that our claim was just, that we five girls would stand like sons to our father and inherit his land. It was all we had asked for. We danced that night and all the women came out, hundreds! Not since the great Miriam was alive had the women danced with such joy. Something great moved within them, a great joy and a great hope.

Ken B'not Zlafchod Dovrot (Num. 27:7): Rightful was our claim! These words babbled like a brook from the mouths of everyone for days as the word passed amongst the tribes. I have said it made the women laugh with hope. *Adonai* had said we too could inherit the land, that we too can hold a place in the tribe. This women know in their bellies. But now *Adonai* had spoken it. And some men rejoiced as well. There were those that wished us well. But the men of M'nasheh, the Giladi cousins, were sour and grumbled amongst themselves. I did not heed this omen.

Instead, I ran to my Gadi lover. You may know him? The chanter with the ruddy face and tousled fair head. His voice is utterly melodious and he carries on his hip a small drum, beloved to him as a small child riding on his mother. This one is my love. And on that day we ran together and laughed in great innocence thinking that one fifth of my father's land would be ours together and dreaming aloud of the beautiful children to spread out from our loins.

As we walked back to the tents my uncles stood glowering. They detested our joy. To them it meant their loss. For we would seek husbands apart from our staff of M'nasheh. This they knew. And this would lessen their wealth. A greedy wealth it is. I hid my face and scurried away to the sisters' tent. Already there I found an air thick with foreboding. Noah and Chaglah wore furrowed brows. They too had exchanged eyes though not vows with young men of other tribes. Machlah, our eldest sister, spoke what we knew in our hearts; our uncles were to have a hearing with Moshe and the Elders at sunrise. They were to question the gift of *Adonai* to the womenfolk, to ask for a new decree to keep us from taking men outside of M'nasheh. They would ask to hold on to the land of their brother, our land, by restricting our marriages.

Woe to me. I had made a vow to my Gadi lover. My heart had already seen a home with him and our joy was double. Just then I heard his happy palms hit the drum hide in the distance. It ran together with the knocking in my heart. He would not know until the following high noon what I knew, what we all knew at that moment. My uncles would rob us of our small gain. Indeed, they would rob me of my heart's love.

I did not sleep that night but watched the white moon sail around the top of the tent. I was as a trapped animal. I had vowed myself to the Gadi youth. A vow in the name of *Adonai,* the holy One. Was it *Adonai* who had betrayed us, daughters of Zlafchad? Or was it the meanness of my father's brothers and nephews? My sisters and I, all of the women it seemed, had celebrated at the sign of our small liberation. But now this, too, seemed to have waned. *Adonai's* words rang out bitterly the next day as we knew they must: *Ken Mateh B'nei Yosef Dovrim!* (Num. 36:6) Rightful is the claim of Joseph's tribe! If women of the tribe inherit the wealth of the father, their marriages must be restricted to their tribe. There is no Giladi man, indeed, no man of this staff that I will have, I cried! My teeth set themselves. They could not force me to break my vow. I had promised myself to another.

By the full moon, when my blood flowed, I sought the counsel of the old seer from Asher, the crippled crone with the great lips. She told me this. That my vow would be unloosed before *Adonai;* indeed, that a new law would be given, and soon, whereby a daughter would be cleared of her vow by the words of her father. And in my case, it would be my uncle.

These words made me wail. I felt my life, my very vows, were suddenly not my own. And a boiling heat took me over and with it came angry, hot tears. After a time, for the crone knows the cleansing power of tears, she continued. She said that in the far distant future, well after our people were established in our land, my name would be remembered. How could this be so, I asked. Then she spoke of the love that my truest of loves holds for me. In his way he would remember my vow to him. For he would set my beauty to music, and though the songs would not last forever, my name—Tirzah—would come to mean great loveliness. She said it would be scribed into hides for all generations to remember. This made me wail as well. But now a different sort of cry, a deeper one. Would that no one ever heard my name again! That a lamentable fate such as this one be dissolved into ordinariness. That I could carry out my simple vow.

The crone's words have returned to me often in the days and nights since that moon. Always with pain do I hear them. Yet, too, they hold a sort of sweetness within their bitterness.

I know that soon I must think of a M'nahseh husband as my sisters do. But I cannot bring myself to cross those waters as yet. For I am thick with grief and with questions. Will it always be so, I ask myself, that our women be the subjects of the menfolk? Could this truly be the will of *Adonai?* Will *Adonai* someday feel our pain as women just as our pain as slaves was felt in *Mitzraim?* For the song and joy of the women on that one night of celebration has kindled within me a hope and a vision. And I wonder if it is not still found, buried very deep, in the breasts of other women as well. These are the big questions that raise my head while the groan in my heart asks others. Will my Gadi youth soon find another? Is his lament as deep as mine? Is it to him the same cool relief that he and his tribe will hold their land on the opposite side of the Yarden from us? Or would it not pain him to see me through the coming times carrying another man's children? These are the questions in my heart. And this is my bitter yet unfinished story.

Julie Heifetz-Klueh
Why the Butterfly is Never Mentioned in the Bible

God created many universes before this one. When He started over, He brought her from the last to this firmament, bright-eyed, wings shimmering, God's first child. He placed her a little lower than the angels, a messenger between God and His new universe, and she saw that it was good; light and evening, earth and the seasons and stars, creeping things, wild animals and fowl. And she saw when God rested, and she saw the mist and watering of the ground, and the garden eastward in Eden, the tree and the river in the garden. And she heard man name the animals, and watched woman drawn from Adam's sleep. She heard God bless them and command. And she thought of children, one flesh. She was in the garden when the subtle snake and the woman argued, edging closer to the tree. Her eyes were open as the man began to eat. And she watched silent as the cool of day, shouting out no warning, no protest, no rage. And God, walking in the garden cried out "Where art thou?" And she hid herself in leaves. God found her and said, "Because you saw and did not speak, I will never say your name. From this day forth you will be without language of cattle or cricket or bird. You and your children and your children's children have nothing more to say." And He sent her through the gates, the first leaf driven from the garden.

Jerred Metz
Angel Rolling the Heavens Together

At the end of time this will happen: when the souls of air, dust, stone, plants, creatures and men stream toward the gate and all the words and sounds and letters signing sounds crown the sky, when everything seeks gate and passage through the sky, in a place of the world, a point in air where no one looked, an angel appears. Other angels surround him—some no bigger than fleas, but white and whose wings beat loud as thunder, some the size of men and women, robust and smelling of work and long flight, some big as stars, showering the sky with threads of light. One angel tears the tongue from a liar's mouth, another buries living sinners in dust, a third drops a ship on a courtyard filled with thieves. But this angel does not move with the other angels toward a distant point singing as they fly. This angel will roll the heavens together and so stands still, his eyes burning, his jaws shut against the strong and growing stink.

Skilled in knots and cloth, a sailmaker or one who coils baskets from plaited straw, he bends to his knees and winds and furls the air. As he furls, he names God from the least name to the most secret and when he speaks the last the world becomes a snail shell, the moon and sun at the rim, the planets and stars clustered in tight swirls at the center. Coiling backward, the angel enters the shell and comes out an eon later, horns on his head, himself a snail now, who drags the heavens slowly toward the Ever Present.

Bert Minkin
Feet First

Moses left his princely chariot behind when he fled Egypt to labor as a shepherd in the land of Midian. His feet became his sole means of transport and supported his weight as he guarded Jethro's flock, but they didn't receive their due respect.

His eyes thought feet were too large, and scarcely cared to look upon them. Ears complained that feet made too much noise while walking. That mouth never spoke kindly of feet, and the hands seldom bothered to touch them. His nose was particularly harsh in its judgment of those hard working feet.

The sense of sight resided in his eyes. Ears claimed hearing. His mouth bragged about its exquisite taste, and Moses relied upon his hands for touching. We all know what sense his nose claimed.

Those feet felt low down and left out until God's first commandment to Moses as he trembled before the burning bush on Mount Horeb: *"...put off the shoes from your feet, for the place where you are standing is holy ground."* The God of the high and the low wanted all of his prophet to behold the miracle.

The feet that would carry Moses to the River Jordan felt totally involved! God raised them to new heights. In every sense, they rejoiced!

Rabbi James L. Sagarin
Why God Created the Rainbow

*"I have set My bow in the clouds, and it shall serve as a
sign of the promise between Me and the earth."*

—Genesis 9:13

All the colors were arguing one day, bragging about their importance.

Red spoke up first and said, "I am the greatest of all colors, for I am the color of life-giving blood. Without me there would be no bright juicy apples, cherries or raspberries. Red is the color of life, a strong, beautiful color."

Orange exclaimed, "No, I am the most beautiful. I'm the color of the setting sun and the marigold. I'm the color of peaches, pumpkins and persimmons. I glow in the dark; I bring light where there is darkness."

Yellow interrupted saying, "Now look at me. I'm the color of the bright sun of day; the sun that brings warmth and light to all the earth." Yellow continued, "I'm the color of many fruits and vegetables, like squash and bananas, and many precious birds, like canaries and finches. I even bring in the spring with daffodils and tulips. I'm the most special!"

Next green boasted, "Without me, life on earth would be dull and drab. Look around you, the whole world is green, the grass is green, as are the leaves on the trees. Green symbolizes new life. I brighten everything. My color is growth."

Then blue shouted, "No, blue is the most important and beautiful color. The blue above and the blue below; the blue skies and the blue oceans. I am the blue of all water; without my rain, all else would disappear."

And then purple cried, "I am by far the most beautiful of colors, for I am the color of ripe grapes and wine and the rare treasured orchids. I'm also the color of velvety soft robes and nature's violets. I am by far the most important!"

God heard their arguing and declared, "Truly, all of you colors have something to offer, each in his own way. The world I have created would be less complete without any of you. So what shall I do? I shall put you all together and make a rainbow that I will set in the sky—a symbol of my Creation!"

"I have set My bow in the clouds, and it shall serve as a sign of the promise between Me and the earth."

Who's the Best?

The long awaited day had finally arrived. All of the animals gathered together to boast of their importance. God would once again hear their statements and be the judge. Each of them had something very important to say.

First, the lion stood up, very proud, strong and immediately began to roar. He said, "I'm the best of all animals, and am called the 'King of Beasts,' I have a beautiful mane and sharp teeth, and am the most powerful animal in all of the jungle!"

Then the serpent crawled up before God, "No, God, I am the most important of all animals, very cunning as you know. I have smooth skin and slither any place on the earth. My teeth are very, very sharp, so sharp that I call them fangs, and am the most feared of all your creatures. I am the greatest of all!"

And the elephant stood up on is two hind legs and said, "Look at me, look how big 1 can be, I am the largest of all animals. You fashioned me, oh God, in such a wonderful way. I have beautiful tusks that gleam in the sun. When people behold my presence, they see me and run, I have been around this planet earth for thousands and thousands of years. I am the most magnificent of your animals."

No sooner had the elephant finished than the monkey stood up, and said, "No, you are all mistaken. It is I who am the greatest; look what I can do! I can fly from tree to tree and climb to the greatest height. I can entertain put on a show, and mimic humans. I am certainly the greatest of all animals, because I am the most intelligent, the most like your creations, man and woman. Surely I am the best!"

And then the rabbit stood up,. and wiggled its nose, "Look at me, I have soft fur, and a, little red nose. I am a nice animal. I do not hurt anybody. I only eat lettuce and other vegetables. I'm the best of all animals,

God, because I am so kind, gentle, soft and wonderful!"

Then the horse stood up and said, "Well, oh look at me God. I am an animal that cooperates with humans. I give them a ride whenever they need one. I am sure footed and swift and able to accompany people through their ordeals and great battles. I have a beautiful coat and very strong legs. I, too, have been around for many, many thousands of years, and it is I who have given more to this world than any other animal!"

But then the beaver stood up and he said, "God, you know me very well. I'm your hardest worker. I build dams and underground passages, day in and day out. I never stop working. I work for my family and the whole community of beavers. What a wonderful animal I am, so dedicated to the service of others. Truly I am your favorite and the most important!"

There were many other animals assembled, but God had heard enough from these, and began to look around in the crowded forest where everyone stood. Slowly God gazed upon a little animal that was nested in a tree. God asked, "Why do you say nothing?" The animal said, I'm in awe of you and all your wonderful creations." And God said, "Come forward dove, next to God in the presence of all the animals. They all gasped and said, "Ohhh what a beautiful bird!!" God spoke to the dove saying, "You are important to me, yet you remained silent.

"You remember the story of Noah and the flood. You brought an olive branch back to the Ark, symbolizing that people would be saved and that there would always be peace, peace among all of My creations. To you, oh Dove, I give a crown, the crown of peace, made of an olive branch."

And God spoke to those Assembled saying: "All of you animals are great, but those who bring peace are the most blessed of all!"

Hal Schmerer
How the Kaddish Was Discovered

Once there was a man named Avram Ben Joseph who was known to all in his town as being mean and uncaring. He was a merchant and many times had overvalued his goods and sold them for more than their worth to unsuspecting customers. He had never married because he did not want to share his money and possessions with another, but he lived with his nephew, an orphan named Hershel who did the chores around the home. For room and board, he cleaned the home and did other tasks for his uncle. Hershel never went to school because Avram did not want to spend the money for the teacher.

Avram Ben Joseph died one day of an unknown illness and was buried in the town cemetery. About a week after the headstone was placed on the grave, Avram appeared to the rabbi of the town in a dream. "Why have you returned?" the rabbi asked. "Because I have to tell you of my plight so that you can help me," replied Avram. "I am in *Gehenna* and am being punished for the sins I committed while on Earth. There is only one way that I can leave this place for *Olom Habah,* Heaven," he said. "And what is the way?" asked the rabbi. Avram replied, "My closest relative must cause the congregation to praise God's name three times a day for twelve months. Since I have no son, this must be done by Hershel, my nephew." Avram Ben Joseph then taught the prayer to the rabbi and told him the proper congregational responses. Then he departed.

When the rabbi awoke, he went to Avram's house to find Hershel. He tried to teach the special prayer to him but without success. Hershel was ashamed and told the rabbi that he could not learn the prayer because he could not read and write. After overcoming his surprise at this, the rabbi said that he would have to learn. Over the next five years, the rabbi taught Hershel how to read and write both Hebrew and Aramaic, and how to pray in the synagogue. After this was done, Hershel faithfully said this prayer at *Shacharit, Mincha* and *Ma'ariv,* the morning, afternoon and evening services every day for a year. Upon hearing the prayer, the congregation responded with praise of God. When the year was up, Avram

Ben Joseph appeared to the Rabbi again in a dream and thanked him for all he had done in teaching Hershel and showing him how to pray. Because of this, Avram was now out of *Gehenna*.

This prayer that freed Avram from *Gehenna* was the *Kaddish*. In this prayer, the congregation says "May His great name be blessed for ever and ever" and responds "Blessed by He" to the phrase, "Exalted and honored be the name of the Holy one." Because of this, we still say the *Kaddish* for our dead to help them in their way to *Olom Habah*. But, since we do not like to think our loved ones committed enough sins to be placed in *Gehenna,* we only say the *Kaddish* for eleven months.

Howard Schwartz

Adam's Soul

Before God created Adam as a man of flesh and blood, He created a dream Adam, whose name was Adam Kadmon. And God called forth this dream Adam and said: "Alone among all creations, I am going to permit you to choose your own soul." And God brought Adam Kadmon to the treasury of Souls in heaven and opened its door. And when Adam looked inside, he saw a sky crowded with stars. And God said: "Every one of those stars is a soul. Which one do you want?"

And as he gazed out at that constellation of souls, scattered like sparks, Adam wondered how he could possibly choose one from among them. Every one glowed with a light of its own. Every one was equally beautiful. Then Adam saw that the constellation formed a great Tree of Souls, which branched out in every direction. And Adam replied to the Holy One, blessed be He, and said: "I want the soul of the Tree of Souls from which all of the souls are suspended." And God was delighted, and brought forth the soul of the tree of Souls and gave it to Adam.

And that is why the soul of Adam contained all souls, and why all souls are but a part of Adam's soul.

The Yoke of Moses

For Charles Larson

When the children of Israel were still slaves in Egypt, and Moses was a prince who was also their leader, the people saw Moses join the line of the slaves and receive a great yoke, which was tied to his back, and which he bore to the top of the pyramids like all of the others. This seemed very strange to them. On the one hand, they greatly admired and respected Moses for sharing their suffering, but on the other hand, Moses was very precious to them and they didn't want to lose him. They wondered about this and came to him, saying: "Moses, Moses, you are free from this. Why are you taking it upon yourself anyway?" And Moses said: "I'm carrying it for the great relief that will come when they cut away the yoke."

The Fiery Serpents

Once again the people murmured against God and his servant Moses. This time they had grown tired of the long journey. They had even come to abhor a diet that consisted solely of manna and fresh water from Miriam's Well. For the manna fell fresh every day at dawn, and the well of Miriam followed them everywhere they went. But these miracles were not enough for the people. And when the Lord saw how they had even wearied of miracles, His wrath turned against them, and He punished them with the fiery serpents.

These were not serpents like any others. They were not made of flesh like a living serpent, but consisted entirely of fire. In fact, these serpents leaped out of the flames of the campfire at night, and slithered through the camp, until they reached the tents. There the fiery serpents bit them as they slept, rarely waking anyone, but bringing on a nightmare so terrible that those who awoke from it were grateful to be alive, while for many others there was no waking. That day the men and women staggered around pale and confused, and their anxiety turned to terror as they discovered how widespread was the nightmare among them. For they knew that this must foretell some terrible danger that loomed ahead. And their fear was even greater because they could not imagine what it was.

The next day brought no relief from the nightmares. Indeed, even the children fell prey to them. It was on the third night that the fiery serpents were finally seen slithering out of the campfire and throughout the camp. At first the people refused to believe it was possible, but when enough of them had seen for themselves that this was indeed happening, they decided to move the campfire a greater distance from the camp. But no matter how far they moved it, the snakes still reached the camp and bit the sleeping Israelites and brought on those relentless, unbearable nightmares. Finally, the people, in their desperation, put out the fire all together and still the fiery snakes crawled out of the ashes, like long-lost embers, and the nightmares that night were the worse of all.

When it seemed that no escape was possible from the bite of the fiery serpents, the people prostrated themselves before Moses, begging him to carry their plea to God to release them from these nightmares, whose grip had now carried over from sleep and possessed them during their waking hours as well. Moses prayed for the people. And the Lord revealed to Moses: "Make a brass serpent, and set it upon a pole; and it shall come to pass, that every one that is bitten, when he seeth it, shall live."

And Moses made a serpent of brass, and set it upon the pole; and it came to pass, that if a serpent had bitten any man who looked unto the serpent of brass, he lived. For the presence of that brass serpent, and that alone, put out the last flames of the fiery serpents, and freed the people from their terrifying grip.

The Dream of Isaac

For Tom and Laya Seghi

It is said that as he grew older, Isaac put the journey to Mount Moriah out of his mind. Even to Rebecca, his wife, he would not speak of what had happened. So circumspect did he become, that by the time of his marriage at the age of forty no one could remember the last time he had been heard to speak on the subject. So it seems likely that during the period in which his wife was expecting a child the old memory came to his mind even less often, for Rebecca had grown ripe with her waiting, which was already much longer than the old wives had estimated.

On one such night, while he and Rebecca were sleeping side by side, Isaac dreamed for the first time of the sacrifice that had taken place almost thirty years before. But this dream was even more real than the actual incident, for then his confusion had saved him from his fear, and now all the terror he had not noticed was with him, as a faceless man chained him to a great rock and held a knife against his neck. He felt the blade poised to press down when the sun emerging from behind a cloud blinded them both, and at the same time they heard the frantic honking of a goose whose grey and white feathers had become entangled in the thorns of a nearby bush. It was then that the fierce and silent man, whom Isaac now saw was his father, put down the blade and pulled the bird free from the thorns and berries, and as he brought it back, Isaac saw how it struggled in his hands. Then, when the goose was pressed firmly to the rock, Isaac watched as his father pulled back the white throat and drew the blade. He saw especially how white was the neck and how cleanly the blade cut through. At last Abraham put down the blade and unbound his son and they embraced. It was then that Isaac opened his eyes, felt the arms of his wife as she tried to wake him, and heard her whispering that the child was about to be born.

When Isaac understood he sat up in bed and hurried from the room to wake the midwife, who had been living with them for almost three weeks. Two hours later Rebecca gave birth, first to one son and then to another, the first who was hairy, his skin red, and the second who came forth with his hand on his brother's heel. Isaac found himself fascinated as he watched the midwife wash the infants in warm water. The first son, whom they came to call Esau, was born with an umbilical cord that was dark purple, the color of blood. But his second son, whom they named Jacob, had a cord that was soft and white as pure wax. It was this perfectly woven rope that Isaac found most intriguing, for reasons he could not comprehend. And he sensed a strange terror as he unsheathed a knife and drew the blade to sever this last link between what was and what will be. For it was then the dream of that night came back to him, and he saw in the same instant how the hands of his father had held down the goose, and how the sharp blade had cut across its neck, soft and white, like the severed cord he held in his own hands.

Laya Firestone Seghi
Rivka on Mount Moriah

When Eliezer journeyed in search of a wife for Isaac, he came to Aram Naharaim at dusk, stopped with his camels, and had them kneel at the well from which the women drew water. There he prayed for God to reveal the chosen woman: she would be the one willing to draw water, tirelessly, for those who thirsted.

And Rivka drew water for Eliezer and his camels, until all had drunk long draughts and finished drinking. In gratitude, Eliezer knelt before Abraham's God, thanking him for continuing to reveal his kindness. Then he followed Rivka to her father's home, where food and lodging were provided, gifts given, and Abraham's mission told. Upon questioning, Rivka did not hesitate or delay. She simply said, "I will go."

So Rivka traveled to Isaac, entered his mother's empty tent, and rekindled its warm glow. And Isaac loved his wife Rivka and was comforted. For almost twenty years, Rivka spread her branches over him, until he no longer thirsted. He wanted fruit. And he prayed to God for his barren wife who, like a tree standing amidst the fragrance of blossoms, withheld her bloom yet another year.

Spring returned. At last, Rivka's roots spread deep underground, seeking out darker waters. The sap from many seasons spiraled within her, gathering in her womb like countercurrents coupled, the fullness of one part filling the slimness of the other, forming a perfectly intertwined circle. Thus she conceived.

But the swirl within terrified her, as if it were the center of a great abyss. She watched as her outer shape expanded, signifying the mystery mingled within her growing beyond reason. She lost sight of her feet and strained to keep them grounded. The new life struggled within her. She could no longer sleep, nor could she rest. As her body became fuller, she felt herself becoming weightless as an empty shell, combustible as tinder. Dark and light fought furiously within her until she thought the friction would ignite her. "How," she asked the other women, "can I bear this?" The women answered with home remedies, tales of pregnancies, miscarriages, and deliveries. But Rivka was not set at ease. She became volatile. She wished first that she had not conceived, then that she herself had not been conceived.

In desperation, she set out to Mount Moriah. She ascended on the path that Abraham had trod with Isaac, cutting her feet on the jagged stones. As she strained to climb higher, she began to labor, holding on tightly to the gnarled and twisted mountain brush. Thus she arrived at the very rock where, years before, Isaac had been bound and a ram sacrificed in his place. The rock was enormous in size, and it radiated a timeless quality. She reached to touch it and lost her balance entirely, falling until she lay stretched out, breathless, upon it. She felt herself tied and bound, one knot upon another, and suddenly she could see Abraham's glinting knife. She heaved in pain. And then she heard the voice of the angel calling, "Abraham, Abraham," and she became calm.

She lay on the rock, at length, as time reeled around her. She watched the stars appear, and then the chilling moon. She waited. When the sun finally burst forth, she rose from the rock and sang to God:

The years have grown in me;
Like wood rings in the tree
They've rounded.
Patterns of winter winds
Swirled tightly,
Circles of summer sun
Spread wide.
The whorls remain within:

Here—coiled like a spring,
There—extended like an open hand.

I'm getting thicker now.
It takes more than a breeze
To rustle me.
I stand impervious to the rain
And rarely do I chill.

The sun itself must wage battle
To dry or drain me.
Surely I could make a brilliant fire—
I would crackle in a blaze,
Snapping as I burned.
My years consumed would render
A final pile of ashes—
Soft as chalky dust
And caustic.

But don't reduce me to ashes.
Let me rise among the green,
Tall and rooted,
Abundant with seed.
Let me bear fruit,
Let it ripen,
One, and then another,
Until
There will return to earth
What has been turned in me—
The years,
Patterns,
And circles—
To unwind
Endlessly.

And God said to Rivka: "Two will come from you, one stronger than
the other. The elder will serve the younger."

Then Rivka descended from the mountain and returned to her tent.
She lay down to rest and, for the first time in months, she slept deeply. She
dreamed of a storm, thundering in her being, and a violent thrust shook
her from within. A torrent streamed down her and she awoke. Her body
convulsed with its bittersweet fruit, and she watched as her blood-red son
emerged, followed by another holding fast on his heel: Esau and Jacob,
unwinding from their double coil.

Rabbi Susan Talve
A Midrash on the Moon

R. Simeon ben Pazzi pointed out a contradiction in the verse: At first it says, *And God made the two (equally) great lights,* and then it immediately follows, *the greater light and the lesser light* (Genesis 1:16). What happened in the breath it took to finish the verse that caused the moon to be diminished in size? The moon dared to wonder, "Is it possible for two rulers to wear one crown?" and, in the moment it takes to wonder, the Holy One responded by shrinking the moon to its present size, ever smaller than the sun.

"Just because I questioned the wisdom of Creation, should I be punished for all time?" asked the moon.

The Holy One recognized the injustice done to the moon. *"The sun shall rule by day, but the moon shall rule by night."*

"Good but not good enough," said the moon.

"The nations of the world will set their calendars by the sun but the people of Israel will set their sacred times by the newness and the fullness of the moon."

"This is good but not good enough. They will also need the sun for the establishing of their seasons."

"The righteous shall be called small, like the moon. Jacob, Samuel and David will all be called small to bring humility into the world. It will be for the sake of the Small (the young), that I will give Torah and mitzvot, the path for bringing peace to the world."

"This too is good but not enough. You must atone for the imperfections and the mistakes in Your creation."

"When all creation will learn to live together, each one a ruler crowned like the letters of the Torah, and when all have an equal share in the blessings that fill the world, then you will be restored to your rightful size."

"This is good," said the moon, "for this I and your smaller creations will wait."

And so the Holy One atoned for the mistakes in creation with the promise that one day, with creation's help, all children will grow to be old, all the oppressed will be free and all will be *shalem,* whole again, and the world will know *shalom,* peace. And once every month when the moon is full we will sing and dance in her glow and remember the Holy One's promise. May it come soon.

And Abraham Rose Early in the Morning

Sara studied the portion over and over again. "Male and female God created them..."(Genesis 1:27). In the beginning both male and female were created in the image of God. The Commentaries suggested that they were both essential parts of one whole. Each one reflected attributes that created *shalom:* peace and wholeness. What did it mean? Surely in this passage there was a secret to help her to bring peace to herself, her home, her world. She thought of Abraham, her husband and partner in leading their tribe. She and Abraham had such different strengths. Again and again she saw how both were necessary for keeping their history on the right track. There were differences that were more obvious. Her intuition was one they often spoke about. Sara always knew when a change or a trial was in store for them. But she knew that the greatest difference, what was uniquely hers as a woman, was her connection to life and life-giving. She often wondered why there was this great difference between them. Why Abraham wasn't driven as she was to make every decision, every choice for herself and her people on how it would affect the children and the welfare of the next generation. She knew it was not because she had physically given birth to Isaac. She felt this way long before they wanted to have children and even after she had given up all hope of having them.

Perhaps it was because of her *rechem,* her womb, that she had such *rachamim* (compassion). Then she thought of the expression, *Av ha Rachaman,* Father of Compassion, one of the many names for God. Does this mean that fathers are supposed to feel the connection of the womb, the *rechem,* too? Yes, of course, that must be her next challenge. She must share with Abraham the joy and responsibility of giving life. When she and Abraham, partners in parenting a child and a people, were both equally connected and devoted to giving life, then and only then would *shalom,* peace, be possible. With God's help she would think of a way for Abraham to give life as she did; with risk, with pain, with labor and with blood.

So it says, "And after these things God tested Abraham one more time and said unto him, 'Abraham,' and he said, 'Behold here I am.' And God said, 'Take your son, your only son, whom you love, Isaac, and go into the land of Moriah and make him an offering on one of the mountains which I will tell you.'" (Genesis 22) So Abraham rose early in the morning and through the Binding of Isaac labored to give life to his son.

III.
Jewish
Folk Tales

Rabbi Maurice Lyons
Missing the Mark

At times, even some of G-d's heavenly hosts sin thru failure to properly obey their Creator; as happened in the case of the Angel of Death. His punishment? G-d ordered him to fly down to earth, and marry a most wicked woman; such a woman who is described by King Solomon (Eccl. 7:26) as being more bitter than death!

Down from heaven he flew, his black wings spread, to fulfill G-d's grim punishment. He found, and married, such a shrew. However, he found it possible to live with her for only a year. After which he absconded.

Meanwhile, this evil woman gave birth to the Angel of Death's son. The father knew of this and, after some years passed, his heart beat in longing for his son. Stealthily he met the young man, to whom he revealed his parentage. "It is time," he said to his son, "that you contemplate your future. You must have a profession. I suggest that you become a doctor; and I will help you in this profession."

The son protested, "But, Dad, I know nothing about medicine!"

The Angel of Death replied, "That is no problem. Even to become a doctor, you don't have to know medicine. This is my plan: I will always accompany you to your patients. I shall remain invisible to everyone, except you. When you will see me at the foot of the patient's bed, you are assured the patient will recover, no matter what medicine you will give the patient. If, however, you will see me back of the patient's head, that will be an indication that the patient will die.

The son was persuaded and, with the help of his father, his practice grew voluminously; likewise his fame. His pronouncements concerning the fate of his patients were oracular.

It happened that the King's lovely princess became gravely ill.

The famous young doctor was called in on the case, and was promised one-half the kingdom by the distraught father if he would but cure his daughter.

The King and his entourage led the doctor into the princess' chamber, where she lay upon the bed, white as a sheet.

What horrified the doctor, however, was not the grave condition of the princess, but that at the head of the bed stood the Angel of Death!

The doctor asked the King and his entourage to leave the room, as he wished to be alone with the patient.

As soon as they left, the son began pleading with the Angel of Death, "Papa, you must leave the patient immediately! Please!"

However, the father stubbornly refused, despite the son's entreaties, saying, "The patient must die."

When the son realized that all his pleadings were to no avail, he angrily shouted, "Papa, if you don't leave the patient immediately, I shall call Mama!"

Upon hearing this threat a great fear gripped the Angel of Death and, spreading his black wings, he made a fast getaway; and the princess recovered!

Jewish Tales of Illusion

Retold by Howard Schwartz

There is a fascinating type of Jewish folktale in which one of the characters experiences an illusion out of time, where many years seem to pass in the space of a minute. These can be described as Jewish tales of illusion, and the world that these characters are cast into is known as *Ahizat Einayim,* the World of Illusion.

In each of these tales, the rabbis use their powers as conjurers to create spells of illusion. Those who experience these spells are astounded when they discover that they have been living in a world of illusion. But in each case they learn an important lesson that transforms their lives.

Some of these tales are found in early rabbinic sources. But this type of tale is most often found in medieval Jewish folklore and among the tales told about certain Hasidic rabbis, including the Baal Shem Tov, Rabbi Pinhas of Koretz and Rabbi Elimelech of Lizensk. Of the following three tales, "The Enchanted Inn" is of folk origin, while "The Underground Forest" is a Hasidic tale about Rabbi Pinhas of Koretz, and "The Tale of the Kugel" is also of Hasidic origin, and concerns Rabbi Menachem Mendel of Lubavitch I.

"The Enchanted Inn" combines two basic tale types: the illusion tale and the test tale. Ultimately the enchanted inn is a blend of a haunted house and place of illusion, a kind of juncture between this world and the Other Side. One interesting aspect of this tale is the explanation of all the mystifying events by the rabbi at the end. Here everything has a very clear meaning, and the rabbi demonstrates great powers of understanding.

"The Underground Forest" is a classic example of Reb Pinhas of Koretz in the role of Jewish conjurer. Reb Pinhas was an early Hasidic rebbe who was contemporaneous with the Baal Shem Tov. Here Reb Pinhas sends a student into a world of illusion, requiring a great struggle, which appears to last for ages, then breaks the illusion and reveals that only a short time has passed. But in the end the student comes to realize that it was all for a very important purpose.

"The Tale of the Kugel" is another fine example of the illusion tale. This tale portrays Rabbi Menachem Mendel I of Lubavitch, the Zemach

Tzaddik, as having great powers of illusion, as well as the powers to show a man a vision of the future path he will take. These tales are from the book, *Gabriel's Palace: Jewish Mystical Tales,* selected and retold by Howard Schwartz, published by Oxford University Press in 1993.

The Enchanted Inn

There once was a wealthy man who was very generous, but his wife was very stingy. From the front door her husband would welcome every guest, while she turned away every beggar from the back. Only once did she ever give any kind of charity. Then some sisters came to her house, crying out that their mother was about to give birth, and they were so poor they didn't have a sheet. That day the wife of the wealthy man pulled the white satin cloth off the dining room table, and handed it to the girls without saying a word. They thanked her profusely and hurried off.

This man and his wife were the parents of three sons. Then tragedy struck the family, and within a short time both the father and the mother died. Only the family servant, an old woman whose name was Miriam, was left to care for the children.

Now it had always been the dream of the merchant to ascend to the Land of Israel with his family, so the old woman decided to take the boys there, where they could be assured of receiving the finest training in the Torah. So she sold everything and traveled with the boys to Jerusalem. There she purchased a fine home for the boys, and continued to serve them.

Miriam wanted to choose the best possible teacher for the brothers, and she searched for one with great care. Then she had a dream in which an old man came to her and told her to go to seek out a certain Rabbi Nachshon. On waking the old woman remembered this dream clearly, and she set out at once to find this rabbi, for she had great faith in dreams. When she did, she told him her dream, and he said: "Send me the oldest one."

The next day Miriam brought the boy to the rabbi, who welcomed him and said: "Go and fast for today and come to me tomorrow afternoon and I will teach you Torah."

When the boy came back the next day at the appointed time, the rabbi showed him a goat that was tied to a tree outside his house, and said: "Untie the goat and follow it wherever it leads you. But remember this: if you are hungry, you may not eat, but if you are thirsty, you can drink."

The boy did as he was told. And as soon as he untied the goat, he had to hurry to keep up with it. The goat led him on a long chase, and at last they came to an inn, one he had never seen before. No sooner did the boy reach the inn than the goat leaped in through an open window. The boy followed the goat inside, and found that the inn was empty. Still, the scent of fresh food reached him, and he saw a delicious meal waiting on the table. He didn't wonder where it came from, but he was so hungry from fasting and the chase that he sat down and ate the entire meal without once remembering that this had been forbidden. While he was eating, the goat leaped back outside.

When at last he finished, the boy discovered the goat was gone. In shame the boy returned to the rabbi empty-handed. He confessed that he had lost the goat and had failed to keep his fast.

The rabbi showed the boy the goat, which was tied to the same tree. Then the rabbi said: "As you can see, the goat came back on its own. Now go home and send me you brother. You don't deserve to study Torah because you ate during the day of fasting."

The same thing happened with the second brother. Rabbi Nachshon gave him the same instructions, and he too followed the goat to the inn and could not restrain himself from breaking the fast. And when he returned, the rabbi also sent him away, and asked to see the youngest son.

When the third brother came to him, Rabbi Nachshon asked him also to fast and sent him to follow the goat, which led him by a long route to the same inn. There he saw all the food set at the table, but he didn't touch it. Instead, he went into a different room. That room was full of burning candles. He saw among them one candle that was about to go out, so he added oil to it and fixed the wick so it would keep burning.

Then he came to a third room from which seven stairs descended. And he saw a woman sitting at the bottom of the stairs, before an open pit. From where he stood he could not see her face. While he was watching, two men came and threw the woman into a pit filled with snakes and scorpions. Then they pulled her out of the pit and cleansed her with a white tablecloth. After that they threw her into the pit again. They kept repeating this over and over.

The boy became very frightened and left that room and went into a different one. There he saw an old man coming toward him, who offered him a cup of fresh water. And the boy remembered that he was permitted to drink if he was thirsty, and his thirst was very great. And when he drank of those miraculous waters, his heart opened to the Way of the Torah, and it was as if a hidden palace had been revealed. That is when he noticed that the glass was still as full as it was when the old man had given it to him. And he understood that it would never run dry. And as his eyes opened wider, he became filled with the wisdom of the Torah. That is when he saw the door to another room. He was drawn to that door, and when he opened it he saw an old man wrapped in a white *tallis,* which covered him so that the boy could not see his face. He was teaching Torah to students, and while the boy stood there and listened, the rabbi and his students discussed a fine point of the Law, which the rabbi interpreted one way, and the students another. And the boy was amazed to find that he understood what they were saying, and he couldn't help but get involved in it as if he were a true scholar. And in the end he not only joined the rabbi in his opinion, but convinced the others that the rabbi was right.

At that instant everything disappeared. The inn was suddenly gone, as well as the goat, and the boy found himself standing alone in a field. He was filled with dread. For a while he stood there, lost in confusion, then he caught sight of a path and decided to see where it would lead him. And before long he found his way back to the city.

When the boy entered the city, he went to the rabbi and told him what had happened. And the rabbi said: "You must know that the room of the food and drink was this world. And every candle that burned in the next room was a living soul. And the candle you preserved is your own, and now your life has been greatly lengthened. Know also that the room with seven stairs was *Gehenna.* As for the woman that you saw, she is your mother, who was stingy all her days and only gave a gift to the poor once.

That was a white tablecloth she gave to a woman about to give birth. And with that tablecloth they cleanse her from the pit. Thus is she punished, until her soul shall be pure enough to ascend the seven stairs and leave *Gehenna* behind. And the old man you met, who let you drink, that was Elijah, and that water, the water of the Torah. That is why the glass always remained full—for the wisdom of the Torah is inexhaustible. And last, but not least, there was the rabbi and the students. Know that the rabbi was your father, who gave charity all his days. And when he died he came to the World of Truth and received his award. And he sits in the yeshivah on high teaching Torah, blessed be he."

And the rabbi blessed him to continue in the ways of his father, striving equally in Torah and in good deeds. And before he gave him a final blessing, he told him to fast for seven days, for on each day of the fast he could raise up his mother another of the seven stairs, and thus save her from the judgment of *Gehenna*. And this, indeed, is what the young man did.

Eastern Europe: Nineteenth Century

The Underground Forest

On the eve of the third anniversary of his father's death, the student Reuven dreamed that his father came to him and told him to go to the town of Koretz. When Reuven awoke, he marveled at this dream, and how real his father had seemed to him. And he wondered about the strange message: to go to a place where he didn't know anyone. To whom and for what purpose? And how could he leave the Yeshiva? Surely they would forbid him to go on the basis of a dream.

All day Reuven strongly felt his father's presence, and the next night the dream was repeated, except this time his father told him when to go to the town of Koretz: for Rosh Hodosh, the Feast of the New Moon. Now Reuven realized that a decision must be made —whether to act on the dream or not.

The dilemma resolved itself the third night, when the dream recurred, except this time Reuven's father told him to go to Koretz for Rosh Hodosh and seek out Reb Pinhas.

After this third dream, Reuven decided that he must go, no matter what. His father had compelled him. He understood that. And he wrote a letter to the head of the Yeshiva explaining that he had left on business, to claim an inheritance in Koretz. This, he reasoned, would be more acceptable to him than his father's command in a dream.

Reuven took a carriage to Koretz. In the carriage were two Hasidim of that town. As Reuven listened, they spoke about Reb Pinhas. "It is said," said one Hasid, "that Reb Pinhas can read the thoughts of men." "This is true," said the other, "for I myself have heard of a man who came to Reb Pinhas when he was full of doubts that God could read his thoughts. When he knocked on the door, Reb Pinhas opened it and said: 'Young man, I myself know what you are thinking. And if I know, should not God know?'" And Reuven wondered what kind of man he had been sent to, who could read the thoughts of men.

Reuven arrived only a few hours before the eve of Rosh Hodosh. Reb Pinhas greeted him and told him that he would be welcome to use the *Mikveh* before the Feast of the New Moon that night. The young man thanked the rabbi and took his leave. He asked one of the servants where the *Mikveh* could be found, and he was directed to a hut behind the rabbi's house.

The young man walked to the little hut and stepped inside. He saw a stairway, but from the top of the stairs he could not see the water below. Instead, he heard a deep warbling sound, like the call of an exotic bird. "How strange," he thought to himself, "that this calling seems to come from within the *Mikveh*."

Curious to see for himself, the student descended the stairs, still wearing his clothes. Much to his amazement, the stairway was very long, much longer than that of any other *Mikveh* he had ever seen. And he soon found that he could see neither the top of the stairs nor the bottom from where he stood. He feared that something strange was taking place, as if he were descending from one world into another. "Surely," he thought, "no stairway could be this long!"

Each step of the way, the noise from below grew louder. Soon he could make out a cacophony of forest sounds—birds whistling, wolves howling, the wind shaking the trees. But the sound he expected, that of flowing water, was not among them. All at once he wanted to turn back, but he controlled himself and continued onward. "Surely," he thought, "I am almost there."

At last the student reached the bottom of the abyss, but he found no sign of a *Mikveh*. Instead, he found himself standing on the floor of a dense forest. Had he entered the wrong hut? The young man decided to turn back. But when he turned around, the stairs were gone. There was no sign of them at all. How would he ever return to the world above?

With no other choice, the student peered around him, and saw that it was growing dark. He knew that it was unsafe to stay where he was, so he looked for a tree in which to spend the night. He found one in a nearby clearing and pulled himself up into the branches. He was comfortable, but he knew he must not fall asleep or he would tumble to the ground.

When it was completely dark, a band of robbers came into that clearing and made a campfire not far from the very tree into which the student had climbed. He was well hidden in the branches, but he was terrified that the robbers would find him and strip him of everything, perhaps even his life. And it was true that they were a vicious band, for they bragged about their exploits, how many men they had killed and who among them was the most ruthless. They bragged half the night, until they fell into a drunken sleep. And all the while the poor student trembled in the tree, holding his breath for as long as possible, and then breathing very quietly. When they were asleep at last, the student was exhausted. He would have loved to have slept himself, but he knew his life depended on remaining awake.

So it was that the student in the tree saw a serpent slither toward the branch on which the robbers' wineskin had been hung, still open. The snake slid inside the wineskin, and stayed there a long time, filling itself with the wine, till it was so engorged that it spit up the wine, mixed with its own poison. Then the snake crawled out and disappeared into the forest.

When the robbers awoke in the morning, the student watched them take swigs of the wine. Then one after another they began to choke from the poison, and soon they all lay dead on the ground.

Now the student carefully lowered himself from the tree and made sure every one of the robbers was dead. Then he looked for something to eat. In one of the robber's bags he found a loaf of bread, but mostly the bags were crammed with stolen riches, with gold and silver and jewels of every kind. Reuven emptied bag after bag onto the ground and was amazed at all they had carried away. But when he shook out the last bag he could feel that it still had something in it. It occurred to him that the bag might have a false bottom. He took a knife and cut it open, and all at once a shining object came tumbling out—a round, glowing jewel. But try as he might, Reuven could not see the source of the light inside it. Surely, he thought, that was a priceless treasure. And he recognized that such a precious object could be owned only by a king.

Now this student cared little for material goods. His concerns were those of the spirit. He would not have minded leaving all the gold and silver behind, but he could not abandon that glowing jewel, so he put it into his own bag. Then he buried the robbers and said a prayer over their souls, for surely had they found terrible punishments for their evil deeds in the World to Come. And then he went on his way, going in the direction the robbers had come from, in the hope that he would find a city or town of some kind. And he gave thanks to God for letting him survive that dangerous night.

Little by little the faint path he followed became well worn, and that, in turn, led him to a road wide enough for the king's horse and carriage. Soon he reached the gates of that underground city.

There the student saw that the people of the city were dressed for mourning, and he asked a young man passing by what had happened. "Two tragedies have struck our kingdom at the same time. First, our king died without leaving any heir except for his daughter, the princess. And second, the king's enchanted jewel was stolen by thieves. Now this glowing jewel always sought out each king's successor. But now no one knows where it is. Even so, the princess has declared that she will marry whoever brings that glowing jewel to her, for the jewel has always succeeded in reaching the one who was destined to be king. For that jewel is guided by the Dove of Fate."

Now the student shivered when he heard this, for he was carrying the glowing jewel in his pack. He took his leave of the young man, and set off for the palace. And when he reached it, he asked for an audience with the princess, saying that he had news of the glowing jewel.

When the guards heard this, they took him to the princess at once, and he was overwhelmed by her great beauty and by the wisdom and radiance of her eyes. "Tell me," she said, "what you know about the golden jewel."

The student was speechless, but he pulled the jewel out of his pack and gave it to her. The princess looked at him with amazement and said, "Then it is you who is destined to be my husband, and you who are destined to rule. But how did you come into possession of the jewel?"

So the young man told her of his night in the forest, and all that he had witnessed. He offered to lead guards to that very place, to confirm his account and to recover the other items the robbers had stolen along with the glowing jewel. This was done, and the guards confirmed everything he had said. So it was that the wedding soon took place, and the young man, who had been a poor student, now found himself a great king in the underground country.

Now the young man ruled using the principles of the rabbis, as he had learned in his studies of the Talmud, and the kingdom flourished. So too did the young man fall in love with the princess, now his queen. Together they had three children, two boys and a girl, and he loved all of them as much as life itself.

Then one day it happened that there was a sudden downpour that grew into a great torrent. A great wave washed through the palace and carried the king out an open window and away from his family forever. For a long time the current carried him further and further downstream, and suddenly it thrust him into a great whirlpool. As he was pulled down, the young man was certain that his life had come to an end. Still, he fought against the whirlpool and tried to rise to the surface as best he could. All at once the young man found himself above the water, and he saw that he was standing in a *Mikveh*. That is when he recalled having descended the stairs in search of the *Mikveh* just before coming to the underground forest. Now he looked up and saw a short stairway nearby, with no more than ten steps. He climbed out and saw that the clothes he was wearing were not those of a king, but those of a student. And he was greatly confused.

The young man stumbled back to the home of Reb Pinhas. The moment the rabbi opened the door, the student burst into tears and asked the rabbi how long he had been gone. "Why, no more than an hour," Reb Pinhas said. Then the student told the rabbi of all the years that he had lived through since he had gone into the *Mikveh,* and poured out his heart and begged the rabbi to explain how such things had happened to him. For it seemed to him that the world had been turned upside down.

Reb Pinhas said, "Let me first introduce you to my daughter, and then I will explain." He called forth his daughter, and when the student saw her, he almost fainted. For she was the very princess he had wed in the underground city! The rabbi saw that the young man was overwhelmed, and he quickly said: "Listen carefully to what I tell you. I learned from a heavenly voice that it was you who were destined to marry my daughter. And when you arrived here, I recognized you at once. That is why I sent you to the *Mikveh,* for in this way you traveled the path of your own destiny, and now you can understand that you are indeed destined for my daughter."

So it was that the young man married the daughter of Reb Pinhas, and they loved each other as if they had already been married in another life. And they had three children, two boys and a girl, who were identical to the children he had had when he was king. And Reuven loved all of them with all his heart, and thanked God for restoring his family to him. And at the same time he held them dear to him at all times, for he remembered well how quickly they had been lost.

Eastern Europe: Nineteenth Century

The Tale of the Kugel

A Hasid who was a wealthy merchant once came to Rabbi Menachem Mendel of Lubavitch for permission to divorce his wife. The Hasid was worried, for he knew the rabbi regarded marriage as one of the pillars of existence and rarely gave his blessing for divorce. Nor would the man do anything without his Rebbe's permission, for the Rebbe was the pillar of his life. So he was quite tense when he came to the Rebbe's house and requested an audience.

The Hasid arrived just before breakfast. Indeed, the first thing that struck him as he walked inside was the delicious smell of the food. He had left before dawn in order to reach the Rebbe's house, for he hoped to return to his work before the end of the day. The Rebbe's wife seated him in the living room, but she did not invite him to join them for breakfast.

From where he sat the man saw the rabbi enter his study to put on his *Tefillin,* and heard him chanting his prayers. Even though the rabbi twice passed by the door of the living room, he did not look up, and he did not seem to notice the Hasid sitting there.

The morning passed. The Rebbe did not emerge from his study. Nor did any others come to the house. The man wondered why no other petitioners came that day, and why the Rebbe did not call him into his study.

Before long it was time for lunch. The man, who had not eaten since the night before, was tormented by the tantalizing scents of the cooking food. But still he was left to sit alone. Again the Rebbe passed the doorway twice but did not give any indication that he had seen him.

By evening the man was exhausted with hunger and waiting, but still there was no sign of the rabbi. Now the delicate smells of dinner reached him, tormenting him, in particular the smell of kugel, which he loved. If only they would take notice of him and invite him to join them for dinner! But they did not.

By the time the dinner ended, the man was deeply worried about the meaning of the rabbi's actions. So he was greatly relieved when the rabbi's wife came to him shortly thereafter, and led him to the rabbi's study.

When the man walked in the study, he was struck again with the smell of kugel, even more potent than it had been in the living room. At the same moment he saw the rabbi with a plate of kugel before him. Rabbi Menachem Mendel looked up at him, his eyes gleaming, and asked him why he had come. Then the Hasid poured out his heart about his wife, who had failed to give him a child in almost ten years, so that there would be no one to say the *Kaddish,* the prayer for the dead, for him. And since it is permitted to divorce a childless woman after that time, he had come to seek the Rebbe's permission.

The Rebbe stood up taking the plate of kugel in his hand, and offered it to the Hasid. "Here," he said, "first eat some kugel, then we will talk." At that moment the man remembered he was famished, and he gladly took the plate of kugel, picked up a piece, and took a bite of it. It was the most delicious food he had ever tasted. And yet, strange to say, he had taken no more than a single bite, when his hunger was gone.

At that moment the rabbi spoke: "Go now and know that I have approved your request. There shall be a *Get,* a bill of divorce, on your tenth anniversary. Be there with your wife on that day, and bring your wedding contract."

Amazed at how the Rebbe had agreed without any objections, the man left, and he was back there on his tenth anniversary to divorce from his wife. Not long afterward he remarried, and before a year was out he was the father of a beautiful girl. Indeed, every year after that he became the father of another daughter, until he had six girls but no boy who could say his *Kaddish.* And in despair he went back to the Rebbe.

This time he was given an audience as soon as he entered the door. Back in the Rebbe's chamber, the smell of kugel again struck him, and soon the Rebbe was standing, offering him to taste some. Remembering the good luck it had brought him last time in obtaining the Rebbe's approval, the man took a single bite, and at that very moment the Rebbe again gave him permission to divorce his wife.

By the time he had left his wife and six daughters, he was a much poorer man in silver and in spirit. But at least he was free to seek out his *Kaddish.* And in less than a year he was married again. This time his wish came true, and his wife's first child was a son. The man knew that he had been right all along to persevere for his son, even at the price he had paid, and he lavished love and gifts on him. And by the time the boy was three years old, he was recognized as a prodigy, and all who saw him predicted that he would be a great scholar in Torah.

It happened that the Hasid had to travel by ship for business. He could not bear the thought of leaving his son behind, so he hired a tutor and brought the boy with him on the voyage. Then one day there was a storm at sea, and the boat started to sink. It all happened so fast that the man was not able to save his son. He watched in horror as a great wave carried the boy off, and that was the last he ever saw of him. So great was his grief that he almost welcomed death, so he could be with his son again. But just then the mast of the ship floated by, and the man's instincts to save himself took over. He grabbed on to it just as a giant wave picked up the mast and bore it across the water for many hours, until the man found himself washed up on a distant shore. Eventually the heartbroken father made his way back to his home town, but he could hardly bear to break the terrible news to his wife. So he went to see the Rebbe first.

This time the Rebbe himself opened the door, and he recognized the man's grief at once. He gently led him into his study and gave him a seat. Then the Rebbe brought over a plate of food. "Would you like some kugel?" the Rabbi asked. And the man, remembering all the misery that his divorces had brought on, whispered, "No" and began to weep. And he wept with all his heart. When at last he looked up, he heard the Rebbe say, "No, you may not have a *Get*."

This greatly confused the man, and he said: "What do you mean, Rebbe? I have not come to you for a *Get*. Far from it. I have had enough of divorces. After two divorces I finally got the son of my dreams, and I lost him, due to my own foolishness in taking him with me on a dangerous voyage. If only it had been me, and not him, who had died!"

"Let me assure you," said the Rebbe, "that you have not been divorced even once. It is only now that you have requested your first divorce. Nor do you have any children."

"What do you mean!" the man shouted. "My first divorce was many years ago. Oh, if only I had not been divorced, my life would not have been ruined."

"Here," said the Rebbe, picking up a copy of a newspaper and showing it to the man. And he saw that it was the same day that he had come asking for his first divorce. And then he realized that only a short time had passed, while for him it had seemed like half of a lifetime. And he realized that a strange miracle had taken place, for he had seen the futility of divorcing his wife, whose only flaw was a failure to give him a son. The man was awed by what had happened to him, and he took leave of the Rebbe.

So too did he remain married, and before the twelfth year of marriage had passed, he was the father of a fine son, much to his amazement. And he loved that son with all his heart, and from the day the boy was old enough to understand, he made him take a vow that he would never set foot on a ship. So too did the boy keep this vow, and his life flourished. And when the merchant died, his son said *Kaddish* for him and always kept his memory alive.

Eastern Europe: Oral Tradition

IV.
LIFE
STORIES

Diann Joy Bank
Grandma Annie's Gourmet Delights

How can I describe the indescribable! That indescribable taste from your past that you can never forget—the one that takes you back, way back to your childhood.

I was only 12 when I began walking home everyday from Hanley Junior High always past that same warm, cozy, brick house at 1236 Midland Avenue in University City. When I least expected it, that's when I lost all control as my freckled nose was captured by that succulent aroma. "Wow! Grandma's done it again. She's made her gourmet delights. Just for me."

My brain didn't have to tell my feet what to do. With my heart thumping fast, my mouth watering, my feet raced down the white pebble rock driveway, down the side of the red brick house, around the worn wooden porch, up the three cracked steps, and right to her old screen door. This magic concoction rose up from the iron skillet on Grandma Annie's white porcelain stove and that aroma danced in every corner of her small square kitchen.

BAM! My nose pressed into the screen door when that smell hit my brain like a warm, wet kiss! "Hi, Grandma! It's me. Your Diann!" There she stood, my Grandma Annie, holding her fifty-year-old long handled spoon in her hand. Only four feet, eleven inches tall, with her salt and pepper hair, round small face with a *shmachel* (smile) that made you feel so safe and loved, and her pink flowered apron wrapped around her feather-stuffed pillow shaped body.

"*Nu* (so), have a *nosh* (snack). Sit! Eat!" There was a twinkle in her dark eyes. I wrapped my lanky arms around her, and squeezed all my love into her, smelling that special "grandma" smell. I watched her spoon her gourmet delights into the white china plate encircled with red strawberries on her square metal table.

"*Nu,* vhat are you vaiting for? Sit! Eat!" Such a *shmachel* flowed gently across her soft wrinkled face. I dipped my skinny fingers into her gourmet delights. So slippery, so drippy, so greasy, so perfect! Each bite slid down my throat, then dribbled down my chin. What ecstasy!!

Have you guessed what it is yet? I'll give you a hint. First, she spooned the greasy yellow glob of *schmaltz*-chicken fat (flavor is all that mattered then) into her skillet. Next she fried up onions (burnt onions are even better) and chicken skins and let them swim playfully together in the *schmaltz*. That's it.

You've guessed it? Maybe. Maybe not! Something you never see, would never eat (unless you had a grandma like mine), and you would never forget.

Of course, it's *Gribinas!* My Grandma Annie's Gourmet Delights! Was I blessed! Thanks, Grandma!

Gloria Shur Bilchik
The Ark and the Poet

A year later, I still wonder if anyone else noticed, or if it meant anything at all. I thought a lot about it, at first. Then I let go. For a while. This year, on Rosh Hashanah, the scene replayed itself in my head. The ark, the rabbi, so many of those celebrating around me were the same as last year, when it happened. Only I had changed, stronger, seasoned by Year 2 of my new life; more rational about what I'd lost and what, I could finally admit, I never had.

He died, suddenly, out of sight, alone, hours after our evening together. At his funeral, the rabbi read one of his poems. He wrote one every year for the High Holidays.

This poem was about questions, incompleteness, doubts. The impression it left was very strong, like his opinions, like his personality. It was a defiant poem, a challenge issued by an atheist with an ironic sense of humor and an incongruous urge to communicate with God. His personal version, perhaps, of *Avinu Malkeinu*. He had wanted it to be read at *N'ilah*.

"Are you listening, God," he wrote, undoubtedly scrawled on a scrap of paper that some unlucky decipherer had struggled to transcribe. "This time, we're not closing the ark at the end of services. We're not closing the ark until you give us a sign that you've heard us. We're waiting, God. We're keeping the doors open until you answer."

My memory of the exact words is imperfect. (A better journalist would call the rabbi right now and ask for a copy, to ensure accuracy.) It was part poem, part prayer, part debate. No nonsense. Like him.

On the Shabbat morning after his death, his presence, his aura, if I can be permitted a new-age image to describe a man steeped in tradition, was everywhere in the church library with a twice-a-month Jewish identity. Some of what I sensed, I think, was spiritual spillover from the night before, when they read his poetry, alluded to his philosophies, paid tribute to him through personal testimonies, and reminisced affectionately about his disapproval of rituals he regarded as "pagan." Friday night services had been, to a great extent, dedicated to him, his life, his memory, his philosophical and intellectual impact on the congregation.

Everything was as expected during Friday night services. It was about Shabbat, tradition, memories, new beginnings. I came back Saturday morning wanting a little more time in this comforting environment.

Our semi-circle of 10 or 12 read prayers, sang the songs. As usual, I suppose. I'm not a regular. Sitting, unpretentiously, in a metal folding chair next to the ark, the rabbi led us through, explaining the prayers, extrapolating meaning from the Torah portion, digressing, rhapsodizing.

The ark. I had noticed it the night before. Obviously hand crafted. Probably, I speculated, the inspired work of a congregant. Not at all like the automated, chrome-plated, over decorated affairs of the more establishment congregations he disdained. Its simplicity reminded me of the unadorned coffin in which he had been buried earlier that week.

I don't remember the Torah portion under scrutiny. (Another journalistic lapse.) I followed the Hebrew. The explanation, I missed. I was distracted.

That was when it happened. Listening to the rabbi's commentary, I watched as one of the ark's double doors slowly swung open, silently, unceremoniously, unannounced. Without missing a beat, without even looking up, almost absent-mindedly, the rabbi extended her arm, touched the door, and casually pushed it shut. Moments later, it unlatched itself and opened again. Again she closed it. And again.

That's all. For everyone there but me, it seems, it was an unremarkable sequence. Maybe this mechanical scenario happened often, and I'm attaching more to it than it deserves. Maybe a faulty hinge or an out-of-plumb floor was a familiar fact of life on Saturday mornings. It could have been an air current. That's rational. That's probably why the rabbi was so offhanded in her reaction. Yes, that must be it.

I'm a pragmatist, a realist, a non-fiction person all the way. It takes a lot to get me thinking mystically. That there are forces afoot arranging coincidences and symbolic serendipities is not my usual way of viewing the world. I read Jewish folk tales with a mixture of wonder and distance. So, I keep trying to convince myself, I should simply take this occurrence literally. Chalk it off to the broken-doorlatch theory and put it away forever. But I can't. Or I don't want to.

And so, reluctantly, I am drawn to the illogical. I can't shake the image of a very determined spirit, invisibly, persistently forcing that ark door open from within. I can't help thinking that, somehow, it was him. Pushing back, telling us—telling the God he didn't believe in—that he was still there, still questioning, still debating, waiting for the answers that will never come. Not ready to give up the fight. Not finished, not ready to admit that it was over, unwilling to concede the final point. Radiating energy. Stubborn to the end, and beyond. The very characteristics that both enlivened him and probably helped to kill him.

Go ahead. Tell me I'm wrong. Convince me that I'm over-romanticizing, over-analyzing again, making this all up, superimposing symbolism for the sake of a good story. Maybe the rabbi will read this and call to say they've had the ark door fixed. Case and ark closed. But maybe you were there that day and felt the connection, too. Or some other day since. Let me know. I'm still wondering.

Irving H. Breslauer
The Tenth Man

He was the last person through the door before they slammed it shut. He slid into the seat next to my own, buckled the safety belt and looked over at me triumphantly, if short of breath. "Made it."

"Just," I replied. "I thought you military people were more organized than that and only O.J. Simpson ran through airports."

He almost smiled. "He doesn't have to go as far as I did. Last night, or was it the night before, I was half in the bag, sitting in a restaurant on Tudo Street with my friends." He paused, "Tudo Street is in Saigon. I'm stationed there. Not in Saigon really. I'm at Tan Son Nhut Air Base just outside the city. That's headquarters for U.S. Air Forces in Southeast Asia."

"Should you be telling me this?" The newspapers were full of the war, I was against our being in Vietnam and I wasn't really interested in listening to some Air Force Colonel talk all the way from San Francisco to New York.

He shook his head from side to side, "Oh, that's not classified. I wouldn't talk about classified stuff."

I grunted acknowledgment and closed my eyes. A 10 PM take off from California meant getting into New York at about 7 AM. I had hoped the seat next to me would be empty so I could stretch out but now that was out. It was going to be a long uncomfortable night.

My closed eyes didn't deter him. He continued to talk. "I've only been over there three months. Hardly enough time to need a haircut. I'd been in Nam before but only as a crew member on airlift missions from the states. Now it's different. I'm on the headquarters staff, Director of Public Affairs."

I wasn't interested. I tried rudeness. "I guess you're going back East to report how well the war is going or something like that?"

"No, I'm going home on emergency leave, my father died. I don't think I'll make it in time for the funeral, but I'll be there to sit *shiva*." His voice trailed off. Then after a moment, in a firm voice as if he were giving a briefing. "*Shiva* is a ritual that Jews go through after someone dies. It lasts about a week." An afterthought, "I'm Jewish."

I sat up. "I'm Jewish too. You don't have to explain *shiva* to me, but what's half in the bag?"

His laugh caught in his throat. "No big deal. It just means I was a little high." I must have looked uncomfortable. He rushed on. "Not drugs, I don't do drugs, just some wine with dinner, I was at a party in town. Anything to get away from the base."

His father had just died, he already had traveled halfway around the world, he probably needed someone to talk to. I could put aside my feelings about the war and the military and listen to him for a little while. Besides, he was Jewish. But what was a Jewish boy doing in Vietnam, in the Air Force, a Colonel with wings and ribbons on his jacket and clouds and lightning on his hat brim? So I asked him.

"I was in WW II, got out in '45. Went back to college, got recalled for the Berlin Airlift and then there was Korea. By the time that was over I had ten years in so I decided to stay. Vietnam is where my job is right now so I'm there." His voice choked just a little. "That is I'm there when I'm not going home on emergency leave."

I thought maybe I should shift the conversation a little bit. "You said you were a director of public affairs. What is that job? What do you do?"

"I'm responsible for troop information and community relations but the most important part is getting the news out, media relations we call it. I haven't had a chance to meet most of them but there are more than 400 news people covering the war."

"Have you met any of the ones we see on TV all the time?"

"Some of them. In fact I was at a party with news people when I got the word my father had died. I just had time to rush back to the base, change into my blues, throw a towel over the mirror in my bathroom and catch the freedom bird out to the Philippines."

I must have looked confused.

"I know you probably know about covering the mirrors so it must be the freedom bird you don't understand. That's what we call the planes going back to the states, Japan, the Philippines or Australia on R&R."

I nodded understanding and he went on. "You asked about the news people. I made friends with several of them and got along with most of them. I wasn't at war with the media, I wasn't even mad at them. They were doing their job like I was doing mine. I'm sure they didn't want to be in Vietnam any more than I did. In fact, I enjoyed the chance to go downtown and meet with them in what passed for a good meal in a decent restaurant."

"You said you got called away from a party." I interrupted. "What were you celebrating?"

"Well, Abe Rosenthal, the editor-in-chief of the *New York Times* was visiting and the local *NYT* team was hosting a small dinner party for him at the Mayfair restaurant. Al Shuster, the *Times* bureau chief called me and invited me to join them.

"I got to the Mayfair a little bit late and the *mamasan* there told me the Rosenthal party was upstairs in a private dining room. I went up and when I got in the room I saw only a few people there.

"I recognized Rosenthal from his pictures and I had met the other eight. Al Shuster, Ralph Blumenthal and Henry Kamm were from the *Times*. Joe Fried was from the *NY Daily News,* Dave Miller the bureau chief of CBS, Jack Klein from NBC, Mike Horowitz from ABC and Peter Jay was from the *Wall Street Journal.* I didn't see any other military people.

"'I'm honored to be here,' I said, 'especially when the Army guy is a Brigadier General and outranks me.' 'Hell,' Shuster said. 'We didn't invite you because you're a Colonel, we invited you because we needed a tenth man for a *minyan.*'"

Rabbi Helen T. Cohn

Esther's Place

I had two exams in the morning, easy ones that have left me ready for adventure. So I call Esther, my best friend from college who has lived in Jerusalem these past 20 years. She invites me to spend the afternoon with her.

We meet in the center of town and drive to the Ministry of the Interior. On the outside this is an ordinary building; in the inside it is clearly government offices. The building does not inspire feelings of efficient or courteous service. In a week, Esther and I are taking our children to the Sinai for several days. She has four children, I have two whom I haven't seen in the six months that I've been studying in Jerusalem. This morning she thought to check her passport. It has expired. She has a week to accomplish what normally takes months.

Esther's Hebrew is fluent and her manner is perfect for the occasion: polite and firm with a hint of playfulness. She does not back down, she is not deterred by forms and problems and long-winded explanations. I don't understand the rapid Hebrew, but she's clearly succeeding as she threads her way through the bureaucracy, leaving each clerk smiling.

By tomorrow she needs to get photographs and her ex-husband's agreement that the children can leave the country. They divorced when he became religious. He now dresses in black and has changed his life utterly. She loved him very much. She still shakes her head when she speaks of him. There is a question about whether he will give his permission.

Back at her house, her oldest daughter is unexpectedly home from high school, having lunch with a friend. A teacher was absent, so the class was dismissed for several hours. The school cannot afford substitutes.

Esther's house is never empty. The girls go upstairs and James comes over. James is an Englishman who has lived in Jerusalem for many years. At one time he was Esther's lover. Now he lives down the street and daily stops by to borrow three cigarettes and a lemon. Or some garlic. Or a tea bag. Once he came over and said, "I don't have any food. Could you give me a potato or something for dinner?" "Of course," Esther said, "how about some broccoli too? Some herring? Bread? There's chicken from last night. Cheese?" He had the grace to leave with just the potato and broccoli, but came back later to borrow a canister of gas for his stove.

How do you put up with it? her friends ask. "Oh, it's ok. He's nice to the kids."

As I make coffee and James lights his first cigarette, Deborah and Sue walk in. They aspire to fame in international fashion, the two of them, with Esther helping behind the scenes. She's the one who knows the secret of transforming ideas into colorful reality. Deborah and Sue have come for a consultation.

James and I go into the kitchen, since the living room is also the sewing room (and the dining room). We help ourselves to pieces of sugared citrus rind in a jar. I say that the woman with the dog made it. "Which woman," he asks, "the lesbian?" "No, the other one—the lonely one." Both women have dogs that look the same to me. Frequently when you sit in Esther's living room, you will hear the front door open and someone come in. After a while, if no one appears, you call out, "Who's there!" Sometimes it's James, already leaving with borrowed food. Sometimes it's a stranger, or an old friend from the States. You never know. But when it's one of these women you know right away because the dog bounds into the room, sniffing for food and affection. The lonely woman is a neighbor, originally from Russia, who occasionally comes to Esther's place unannounced and sits in an old armchair for several hours. She doesn't say much. She surreptitiously feeds crumbs to the dog from a plate of cookies. Only when he whines to go outside does she get up heavily and say a reluctant good night. Afterwards, Esther sighs and says to the air, "Well, I feel sorry for her. She's all alone, you know."

Deborah and Sue ask Esther's opinion on the rug for their new store. A grey square passes from hand to hand. In the kitchen James explains to me his latest spiritual excursions. In the middle of a sentence he lifts his head and says, "I have to see if there's a phone call," and leaves. Soon after, Deborah and Sue breeze out, just in time because Esther's two youngest children are now home from school and are asking for lunch. The phone rings. Carol Ann wants to know if she can borrow Esther's car for the afternoon. The phone rings again. Someone wants to buy the piano, which is currently disassembled in a corner of the living room, near the sewing machine. The piano is a separate story. So is Carol Ann. Meanwhile lunch is a bit burned. Esther is usually an excellent cook. Her Friday night dinners would delight the Sabbath Queen, so her daughters do not complain about blackened hot dogs.

I go with her to a brief doctor's appointment, a check-up for an insurance form. I wait in the hall of the Public Health Service building and get a glimpse of the doctor, an elderly man from Eastern Europe. She covers her mouth as she leaves his office, to hide her amusement. During the exam he asked if she has had a mammogram recently. She commented about the smallness of her breasts. The doctor gave each breast a friendly squeeze and said, "They're not too small, they're nice!"

When we return to her house, Angela and Isaac are there. Twenty years ago Angela and Esther opened Jerusalem's first boutique, The Gypsy. After a while Angela married and left Israel. She now lives in her native country, Switzerland, with her second husband Isaac. He is Israeli. They have been here for several weeks on vacation. They love Israel but cannot resist Western efficiency and easy Swiss francs.

Esther's house has been chosen as the meeting place. Tzvi, Angela's first husband, is in town and coming by to say hello. Tzvi is the middle-aged son of a well-known Israeli politician. Years ago he fled to New York (with Angela) to escape his father's fame. He was a writer, now he makes movies. Angela saw him a while ago and said he was fat and balding.

He's not fat now. He's tall and emits a certain power. However his face is pale. He seems a brooding person. He and Esther haven't seen each other in 15 years. They talk about his films. She is animated, curious. He slouches in the old armchair and responds slowly. Still, he's an attractive man.

The front door is ajar. A cat wanders in. Esther gets up and shoos him away.

Angela and Isaac bring out Arab bread from the *shuk,* large circles of soft fresh bread with toasted sesame seeds on top. Esther prepares a tray with two saucers; olive oil in one and the Middle Eastern spice *za'atar* in the other. I make coffee for everyone. Tzvi says, "You must promise me you'll give me decaf, and no mistake." The front door opens. You never know. This time it's Esther's teenage son, Leib. He's practiced in dipping pieces of bread first in the olive oil then smearing it in the spice. He eats an entire roll and after the *za'atar* is finished he continues to dip bread in olive oil. Leib is tall and slender and serious. He seems burdened. An Israeli teenager three years from the army.

Tzvi rises to leave. He had hardly spoken to Angela and Isaac. As he and Esther finish their conversation, Isaac puts his hand on his wife's thigh. Tzvi says to Esther, "I'll give you a call." She nods her head.

Angela stands, kisses each side of Tzvi's face carefully, and says, "If you're ever in Switzerland..." An awkward moment; we try to laugh.

The children have drifted away, I sense Esther's desire for a quiet moment with Angela and Isaac, so I prepare to leave. She walks me outside, into the vast blue afternoon.

"One of these days I'm going to write about you," I tell her.

"Really?" she says, surprised. "Why me?"

Robert A. Cohn
Note in a Bottle

"It was like putting a note in a bottle and throwing it into the sea and having it arrive in the right place as by a miracle."

The above are the words of Lazarus Rubanovich, a 90-plus Moscow Jewish resident, in response to the incredible coincidence that unfolded when he addressed a letter in January 1988 simply: "Jewish Community, Saint Louis, USA."

The U.S. Postal Service thoughtfully forwarded the letter to the Jewish Federation of St. Louis, and because it was seeking to make contact with long-lost relatives, it was forwarded to my office for publication in the *St. Louis Jewish Light.*

As I prepared the letter for publication with an appropriate editor's note, I was struck by the fact that the letter writer, then a 90-year-old Moscow resident, indicated that two of his uncles, Abracham and Eizer Rubanovich, moved to St. Louis from Russia in 1906 and 1908— years in which I recalled several members of the family of my mother, Lillian DeWoskin Cohn, moved to St. Louis from the Ukrainian town of Glukhov.

To make a long and complicated story very short, I discovered to my utter amazement that Lazarus Rubanovich's uncles were none other than the late Abe and Ezra Rubanowitz—both of them uncles of my mother by marriage to different members of the DeWoskin family! If ever there was proof of the Jewish concept of *bashert,* a coincidence so astounding that it suggests divine intervention, something which C.G. Jung called "synchronicity," this certainly had to qualify.

Abe Rubanowitz, remembered fondly for his poems at DeWoskin Club family meetings, had worked as an insurance agent in St. Louis. His brother, Ezra, began in St. Louis as a paper hanger and later operated a local restaurant. Both Abe and Ezra have surviving children in St. Louis and other parts of the country.

Lazarus Rubanovich's letter, written just a few months before his 90th birthday in June 1988, was written in Yiddish, and accompanied by a translation into excellent English by his granddaughter, Julia Rubanovich, who had recently completed her medical education at Moscow University. Her parents, Grigory and Bella Rubanovich, also lived in Moscow. As a result of the original letter and its subsequent publication in the *Jewish Light,* Julia Rubanovich was to be united with cousins in Chicago, where she completed medical retraining and the first steps toward eventual U.S. citizenship. Her parents and grandfather also moved to the United States.

In his original letter, Lazarus Rubanovich said that he had corresponded regularly with his St. Louis uncles until 1943, when the pressures of World War II interrupted such communications. Until Gorbachev and *glasnost,* it was extremely risky for Russian Jews to write letters abroad.

"I hope that my cousins or their children still live in St. Louis," wrote Lazarus. "If you have any information concerning my relatives and if they want to renew our relations, it would be very kind of you to help us. I am very grateful for your attention."

Conversations with my mother and other relatives put me in touch with Meyer Ruban, the son of the late Abe Rubanowitz, whose wife was Sima DeWoskin, daughter of Naphtoli DeWoskin, my great-grandfather. I also heard from Marlene Rubanowitz Miller, the granddaughter of Ezra Rubanowitz.

In the Jan. 18, 1989 edition of the *St. Louis Jewish Light,* I published an article headlined "Letter by Soviet Jew seeking cousins gets immediate results."

Many of the cousins from around the country excitedly wrote to their long-separated relatives in Moscow. I sent copies of the article and numerous family photographs of the family members in America, many of which had been taken by our late uncle Philip DeWoskin, a master photographer.

Ultimately, all of us received warm and almost unbelieving replies from Lazarus, Grigory, Bella and Julia. In response to the fact that by coincidence the letter landed on the desk of the editor of the local Jewish newspaper who happened to be among the cousins, Lazar said, "It was like putting a note in a bottle and throwing it into the sea and having it arrive in the right place as by a miracle."

Miracle was also the word used by Meyer Ruban, son of Abe Rubanowitz, who now resides in Covenant House Apartments, to describe the reconnection with the Russian branch of his family after so many years. (Meyer Ruban died in early 1997.)

Several cousins continued to correspond with their Moscow relatives, and one very happy result was the decision by Julia Rubanovich to move to the United States to continue her education and take steps toward American citizenship.

Julia, 26, has a smile as sunny as her burnished hair, and reflects both intelligence and sensitivity in her conversations—traits that were also present in her translation of her grandfather's original letter.

After a brief stay with Frieda Rubanowitz Schwartz, daughter of Ezra Rubanowitz, in Los Angeles, Julia moved to Chicago, where she was the guest of Barry and Linda Newman in the suburb of Woodridge. Linda Kotlicky Newman is the daughter of Celia Rubanowitz Kotlicky, also of Chicago, another daughter of Ezra Rubanowitz.

In May 1991, Julia accompanied the Newmans on a visit to St. Louis, where the Newmans attended commencement ceremonies at Washington University, where their daughter, Lisa, was a student. The following Sunday, they were the guests of Mel and Marlene Rubanowitz Miller, where Julia met several of her local relatives for the first time, including Meyer Ruban, the son of the late Abe Rubanowitz. As a relative by marriage, I was among those privileged to attend.

We met a vivacious, soft-spoken and highly intelligent cousin in Julia, who had trained as a nurse before becoming a physician with a specialty in internal medicine. She enjoyed a quick tour of St. Louis, which included a ride to the top of the Gateway Arch, and was excited to learn that Mark Twain, whose novels she had read in the Soviet Union, was originally from Missouri.

Julia said she regretted that her grandfather, Lazar, had been unable to accompany her on the trip as originally planned. "He is a very determined man, but we decided that the long trip was not a good idea for him, and I feel it was a right decision after the long airplane trip," said Julia.

It was that same kind of determination that caused Lazar to insist that his granddaughter translate his letter to his long-lost cousins and send it to St. Louis, where it landed in the right place.

"I told him that there was almost no possibility that the letter would reach our cousins," recalled Julia. "But I am so glad that he insisted, so that I could be united with our cousins after so many years."

We learned that the Rubanowitz family survived World War II and the Nazi invasion by a series of evacuations from their original hometown of Glukhov in the Ukraine and the Russian town of Samara, before moving to Moscow in 1972. The Rubanowitz family does not know of any members of the DeWoskin family who might have remained in the Soviet Union through the war.

From Glukhov and Moscow to Los Angeles, Chicago and St. Louis— across a span of over 60 years—is indeed a long journey for Julia Rubanovich. "We cannot figure out this miracle, but we are very thankful for it nonetheless," said Meyer Ruban of the *bashert*-caused reunion. "We are not supposed to figure such things out, but we are entitled to thank God for them."

Shelly R. Fredman
Between Two Worlds: Leah's Story

Ten years ago, I was given the daunting task of playing Leah, the young girl whose body is inhabited by her dead lover in the second act of *The Dybbuk*. A Jewish Theatre Group was performing the play at Hillel. Our director told us, "Seek your own life within the circumstances of your character," but I wasn't sure if I had any experiences with death that I could call upon. One set of grandparents had died when I was a child, but I barely remembered that. Although my remaining ninety-year-old grandfather threatened to die every day, the sheer force with which he threatened convinced me he would go on living forever.

My husband, who I had only recently married, had buried his first wife, Elly, only three years before. Elly had been a disturbing presence in my life ever since I met my husband, but I was too young and inexperienced to understand her power. A while ago, he had given away most of her clothes and jewelry, but I kept coming upon her spices on the kitchen shelf as I tried a new recipe. It was as though some parts of her were being poured into my soup, my pasta, my rice. But I hadn't known her. How can you reach back to, seek out someone you have never known?

Our director brought in a rabbi to supply background who told us that the mystics of Safed believed that the soul hovers after a person dies, reluctant to leave the body, the vessel that contained it, and the place it once called home. I began to sense Elly around me. Candles on the night stand flickered when my husband reached for me, though there was no breeze, not a hint of wind in the room.

And then on opening night, in scene eleven, as I began speaking, about three lines in, something happened. At the edge of that blurred line where the stage lights gave way to the audience, something, or shall I say someone, stood. At first she was a bare presence, no more than a shadow. But as I continued speaking my lines, she became something more.

If I could have stepped out of my role, I would have seen the edges of people's shoes, the thin, silver legs of their chairs barely lit, the wash of the lights spreading out just beyond the stage. But I was Leah, completely at one with her, and just beyond that darkness, someone was waiting, listening to every line. I knew she was there, impossible as it was, among the rows. Quiet, but as real as the silver legs of the chairs, and listening to me. A heart feels a heart, my grandpa had once told me, and there was mine, beating, and hers there, too, like an echo.

Our language, unlike the lines of the play, is not transcribable. What happened on that stage went beyond language, more idea and feeling than words. It was a silent murmuring, and exchange of heart beats and pauses.

After the monologue was over, I drew back a few feet, my legs quivering. As I made my way offstage, I was hoping no one had noticed I had been addressing my lines to someone not even remotely connected to the play. I knew I could never explain what had happened out there.

Now, ten years later, with this production presented by Hillel and Washington University, I have been given a chance to revisit *The Dybbuk*. I no longer believe this is strictly a coincidence. I have spent a good portion of the last ten years living as a traditional Jew, shaping *challahs* just before *Shabbat,* my hands turning and turning the round loaves of warm dough, much the way Leah would have. I have sat in other people's living rooms, listening to rabbis share the rich legacy that is my people, listening to the stories and lessons that inform Anski's play. And I have finally had those death experiences I naively wished I had had all those years ago, so I could perform the role.

I have sat at the bedside of a friend who was dying, watched her eyelids flutter and felt the presence of *Hakadosh Borchu* in the room. I have stood at my grandfather's grave (the one who was always threatening to die and eventually, of course, did) and read a letter I wrote to him, felt the wind curl around us, watched the sycamore leaves dance in the breeze and felt absolutely certain he was there, listening to me tell his story for the last time.

I have spent much of the years since I performed Leah learning that the physical does not last, but the spirit goes on forever. I have lived the cycles of the Jewish year, and worked to attain that "heart of wisdom" the rabbis speak of. I have discovered that death is a part of life, that it all turns as certainly as the red leaves drifting from the maples that will be green again in the spring. And I have come to believe that in strange and unstranslatable ways, there are connections between us that are beyond our imagining.

I approach *The Dybbuk* differently now, having come to believe, like Anski, who originally titled the play *Between Two Worlds,* that there is a realm of the spirit and sometimes we bump up against it. The leaps we can make in connecting to that world, whether taken by faith or imagination alone, are astounding. Sometimes, though, we are led along by the unseen hand of someone we have loved and lost.

In the dim rehearsal hall where they are running the last scenes of the play, I sit, envying this young Leah. I would be thrilled to play the part today, because I believe her so much more than I used to, but I am too old. I can only sit in the audience on the night of the performance and watch, daring myself, as we all must, to take the journey with her when the lights dim. Hers is a landscape of spirits and demons, strange messengers and angels, but when the lights finally come up, if we have truly gone along, we stumble between too-brightly lit aisles, still traversing two worlds.

Gloria Rudman Goldblatt
Tricking the Angel

For thousands of years, the battle has been waged—*Malach ha-Moves,* the Jewish version of the Angel of Death, versus man trying to avoid the inevitable. Traditional tales record that trickery has worked better than hand-to-hand combat for man to postpone being taken by the Angel with his poisoned sword. Legend has it that King David himself tried to avoid his death after God told David he would die on the Sabbath in his 71st year, though He refused to name the day. During that year on Sabbath, David would diligently study the Torah, as it was believed to be a way to keep the Angel at bay. When the Angel came at the fated time, he could not enter David's room while he studied pious works. However, the Angel went to the garden and started shaking a tree. David heard the noise, and left his studies to seek the cause. The stairway to the garden collapsed, killing him. If King David's trickery was not successful, what hope for ordinary people?

And yet, ordinary people, too, have tried to trick the Angel of Death, according to customs that survive in Jewish folkways. I did not realize how the thread of these customs was woven into the fabric of so many lives until I began to ask questions while gathering family records and stories. One record leading to questions was the February 27, 1912 ship manifest of the S.S. Pennsylvania which brought many Russian immigrants, including my father, Morris Rudman, his mother, Temma, and his two sisters, Helen and Frieda, to the U.S.A. But Frieda's name is listed as "Alta," not Frieda. I asked Dad to explain.

Morris Rudman remembered that the name "Alta," literally "old person" in Yiddish, was given to young Frieda when she and her twin brother suffered a childhood illness in Bilhorodtka, Russia, and Frieda's twin died. Frieda barely clung to life. It was the custom to give a seriously ill person a different name to trick the Angel of Death. They re-named Frieda "Alta" so if *Malach ha-Moves* came looking for a child named Frieda, he would find "Alta"—an old lady! Though Frieda was critically ill, and her fever did not go below 105 for a week, she did survive. She did not use the name Frieda again until arriving in the U.S.A.

My husband's aunt, Ruth Goldblatt Goodman, remembers tricking the Angel in another way—by changing her place of residence. Earlier in Lublin, Poland, her parents, Rachel and Boruch Goldblatt, lost several infant daughters to childhood diseases, though their two sons survived. After Boruch and Rachel came to the U.S.A., they were overjoyed when their daughter, Ruth, was born. However when she got measles, they saw it as a death sentence. Before the County Health Department came to put up the quarantine signs, they moved her to their son Ben's household. The Angel of Death would not know where to find Ruth when he could not find her in her parents' household. Conveniently, Ben and Fanny's two sons, Sam and Stanley, had developed measles the same day. So the children stayed in a dark room for two weeks, as was the custom in the 1930's, "to save their eyesight." And Ruth survived, too.

Those who study names of older generations of family will often find a double first name, only one of which is a birth name. A favorite seems to be "Chaya" or "Chayim," literally "full of life." There are also other names that reveal a family's efforts to guard their lives in a crisis by tricking the Angel of Death.

From the Shtetl to St. Louis in 1912

Two million immigrants came to the United States from Eastern Europe between 1880 and 1914, the beginning of World War 1. Many were Russian Jews escaping religious persecution and harsh economic conditions decreed by the Czars. The journey from the old world to the new becomes personal as retold by Morris Rudman and his sister, Helen Rudman Polinsky, in their later years. When they left their town, Bilhorodtka, Ukraine in 1912, Morris was 12 and Helen was 17.

Their father, Louis Rudman, had left in 1905, ending up in St. Louis, where he had *landsleit*. The older sons, Harry and Jake, soon followed. Louis found work in the egg business, and did well enough to send for his wife, Temma, and the other children. He even had a little bungalow on Bacon and North Market Street ready. Temma would not leave because Louis' mother, Reva, was too ill to travel. But in 1911, a grandchild was born in the U.S.A., and Reva died. Temma was ready to leave.

Leaving Russia

MORRIS: We prepared to leave Bilhorodtka. First we stopped in Lacherwitz to spend our last night with Mama's mother, Bobbe Bessie. She knew we were leaving for good, but was cheerful. From there it was a tough journey to the border, first by wagon—at the end, we had to walk probably 30 or 40 miles in snow and ice.

HELEN: We had to cross the border at night where armed guards patrolled. Our group had a paid guide who bribed the border guards. Then he hid us in a shack with straw on the floor where we rested. In the middle of the night they signaled us to go to the train for the port of Hamburg. A lot of our baggage was lost or stolen during our train journey.

MORRIS: We had to stay in Hamburg four days to wait for our ship to leave. The people who sold the boat tickets arranged places for everyone to stay. There were plenty of immigrants waiting to leave.

On Board the Ship

HELEN: We didn't understand. We had first-class tickets—when we boarded S.S. Pennsylvania, the porters put us in steerage—it was terrible. I made friends with a young lady in first class, and she invited me to visit her stateroom. I felt like I was in heaven!

MORRIS: I needed a vaccination to get in the U.S.A. I went all alone down those strange hallways to the ship's doctor to get it. At first I was afraid of the gruff German doctor, but he became friendly. After 18 days of rough weather and being seasick, we entered New York harbor, February 27, 1912. Everyone rushed to the side of the ship—we were excited to see land, and the Statue of Liberty!

Ellis Island and a Train Journey

MORRIS: We arrived at Ellis Island at night. It was like the airport nowadays—people running and pushing. Then we had to get the health examination. Fortunately our family passed. Some didn't, and were sent back. Many had eye trouble. In the morning we went by cab to the train—we didn't get to see much of New York.

HELEN: We got on a beautiful train, and as we were sitting, we noticed people getting up to leave. We later found out they were going to their sleeping compartments. We had tickets for that too, but no one told us, and we could not communicate.

MORRIS: We were dressed like immigrants—they put us in second class. I don't think the other people wanted to ride with us!

HELEN: I thought we would be in St. Louis by morning— I tried to look nice. I opened my suitcase and put on a fresh blouse, and a ribbon in my hair. Suddenly the train stopped, and they put us on another train that was dirty and hot like a cattle car. When Papa met us at Union Station, he asked why we were on such a train. And when he found out we came over steerage, he complained to the ship line, and got a refund from them and the train.

<u>A New World</u>
MORRIS: Papa took us to our home—it had nice furniture, and everything for the kitchen. But Mama cried. She noticed Jewish women who didn't wear *shaitels* (wigs)—how shameless to leave their hair uncovered! She said America was a country where the Jews would lose their religion.

HELEN: Papa prepared the cottage on Bacon Street with new furniture, jewelry for all the women, and new American-style clothing. He welcomed us in style. Our family was happy to be together again.

(Edited by Gloria Goldblatt from interviews with her father, the late Morris Rudman, and from Joanna Polinsky Berens' interview with her grandmother, the late Helen Polinsky.)

Rabbi James Stone Goodman
In Israel They Speak Hebrew

We moved into what was formerly an Arab neighborhood in Jerusalem. It has a Hebrew name now, but everyone calls it by its old Arabic name. The streets are narrow and even the new building and renovations preserve the style, square houses, decorated with ceramic, the courtyards and small gardens, of an Arab village. There is a perfect example of one such house at the end of our street. When we first moved in, I noticed an old man sitting on the balcony of the second floor of the house. He sat in the sun, with his hands folded over a cane. He wore a large black hat in the North African style, a long beard, and even from a distance, I saw a beautiful dark Mediterranean face.

The next day, I watched him slowly walk up the street to the synagogue in time to pray *Mincha* and *Ma'ariv* (afternoon and evening prayers) in the late afternoon. And the next day, and the next.

A few days later, we were walking our daughter Adina to school early in the morning. We met him in the street. He stopped and took Adina's little face in his wrinkled hands, he smiled and repeated one word, laughing as he said it, "*mal-kush,*" or something like it. I didn't know the word "*mal-kush,*" but he stood there in the Jerusalem sun, holding Adina's face in his wrinkled hands, the perfect symmetry of his wrinkled hands and Adina's peanut face, giggling and saying "*mal-kush, mal-kush.*"

A few days after that, I ran into him again on our street. This time he was with a younger man who introduced himself to me as his son. I told his son the story of the encounter of his father and my daughter, and I asked him, in Hebrew, "What language was your father speaking? What was he saying?"

His son laughed, much like his father, and said to me, "Probably Arabic. He was born in Algiers but he has been in the Land for a long time. My father has seen many things in his life," his son said to me. "He speaks many languages, and sometimes even I don't understand him," and he laughed again.

Two weeks after I arrived in Jerusalem, I went into the post office to retrieve a package sent to us from a friend in the States. In the post office, an old Russian man was standing at the window next to me trying to mail a large box to the States. An Israeli (a former Russian, I assume) was helping him fill out the form. They came to the part where they have to declare what is in the box and the Russian was explaining to the Israeli who was trying to translate it into English for the form to accompany the package to America. Finally, the post office clerk became frustrated and asked the room, in Hebrew, was there anyone here who could write English? I said yes, and the Russian told the Israeli who told me that there was a "*tik g'veret*" inside, at which time a whole post office full of people announced their interpretation of this Hebrew phrase.

The guy behind me was yelling "handbag for ladies! handbag for ladies!" and I shouted, with revenge in my voice for all the Israelis who correct my Hebrew on much subtler points of style, "purse!" I wrote purse, then chocolate, then coffee, then book, and the last entry stumped everybody in the post office until I realized that the Russian was saying the brand name of a dog food. "Dog food!" I hollered and inscribed dog food on the form. Everybody in the post office, except "ladies handbag," thanked me for the help and I started to leave. "Hey—professor," the clerk behind the post office window yelled at me, in Hebrew. "You forgot your package," and the whole place erupted. I had left the package I came in for at the window.

I left the post office and a block away a young Russian man with a Solzhenitsyn beard stopped me and said, in English, "I eat all morning...give me three shekels for food?" I said, "I haven't eaten all day myself." "Yes," says the Russian, as if to say "that's what I mean." I gave him three shekels (about one dollar) and he looked at me, touched his chest, touched my chest and said, "from my life to yours, from my life to yours" and thanked me, to which I replied, in Russian, "you're welcome."

Two weeks earlier, I had just arrived in the Land. I hadn't lived here in eighteen years but I remembered my Hebrew well enough, I thought, to jump in right away. I went shopping at the Hypercol, the local supermarket. Everything was copasetic until check-out. The check-out woman asked me something and I answered her without hesitation. I wasn't quite sure what she said, but she responded immediately with a little piece of paper and pointed me toward the supermarket office. I took the paper to the office. The clerks behind the counter began to discuss me in an animated fashion, then they shrugged their shoulders, fished into a box and gave me a pair of panty hose.

What question did I answer? Maybe it was whether I preferred men's or women's clothes, perhaps if I was married or not, maybe it was if they gave me a pair of panty hose would I wear them? The fact is, I didn't know. But I wanted to. I want to so badly that every day I am in Israel, I suffer a similar indignity. But I have radicalized even more. I tell them now when they try to speak to me in English, I speak no English. "What language do you speak?" they always ask me—"French, Russian, Spanish?" "Samoan," I say, and we continue in Hebrew.

How Reb Shlomo Gave Me My Name
Dedicated to Reb Shlomo, of blessed memory

I had never met Rabbi Shlomo Carlebach, but I had been hearing about him for years. "What — you don't know Shlomo?" people who knew him would say to me. "You of all people should know Shlomo." We were two musicians who should know each other. People who knew us both were surprised that our paths had not crossed.

In a sense, our paths had crossed. On my first trip to Israel, in 1976, I stayed in an apartment that was once inhabited by Shlomo some years earlier. I knew this because people would show up at all hours looking for him. "Is Shlomo here?" they would ask, and stand there in the hallway forlorn when I explained he no longer lived there. I understood from the people who showed up looking for him that Shlomo attracted unusual people. Still, I never met him.

Shlomo was well known in Jerusalem, so well known that wanderers continued to show up at 16 Lincoln looking for him years after he had moved out. While I stayed at 16 Lincoln, I scheduled a trip to Europe. In those days, the planes left very early in the morning from Ben Gurion airport to Paris. You had to hire a cab to pick you up at about 4:30 in the morning to make the plane. We didn't have a phone, so I went down to the local cab company to reserve the cab. "What's the address?" the man at the cab company asked me (in Hebrew), "*shesh esrei Lin-co-lin*," I replied. "Ah, Shlomo's place," he said. Even the cab drivers knew him.

Fifteen years later, I heard Shlomo was coming to St. Louis. Though we had still never met, I felt connected to him somehow, through the apartment in Jerusalem, through everyone who showed up at the door looking for him, through the many friends who said "you don't know Shlomo? You, of all people. . ."

So I determined to meet him. His concert in St. Louis began at eight o'clock, and I found out what time he would be doing his sound check. I went to the auditorium at six. There was no one around, only a young woman running up and down the aisles taking care of details, I walked through the door into the dark auditorium. On the stage was Rabbi Shlomo Carlebach, under a lone spotlight, speaking into the microphone and testing the sound levels.

As I opened the door, he stared at me from the stage, stopped what he was doing, and said into the microphone, "Nachman? Is that you?" "Yes," I said a little hesitatingly. Nachman was a variation of my Hebrew name, given to me in a rather confused fashion by my mother. My mother had always told me that my Hebrew name was Nachman. I was named after someone in the old country that no one in my family seemed to know anything about. Nachman was close enough, as far as I knew.

There was music in Shlomo's voice, "Nachman, my holy brother, is it really you?" "Yes," I repeated. He put down his guitar, came down from the stage and walked up to me, held me in his arms, kissed me on both my cheeks, and said, "holy brother, it is really you." "Yes," I said, feeling very much me, at that moment, in his arms. "Where was it?" he said, "Jerusalem?" "Yes," I said, shrugging my shoulders, remembering the 16 Lincoln connection, "Jerusalem." "It's been so long," he said. "Yes," I said. I hadn't been in Jerusalem in fifteen years.

My mother had a rather confused sense of identity. She conferred on me the Hebrew name "Nachum," told me it was after a relative who died in the old country, and left it at that. There was a problem with my middle name as well, her family name, Stone. "Stone" was the given name at Ellis Island. She gave me the middle name "Stone" because it was a source of pride for her. We all identified the name with my grandfather, Art Stone, a former vaudevillian, a kind and charismatic leader who was the last glue that bonded the family together. I, too, was proud to carry his name.

When my mother got mad at me, she would refer to the name as she knew it before Ellis Island, "*stavisker.*" "Nachum Stavisker — get in this house immediately!" I can hear her bellowing. My attachment to all my names was complicated.

So it was easy to answer to Nachman, to fall into Shlomo's arms, to be whoever he thought I was, believing that maybe it was me after all, somehow a part of Shlomo's circles, even though we had never met. I was indeed the kind of person that might show up in the middle of the night looking for him, and who knows, perhaps we were connected in ways I myself was unaware. Perhaps the force of *bashert*—"what—you don't know Shlomo?" was strong enough to change fact. I had never before that night met Rabbi Shlomo Carlebach, but that didn't mean, to me or to him, that we didn't know each other. So for the rest of that evening, I was his holy brother, Nachman from Jerusalem. I sat in the first row of the concert. I sat with him later while he greeted fans. I sat next to him and held his hand when we learned a Chassidic Torah about Pesach.

I never saw Shlomo again, but the connection we made that night was strong enough for me to regress our relationship into history. I felt as if I had been tied up with him, as were so many others, for decades.

About a year later, I received a letter from a distant relative I do not know. He had been doing some genealogical research on our family. He had all the information on the few branches of the family that I do know. I saw my name, my wife's name, my children, the name of my brother and sister-in-law, their children, my parents, my grandparents, my great grandparents, and then in a lone box, by itself in its generation, the generation before we had come to the United States, a lone name in a single box, one generation deeper in the history of my family than I had ever any knowledge. I stared into that box until the box itself expanded and threatened to drag me in with it, for in that box was my name: Nachman

Stavisker. This was the man I was named for, my great, great, grandfather Nachman Stavisker, whose name became Stone when his son came to the United States. I became Nachum Stone through carelessness or forgetfulness or ignorance, but this was the person whose name I carried, and not as I remember it, not even as my mother gave it to me, but just as Shlomo knew me, Nachman.

Several years later, we took a sabbatical and went to Jerusalem. The purpose of the sabbatical was not at all clear to me. Like all such activities, there was a vague sense of life review, of renewal, of the necessity to reclaim something that may have been lost, or the hope of finding something for which we may not have been looking. I don't think any of us were quite sure why we went on sabbatical, but we were drawn to Jerusalem, and we made jokes about learning new stories because our audiences were tiring of the old ones.

Less than a month after we arrived in Jerusalem, just before Pesach, we were learning at the *yeshivah* where we had found a home. Every so often, during the course of one of the teachings, someone would mention a teaching or a story or sing a song that came from Shlomo Carlebach. I came to understand that some of the people involved with this *yeshivah* were students of Shlomo. My first teacher at the *yeshivah* was a student of Shlomo, and often quoted his teachings or the teachings of others in Shlomo's name.

One night my new teacher asked us to dinner. We went to a vegetarian restaurant in a newly gentrified neighborhood in Jerusalem. During the course of dinner I told this story, the story of how Reb Shlomo gave me my name, this story, like it was dinner drivel. I saw my friend's eyes widen and he and his wife began to rise from their side of the table and by the time I had finished the story we were all ten feet above the table in complete silence staring at each other under the dome of truth.

To tell a story of a *tzaddik* or to sing a song of a *tzaddik* is to invoke their presence. The story became not only the story of the restoration of my name, but the ritual invocation of the presence of Shlomo, of blessed memory, and we all breathed in Shlomo's presence in unison.

"Thank you for the story," my friend said to me after dinner. "Shlomo gave me my name, too." I could see in his eyes love, and awe, and mystery, and hurt.

I come from a generation in which many of us lost our names. I came to Israel on sabbatical not searching for my name, but finding it nonetheless. All journeys have secret destinations of which the traveler is unaware. I came not looking for Shlomo, but finding many of his students who are fellow travelers along similar roads. Shlomo worked some repair on me, although we may have met only once. Although he has passed to the next world, I am one of the pilgrims who came looking for him in the middle of the night. In the course of my journey I have found my private name, Nachman, given to me before I knew it was missing, by Shlomo, on a journey of secret destinations of which I was unaware, fixing a part of me I didn't know was broken, finding a part of me that I didn't know was lost.

Felicia Graber
Metamorphosis

The rear lights of the car disappeared. A second later even the faint growl of the motor was engulfed by the silence of the night.

I was brutally dumped into a cold, dark, isolating solitude. The bright stars were staring down coldly, indifferent to the plight of men. For them life was a spectacle viewed from such distance that any feelings or emotions were lost between actors and viewers. Their cold light made me shiver. Nothing interrupted the unbearable silence of the lonely night. The lightless houses around me seemed skeletons, props, set up to create a dark, mysterious and gruesome atmosphere for a detective story. It was difficult to remember that behind those repulsive facades people were blissfully asleep, happy, content, unaware of any disturbance in their midst.

The only light came from behind me, from my house—our house— from the house we had spent so many happy days and nights, from the house that was sheltering the dreams of two little angels. Slowly, I turned toward this place of happy memories, hoping to find some mute consolation within these familiar walls, hoping to find a warm embrace of comfort in the cozy rooms. As I walked, however, the light pouring out of the gaping door suddenly lost its warmth. It seemed just as indifferent as the stars above. The house seemed as repulsive as a cold, lifeless carcass. Like a sleepwalker, I crossed the unwelcoming threshold and locked the door behind me.

What now? I looked around, amazed to find the room intact, in the same condition it had been for years. I had expected to see everything shattered and broken. I had expected to find the house in the same turmoil I found myself. Yet, nothing had changed. The couch still showed the contours of his body which had rested there minutes earlier. His deserted socks lay on the floor. The empty cup still stood on the end table. The home reflected a frigid air of desolation and loneliness that was accentuated by the ticking of the clock. 3:30 a.m.!! You could not hear a stir in the whole neighborhood. The children slept peacefully like only the very young are capable.

I realized that I was still standing, my back against the door, numb with loneliness, like an abandoned child. I tore myself away trying to decide what to do next. The large bed looked too cold and foreign to go to sleep in, so I first sat down trying to collect myself. After all, I was supposed to be a mature woman. I was not a child anymore. I was now in charge of our children. The whole burden lay on my shoulders until his return. I shuddered. "His return—when will that be? In a day, a month, or in a year? Why did he have to go anyway? What was the purpose of this war? What was he going to help? Will he be under fire? Oh God! What if he gets hit!!?" Maybe that would help to bring him back? What thoughts! I was being childish. But what was the purpose of his being hit by an aimless bullet? What was the purpose of anyone being hit? Why couldn't men talk their differences out? Let them even scream—nobody ever died from words. It is the bullets, the bombs that kill!

The whole atrocious reality of war hit me like a dagger in the back. Every single individual in those gruesome, merciless jungles had a home, a wife, children, parents. Every single soldier's death meant a young life uselessly cut at its roots—a life which could maybe have brought to the world some hope of peace, a life that could have served humanity far better by living, a life that could have been giving his family support, comfort and leadership.

"Mommy! Mommy!" I jumped up with a start. I must have fallen asleep without realizing it. "Where was I? What was I doing on the couch?" I ran to help the baby out of the crib and then to console my three-year-old who had been bewildered in finding an empty bed when she came for her daily cuddling. "Where is Daddy?" she wanted to know while I was wiping her tears away. This innocent question flew like an arrow through my heart. How do you tell a three-year-old that her father has gone to war? That he was killing people and that he himself might be killed. What do you tell her when she asks her unsuspecting "why?" You don't want to deceive her, yet you want to spare her feelings, so you throw in a casual, "he had to go away for awhile," while your heart is torn to pieces by anxieties, fears, and loneliness.

Children are luckily naive and trusting. They take things in stride. So soon my two temporarily fatherless children were back to their daily routine of playing, eating and sleeping, in that order of importance.

How does a grown woman, though, who had been spoiled like a child, adjust to her new role as head of the family? How does she conceal her weakness, solitude, aches, and lead a "normal" life? Things are not that easy. At every step I encountered difficulties. I had been, as I said, treated like a Dresden doll. I had no responsibilities outside the running of the house. I had no idea even how to write a check ....

Thirty years have passed since I wrote those words, thirty years since I even remembered writing them. I found the paper while on a routine search for a lost document. Had that really been me who had written those words?

Yes, I do remember that night. I remember the pain in my chest as if it were yesterday. I remember the loneliness, the feeling of being deserted, the oppressive cloud of responsibility to the children, the fear, the running to the t.v. set every morning to hear the news of the war ..." There were only two casualties last night," a calm even voice was saying. ONLY TWO!!? ONE of them could mean the end of my world! I can still hear those words and feel their impact. Never before had the word "only" been so misused!

How this experience, however, had changed my life! How this traumatic time had propelled me into a different way of life! It had been a catalyst, had made me see and appreciate my life as a mother, a wife and a human being. It changed me from a "Dresden doll," a submissive follower, a woman of the '50s, into a woman of action, a woman who was able to stand on her own two feet. I went back to school, got a degree, a career, and took charge of my life. I became a woman who could share together with my husband the shaping of our future together.

Julie Heifetz-Klueh
The Blue Parakeet

They knew what was coming to Radom, to all the Jews. My parents paid to send me to a farm in the country with a Gentile family. They treated me like I was one of them. I learned to milk a cow and churn my own butter. In the woods there were mulberries and sweet clover. In the evening I went to the edge of the property where Gypsies played their violins and danced. I never saw so much jewelry.

Because I talked to trees and said I heard my Father singing, they called me Dreamer. I like to play games by myself, the games I used to play with Papa. Especially the game we called the Color Game. "I'm thinking of something blue," I'd say. Papa had to guess what I was thinking. "Your dress? Your eyes? The book on the library table?" Until finally I'd tell him "I'm thinking of the color blue. Blue as the moonstone on your finger." All the colors of home came back to me playing the Color Game. The pale yellow grass tall enough to hide in, Papa's cotton shirt, embroidered like a silk bouquet with every color of the rainbow.

Winter came. I heard Papa tell me, "Look how the icicles are candles in the starlight. Think of them as friends. Also, slap yourself, move around, keep active. You'll be warmer." With the first snowfall I thought about my cousin Helga. We visited winters in Cologne, flirted with boys at the skating rink in our sophisticated dresses. Helga was prettier than I was. I hoped she was still pretty that Winter.

Many nights the same dream came back to me. I was in the forest, alone. On every tree a sign with candy-striped colored letters. LOST. A BLUE PARAKEET!! I tried to see the treetops, a little spot of blue in green leaves, but the limbs were twisted fingers reaching out to grab me. I ran faster and faster, until I woke up whimpering, sad for the bird alone in the world she hadn't been born to, sad for the child who'd lost her. Of all the nights I had the dream, I never saw the bird.

One day some neighbors came. While I was gathering eggs they saw me. "She has a Jewish nose. You have Jews hiding here." After that I hid in the hayloft, but eventually the Germans found me. I was sent to Auschwitz, the youngest in my lager. Some would take bread from the dead. I could never do this. There was even cannibalism there. One old woman tried to protect me. She put her arms around me. "Cover your eyes. Nothing important is happening." What I saw I did not see. What I felt somedays I could not feel. I became like a robot, empty, except for dreaming of hundreds of faces streaked with color, melting in the rain.

To keep my spirits up, I started rumors. "The war is over, someone with a radio told me the liberators are coming." After a while, whatever I said, nobody believed. The Lagerfuhrerin, our camp commander, had the prettiest hair, hair like cotton candy. You couldn't paint a doll that beautiful. She loved to torture. The minute our hair would grow a quarter of an inch, she'd cut it. When she walked by, I imagined her bald and naked, me holding the razor.

In 1945 after the war, I went back to Radom. Our house was there, the Gentiles gave it back for me to live in. Someone told me while I was in the country they saw my Father on a transport. He was strong. He was young enough to make it. I knew where my strength had come from. Three months I waited. One day I went to an open window. Down below my Mother was walking. I must have screamed. She turned around. I ran to the street where she was waiting. Her hands were all over me. She was crying, so much smaller than I remembered. I thought she was a lie I wanted to believe in. I held her very gently, the way a child would hold a tiny bird in her hands.

Rabbi Robert P. Jacobs
Stephen Wise Takes Command

Of course Stephen Wise took command. But of my taxi? Never. It was not only my taxi but my wedding day, and I had told him the cab would be waiting at a quarter to twelve at the door of J.I.R. I would come up to his office, help him on with his coat and off we would go. The wedding was to be at 12:15, call it "high noon," on Wednesday, April 19th, at the Hotel White, fifteen minutes by cab from J.I.R. It was so well planned, so simple!

The cab was five minutes ahead of time. Good. The wedding party was ready at the hotel. Good. I mounted the stairs to Wise's office on the second floor, walked down the hall to his door, put my hand on the door-knob and heard a shriek. "Don't go in there!"

Across the hall in his secretary's office a rising female form commanded my attention. "He's in conference! He mustn't be disturbed." I was dumbfounded, "But Gertrude, it's my wedding day. We planned it this way. I have a cab waiting downstairs."

I knew the answer before she replied. "But he's in conference. We never disturb him. You'll just have to wait."

"O.K.," I said. "You wait. This is my wedding day. I'm getting him." While she shrieked I walked across the hall, opened the door and walked in.

Wise was sitting in his huge tall-backed chair, leaning forward on his long walnut table, hand holding his chin and concentrating on his companion's speech.

Startled, he looked up. I walked directly to him. "Dr. Wise, this is my wedding day. The cab is waiting downstairs."

There was anger in his face. In an instant it was gone, and he roared with laughter. "Of course. Of course. So it is. We mustn't keep the bride waiting. Here, let me introduce you to my friend." His friend arose abruptly. A short, stocky man, maybe five feet tall. Wise said, "This is Eduard Benes, the president of Czechoslovakia." My mouth stayed open. "Hello," I said. "Hello." The little man was smiling. "A student, Dr. Wise?" "Yes,"

Wise muttered, "a *chutzpadik* student." I went for his coat, and heard the man chatting quickly about another appointment. As I held the coat for him he shouted, "Gertrude!" She came in and he said, "Tomorrow at 10:00 for Dr. Benes." She nodded and looked at me with scared eyes. I stuck out my tongue. Wise shook hands with Benes. I did too. He smiled and said, "Good luck, young man." I muttered, "Thank you," and hurried Wise out of the door.

The cabby was holding the door open for us as we emerged at the entrance. A voice called, "Stephen! Stephen!" He glanced down the street. "Come on," he said. "Come along with us!"

I held the door for the man who joined us. Familiar face, somehow. A square jawed, grey-haired man, holding his coat. The three of us sat in the back seat; the cab lurched and was off. The two men fell into a heated conversation. "We've got to see Brandeis...No, no. Let's cable England ... Listen to me, Stephen...... The man jabbed Wise's chest with a pointed finger. The voices rose in heated debate. I sank into a corner. My cab. My wedding day.

The cab stopped. The Hotel White. I opened the door. They sat there, talking. I put my head in. "Oh yes. Yes. I'm coming." I helped the two men out. They were still talking. I took Wise by the arm. He looked at me, and smiled. "Bob, this," he said as the other man stood silent, "is Felix Frankfurter." I think I said, "Happy to meet you." We shook hands, and Frankfurter bounded off as Wise looked after him. He turned to me.

"Well, Robert, so you're getting married. Let's get you married." The smile was there. I ran ahead to open the door for him.

Cissy Lacks

Miriam's Way

Miriam's Way is a fictionalized account of the life of
Miriam Kenisberg from 1941 through 1946, based upon her true
life experiences. The following excerpt is the first chapter of the novel.

Miriam's father, Nathan Kornitsky, believed in truth. Lying to his daughter was for him an act of bravery, but one that did little to console Miriam. She only knew she had seen her brother Jacob taken away by Russian soldiers and now she was being sent away because of German soldiers. Her brother never returned and no matter what her father said, she knew that he thought she would not return either.

It was a warm day in early September when he told her he was going to send her away. They had hiked through the Vilna countryside for at least twelve kilometers and were on their way home when he stopped her.

"Papa, I'm not tired and we're almost home. We don't have to rest here."

"Miriam, I promised your mother I'd talk to you before we got home today but now we're almost back and I haven't done it."

"Done what, Papa?"

"Talked to you about the war, about Jacob and about what's going to happen to us ... and to you."

"What if I don't want to hear, Papa?"

"I'm afraid you have no choice and neither do I."

He put his arm over her shoulder and rubbed it as he talked.

"This countryside you and I love so much is much more than beautiful. The black soil is so fertile that crops almost grow by themselves. The Germans want this land and these crops to feed their armies, and they don't care what happens to any of us. I want you to remember Poland the way we see it today, but you've heard the planes and everyone says the soldiers will be in Vilna within days.

"I know you'll take care of me if they come," she answered.

Nathan squeezed his daughter's shoulder so tight it hurt.

"I can't. I couldn't help Jacob, and the Germans are worse than the Russians. They don't like Jews, even pretty little Jewish girls."

He stroked her cheek with his large, calloused hand.

"I'm thirteen, Papa."

"Miriam, I'm afraid for you. Your mother and I have decided to send you away ... someplace where you'll be safe. When it's better, in a few days, in a week, you'll come back."

He blurted out the words and just the sound frightened her. He had taught Miriam that to be calm was to be able to handle any situation. This time his eyes scared her. Sometimes she could get him to change his mind, but this time when she looked at him, he turned away from her. His rejection was worse than the threat of separation.

"Your cousin Sonia is coming tonight and tomorrow you'll leave with her."

"No, Papa."

"We have no choice."

"Where is Jacob? Can't I go to Jacob?"

"Jacob was strong, like you, and the Russians took him. They needed workers so Russian men could be soldiers. Your mother and I are not going to let the same happen to you or your other brothers."

"Why can't Joseph go with me tomorrow? Why can't we all leave together?"

"And when we'd return, we'd have no farm. If we have a future together, we must separate now. Don't ask your mother these questions. She can't bear to send you with Sonia, even though we have decided we must."

Miriam wanted to cry but she didn't.

That evening supper was a few mouthfuls of *bulbous,* potatoes cooked with milk, since they had no meat, and some tea without sugar or honey. In the middle of dinner, Nathan leaned both hands on the table and pushed himself to a standing position.

"I've talked to each of you about the war and what it's doing to our family. We aren't sure where Jacob is, and tomorrow Miriam is leaving with Sonia. We are like a herd of sheep grazing in a field when a wolf comes and scatters them. The flock is never the same but it disperses to save itself."

He cleared his throat and ran a finger along the edge of his mustache. His eyes went around the table, stopping to look at each of them.

"I have tried to be a good father to you. At times there hasn't been enough food, for I haven't been as lucky as some men, but I've done my best. I don't have anything to give you but advice. Let your heart guide you and don't fear what it tells you. Be careful of people. Don't go with them, not because they'll harm you, but because they'll be confused. I've taught you to be self-reliant, to respond to nature, and to use your intelligence in a crisis. Count on yourselves. Keep your head clear and remember to trust your heart to lead you.

"*Yiv v rachecha adonoi vayishmaracho, Ya air adonoi panov alecha vechunacho, Yesaw adonoi panov alecha veyasame lecha shalom.* May the Lord bless you and keep you. May the light of the Lord's presence shine upon you and be gracious to you. May the Lord bestow favor upon you and give you peace.

"May we each find our way back. I have nothing more to say."

Miriam's mother, Rebecca, swaying slightly from side to side, started her familiar, almost silent humming. Nathan sat down and pulled the plate of potatoes toward him, but he couldn't swallow even a mouthful. He left the table to go outside and Miriam started to cry. Her mother hugged her, but the arms around her only reminded Miriam that tomorrow they wouldn't be there. She pressed herself into her mother's lap and cried harder.

Miriam didn't want to sleep that night and her parents didn't force her. She stayed up as long as she could, sitting in front of the fire and watching her mother and father. As much as she resisted, she fell asleep on a small rug in front of the fireplace and when she woke, it was to hear her cousin Sonia talking to Nathan.

They were discussing the safest places to go, deciding together that the forest was the only alternative. Sonia told him about what she had seen on her way to the house; refugees filled the streets and roads, making their way toward the East, toward Russia. German soldiers were everywhere, and neither Nathan nor Sonia thought the refugees would make it to Russia. Hiding in the forest seemed to be the only solution. Nathan suggested they start east toward Russia on the Vilna-Oshmyany Minsk Road, as everyone else had done earlier that day. Then they should go into the Rudnicka Forest as soon as they could.

Miriam pretended not to hear, but when she could no longer control herself, she shouted as loudly as she could, "I don't want to go."

They turned to look at her still curled on the rug with tears filling her eyes and her long blonde hair falling over her face. Nathan walked to her and bent down to push the hair from her face. He moved his fingers over her cheeks and rested them on her shoulders.

"Miriam, my only daughter, don't worry. The war won't last for more than a few days and you'll be back."

She wanted to believe the words, but her cheeks felt the pressure of her father's fingers. From the other side of the room, she heard the low, sad singing of her mother. Her father couldn't comfort her. He only gave the advice he had repeated several times in the last twenty-four hours.

"You'll go with your cousin and you'll be all right. You have a horse, a wagon, food and clothes. I know you'll be able to handle any situation because for thirteen years you have been my best student, better than your brothers."

He began to list the things he had taught her, as much for himself as for her.

"You know how important it is to wash, to keep clean; you know what berries and roots to eat if you have to; you can make shoes from leaves and bark; and you can keep warm in the cold.

"Most important, I have taught you to listen to yourself. People will be confused. Don't follow them, follow your heart."

He pressed her hand, kissed her on the forehead and returned to his conversation with Sonia. Hearing that Miriam was up, her mother stopped her work in the kitchen and came to the fireplace. "Miriam, I want you to wash and look nice." She rubbed her daughter's back as she talked. "First, I'll braid your hair, then you'll take a bath and get dressed."

She brushed Miriam's hair until the tangles were out and she could run her fingers smoothly through her long hair. All the while, she hummed a sad melody Miriam had heard often. The words were even worse, and although her mother didn't sing them, Miriam heard them anyway.

The sky grows dark and overcast.
I seek to walk a different way

Where loving arms will lift me close
And guide a child who's gone astray.

After her mother finished braiding one side of Miriam's hair, Miriam turned to look at her. Rebecca smiled but kept humming. The soft melody was so much a part of her way of handling sadness that she didn't even know she was singing. Miriam would carry this image with her. Her mother was bending over her, and they were both surrounded by the familiar sad music of Rebecca's songs.

Sonia didn't talk at the breakfast table. The two brothers sat across from Miriam, and she would miss them, but she already longed for her parents, even though they were still at the table with her.

Nathan told them it was time to go. He wanted them to be in the forest before sunrise so that no one could see them on the road, and he thought the way could take three hours. He carried the suitcases to the wagon and asked Miriam to follow. In the dark, she could hardly see her father walking, much less her cousin's horse and cart.

Rebecca turned to her husband, "Nathan, I have my wedding ring in the house. Get it and give it to Miriam for good luck." She had already given Miriam her coat. Miriam didn't want to take it because she didn't need it in September. Her mother said she could bring it back and they would share it over the winter. When Miriam turned to her mother, Rebecca turned her head away and said to Miriam, "I love you. Don't worry, it's not going to take too long." Then she stroked Miriam and embraced her. She held her until Nathan came back with the ring.

Nathan told Rebecca to sew the ring into the coat lining. When the ring was hidden in the bottom of the coat, he lifted Miriam up to the wagon seat. She wanted to throw herself back down into his arms, but she knew not obeying would make things worse. She wanted her parents to remember that she was good.

Her father smacked the horse and as the wagon started up, he called out, "Keep the ring. It will bring you good luck. Just remember, you are going to be back with us soon."

Miriam tried to watch her parents as the wagon pulled away, but because of the dark, she lost sight of them and of her house after only a minute. By the time the wagon reached the outskirts of Vilna, she didn't recognize anything. She began to cry and for the first time, her cousin talked to her.

"Miriam, don't worry. We'll just be gone for a few days. We're only going because the German soldiers are coming. When they leave, we'll come back home."

Miriam started shaking. The farther they went, the more she cried. Finally, Sonia reached over and pulled Miriam to her, keeping an arm around her. The wagon started to rock back and forth in the holes and ruts of the dirt road because Sonia needed both hands to control the horse, but Miriam's body stopped shaking only when Sonia held her. In one last effort, Miriam begged Sonia to turn the cart around and take them both back to Vilna.

Sonia tightened her grip around Miriam's shoulder but didn't answer. Miriam wept until she was exhausted, finally falling asleep on Sonia's lap. Sonia had to shake her to wake her up. They had pulled off the road and stopped beside a large lake. The sun was just beginning to rise and in the early light Miriam took a good look at her older cousin. She had only seen Sonia once or twice a year and hadn't talked with her much, being so much younger.

Now she watched Sonia carefully and listened to every word. Sonia was big and healthy-looking, even plump. Her long blonde hair, which was braided and pinned against her head, escaped in wispy tendrils everywhere. Her face was red, maybe from all the work in keeping the cart straight on the rough road, and she was talking to the horse as if he were a friend.

"You're very good to us, Lisper," she said to the horse.

"You earned this drink and a good breakfast too. We're counting on you."

Sonia handed Miriam some food. "Take this to the lake and we'll eat when Lisper does." She unhitched the horse and took him a few yards to a shallow watering place. While he grazed, they ate, too.

"Where are we going, Sonia? When will we get there?"

"I don't know. I only know we must keep going and that once we get in the forest, we'll travel in the night and sleep in the day. Day will become night to us and night will become day."

"Why must we do these things? I don't understand."

"Look at old Lisper. See how happy he is with a little grass. He knows that after he eats he has to pull the wagon, but he doesn't protest. He has no choice, so he does what he has to do. We are the same."

"But why must we travel at night? It will be so dark and we won't have any way of knowing where we're going."

"Miriam, do you hear the planes?"

For the first time, she realized she could hardly hear anything else.

"Those planes fly during the day and soldiers march during the day. We'll avoid them by traveling at night. Let's hitch up, and I will teach you how to drive so that I can sleep."

When they were on the road to the forest, Miriam started her questions again.

"What is going to happen to us, Sonia?"

"We'll survive. Just do what your father told you."

"But how far can we go?"

"You remember what your father said. Don't ask questions. We'll just keep going."

It wasn't until Miriam held old Lisper's reins that she noticed the road was one long path of carts, bicycles, and wagons. She thought that her parents should have left with her, just as these families had gone together. Almost as soon as Miriam noticed everyone, Sonia said it was too light to travel on the road. They would have to go into the forest.

The forest was crowded with the same people she had seen on the road. No one talked to anyone else, except Sonia. She talked all the time to Lisper. "We're depending on you, Lisper," she'd say over and over again, and snap the reins gently.

They couldn't stay in the forest all the time because they needed to water Lisper and to bathe themselves. The lakes were outside the forest. The first time they crossed the open fields to the water, they saw dead animals, cows and sheep, lying everywhere.

Sonia told Miriam to look the other way, but everywhere she looked she saw dead animals. The grass was more red than green and the stench of rotting flesh made her sick to her stomach. For awhile she tried walking with her eyes closed but then she tripped over a dead cow. She was lying face to face with it and its eyes were open, even though it was dead. Right next to it was one still alive, making groaning sounds.

The animals still alive had turned on their sides and were trying to lift their heads, but none could. The straining of the dying animals didn't bother her as much as the groaning; it started out loud and agonizing, then faded, and finally stopped when the animals had no more energy to fight or complain. At the quiet, she knew they had died. As she walked, she'd hear groans, then whimpers, then silence. Miriam didn't see or hear any planes, but she knew they had been there.

The next morning, safe in the forest, they heard explosions in the distance. Soon after, a formation of planes flew over, followed by another that came low over the trees. With only that short warning, a sudden burst of gunfire fell through the trees and onto the open field a short distance away.

The people on the road and in the field were easy targets. Even people in the forest were hit as the bullets came through the trees. For the first time, Miriam heard the screams and groans of dying people, and she screamed, "We have to do something. We have to help. We have to."

Sonia ignored her. She slapped the reins on the horse's back, trying to get the wagon away, but they were unable to escape. The drone of planes flying over and the explosions from bombs falling everywhere were not as frightening as what they saw and heard around them. People were going wild from fear, running in all directions. Some were screaming, some were crying and some were singing in pleading prayers. Miriam knew the song." *Eli-Eli, lama azautani?*" "God, why have you abandoned me?" They were begging God not to let them burn and asking God to forgive them anything they had done wrong.

Sonia kept talking but Miriam couldn't hear the words over the noise. She was able to make out only one sentence that Sonia kept repeating, "Don't worry, we'll survive."

When the noise from the planes stopped, Sonia pulled on Lisper's reins to slow the cart. She and Miriam looked at each other not speaking.

Finally, Sonia began as if nothing had happened. "Let's find some berries and nuts and eat our lunch." While they were sitting, Miriam asked questions. She always asked questions even when Sonia wanted her to be quiet.

"Did they mean to kill us? They flew down over us and shot right into everyone."

"It's better not to think about what just happened, Miriam. It gives us good reason to stay in the forest."

"But Sonia, they killed the animals and now they're killing us."

"The Germans are in Poland," she said. And that is all she said. For the first time Miriam was more frightened than sad.

"How far can we go?"

"We'll go as far as the horse will take us."

"But can Lisper take us away from all this, and when will we be able to come back?"

"We'll return soon."

Her answers did not give the reassurance they were intended to. Finished with their meal, the two girls climbed back on the wagon and the steady plodding of horse and wagon through the dark forest began again. The trees were so thick they kept light from entering the forest, even in the daytime, but Sonia and Miriam traveled through the night as well. At sunrise, they saw a little light ahead and knew they were close to the edge of the forest. When they took Lisper out of the forest to drink at a lake, Miriam saw the gold and red colors of the sunrise against the field and in reflections on the water. The beauty comforted her.

While Lisper drank and ate, the girls bathed in the lake and washed their clothes. Miriam's father had told them over and over that cleanliness was important. No matter what happened, they were to bathe as often as they could and keep their clothes as clean as they could.

In the quiet of the early morning with the pleasure of the cool water against her body, Miriam almost forgot what she had seen the day before. They ate breakfast slowly deciding to give Lisper a much needed rest, and then walked the few steps to where their clothes were drying. Together they hitched the horse to the wagon, and once Sonia even looked up to smile at Miriam.

They decided to lead the horse back to the woods instead of riding. They wanted to enjoy the short walk through the field. As they began, they heard a single plane flying overhead and then short bursts of sharp, cracking sounds. Before they took two more steps, Miriam felt a heaviness leaning against her hands, and she turned to find out why Lisper was pressing so hard against her. She saw blood gurgling from his throat and she watched him drop, rolling over on his side. His eyes got big and she heard him groan. Sonia saw Miriam staring, frozen, at the horse, and shouted, "Run to the forest. Don't stay and look." She reached over and pushed Miriam from behind but even as Miriam ran, she heard the groaning subside, and the gasping for air became more desperate.

Then the noises of more planes drowned out the sounds of the dying horse, and Miriam and Sonia were back in the forest. Although they knew they should continue running, neither could move. They sat under a tree and talked to each other.

"Sonia, they killed Lisper on purpose. He groaned and gasped for air just like those cows. They are going to take everything away from us."

"Miriam, Lisper served us well. Forget what you saw and heard. Remember him in front of the cart, pulling us even when he was tired or thirsty. We'll have to leave our belongings with the cart and walk. We'll be okay."

"But I'm tired. How can I walk. I can't even see. The forest is so dark. How will we know where to go if we can't even see?"

"We'll be like blind people. In a blind person's mind, he can see everything. Now we must begin to travel again because we protect ourselves when we keep moving."

Miriam was lucky to have Sonia with her. Other people were already giving up, going out of the forest to walk on the roads. Many were being killed by artillery or bombs. Or else they were captured by the Germans and sent to labor camps. Neither Miriam nor Sonia knew the fate of those who left the forest, but they knew about the bombs and the artillery. Their fear was enough to keep them in the forest. Now Miriam knew why her parents had sent her away, but still, she wished she were home with them.

At least she had Sonia and Sonia would tell her what to do.

They traveled a week before they left the forest again. It was hard to stay in the forest when even in the day the leaves blocked out the sun and created night. Their view had no sky, no mountains, no flowers—all the sights they treasured when walking across a meadow to drink water or wash in a lake.

They had no problem finding food. Even late summer was a good time to be in the woods. Wild berries grew everywhere. Nuts, which had fallen from the trees, were soft and easy to chew because no sun came through to dry them. Nathan had taught Miriam what to eat in the woods, and she knew there would always be enough. She would get the food for her and Sonia.

The two didn't talk much anymore. The constant noise of planes and bombs made it almost impossible to hear. And they didn't want to talk about the hundreds of dead bodies, which they saw everywhere. In a month, routine had become everything. They knew when to walk, when to stop, when to eat, and when to slip out of the woods.

Trips out were necessary. They had to find drinking water, and they could only find it outside the forests. They looked to these outings with both pleasure and fear. They enjoyed the brief escape from the forest, a reminder of the outside and a more normal life, but these were also the times they were open to attack. The trips out were in the daytime because it was the light that guided them out of the forest. They would see a shimmer from the darkness and move toward it, knowing they were walking to the edge of the forest.

The pattern of walking was always the same. Sonia led the way and Miriam followed a few steps behind. They could have walked together but Miriam respected Sonia's age and Sonia wanted to protect Miriam. On the sixth trip out, Sonia had almost reached the water with Miriam her usual five steps behind when the planes came. As soon as they heard the noise, Miriam saw Sonia turn, frantically looking for a place to hide. But before they could move, the bullets sprayed everywhere. Miriam saw the bullets hit Sonia. She fell, just like Lisper, with her head rolled sideways and her eyes open. When Miriam bent to help her, Sonia rasped, "Run to the woods, Miriam. I can't help you."

Miriam bent over to touch Sonia's face. Sonia repeated the words, until they were only an imperceptible hiss. A gurgled, choking noise sputtered from her lips and finally voiceless gasps for air.

Miriam couldn't move as long as Sonia was alive. When she died, no more than a minute or two after she had been hit, Miriam ran back to the forest. She sat down on the roots of a huge oak tree and put her arms around its trunk. For an hour she couldn't move or think, only cry. She stopped crying to listen; she thought she heard her father talking to her.

"Remember to follow your heart and your feelings, no one else's."

She was startled to realize that the planes were gone. Even the sound of birds, familiarly calling each other across the forest, had disappeared in the aftermath of this last attack. She heard the sound of leaves brushing against one another as the wind gently blew through the trees. Only the conversations of the leaves would accompany her now. She could listen to them but she couldn't ask them questions. She thought about going back to see Sonia but she didn't.

Miriam had survived, but she was alone. She had always had someone to check her decisions, but now she was alone. Now she would somehow have to make them for herself. She got up deliberately, and began to walk. Her first day alone ended only when she could no longer move. She walked and walked until she couldn't do anything but fall to the ground and escape into sleep.

When she slept, she dreamed. She recalled her life in Vilna, her father's teachings and her mother's songs. When she woke, she could still see light at the edge of the trees. Afraid to move until night, she remained hidden and still under the oak.

Dos Iz Mishuga

My mother was the sixth child in a family of seven and the third born in the United States. One result of this history is that my grandmother was always old, old, very old to me...old and different...because she spoke Yiddish, not English.

When she moved in to live with us, when I was nine, she and my mother went into a separate world of which I could eavesdrop but never enter...the world of Yiddish.

The only world my grandmother entered of mine was my bedroom and then her language was snoring. And I wanted her to stop.

I had watched her and my mother pray over candles every Friday night and I decided this flame must get you what you want. One night I took out a cigarette lighter and told my grandmother, my *baba,* she had to pray to stop snoring—over the cigarette lighter. I showed her what to do and then said in simple English, "No snoring tonight. No sounds." And I made a snoring sound. "Blow out the lighter." And I showed her how to blow out the cigarette light. "No snoring." Say "No snoring." It took about 15 minutes to get her to do it.

Finally she said, "*Oy klana madela, dos iz mishuga.*" (Oh little pretty one, this is crazy.) And she blew out the cigarette lighter.

Now that I am older, I wonder what my *baba* thought about me but she never learned English and I never learned Yiddish to find out.

Edward M. Londe
Half A Dream
To My Father, His Brothers, My Son and His Sons

It began with a dream, a dream in which a young Rabbi came forward from a group of other younger men, among whom was my son Gary, (Gershon Shimon Londe), who was looking at me sadly. The young bearded blonde rabbi said to me, "Don't worry, he is with us."

He and his fellows were going into what I felt to be a *Yeshiva.* It was much later in reality that I read that mystics have long talked and wrote about a celestial *Yeshiva,* and *Beth Din.* I do believe from this experience that they must exist in another dimension that is beyond time and space.

Whatever the truth, this dream made my heart much lighter, for I believe most certainly that my son is in good company.

Now in a half dream, I imagined that my son has completed his course at the *Yeshiva,* and gathered around him in a great hall are all my deceased relatives, and my father, Simon, and his brothers Sam, Harry, David, Charles, Bill and Abe, are about to to celebrate, and the man of honor is my son Gary.

Just as the Hasidim dance and celebrate, so they dance around Gary. He smiles shyly at me, for he was always so modest, and this attention moves him and I deeply. My heart beats with joy and I am caught up in the dance, and now Gary is lifted upon their shoulders. I wonder will they meet me in such a manner when I go to the *Yenne velt* (the other world). If that would be case, then death is not to be feared, for it would be a celebration.

Bill was the baby, and he used to call me the Lion. He was always so good to me, taking me to the firehouse, where they still had horses with the harness that dropped when the fire gong was sounded and taking me on deliveries for the old Knight Drugstore, in his model T, way out to Creve Coeur. How I loved him and all my uncles and aunts and cousins.

Now I see Nathan with his handsome dark looks, very black hair. What a contrast to his brother, Arthur, six foot tall and blonde, and their younger brother, Leo. They are my cousins, the sons of David who lived in Belleville.

There is Leonard, who we called Sonny, such a sweet, good man who endured so much pain being confined to a wheel chair, so young, but first had beautiful children, among them Ricky, who dances with them. Ricky, who died so very young, and had his father's same good natured handsome appearance.

On the other side of the hall, as is the custom, I see my mother, her sisters, her mother, and all the other women of our family for they are all here.

Uncle Sam, whom I loved so much, had a special feeling for me. I loved his husky accent, and will never forget how he took me, a poor boy whose father had died at the age of forty-two, leaving six children and no insurance, but a legacy of such deep love as no children and wife have ever experienced. Yes, he took me to the wholesale row and filled my arms with underwear, shirts, and clothing. He gained a place in paradise.

Look, Eva is here, and her face is restored to its original beauty, no longer sunken from the operation which had removed the cancerous jaw, caused by a fall when she was very young.

My mother is young again. They are playing the Vienna waltzes she adored, and she dances, her face is radiant.

The looks of deep affection adorn the faces of all here, for this is their souls now, and the love is genuine. How can one fear death if this is what will be seen.

That is what is meant when in the Bible it states, Moses joined his Fathers.

Ah, now entering the hall have come my wife's family, Leo, Ann and her two younger brothers. No longer do they dwell in the Valley, victims of Hitler, now they have come to see the family of the man who their surviving daughter Mulcah, my wife, has joined.

They like what they see, for these are the sons and daughters of *Tzaddikim,* and they may now join in the revelry.

A dream perhaps, but what man can dream, can be and is, and over it all God watches and a tear does drop from His Hidden Face, a tear of joy and I feel the depth of His Love for all his children.

Marcia Moskowitz
Charlie and the Angel of Death

I came into the kitchen early in the morning to find my older son, Steven, then twelve and a half years old, already eating his breakfast. I asked him where his younger brother Michael was, because it struck me as strange that Mike was not with him. Michael, two months shy of his ninth birthday, was always the earliest one to awake. Steven's answer startled me. "He's praying at the guinea pig's grave." Yesterday morning one of the baby guinea pigs (born just two days before) had died. My suggestion that we put the dead guinea pig in a bag and then in the garbage was rejected immediately as disrespectful. Instead Mike dug a grave in the middle of the garden and buried the guinea pig. He placed a rock on the grave and wrote on it "R.I.P." He explained that he had refrained from placing a Jewish star on the rock because the animal might be considered a form of a pig. "Pigs can't be Jewish," he told me. A cross, he had decided, was simply inappropriate in our garden. Logically, he had come up with "Rest in Peace." It was at this grave that Mike was now praying.

The whole incident, so important to Mike, was bothersome to me. I despaired that he should have to deal with so unimportant a death when we were in the midst of facing death in a much larger framework. Downstairs in the children's playroom lay my father-in-law. The hospital bed had been rented. The homemaker spent each morning with him to bathe his helpless body and cleanse his bed sores; the wheelchair needed when he first came to us three weeks before now stood unused. My mother-in-law slept in a bed next to his, and the various medicines lay neatly displayed on what was the children's old dressing table. Before he had arrived, the boys had tried to brighten the room with things to cheer him and so college banners, a Sesame Street poster, and a scientific one explaining the sky, sea, and land hung on the walls.

My father-in-law had come to spend the last weeks of his life with us as we all waited for the cancer which had begun its work years before to win finally, completely. Medical science had borrowed years for him, but the beginning of this last phase had started Memorial Day weekend. Now it was November. How he came to spend these last days with us was a circuitous route. From that hospital stay in the spring, he went to a nursing home. Unable to walk or care for himself, he looked forward to my mother-in-law's visits each day. But he missed his children, and so each of us, during the course of that hot summer, made pilgrimages to Florida. My visit was in August. His manner during his life was to avoid painful issues; my mother-in-law's was to deny. So they never discussed his cancer or his eventual death. He cried when I sat with him, and when I kissed him good-bye, he said, "Take me home to my children to die. Take me to New Jersey." I decided to make his wish my task. Somehow this wish would be mine and I would find a way to achieve it. When I suggested to my mother-in-law that she and Dad come to stay with our family, she vetoed the idea as too difficult. "No one does that anymore." Suffering and waiting for death occur in hospitals and nursing homes in the modern age. For many years now, I had felt this was not only wrong; it was unnatural. It was a violation of man's basic need: the support and care of loved ones. The need is double-edged. Not only does the dying man need love and care, but those who love him need to do something to comfort and support.

In mid-October my husband Carl went to Florida, and he and his mother brought my father-in-law to Passaic, New Jersey, the town he considered his home. The arrangements for his stay at the hospital were facilitated by my husband's older brother, who is a cardiologist. We brought our sons to see Grandpa Charlie, and they cried and held his hand. It was difficult for him to remember many things of his life, but his love for his grandchildren was apparent in his tears. I dutifully explained to the children that Grandpa's death was imminent. Uncle Bob and the other physicians had already explained that to us. At our nephew Richard's bar mitzvah the last week in October, the rabbi's prayer was that Charles Moskowitz should soon be with his family again. It was an empty prayer, because we all knew it was never to be. All we did know was that Charlie was not with us at his eldest grandson's Bar Mitzvah. But Charlie did live on, and the rabbi's prayer came to be.

My father-in-law didn't die when the doctors said he would. The hospital could no longer keep him, and everyone investigated local nursing homes. I appealed to the family and asked that my father-in-law be brought to our home. Family and friends seemed to think I had lost my usual clear thinking ability. My husband was overwhelmed that I felt so strongly about caring for his father. My own parents questioned the wisdom of my decision to expose their grandchildren to suffering and death. I answered my father's query "Why?" with "Would I do any less for you, Father?" His embrace was his approval. Carl and I asked the children for their support in what we wished to do. We explained that we saw this as an opportunity to do something for Grandpa Charlie. That his death was inevitable we never sought to deny. Instead we were in the unique position of granting his last wish—to be with his family as he faced his death. We assured the children that it would be difficult but that we would have each other for comfort.

Grandpa Charlie arrived at our house the first week in November. He was wheeled from the ambulance and looked small and cold under the gray blankets. His face, so ashen, seemed in stark contrast to the crisp fall day. He was crying and saying it was a miracle that he was "home." He was more lucid than we had seen him in months. I had cooked his favorite soup; the boys served him lunch. We didn't stay death's hand; we made the waiting for him bearable.

Our life in those first two weeks developed a pattern and a coherence. Luckily, I was not working and so I handled the management of the house. Carl went to work; Mike and Steve went to school. My mother-in-law cared for Charlie. Medicare sent a homemaker who came each morning to bathe him, change the linens of his bed, tidy his room. Twice a week a nurse from Hackensack hospital came to cleanse the catheter and treat the advancing bed sores. Bob came three to four times a week in his dual role as physician and eldest son. The children would visit Charlie before they left for school and when they came home. They fixed his pillows, straightened his blankets, fetched drinks for him, but most of all they talked with him.

The second Sunday after my in-laws were with us, a psychiatrist friend came to visit. He, as one would expect, was eager to understand how I was coping. I turned to the ancient symbols of my people to interpret metaphorically what I was experiencing. As a child I had heard the stories of the *Malach ha-Moves,* the Angel of Death. He stopped at the houses of the Egyptians and passed over the houses of the Israelites. Now the Angel of Death had taken up residence in my house. I had met him before in the lonely corridors of hospitals, and he always frightened me. But in my home, he seemed less threatening, more natural. He had his work to do and I had mine. I had agreed to accept his presence and his task, and as his initial quarry, the Angel of Death had taken the baby guinea pig.

The Angel of Death sat in the corner of Charlie's room, and I would nod respectfully in his direction when I entered. But his hold on the Moskowitz family was even greater than I suspected. Charlie's older sister, Sophie, also lay dying of cancer. Neither knew of the other's plight. During the third week of his stay with us, he began to call for his mother (dead now some thirty years) and for his younger brother Moe, who was killed in France in World War II. My father-in-law was seventy-two years old; he had a wife whom he had loved for forty-nine years, two sons in their forties, a daughter of thirty, two daughters-in-law, one granddaughter, and three grandsons. But he called to his mother to ease his pain and stop his suffering. Sophie died the last week in November, and, the day of her funeral, Charlie rambled incoherently of a procession walking in the cemetery, of a fresh grave, of his sister Sophie. He then called for his mother, his brother, and his sister. It seemed to me his dead were calling to him. They were waiting for him.

It was at this time that I had a dream. The Angel of Death appeared to me like someone from a 1930's gangster movie. He wore a trench coat with its collar turned up; his hat covered his eyes so that his face was indiscernible. Like a thief, he was trying to enter our house by prying open one of the windows. Somehow he made it into the house and was walking down the long hallway to the children's bedrooms. I ran out of my room, blocked his path, and screamed, "No, not one of us, not the children. Charlie's waiting for you in the downstairs bedroom. You're supposed to take him, not us. Don't make a mistake!" My screams awakened both Carl and me.

Charlie's mental and physical condition deteriorated, and we marveled at how long life could go on. He ceased to recognize Carl and Steve. He prayed for the pain to cease. It was impossible to touch or move his body because the bones of his back and legs were riddled with cancer. The bed sores, in spite of constant care, had exposed the flesh on his legs. They bled and festered. All quality of life had been destroyed.

When we first started out on this mission, Bob had assured me that he would have Dad moved to the hospital for the final days. We were obviously at this point now. Bob, my mother-in-law, and Carl all felt this decision was mine. If I did not want the children exposed to death, if I did not want the death to occur in our house, Charlie would be moved. I know I have never felt such determination and resolve; Charlie would spend his last days at home.

Charlie spoke his last words Friday afternoon and then slipped into a coma. The pain had finally stopped; his breathing became shallow; all the muscles relaxed. We began the ancient death vigil. We took turns sitting with him. Saturday, Ruth and I potted plants that I had been rooting from the summer. Saturday evening Bob and Bernice and their children, Lisa and Richard, arrived to have dinner with us and stayed late into the night. They went home after midnight; Carl cancelled his trip to St. Louis and asked his older brother, "How long?" Bob confessed his inadequacy and said, "I don't know but it can't be much more."

Sunday, December 12th, was a bright and bitterly cold day. Bob arrived early in the morning and sat by his father's bedside. During the many years of his illness, Charlie had looked to Bob to make him well. Bob sat now with his eyes filled with tears. He went home at mid-day. Mike spent the day with our cousins. Carl paced the house; Steve wandered after him; Ruth and I drank endless cups of coffee.

The rabbi came and we sat and talked together. He asked if we had any unanswered questions about what we still had to face. Steve said "yes," he did indeed have a question. "What is the purpose, what is the meaning of life?" Hesitantly the rabbi went to Ecclesiastes for his answer. He spoke of life as a gift that is given to each of us, of the mysteries and complexities of life, of life as it continues from generation to generation. He asked if he might say the ancient prayers of our people by Charlie's bedside. Carl asked to stand by his father's bed for the prayers; Steve asked to stand by his father's side.

As the afternoon came to its close, the moment we wished for, we longed for, arrived. In spite of all the preparation, we were still unprepared. Ruth sat by Charlie's bed crying that she had lost her best friend. I held his still-warm hand and spoke of my love. Carl began to cry; Steven's eyes filled with tears. As I went to comfort my husband, I heard my cousin's voice at the door. Mike was returning home. I ran out the front door to stop my young son before he could enter. As I held Mike in my arms, I explained that Grandpa had just died. Mike and I entered the house to find Steve, his arms barely long enough to reach around Carl's shoulders, holding his father, seeking to comfort him. Life moves from generation to generation.

Bob, Bernice, and their children arrived within the hour. The men from the funeral home came and did their necessary work behind the closed playroom door. When Charlie's body, now shrouded in the gray leather case, was wheeled out to the waiting station wagon, his wife, his sons, his daughters-in-law, his grandchildren stood silently. Bob and his family stayed a bit longer as we made the necessary plans together. Ruth would stay with us for this night.

Late that evening, after the friends who had come to offer solace had left, my mother-in-law came to me with two gifts. Earlier she had sent Charlie's prayer shawl with his body. After the ritual cleansing, his body would be wrapped in a shroud and then the shawl placed around it. The round silver clips he used to wear to hold the prayer shawl in place, Ruth offered to me for Steven. The blue velvet case with its gold embroidery, in which Charlie carried his prayer shawl to and from the synagogue, she offered to put aside for Michael.

We had completed our task and I felt a sense of relief. Throughout the five weeks Charlie had been with us, the words of the Twenty-third Psalm echoed and re-echoed through my head as a form of prayer. I felt as if I were journeying through the valley of the shadow of death. Tuesday morning when we gathered at the funeral home, the rabbi opened the service with King David's words, "Yea though I walk through the Valley of the Shadow of Death..." and I felt the end of the valley was near.

On a bitterly cold day—so cold I wondered how the grave had been dug in the frozen earth—we buried my father-in-law under the skeletal branches of a dogwood tree.

We returned to Bob and Bernice's house to begin the period of mourning, and ate the hard boiled eggs, symbols of life, which neighbors had prepared for us. Friday evening, we entered the synagogue, sat in the front pew, and were greeted with "May you be comforted among the mourners of Zion and Jerusalem." The service ended as it always had with the memorial prayer for the dead. The rabbi asked for "those who mourn and those who would stand with them" to rise. Carl stood; the children and I stood with him so he would not mourn alone.

Our lives slowly returned to normal. The hospital bed was gone; the children's paraphernalia reappeared in the playroom. Ruth went home to Florida; I started teaching again. The pain began to lessen, and I found I measured time by Friday services. I could see from each Friday to the next that we were better. The winter was long and cold, and snow lay on the ground until late in March. By April, the new season seemed to reflect our greater commitment to life.

Steven's Bar Mitzvah was the end of April. Ruth arrived from Florida, and again our family assembled. Steve had worked many hours in preparation for this day. He agonized over the injustice of life: his grandfather would not see his accomplishment. He asked if he could talk about Grandpa Charlie in his Bar Mitzvah speech and we agreed.

Charlie's silver prayer shawl clips, which Steve had refused to accept until the morning of the Bar Mitzvah, the rabbi lovingly placed on the new prayer shawl. Steve led the congregation in prayer. He read from the Torah the passage from Leviticus describing the code for holiness. In ancient melodies he chanted verses from the prophet Amos. He spoke to the congregation of what he had learned of life, of sorrow, of suffering. He spoke of being able to bear life's pain when one has the support of others. He spoke of Ecclesiastes and of the rabbi's words three months before. He spoke of the obligation he felt to do something with his life. He spoke of his memories of his grandfather, and to him that was how his grandfather would live on.

That summer Carl, the children, and I moved to St. Louis. We took the plants Ruth and I potted with us. The following year Bob and Bernice moved to another town in New Jersey, but Bob returns to Passaic regularly to tend the white heather he planted on Charlie's grave. Each spring the dogwood blooms by the gravesite; each winter on December 12th we light a memorial candle. The blue velvet prayer-shawl case waits for Mike's Bar Mitzvah.

Sheldon

Restrained against her own violence, my mother sat in her wheelchair in the nursing home: hair ill-kempt, clothes disheveled and stained with food, hands constantly agitated. Although she recognized me, her eyes were distracted and vacant. "Where's the baby? Who has my baby?" she asked. Assuming she meant her new great-grandchild born the previous year, I explained that Shira was in New York with her parents, Susie and Steve. But Shira's name did not seem to evoke recognition and my mother's gaze looked through me and beyond me. Again she asked, "Who has my baby?" As she searched the broken fragments of her mind for the answer, the shards of memory splintered and shattered. And although I asked which baby she meant, I could not bring myself to utter aloud the one name I believed she was asking for.

His spirit hovered over my childhood. My parents' first born—a son whose brief life ended four months after his birth. He died from spinal meningitis and there were no children from his death to my birth nine years later.

I can no longer remember my first knowledge of his existence, just that my mother talked of him, always referring to him as "the baby" and somehow allowed me to feel his presence. When I was about six, I had my first theological challenge as I sought to understand why God had allowed the baby to die. I asked my mother who responded that she did not know. Because unanswered questions always bothered me, I sought to answer the question myself. My theological explanation was that God must have needed a good baby soul and so he sent for Sheldon. I can still picture the room as I carefully explained my theory to my mother. She seemed to accept my explanation until I told her to "tell Daddy." My father was the arbiter of all intellectual ideas in our family. I do not know if she ever told him, but the skepticism in her response told me that she did not believe my father would agree with my explanation. What I did learn over the years was that my father never spoke of "the baby," never mentioned his name, and did not respond verbally to any questions about his son's brief life. There were no pictures of Sheldon nor any mementos from that time.

Once when I was about nine, we went to the cemetery to visit my grandfather's grave and walked the short distance to where the baby had been buried. I was taken with the small headstone, the name which I had only heard, now visually powerful and the beautiful wild purple flowers that grew from the grave. My mother, always practical, insisted they were weeds and cut them down. My father walked away.

Over the years I collected a litany of tales about this infant child. My mother told me that after the baby had been taken to the hospital, she was told that if he lived, he would never be "normal." She said she did not know what to pray for at that moment. She talked of the nurse from public health who came to the house after Sheldon had died for a required health inspection. She told me of their poverty and how they had no money to pay for the funeral. Her brother lent her the money; her father bought the grave site. This was New York in 1930 and the deepening Depression had far reaching effects on the entire family.

My parents were twenty-five when they were married; twenty-seven when the baby was born and died—a young couple whose lives seemed to cease in response to the grief and emptiness of the next nine years. Mother told me that after Sheldon's death, my father sunk into a deep depression and would not talk. He stayed that way for months. Since I was well aware of his black moods when he would withdraw, cease smiling, refuse conversation, I understood what she was describing. Evidently, the death of his young son was the first time the deep funk appeared. It was to reappear many times in my childhood and adolescence. For my mother, the weeks following the baby's death were complicated by health problems. The milk in her breasts did not dry up naturally and she developed an infection. Unlike my father who was emotionally unable to work, she returned to her job as soon as her health allowed.

The Baal Shem Tov taught that a child who died had a soul that had completed its earthly tasks and could therefore return to God. I do not know if my parents knew that story, but I know that if they did, it would have been meaningless to them in the face of their overwhelming grief. Although they rejected completely the *bubba meisas* of the old world which to them were superstitious nonsense, the rituals of Judaism remained. And so in five short months, they had experienced a *brit,* a *pidyon ha ben,* a funeral, *shiva,* and *shloshim*—the rituals celebrating the start of life and those marking its end.

Recently I read a story about a young couple who had lost an infant son. Overwhelmed by their tragedy, they went to their support group sessions; each had a therapist. She took tranquilizers. But in 1930, I wondered, what did a poor Jewish couple do when faced with the same kind of loss. No help groups, no therapy, no counselors, and an ancient religion that spoke of strict rules in alien tongues.

I thought I knew all the stories about the baby but there were two more I was to learn very late in my parents' lives. My father broke almost sixty years of silence and told me his tale. One Shabbat evening after we had finished dinner, he came into the kitchen to talk to me. I cannot remember if some part of the dinnertime conversation triggered his story or if it were some inner clue that prompted his confession. He began without any introduction.

"After Sheldon died, the doctor came to me and asked if he could perform an autopsy in order to better understand what had happened. He wanted my signature on an official form. I asked if he thought the knowledge gained might help another infant someday and he answered that he would hope so. I said yes and signed the paper, but on the sole condition that your mother never be told. To this day, she does not know. You must never tell her and you are the first person I have ever told."

I looked into his 85-year-old eyes and saw the pain of the young father. He asked if I thought that he had done the right thing. Although I wasn't really sure and certainly did not have time to formulate an educated response, I said, "Of course, you did." He shrugged his shoulders, "Perhaps."

I marveled at his courage knowing that his decision was made in the context of the world of immigrant Jewry. The religion of his home was that of the Russian *shtetl,* the rabbis old world figures who knew little English and certainly did not think in modern American ways. My father believed passionately in America, in science and not in the *bubba meisas* of Judaism. But the prohibition against autopsy had its impact. He had lived with the guilt of his decision for close to sixty years.

Later that same evening during services, he looked at me, took my hand, and whispered, "I feel better—as if a weight has been lifted from my heart." My father died less than a year later.

The second secret about Sheldon came from my mother four years later when she was eighty-nine. Hospitalized for what we thought was depression resulting from mourning for my father, but actually was the start of the senile dementia that would destroy her mind within two years, she revealed parts of her life to the psychiatric social worker who talked with her each day. Initially her conversations focused on Dad, but ultimately they turned to that primal grief, the baby's death.

After her conversations with the social worker, she and I would continue the dialogue as she sought to fill in the spaces of memory and grief. When Sheldon was taken to the hospital, she would go there, enter a sterilized room, and have her breast milk pumped into a bottle. Given the milk filled bottle, she would bring it to the nurse in charge of the baby's care. Because of the highly contagious nature of spinal meningitis, Sheldon was kept in isolation and no one could hold him—only look in through a viewing glass. My mother had spoken of the physically painful process of expressing the milk. All this I had heard before but the new story overwhelmed me as we sat together on the bed.

"Carrying the bottle of my milk which had just been expressed in the sterilized room, I went to the nursery and saw through the glass the empty crib. I gasped. I asked the nurse, 'Where is the baby?' and she said, 'Oh, that baby died an hour ago.' I kept asking her if she were sure. I didn't know what to do. I left the hospital and walked and walked and walked. I was afraid to go home and tell my mother. I looked and saw I was still carrying the bottle. I knew I didn't want my mother to see the milk so I stopped, opened the bottle, and poured the milk into the street." My mother stopped speaking.

She wasn't crying but I was. "Where was Daddy?"

"I can't remember. I guess at work."

Eight months after I learned that story, our eldest son, Steve, his wife, Susie, and their six-week-old daughter, Shira, our first grandchild, came to visit.

During the course of their visit, Susie expressed milk using the efficient modern gadget now available and she froze the milk in small plastic containers. One was left when it was time for them to return to New York. I asked what I should do with it and she said "pitch it" with the casualness appropriate to a small insignificant decision. But I did not and I still have not. And I did not understand why until I remembered my mother's story.

The milk is still in the freezer, reminding me of the promise of life when I think of Shira Yael, the sorrow my parents endured sixty-four years ago, and the soul of Sheldon who spent such a brief time on this earth.

Vicki E. Pickle
Schulman's Market

My mother filled a cardboard box with our weekly groceries, and inspected by Grandpa we left with fruits, vegetables, dry goods, and a pocketful of memories. "Taste it and try it before you buy it" was Grandpa's motto, and we did just that, with plenty of apples, pastries, candy, and any other treat a child desired.

I sat in my favorite spot every week, propped upon the butcher's counter, sampling the kosher salami. It was always perfect, yet the sampling still necessary, according to Grandpa's philosophy. My brother, two years younger, opened Twinkies, making sure each one was fresh enough for the eating. We finished nothing, and in our carefree youth, cost or concern never mattered. At Schulman's Market we were royalty in a kingdom of treats. Salami or sweets, enough of both to last a lifetime.

At the butcher counter, Pat smelled like a delicatessen. On rare occasions I followed him to the back of the store where the heavy metal doors of the meat freezer swung open with a burst of frozen air. Inside, meats hung suspended like fixtures from the ceiling. I peeked cautiously into this mysterious place, as Pat grabbed a slab of ribs or a string of sausages to display in the meat case. He lifted me to the counter with one arm and respectfully set me down like a queen awaiting her next visitor. On the best seat in the house, my throne, I feasted and remained seated until check-out time.

Grandpa, the grocery man, was never without a pocketful of cigars and a warm-hearted joke. He greeted customers, boxed groceries, rang up bills, and was the overseer of the market. I hopped off the meat counter when my mother and Grandpa began the check-out ritual. As the bargaining over payment began, my brother and I slid past Grandpa, allowing him to slip a pack of gum into our pockets. Resting on crates outside the storefront, chewing gum occupied our time. Grandpa always said the only thing we needed to bring next week was ourselves (and maybe, of course, the cardboard grocery box). Mom laughed as Grandpa smiled and turned towards the door, holding it open for his next customer.

Seymour V. Pollack

My Mother and Macy's

I started the sixth grade in a new school. In my old school it was okay to do homework in pencil on loose leaf paper or even on pages torn out of our notebooks. (By the end of the term my notebook would be half gone and the white lines of its marbelized cover were completely inked blue.) The new school, accelerated and experimental, said no. We could submit arithmetic homework on loose leaf pages (three holes, wide lines, written on one or both sides, each page properly headed and numbered.) Everything else, though, had to be typewritten. On typing paper, one side, double spaced, each page properly........etc.

My mother greeted the news with guarded interest.

"This is your trick to get a typewriter machine. You always wanted a typewriter machine."

I knew it was going to be an uphill struggle when she switched to the third person, talking to the wall:

"A typewriter machine he wants. A pencil for him is no good. A Waterman fountain pen for him is no good. Must be a typewriter machine."

Finally, she gave in.

"You'll bring me a letter from the principal where it says you must have a typewriter machine."

The principal preferred to call my mother. I told her we didn't have a phone at home. When I said she could call the candy store and Mrs. Dworkin would get my mother, she rewarded me with a desiccated smile:

"All right, dear, you'll have your letter."

The letter did it. We made up to go to Macy's that Saturday and I would pick out a typewriter. (Meanwhile, my teacher agreed to let me turn in handwritten homework—in ink, no crossing out, each page properly........, etc.—for two weeks.) There were a couple of stores in our neighborhood that sold typewriters, but my mother wouldn't hear of it.

"Something like that you buy in a department store. By Macy's. By Gimbel's. We'll go in Macy's."

That didn't stop me from going to the Stadium Stationery Store

(Pitkin corner Chester) and using each of the floor models to report the exploits of the quick brown fox. By Saturday morning I knew what I wanted—an Underwood Champion portable (portable because it had a case with a handle). When I told my mother how much it would cost ($87.85 including the tax), she said "*Oy.*" That *oy* took in three thousand years of Jewish suffering on top of her own burden. But she didn't back out. In fact, she made a big show of hurrying as I continued to nag and, at last, we were out the door.

A half-hour subway ride got us to Macy's just as the doors opened. I ran to the first salesperson I saw and asked where the typewriters were. (My wife insists that this was the last time I asked anyone for directions.) By the time my mother caught up with me I had already told the skeptical salesman what I wanted. Once he checked it out with my mother, he went in the back and brought out a brand new (my brand new) Underwood Champion.

"How will you pay for this, Madam?"

"I want to pay it out," my mother said.

"Very good. Do you have an account with us?"

"No. But I buy many things in your store."

The salesman smiled. "I'm very glad you do. Take these papers up to the credit office and they'll take care of you."

It was still early, so there was no one ahead of us in the credit office. A man in a nice gray suit asked my mother to sit down and wanted to know what he could do for her. She showed him the papers we got from the salesman and said she wanted to pay out the typewriter. He took her name and address.

"Fine," he said. "We just need to get some more information from you and once we hear from your references, your account will be open. You'll be able to use any of our payment plans. It shouldn't take more than ten days or so."

Ten days?! My gullet caught itself in mid swallow. Here I thought I'd be taking my Underwood home with me. Today. My mother looked at the credit man:

"What?"

He explained that Macy's would need to check her financial situation—where she has her checking account, who she borrowed from, how much she owes, how promptly she pays. My mother didn't like the sound of this.

"I don't have checks. I don't owe nobody nothing! Once I borrowed a few dollars from Dvorah and Benny—my cousins—for a couple weeks. Then I gave them back. From Macy's I bought I don't know how many things. Cash! Always cash! Now I want to pay out this typewriter machine!"

"Mrs. Pollack, you don't understand," the man said. "Without a credit history, we can't open an account for you. I'm sorry."

I felt as if someone had whacked me across the back of my head. My mother, who'd been sitting at the credit man's desk, came around to his side and glared down at him. He quickly moved his swivel chair back.

"I understand. I understand," she said, her voice trembling. "A Jewish widow comes into Macy's who knows how many years and buys and buys and pays cash, that's all right. But now she wants to pay out a typewriter machine so her son shouldn't be left back in school, that's not all right. No. The Jewish widow wants to steal from Macy's, she wants to make this big store go under. LOOK, EVERYBODY, AT THE BIG CROOK HERE!"

Everything in the office stopped. All eyes were on my mother and the credit man. His face was beaded with sweat and redder than the reddest face I've ever seen. I wanted the floor to open up and swallow me, and I'm pretty sure the credit man would've been glad to come along. All he could say was, "No, it's not like that at all. I'm sorry. I'm really sorry."

My mother came over to the side of the room where I was trying not to cry and said, "*Gey aheym un breng gelt.*" (Go home and bring money.)

Then, as if she suddenly realized that there might be Yiddish-speaking eavesdroppers present, she whispered in my ear:

"*Kleyngelt.*" (change).

She settled herself into one of the seats in the waiting area and took yesterday's Yiddish newspaper out of her pocketbook. I headed for the subway.

The train came only a minute or two after I got there, but it couldn't get to Brooklyn fast enough for me. Finally, my station came and I half ran half walked the seven short blocks. Now I was home and on my hands and knees in the bathroom. My mother kept a couple of hundred dollars (her "emergency money") in an old pocketbook which she put inside an even older bedpan that just fit under our claw-footed bathtub. Go ahead, laugh, but each time our apartment was robbed—three times while we lived there—they never got that money.

I took ninety dollars, grabbed a canvas shopping bag from the kitchen, and ran to the Manufacturers Trust branch, a block away. It was just a little after twelve and they were open till one. Good. But standing on line was pure agony. It seemed to me as if the three people in front of me had saved up their whole year's banking business for this one Saturday. The clock wasn't helping either. Then I was in front of the teller. Twenty minutes later I was on my way back to the subway.

When I got to the credit office, my mother still was sitting where I left her, with her newspaper. The credit man in the nice gray suit, busy with a customer, seemed to get busier when he saw me come in. I sat down next to my mother and put the shopping bag between us. My mother nodded, put her paper away, and looked at me.

"Did you get?"

I nodded.

"What?"

"Nickels" I said.

"*Nu,* all right. Nickels. Was the subway crowded?"

"No." I said. "I got a seat."

"Did you eat anything?"

"No. You?"

"I was here. I read the paper."

When the customer got up to leave, my mother went over to the credit man's desk, motioning for me to come.

"*Gib im dos gelt*" (Give him the money.)

The nickels were in a canvas bank bag. I pulled it out of the shopping bag and put it on his desk. Then I reached into it and took out one of the rolls of nickels. I opened it, removed three nickels and put the roll on the desk, next to the bag. My mother held out the salesman's papers.

"Here," she said. "I'm paying you for the whole typewriter machine."
The credit man shook his head.

"Oh. Well. Then you're making a regular cash purchase. You don't need
to do that through our office. Just go down to the typewriter department
and pay them there."

My mother's voice rose as she shook the papers at him.

"No! I'm paying *here*. Eighty seven dollars and eighty five cents. Count
the money. Make sure the whole money's there. I'll wait in case
something's missing. I don't want Macy's to be fooled by a poor Jewish
widow. Go ahead. Count."

"Mrs. Pollack, this really isn't necessary. Our office doesn't even handle
cash sales. Please."

By now we had everybody's attention. A door opened at the other end
of the office and a very efficient-looking man came out. His hair was
almost the same color as our credit man's suit.

"What's the trouble here?"

Before the credit man could say anything, my mother turned to the
efficient looking man and waved the papers at him.

"I wanted to pay out a typewriter machine and he wouldn't let me.
Now I brought him money for the whole typewriter machine and he still
wouldn't let me. Why does such a big store like Macy's treat poor widows
like this?"

"We'll get to the bottom of this. Please let me see those papers."

My mother gave the papers to the boss (I guess he was the boss) and
he took our credit man aside. They talked in agitated whispers, each one
pointing several times to the bag of nickels sitting on the desk. We stood
and waited. After a few minutes, the boss went back into his office. The
credit man took some papers from one of his desk drawers and came over
to my mother.

"All right. We can take payment here. I'll need to fill out these forms
for you to sign. Then you'll take the yellow copy to the typewriter
department and they'll give you your merchandise."

"First count the money. See it's all there."

I could see that the credit man was about to say something and then thought better of it. With a sigh, he sat down and began to remove rolls of nickels from the bank bag, marking on a pad as he counted and putting the rolls in his bottom desk drawer. My mother stood over him, watching. I looked around, wishing this was over. Some of the customers were smiling. One of the other credit people shook her head and went back to what she was doing.

"There's only 86 dollars here."

"Count it again," my mother said.

"No. Wait." I said. "Here's the rest of it."

I picked up the roll that I had opened and handed it to him.

"I took three nickels out of this roll, so that should be the other dollar eighty-five."

"Very well," he said, and reached to put the roll in the drawer with the others. My mother stopped him.

"*Not* very well. Make sure my son didn't take out too much money."

"Don't you trust him?" His tone made me think of ice cubes.

"He's an honest boy," my mother said sweetly, "but who knows what comes into a person's head when there's a chance to cheat Macy's?"

He tore the roll open, spilling the nickels on the desk. In a few seconds they were counted and thrown in with the rest of the money.

"All right. Now I'll make up your receipt. Have a seat over there."

My mother sat down. I took the empty bank bag, put it in the shopping bag and stood next to her. In a few minutes our credit man came over, gave my mother a receipt along with her papers, and turned toward his desk without a word.

"Good-bye," my mother said to his back. I was walking on air.

"Thanks, ma. Let's go get my typewriter."

"First let's eat something."

I can't remember what we ate, or where. I know we didn't go out of the store. My mother, still upset when we left the credit office, seemed to relax as she drank her tea. By the time we finished eating, she had stopped talking about the events in the credit office.

"Okay," I said. "Let's go get my typewriter."

"Wait. I saw something on this floor on our way to eat. I wanna take a look."

"Ma, Please!"

"We took a whole day with your typewriter machine, wouldn't hurt you a few minutes more for your mother."

I stood there, holding her pocketbook, while she pulled garments off the rack, tried them on, brought them back, took others. I almost had to bite my tongue to keep quiet. Finally, she took her pocketbook back.

"That one in dark blue wasn't bad, but not for that price. Maybe it'll go on sale."

We started heading for the down escalator, and she stopped.

"We're here already, let's go to the fifth floor and get a toy for Cousin Heshie. We're gonna be by them next week, for his birthday."

I thought I would explode. Do I say anything? Can I say anything? After all that trouble to get my typewriter? Before I had a chance to decide, she turned to me and smiled. The light finally dawned: — she was playing with me.

"*Nu,* all right. We'll get something for Heshie on Pitkin Avenue. Doesn't have to be Macy's. Come. We'll go for the typewriter machine."

That Underwood Champion is still here, sitting in the back of a closet. Sometimes, especially when I'm working at my fancy word processor, the image of that machine springs into my mind's eye. For a moment, I'm a sixth grader again, back in Macy's credit office with my mother, trying to buy a typewriter on the installment plan.

Miriam Raskin
Forgetting and Remembering

Almost fifty years after Kristallnacht, I went back with my mother to revisit the scene of the crime. When she first asked me whether I would like to join her on a trip to Hamburg, my heart skipped a beat. Go back to Germany? And revive the painful memories I had been suppressing so long?

All the fears of my fearful childhood roused themselves from slumber and contended for expression. I cannot do this, I thought. I will go crazy. My feet will step on German soil and I will lose whatever tenuous hold I have on sanity and go screaming like a Banshee through the streets, wailing against the past which I will misapprehend as a magically preventable future. Don't let it happen, I will be shouting as men in crisp uniforms keep marching towards me guns at the ready so that they can restrain me and enforce the civil order. In my head, which now felt feverishly hot and ready to explode into primal bursts of neurotic energy, I could already hear the chorus of inchoate shrieks I expected to be unable to hold back. I will fall apart and will never get the fragments of my being back together again into a cohesive whole. I will be a helpless child again, afraid of death and untold mortifications again. I will embarrass my mother, upset her no end. But if she can do this, how can I not? She is the one who lost her parents, not I. Perhaps this is required of me; something I must do, must prove to myself I can do. Rationally, in the way I always make decisions, I decided that making the trip while my mother was alive to accompany me was the right thing to do.

"Do you know?" my mother said to me much later, after we had come back largely unchanged, "do you know, when you first said that you were not sure you could face going to Germany, that I did not know what you meant? I thought, Germany is such a beautiful country, why would she not want to go there?" My mother was telling me—can you believe this?— that she had for a time forgotten what happened in Germany. She is even better than I am at forgetting. It is a skill one can develop with practice, I suppose, and she has had lots of practice.

As it turned out, she was right to be unafraid. We saw nothing in Germany to be scared of, nothing reminiscent of the terror we remembered. Hamburg, still one of the most beautiful cities in the world, shows no scars, no evidence of its participation in the dark business of the War Against the Jews. It looks less guilty of crimes against humanity than Washington, D.C., New York City, or even St. Louis. It was easy for us to fall into the admiring tourist's role as we visited the cultural sites, toured the magnificent harbor, and wandered through the old and amazingly still familiar paths in the Botanical Garden. We even managed to handle City Hall (where one can easily imagine all sorts of oppressive regulations to have been dutifully laid down, in their time) as civilized visitors to the city.

My mother enjoyed pointing out the familiar sights. And I, to my surprise, I did not scream, not even once, not even when we walked on the old Grindelallee, the street on which the family had lived, not even when we stood in front of the apartment building in which I used to visit my grandparents. Like ordinary tourists, we expressed wonder that the building still stood, looking much as it had fifty years before, no older, no less habitable. And, look, there is the corner grocer I used to run to in order to buy a forgotten food item for my grandmother's table, still there, still standing. Was there a war? Was there a Holocaust?

One could wonder. It was a peaceful scene, utterly devoid of harsh reminders of the hard years, and we, we were glad just to replay some old familial history, as if we were simply revisiting the residence of some unknown ancestors we had heard about who had lived at this site and who had died in their beds. So happy was I not to be screaming, not to be reminded by any visual clues of what had happened to my grandparents right in that very spot, not to mention what happened after, after they were deported in cattle cars across half of Europe, only to be shot and pushed into mass graves they had themselves been forced to dig, that I made no attempt to visit the actual apartment in which they were living when all this started.

Standing on the street in front of that building, concerned more about surviving what I already knew than acquiring new information, I followed my mother's lead in remembering the good times we had enjoyed in my grandparents' apartment. I marveled at the stories my mother could tell about what went on there and at the stories she had forgotten.

"Why do you want to keep thinking about all this?" my mother asked me after we came back from our trip and I told her that I was writing something about the Holocaust. She seemed surprised, thinking perhaps that not talking about it one time during our trip would have killed that topic once and for all. "What good does it to anybody?" I don't know, I said, and that is the truth.

Is it better to remember or to forget? I don't know that either but imagine it to be the question Hamlet would have come to ponder, had he lived to contemplate the best way to put his sadness behind him. Is it better to remember or to forget? Though rarely asked because we think we know the answer, it may be the most important question of the dying century. Is it better, as individuals and as a society, to recall and to pass on to generations yet to come the awful truths that we were forced to learn when human beings committed the most horrendous crimes ever imagined against other human beings? Survivors of the Holocaust spent forty mute years trying to resolve the tension between the conventional wisdom that it is important to remember and the instinctive knowledge that forgetting is the key to survival.

Forget, forget, forget, said the voices in their heads. Forget me, forget them, forget what happened, don't think about it. Get on with your life. Start over. Put it all behind you. Forget, forget, forget. Don't talk about it. Nobody can believe you. You are wasting your time. It is too awful for words. Put it away, away, away, deeper, deeper, deeper down. Forget it all.

But society said remember and, as if by mutual consent, after forty years in the wilderness of trying to forget and failing, survivors started telling their searing accounts of what, in fact, they had survived. And now that the world knows all about the horror, now that all the godawful stories have been told, all the documentary films made and seen, all the Germans' own meticulous reports of the killings read and analyzed, and all the monuments in stone and film constructed or at least drafted, now the world is ready to remember.

To what end, I ask, echoing my mother. What good does it do? Are people made better by the knowledge of the depravity to which human beings can sink? Is this knowledge worth having, worth passing on? Are the well-intentioned people who declaim "Never Again" better able to defend against a recurrence of wholesale brutality against them or any people than the original victims of the Holocaust were? If there is a lesson to be learned from the Holocaust, I suspect it is a lesson not for you and not for me and certainly not for our children, but for the brutes who will not be persuaded to learn it and who cannot be restrained from defying it.

"Forget it," my mother says. "Get on with your life." I wish I could.

Barbara Raznick
A.K.A. Zelda
In loving memory

My Aunt Zelda was right about nearly everything. She was my mother's older sister and she and Uncle Morrie had no children, so they were like second parents to my brothers and me.

Aunt Zelda had exquisite taste in fashion and knew what was suitable for a young girl to wear so she always accompanied my mother and me on shopping trips, even if we had to take the train to St. Joseph to find just the right outfit. She knew the proper way to write bat mitzvah thank you notes so that you didn't have to write the same thing on every one. Aunt Zelda knew the best recipes and the right way to prepare them. She knew the special ingredient to add to make the most delicious chicken soup. (Don't ask me to divulge a family secret!)

When I had to peel the three dozen hard-boiled eggs for our Passover seder, she knew the right way to do that, too.

"Hold them under running water when you're peeling them, darling. Then the shells won't stick to the eggs."

Aunt Zelda even knew the right places to go in a supermarket or shopping mall parking lot to find those parking spaces that are closest to the entrance. To this day we call those nearby parking spaces "Aunt Zelda spaces."

Aunt Zelda was right about the way to treat people and to love all of her nieces and nephews.

But Aunt Zelda was not right about everything. She was wrong about something very important in her life—her name. She discovered this mistake when she and Uncle Morrie were planning their first trip to Israel. She had never been out of the country, so she had to obtain her birth certificate in order to apply for a passport.

When she picked up her birth certificate at the county courthouse, she was amazed to find out that her real name was actually Ruth, not Zelda, even though that is what she had always been called by her parents and her family.

"You mean to tell me that I've been stuck with this horrible name of Zelda all my life when I could have had a beautiful name like Ruth! After more than fifty years, I guess it's too late to ask all of my family and friends to call me Ruth."

And, of course, she was right.

Her passport was issued and a few weeks later, Aunt Zelda, Uncle Morrie and a half dozen other travelers excitedly boarded their flight in Omaha on the first leg of their trip to Israel.

All went well until she attempted to board the El Al flight to Israel in New York. The agent looked at Aunt Zelda's documents and pulled her out of line and into another room.

"What is the purpose of your visit to Israel?" the agent inquired of my aunt.

"I'm touring with a group," she calmly replied.

"But madame, are you sure that is your only agenda?" he continued.

Aunt Zelda felt that the interrogation was beginning to turn a little nasty, but she tried to remain calm. "Of course," she answered.

"Then why are you traveling under an assumed name—your passport says Ruth while your other documents list you as Zelda! You must be trying to sneak into the country. For security reasons I cannot allow you to board that flight."

Aunt Zelda tried to explain that she had always thought that she was Zelda, but recently discovered that her real name was Ruth. The agent didn't seem to be buying her explanation.

Finally, afraid that the plane would leave without her, Aunt Zelda stuck her face right up to the agent. "Look," she said, "'I'm just a middle-aged Jewish lady from the Midwest. If I were some kind of terrorist trying to enter Israel illegally, do you think I would use a conspicuous name like Zelda?"

I guess the agent decided that she was right and let her board the plane just as it was about to pull away from the gate.

On subsequent visits to Israel, she always had to travel as Ruth. But I knew that was not right. She was really my Aunt Zelda.

Marylou Ruhe
The Storyteller

"Scarlett O'Hara was not beautiful, but men seldom realized it when caught by her charm as the Tarleton twins were…"

These words beginning *Gone with the Wind* reverberate in my memory. I have read and enjoyed the book a number of times, but the very first time I heard these words left a lasting impression.

The time was the winter of 1943, the place a Concentration/Labor camp in Germany The night was frigid and a small group of us — the slave laborers — were huddled around the little stove in the middle of our barracks room trying to coax some warmth for our chilled to the bone bodies. It was Sunday, the only day we didn't have 12-hour shifts at the munition factory.

On Sundays we had time off and could meet the members of the opposite shifts face to face. Otherwise we could see them only in passing, on our way to and from work. Five to a row, 10 rows to a unit, young women dressed in striped prison garb, wearing ragged shoes or wooden clogs, marching under the watchful eyes of the German guards and trained dogs.

Sundays were actually harder on us, because the barracks were not as warm as the factory, where we worked along with the German overseers, who required comfortable surroundings, whereas the barracks housed only the "subhuman" prisoners, and it did not matter if they were freezing. On Sundays we tried to wash our one and only set of clothes or rinse hair with hot ersatz coffee rations, as warm water was not obtainable.

Sunday was also the day for complaining, crying and sometimes quarreling. We complained about our living condition, inadequate food, hard work and the way we were treated by the German guards, especially by the S.S. woman, whom we called "the Lizard."

We were crying because our hearts were breaking when we thought of our families, our parents, sisters and brothers and in a few cases, husbands, from whom we were separated and might never see again.

We were quarreling because any little thing, which in normal circumstances wouldn't mean anything, felt like a thorn in our hurting souls. A smaller food ration, a warmer blanket, an easier job, became a bone of contention.

But one Sunday a young woman changed all that. She was really just a girl, petite with short blond hair and her quiet dignity made her stand out of the noisy crowd. "Would you like to hear a story?" she asked and something about her made us listen as she spoke the opening words of Margaret Mitchell's opus.

The young woman, whose name was Doris, told us in her own words the story of Scarlett O'Hara and her fortunes and misfortunes. We sat entranced, listening to the saga of the American Civil War, the romance and the tragedy of the war unfolding in our imagination. We felt strangely at peace, just listening to a beautiful story related to us by this small, quiet girl whose soft voice was nevertheless audible to us in the unusual quiet.

After a while Doris said, "If you want me to continue, I'll be glad to do it next Sunday."

And so it continued the following Sunday and for many weeks after. When Doris finished the Scarlett O'Hara story, we begged for more, and for many weeks we sat listening eagerly to her soft voice describing to us the adventures, the tragedies, sometimes happy or funny episodes from books, which some of us had read, but which were new to many of us.

Our spirits were lifted, there was something pleasant to look forward to after each grueling week of hard work, of being treated like lower species of humankind. We could always anticipate a new chapter of a great book to unroll upon the screens of our minds.

I do not know what happened to Doris after the war. When we were liberated by the American Armed Forces, we all went our separate ways.

I hope Doris survived the tragic times and leads a happy life somewhere, still bringing solace and pleasure to the people around her.

Rabbi James L. Sagarin
When Our Baby Died: One Father's Story

November 1989

... and we were pregnant. The day had finally arrived. There were the accompanying expected feelings of relief and of joy.

Literally weeks before, Lori and I had been trying to get pregnant. The difficult process had begun to grate on us both, causing great frustration and tension. But now there were only clear skies ahead.

Lori officially told me we were pregnant at the downtown Marshall Field's. So to mark the occasion, I bought our child-to-be a pair of socks. It was Daddy's first gift and a look into the future. (As the months passed, I would buy many such gifts.)

Lori and I had largely formulated our attitude to the pregnancy together. We both wanted "things" to be as normal as possible as we went about the daily business of living.

Work, for Lori, we decided, would only be curtailed the last month or so. Check-ups would occur at regular intervals as deemed fit by the doctor. In fact, we implicitly trusted all our doctors allowing them carte blanche to provide the care they found necessary.

We had tried not to be what many of our friends had become. Many had miscarriages. Each subsequent pregnancy was shrouded in tension and fear. Neither of us would get caught up in this negativity. Nor did we understand it. We both considered it as an over-reaction, detrimental to mental health and our nine months ahead. We felt that life and our pregnancy would go on as usual. And they did for the full nine months.

January, 1990

After the New Year, Lori and I resumed our schedules without flinching. After all, what else was there to do? I continued my work as an associate rabbi in Chicago. Lori went back to her principalship at a suburban school.

At the time, I was enrolled as a student in a Clinical Pastoral Education (C.P.E.) program. I learned "hands-on" what it was like to work as a hospital chaplain. We in our group had access to and responsibility in virtually all areas of the hospital. The cancer and heart disease floors, not to mention the emergency room and dialysis unit, provided us with an unending panorama of human suffering and triumph.

On another note, I heard from a publisher early in the year that one of my books would finally come out in the Fall. How wonderful, I thought, the birth of a child and a new book!

Lori and I had decided not to share the good news until another month or so. For now, it would be our secret.

We went to bed smiling, thinking of days to come.

February, 1990

We finally decided to let "the world" know. We informed our respective families first, followed by our employers. All rejoiced with us. Often, upon hearing the news, people would say *B'sha'ah Tovah,* Hebrew for "at the right time." Almost no one said "congratulations," this greeting being assigned for after the birth. As with everything else in life, my Jewish faith and culture had created an entire folklore surrounding the mystery of birth. Time and timing were both held sacred, "a time for every purpose under heaven."

Despite my uneasy feelings, Lori and I both began to shop for basic baby clothes and furniture. We went to virtually every baby retail and wholesale outlet in the Chicago area.

My in-laws also wanted to get involved and generously offered to buy the baby furniture for us. One weekend they came in especially from Wisconsin. How could we refuse? The furniture was ordered, only to be delivered a few months later. We were well on our way.

My second gift for our baby-to-be was another pair of socks, neutral white socks with Mickey Mouse. I was now getting into the habit of shopping for this "third person," an already integral part of our lives.

March 1990

Lori was beginning to show which further heightened our awareness of the upcoming event. I remember how Lori radiated with that special glow. I had never seen her so happy. She told me many a time that having a baby was a lifelong dream. I felt fortunate that I could share it with her.

Overall, I didn't know what to feel at this point. Fatherhood seemed appealing, but I had lived most of my life alone. Now, with this new life, my life would invariably change. So much for independence, but the new joy?

Thirty-nine seemed a bit old to be a father. Yet it was now or never.

April, 1990

April was yet another month of preparations. Now we would be focusing on converting a den into a baby's room. I'm not at all knowledgeable about interior design, so I left the planning of the room essentially up to Lori.

Since we opted not to know the sex of our child, the room would be painted in off-white, (the furniture also was white). Furniture from the den now found itself in every corner of the house. The attic was literally stuffed to the gills.

We both actually decided on a fish/curtain/cover motif which was quite colorful. I think it was called "Fiesta Fish."

Not too long after, I went out and bought my child-to-be's third gift, a goldfish bowl with its requisite goldfish, gravel, and a small "palm tree." After all, we wanted to create an appealing water environment. Although I remained unenthusiastic about these preparations, I basically went along. I was clearly outnumbered by the women of the family. All was done for the sake of family peace.

May/June 1990

These months were rather pleasant ones. The weather was balmy, and all was going well with Lori's weekly check-ups.

We had begun a Lamaze class out in a suburban hospital. The instructor was excellent and accomplished in her own right, having written numerous books on the theory and practice of having children.

She taught us not only about the expected breathing techniques, but also a bit about the physiology and psychology of becoming parents. We truthfully learned a great deal.

We enjoyed meeting with our fellow class members and began to develop a sense of purpose and camaraderie with them. They, too, were excited and nervous, planning for this life altering event. We shared stories as well as our hopes and dreams. We felt connected.

Work had slowed down for the two of us, as our respective schools let out in mid-May. This offered us the time and opportunity to focus more on the near future.

During this time, I had developed some sort of muscular condition, that grew increasingly worse. I spent a lot of my time seeing my G.P. and chiropractor in trying to get some relief.

It was count down now to Baby Sagarin. (Incidentally, we did agree not to have any baby showers before the birth.)

... up to July 18, 1990

July was hot, as could be expected. Now especially during the heat, I wondered how Lori felt with those extra pounds. She never complained. Pregnancy remained a miraculous gift. Her happiness was evident, and all of us were very supportive.

On July 10th, we and her parents attended "Phantom of the Opera" in downtown Chicago. I remember our walking carefully and having wonderful seats.

It seemed that the baby liked the performance, as he/she kicked up a storm. We thought we had another Mozart on our hands.

The baby's due date was about July 15th, so we began to hold our breaths.

I continued to go to the chiropractor during these auspicious days, trying to deal with increasing pain. One morning, the 18th of July, I saw him as usual in his office on Lincoln Avenue.

During the middle of the session, the phone rang. Normally it would have been nothing. But the doctor called me to the phone. I had little time to think, and suddenly heard the words—"our baby's dead." I jumped and grabbed my shirt. The doctor said, "you'll have another." "Another" was not where I was. I was focused on my dead son. I had to meet Lori immediately at Evanston Hospital.

As I drove in the car to the hospital. I remembered that Lori sensed something was wrong when she woke up that day. I sloughed it off as being nothing. Why hadn't I been more attentive, more concerned? (Questions such as this one would plague me in the many months to come.)

When I arrived at the hospital Lori was already there, waiting in the Fetal Monitoring Room. Chaplains descended upon us but I brushed them away. I could speak to no one.

I literally broke down hysterically and found some solace calling a rabbi-friend who was my mentor during my hospital training. He said he would be there for the child's delivery. Delivery? It hadn't occurred to me that the worse was yet to come.

Lori maintained somewhat stoic throughout this whole, horrible time. She "allowed" me to cry and cry I did. I was so entrapped with myself that I genuinely had not made myself "available" to her. I still regret this today.

I worried that she might explode.

Lori had already called her parents in Madison, Wisconsin, before getting to the hospital. They came immediately to be with us just a few hours later.

I had called my brother as well, as he was my closest relative. The call was automatic, a basic reflex to the situation. I had instinctively wanted my mother, but she had passed away seven years earlier. He, too, flew into Chicago as soon as he could get the next plane out of New York. Yes, the family would be with us.

We were far from finished at the Fetal Monitoring Unit. The requisite ultra-sounds were taken.

And now we both saw our baby dead. Lying in the sac of amniotic fluid. We both were paralyzed, devastated beyond words. I should also note that Lori's doctor had come to be with us, to see the test results for himself. This had never happened to him before, so he, too, seemed at a loss for words. However, he did now outline what had to occur next.

I remember how he spoke. It all made sense and yet it didn't. How could this be happening to us? The nightmare would continue the next day and the next month, and for the rest of our lives.

July 19, 1990

Procedurally we would have to enter the Women's Hospital the following day to have the baby delivered. (Why we couldn't do it then and there still escapes me.) Our doctor would be there to assist in the delivery.

How would we live through that long day of darkness? How could Lori hold our son inside knowing he was dead? I wish I could have felt her physical and emotional pain. I had prayed earnestly that we were one, yet the Creator had made us two, separate yet intrinsically intertwined. Life seemed much too limiting, as our togetherness, I felt, would be in some way challenged.

Who was this Creator anyway? What was he doing to us?

We were placed in a corner room in Delivery, far away from the other mothers and fathers of the day. (This isolation reflected our own feelings of isolation and loneliness.) No, ours would not be the normal, healthy birth we had hoped for. It would be un-sung and un-celebrated, the birth of a death or is it the death of a birth?

How could life and death be so close? Were they not opposites? Here they were intertwined in the life and death of our son.

After awhile our questions seemed senseless. There just were no answers.

As we slept together that night, I recall our silence. We quietly held hands and did not speak of tomorrow. I did sense we indeed were one that night and that there was a "Presence" over us.

The baby's delivery was induced with potosin. Lori was also given an epidural to ease the pain during the delivery.

It didn't seem right to go through all the life-affirming exercises we learned in "Lamaze. We had no desire to make believe. We, each in his own way, began to face the reality of our son's death.

The hours were long and sad. We had little to say to each other. All we did was wait.

The baby was delivered at 2:19 p.m. I sensed that we were both numb.

Our virtual silence was reflected by the hospital staff who went about their business with little or no conversation.

After the child was delivered, our son was cleaned up and wrapped in a small cloth and brought to the both of us. I held him first, pressing his warm body next to mine. I remarked how cute I thought he was, with that wisp of red hair—no one responded.

I handed him to Lori and she cuddled him close to her body. There was bonding despite his death. We would, in no way, negate the nine months he had spent with us as a member of our family, in the security of Lori's womb.

When we offered him to Lori's mother, she felt most uncomfortable and chose not to hold him. This certainly was not the time for any of us to make demands or set expectations.

The impact of the death had barely set in.

After awhile, he was taken away from us to be placed in refrigeration overnight. The thought chilled both of us, but such was hospital procedure.

I knew, from my own hospital experience, that funeral arrangements would have to be made. I called a close friend in one of Chicago's funeral homes. In an unsteady voice, I told him all that had happened. He seemed to listen and "nod" over the phone. Finally he said he would take care of "things," anyway we saw fit.

We were in essence forced to talk about burying our son, literally minutes after bringing him into the world. How could this be?

We decided, rather quickly, that we wanted a small, private committal graveside service. Our son would there receive the name Judah L. Sagarin and an appropriate "farewell." There would be no eulogy and no particular words of comfort. No one knew what to say and silence continued overall to be the best response.

We decided also only to have the four of us present—the funeral director, the Rabbi, Lori and myself. This would not be marked by throngs of people—it would be short and altogether simple.

I remember when they brought Judah back to us early in the morning. A social worker was there to be with us. I remember how cold he felt and how blue he looked. I cried out in agony as I held him. I kept asking—why is he so cold? Why is he so cold? Lori held him too and then we let go. At first, I did not want an autopsy performed. It went against my grain, my entire being. He had been hurt enough, why more unnecessary cutting?

July 20, 1990

Lori convinced me that an autopsy might help her with future pregnancies. After a brief discussion, I acquiesced. They would later inform us that they found no particular cause for Judah's death. We had hoped to find something so we could try to remedy the situation in the future—but now with the coroner's report we were left in limbo. The unknown is a frightful place to be.

We knew there would be no champagne dinner for us, no celebration—we knew a vast emptiness lay around the corner.

We packed our belongings and left the hospital. All the staff was present to say good-bye to us. Their words were most kind, but it was difficult to appreciate them.

When we arrived home we found Lori's parents there ready to greet us. While we were in the hospital, they had managed to call "Lazars," the baby furniture supplier, and had all of our son's beautiful, white, Morageau furniture removed.

Even my goldfish bowl, goldfish and gravel had been taken away. I always wondered what had happened to the Mickey Mouse socks I had bought him.

The baby's room was now closed and I can't remember when we opened its door.

The scene in our home was difficult to say the least. Family and friends immediately began calling to offer their condolences. Lori took most of the calls, since I preferred not to talk at all. I had no energy or will to talk. Silence would protect me, or so I thought.

People just didn't know what to say and we did not know how to respond. They wanted to rush over, but I said no. After all, we had not buried our baby yet.

Was I an "official mourner?" What about Lori? Could we comfort each other? How does one define strength or courage in such a situation? I didn't feel like being strong or courageous; I just wanted to be myself.

Much was yet to occur regarding the roller-coaster nature of our feelings. Even to this day, I know we haven't resolved all the complex, heart-breaking pain. Maybe it's just not suppose to work out. It's just one of those things.

July 23, 1990

I remember the funeral director picking us up at our home with Judah in a small box in the front seat. We both opted not to see him again. The director also told us how cute he was. I'm not sure how I felt when he said that.

Honestly, I wasn't sure what to mourn—the loss of his life or the loss of his life with us? Did I mourn the loss of my hopes and expectations or the little life that would have been?

My own uncertainties taunted me. What was I suppose to feel and what did I actually feel? Was I in tune with Lori?

Frankly many "crazy thoughts" ran through my mind. Why wasn't my life taken instead of his? Intellectually, I knew it would be better if I just stopped asking why, but it too felt instinctive.

The world wanted us to move on, but we weren't ready. I had the fear that we'd never be ready.

The first night after Judah's burial, many people came to visit us, including people I didn't know. Their intentions of course were well-meaning. I wished to live with my silence (to a degree) and my privacy. I was not ready to interact with others, especially strangers. I can recall that I remained "tucked-away" in some corner of the house. There was my haven, my sanctuary.

Subsequently, during the week of July 23, 1990, Lori and I received visitors from our two congregations. They graciously brought dinner, as is generally the custom in a *Shivah* home.

I don't remember really talking about our son's death much. Even for those who came to offer their condolences, conversation surrounding our loss seemed difficult and strained to say the least. So we avoided it. No one, as I said before, knew what to say.

Now mention of Judah's death was replaced with small talk and the general goings-on of the day. Such was human nature.

I remember someone remarking that now it was time for me to go and serve as a rabbi again. In helping others, I would begin to get over this tragedy. I didn't and it doesn't quite work that way. I could no better fool myself than others in thinking I was "ready" to face the world and its challenges again.

August 9, 1990

If I recall correctly, we did go back to work around July 30th, taking the requisite seven days of *Shivah*.

The mourning was particularly strange and difficult in its own right. Was I supposed to comfort Lori? Or was she suppose to comfort me? Who was there to offer comfort to the two of us? As I said previously, our reactions were quite diverse. We had no idea of where to begin with each other.

(The long-term responses likewise brought out and continue to bring out an array of emotions.)

Nevertheless, we entered the every-day world again, basically carrying this burden without receiving any guidance on how to deal with it. We would have to find our own way into the "light."

We decided to attend some infant-loss groups. We really didn't know what to expect.

For our first visit, we readily shared the events surrounding Judah's death. We listened attentively to the facilitator and ultimately felt a bit unburdened when we left.

But during subsequent times, we felt the group never really got off square one. The repetitive nature of the class and its "canned" nature left us both at a loss. We wanted something with more substance, that would take us somewhere.

In frustration, we realized that this would not be the place.

August 9, 1990

In August, we went to Door County, Wisconsin in an attempt at "getting away" from our son's death. The intention had been a good one; the reality was that all was too fresh, too close.

Once again, I don't recall speaking about Judah at all, even though he was ever present in our thoughts. In retrospect we did him a disservice by not talking about him. We needed to recognize him and all he had been to us.

I did write a sermon that Fall about the nature of good and evil, coming to the conclusion that all was relative. Yet if I attributed Judah's death to nature, could I in good conscience consider nature to be evil?

A philosophical, theological dilemma ensued with little resolution. My only solace was in essence knowing that he didn't suffer and that his little life, like our own, remained in God's hands.

True, I asked the eternal question of why and why him, why not me, etc. One friend suggested we stop asking why and begin to ask "how." Unfortunately for us, "how" failed to yield an answer as well.

Even without answers, my writing continued to offer me some catharsis. Pen and paper provided a ready outlet, a vent for my feelings. It continues to do so today.

As the months passed by, the pain of Judah's death seemed less intense. Time was good to us and began to bestow its healing qualities. But manifestations of the event lingered. I began to have increased back trouble and pain. Lori grew ever anxious.

Judah's death now forced us to take a good look at our relationship. We had to reassess, reevaluate. What were our priorities, goals?

Undoubtedly, this event had irrevocably changed our lives. Now it was up to us to turn it into an experience from which we could learn.

Joan Schultz
A Candlestick Blessing

The phone rang once. It was my husband, Sandy, calling from the doctor's office. I heard his voice apologize because the biopsied tumor was cancerous. After our telephone goodbyes, I stood beside, though not touching, my Bechstein piano.

It held a pair of old, heavy brass candlesticks. They had journeyed from Russia to an antique shop in Jerusalem. My parents, on a Hadassah trip through Israel, had seen and admired the simple, burnished beauty of the candlesticks. When they returned, mother told Sandy of the treasure they had found, loved and left. She had kept the shop's name, address and price of the objects of her affection. My husband, wanting to surprise her, wrote the owner and had them shipped to my parents in St. Louis. The candlesticks stayed with them until their deaths. Then the Russian antiques came to live with me. Like a faded romantic image, they graced my grand piano.

Still standing by the piano, silent prayers for my precious partner crackled the still air like electricity. I felt my mother's presence. A loud, dull thud broke the quiet and the intensity of my concentration. On the opposite side of the piano, a fallen candlestick came into my focus. My curiosity instinctively moved me forward because these sentries of love had always remained unbowed. I walked over to the weighted piece, picked up the sturdy balanced base and looked for the dent as I set it upright. The soft, satin wood was completely unmarred. I didn't understand this phenomenon. I did understand the sudden peace and unexplained knowledge from my mother that my husband would recover. Sandy would be well once more.

Howard Schwartz
How I Became a Writer

Before I became a writer, I was a reader. From the time I was eight I loved to browse in the library, especially in the sections on myth and folklore. I read all the books I could find about Alexander the Great, my first hero, then all the books about King Arthur and the Knights of the Round Table. I read Andrew Lang's complete series of rainbow books of fairy tales. I remember reading Nathan Ausubel's huge book of Jewish folklore over and over, laughing hard at the stories of the Wise Men (who were really fools) of Chelm.

By the time I was in junior high, I was reading science fiction. I would explore one author at a time and read all of his books. I started with Robert Heinlein and proceeded to Isaac Asimov, A. E. Van Vogt, James Blish and others. I guess I spent most of my time in my little bedroom, lying on the bed reading. (I still prefer to read in bed.) At an early age I decided to keep a list of everything I read. (What did I ever do with that list?) I was very proud as it grew longer and longer, into the hundreds of books.

In high school I discovered J. D. Salinger's *The Catcher in the Rye,* and this was a life-changing event. Not only did I (and, as I was later to discover, millions of others) relate to this book in a very personal way, but I felt an intense attachment to the author. I quickly devoured his *Nine Stories,* and a few of those stories, especially "For Esme, With Love and Squalor" and "A Perfect Day for Bananafish" haunted me for years. Then I started waiting anxiously for Salinger to write more books. I was fortunate, in that his long stories about the Glass family started to appear in *The New Yorker,* as a kind librarian pointed out to me. Later they were published in book form, and I bought them in hardcover and read them over and over. I felt like I was a member of the Glass family and that Salinger was my buddy. I used to write him letters in my mind. He was a very important presence in my life.

But Salinger just couldn't write books fast enough for me. Every time I walked home through Clayton I stopped at the bookstore and checked to see if there were any new ones. One day there was a little book about

Salinger and his writing. I bought it. That was the first book of criticism I ever read, and I found it fascinating. The author had reached many of the same conclusions that I had about the Glass family, but the most important discovery I made was that Salinger had published quite a few stories in *The Saturday Evening Post* long before he started publishing in *The New Yorker.*

That summer, when I was sixteen, I was a junior counselor at Camp Hawthorn in the Ozarks, and when I had my first a day off, I spent it in the library in Jefferson City reading those old stories of Salinger's on microfilm. They weren't as good as the ones in *Nine Stories,* but they were full of hints of the glories to come. I found the whole experience thrilling, and as I walked out of the library that day I made a decision about what to do with my life: I decided to be a writer, because that way I could leave some part of myself behind when I wasn't around anymore. I can remember that moment vividly, standing on the stairs outside of the library. I didn't tell anyone about my decision, but my life was changed forever after that. I had a secret purpose to my life, and I carried it with me wherever I went.

I had brought my old Royal portable typewriter with me to camp. And at night I would carry it to the rec hall and sit for hours writing letters to my friends, long, single-spaced letters filled with my thoughts. I found the writing of those letters to be a gratifying experience. I felt that I was preparing myself for my future as a writer, and I guess I was.

I continued this secret life for the next couple of years, until I started college at Washington University. One day I was sitting in the office of David Hadas, an English professor I greatly admired. He asked me what I wanted to be when I grew up, and I revealed my secret: I wanted to be a writer. Then he said: "Did it ever occur to you that a writer writes?" I said: "No." And it was true. Up to that time, I really hadn't tried to write anything except for long letters. This unexpected question caused me great distress. It was no longer possible to consider myself a writer, at least until I wrote something. And I had no idea how to go about doing that.

I went through the next couple of years stripped of my fantasy about being a writer. I struggled with my work in college, and the only classes in which I distinguished myself were my English classes. In those classes I had my hand up all the time, and when the teachers called on me (which was less and less often) I almost always had the right answer. Those classes went a long way toward restoring my confidence, but I missed the certainty I had known when I was sure about what I was going to be. Now I was struggling to make a real decision, one that I would have to live with. My parents wanted me to be a doctor, but the truth is that this didn't interest me at all. The matter was finally decided when I failed freshman chemistry. Then my parents came up with an alternate destiny: I could be a rabbi. But I still wanted to be a writer.

Finally, in 1965, when I was twenty, fate intervened, in an unexpected fashion. My girlfriend Hannah broke up with me. We had gone together for a year, and this breakup was very upsetting, especially when I realized that she really meant it. One day not long after that I was sitting at home in front of my typewriter when I started banging out angry lines about her. I would write a few words and hit the carriage return. After writing a few pages this way, I looked at them and realized, with amazement and disbelief, that I had just written a poem. My very first one. From that instant, I forgot about Hannah and started writing poems. I must have written a hundred poems in the next few months. I was filled with inspiration, and thrilled, at the age of twenty, to finally be fulfilling my destiny as a writer. Of course, I thought the poems were splendid. It never occurred to me that they might not be.

I was so proud of those first poems that I put together a little book of them, called *Flowering,* and printed one hundred copies of it at the home of a friend who had a ditto machine in his basement. I gave copies to my family and friends, as my way of announcing my new career. Except for one friend who was kind of snide about it, they all told me how wonderful the book was, and of course I believed them. (Today I would do anything to get those books back and burn them!)

That summer I worked at a camp in Michigan, and I fell in love with Julie, another counselor. I'm sure she knew how I felt, but she didn't indicate the slightest interest in me. I stared at her whenever I saw her in the dining hall or walking around the camp. And then I went back to my cabin and wrote love poems about her. I must have written another hundred poems that summer, and as soon as I got home from camp I published my second book on the ditto machine. Of course I sent a copy of it to Julie, and it did provoke a very nice letter, which I read over and over hundreds of times.

When I went back to college in the fall, I signed up for a poetry writing class with Donald Finkel. I felt far superior to the other students in the class for, after all, I had already published two books of poems. The class was full of young poets, and I made many friends among them. At last I had found a circle of friends who recognized my identity as a writer. With them I became active in the student publications: *Free Lance, Reflections, Crossroads* and *Tambourine*. I remember the day my first poems were published in *Free Lance*. I walked around the campus certain that everyone I passed knew who I was. Before long I began to serve as editor of some of these student publications, and I discovered a joy in editing that I had never expected. This turned out to be the ideal preparation for the editing projects I later undertook.

As for Donald Finkel, he was a truly extraordinary teacher. Although, in retrospect, the poems I wrote for his class were pretty awful, he never even hinted that they weren't superb. Of course, he never said that they were, either. I just assumed that we both knew how good they were. Instead, he made practical suggestions, suggesting that some lines could be cut, some revised, some words might work better than others, etc. At first, I was reluctant to change anything that I had written, as if it had been engraved in stone. But after working with him for a couple of years, he convinced me to regard my words as if they were written on water and were infinitely malleable. I eventually came to appreciate his criticism and that of the class, for it led me to strengthen and improve my poems. In fact, I became something of a maniac about revision, reworking the same poem hundreds of times. Even today I have a hard time letting go of anything that I've written, and I've driven more than one publisher crazy with the changes I've made at the last minute.

Now there were a couple of other teachers of creative writing at Washington University, but one of them was said to have bragged about making students cry in his class, and the other was overheard saying to a colleague, "Well, just crushed another aspiring young poet!" I decided not to risk getting crushed. In retrospect, I think it was a wise decision. At that time my ego was fragile, and I'm not sure my confidence as a writer would have survived a put down from either one of them. Today I'm a teacher of creative writing, and I have never forgotten how vulnerable I was at that time. I've modeled my approach after that of Donald Finkel—the gentle approach. I try to inspire confidence in my students while showing them the possibilities of revision. And I never try to predict who will succeed as a writer and who won't. I know from experience that virtually every young writer (with the exception of Rimbaud, who started writing at fifteen and quit when he was nineteen) goes through at least a two-year period of apprenticeship. During that time they are struggling to define their voice and style and vision. It is simply unfair to make any judgments about their potential during that time.

In 1967 I began to keep a journal of my dreams, and I have continued to do so ever since. I have always been vividly aware of my dreams, and now I began to recognize the possibilities of using dream images as subject matter in my poems. This turned out to be a very fruitful decision for me, as dreams have proven to be one of my primary sources of inspiration. Sometimes my dreams seemed to beg to be turned into poems. I remember one dream in which I was walking outside at night, when I encountered my girlfriend, who was turning into a tree. This dream became the poem "Calling the Moon Closer":

> All at once
> I find her taking root
> In the soft earth beside me
> It is hard to wake her
> Even when her eyes are open
> She cannot decide
> How to breathe
> Whether to draw her breath
> Like a young girl
> Or let her leaves absorb

The light
Still
She is able
To call the moon closer
And lets me hold her
In my arms
And all the while she shelters me
The branches are filled
With a silver light
As if the moon had slipped
Inside.

In 1967 I wrote a poem called "Blind Descent," about climbing down from a fire escape with my eyes closed. At first I included all of the details of the experience, but as I continued to revise the poem it got shorter and shorter, and in the end all I left in it was the motion of the downward descent. This poem was a great revelation to me, because it served as a kind of archetype of descent and could be related to many situations, not only to the one that inspired it. I decided that I wanted to write the poems of the archetypes, and this gave me a specific and unique goal. The final poem reads as follows:

It is night
All the way
Down, the wet
Eyes urge open,
The blind guide
Reaches to
Touch, startling
The flights fall
Down, the steep
Shivering
Begins, the last
Flight, the trees,

The soft ground,
The rocking
Disbelief.

After writing this poem, I realized that I had reached a new plateau in my writing, and that everything I had written before then was not good enough. One evening I made the rash decision to burn everything else, which came to a couple of carton boxes full of poems, and I did it. Later I realized how foolish I had been. Even if most of the poems were adolescent, there might have been a few good lines in them worth salvaging. Now I always tell my students not to destroy anything they write, but to file it away, and when they are stuck for a line or image, to take out their unfinished drafts and see what they can find.

Starting with "Blind Descent" I began to assemble a manuscript of my poems. I started off with that single poem, and every time I wrote another one that I considered as good, I would add it to the spring-back binder I kept the manuscript in. This was a slow process. As often as I would add a poem to the manuscript, I would pull another one out, that I didn't consider to be strong enough.

From 1965-1968 I wrote poems exclusively. During that time my only ambition was to be a poet. My heroes were William Butler Yeats, Theodore Roethke, and James Wright. But in 1968 something happened that caused me to change my mind. I had a very powerful dream in which I played a bamboo flute and became one with the music. I wanted to write a poem based on this dream, but no matter how many times I revised it, it didn't seem to work. At last, out of desperation, I tried to write it as prose, and I was astonished to find that it worked perfectly that way. But I didn't want to include any prose pieces in my book of poems, and I didn't know what to do with it. So, being of an obsessive nature, I decided to write a book of parables to go along with it. And from that time on, I divided my creative efforts between poetry and fiction.

In 1970 my writing took one more crucial turn. On my birthday in April I called my girlfriend, Jocelyne, who was visiting in Israel, to tell her that I would be coming there to join her that summer, and that we could

get married in the fall. She told me not to come, that she was with
someone else, and the bottom fell out of my life. That day I drove out to
the country, to be alone with my despair. As I drove, I was haunted by the
image of the rib that became Eve being extracted from Adam. When I
reached my destination, I pulled out my notebook and wrote, in a single
draft, one of my best poems, "Adam's Dream." That poem, which seemed
to write itself, served me like an amulet during the long period in which
I tried to adjust to this great loss. But it also announced a major
development in my life—a fascination with the myths and legends of
Judaism, which I found to be an endless source of inspiration. From that
time on, I have drawn on these images more than any others, and they have
made a deep imprint on my writing. Here is "Adam's Dream:"

> The blossoms closed into buds
> Singing only to themselves.
> The sweet hand that guarded my heart
> Stirred within my body.
> I reached for you as you pulled away
> And followed the arm's length
> That linked us. I could hear
> The dark pools filling, the breath you took
> Rising over the waters.
> I felt the life leave me
> With a gasp that gave me life.
> No eyes opened to ask or to answer,
> Yet then I knew you were another
> That I had lost,
> That you would never remember
> Why the wound could not heal itself
> Once we had awakened.

Ironically, the first book that I completed was not one of poetry, but
of parables, *A Blessing Over Ashes*. I sent it to David Meltzer, a west coast
poet who edited the magazine *Tree* and published *Tree Books*. He had

published some of the parables in his journal, and then he agreed to publish my first book. That book appeared in 1974, and although it is a tiny one of 36 pages, its arrival was probably the greatest thrill of my life. At last I was a real writer.

Meanwhile, I had continued to write poems, and finally I felt that the book, which I called *Vessels,* was ready to be published. I had always been good about sending out my poems to journals, and as a result a good many of them had already been published, making the manuscript more respectable. There was one poetry imprint I especially admired, Unicorn Press, and I sent the manuscript to them. Much to my amazement, the publisher wrote back offering to publish the book. (Little did I know what an aberration this was, and how difficult it is to publish books of poems.) And in 1977, *Vessels* was published.

With the publication of *A Blessing Over Ashes* and *Vessels,* the die was cast. I knew that this was what I wanted to be doing, and that I wanted nothing more than to continue to write. I felt that I had finally found a voice and style of my own, and I had also started to think of myself as a Jewish writer, and took comfort from knowing that I was working in an ancient tradition. That was twenty years ago, and I am still following the same path, writing poems and stories, collecting and retelling Jewish tales, and publishing books that I hope will be around long after I'm gone.

Maury L. Schwartz
My Father Read to Me

A long time ago, before television, my father read to me. I was an eight-year-old who had finally been given permission to go to the neighborhood library alone, crossing two busy streets. The library looked like a castle high on a hill whose ceilings seemed to touch the sky. It was very quiet. The librarian looked like the queen of the castle. She spoke ever so quietly as she bent over looking into my face. Her glasses hung from her neck on golden chains. Her voice was warm and her smile kind. She made me feel welcome. She looked like I imagined *Shekhinah,* the Sabbath Queen. She told me I could have my very own library card. I had never seen my name on an official document before.

After thanking Her Highness with the kind smile, I wandered around the library palace. There were so many books. Finally, I came across a section of Yiddish books. That was the language spoken at home. I couldn't read the titles or the authors and neither could the librarian. The alphabet is different from English. How could I make my selections?

I finally decided to be guided by the *Havdalah,* a ceremony that separates the Sabbath from the rest of the week. The ceremony uses wine, a special candle and a spice box to emphasize the five senses. We light the candle and feel its warmth. We taste the wine. We smell the spices and see the candle extinguished in the wine. My father says the prayer. Then he looks into each child's face, touches his cheeks, kisses his eyes, almost tasting them. Finally, taking a deep breath, he says *"zesa neshamah"*—sweet soul.

I reasoned as an eight-year-old might that this was how I would select the books—the way my father expressed his love for us. I picked up a book, looked and felt its cover, brought it to my lips and took a deep breath with the book almost touching my nose. I learned then that every book had its own aroma. I selected six books and brought them home to my father. He was overjoyed. He had never been to a library. Maybe he did not know it was available to him.

That evening and almost every evening for many years, my father read the Yiddish classics to me. I was thrilled with the stories of Sholom Asch,

I.L. Peretz, S. Ansky, Sholom Aleichem, Mendele Mokher Seforim and many others. Every time a picture of one of these authors appeared in *The Forward,* the daily Yiddish newspaper, my father would cut it out, frame it and put it on the wall above the refrigerator next to a large picture of Franklin Delano Roosevelt, whom my father considered our family *Tzaddik,* a righteous man.

The stories in the books were magical, better than the radio serials I listened to in the afternoon. Every week I would go back to my enchanted castle and take out more books, selecting them in my own special way. I never learned to read or speak Yiddish, but I did learn to understand it. My father read and spoke in Yiddish and I answered in English. I was not encouraged to learn Yiddish because when my older brother entered elementary school knowing only Yiddish, he was extremely handicapped.

Years later I was told that when I became very happy or upset, I spoke in very clear, classical Yiddish. When this was pointed out to me, I was unable to utter another word in that language. After my father's death, I became depressed and sought counseling. After three months, my counselor pointed out that we had been conducting our sessions entirely in Yiddish. After that we spoke only in English for once again I could not utter a single word in Yiddish.

Today, 37 years after my father's death, I can tell a good Yiddish story but I can't speak a single sentence. I cannot understand why my tongue plays this trick on me. Last year when I visited St. Louis, the city of my birth, I went to the cemetery to my parents' graves. I spoke to them in English and I could hear them respond in Yiddish. I even recited a story by I.L. Peretz, *If Not Higher,* that my father read to me more than 50 years ago. This time I heard myself speaking in Yiddish.

The library, that castle of serendipity, put me on a path of adventure and imagination. I can still see myself browsing in the section of "Yiddish Books." In the quiet of my mind, I can hear my father reading. He closes the book and explains the moral of the story. Then he says, "*Gita neight, mine zunne,*" and I answer, "Good night, Pop."

My Mother Fed Me

I want to tell you about my mother, Mama Leah, who believed that food was the essence of love. The more she loved you, the more she fed you, and my mother loved me a great deal. Looking back on it, there was only one problem. She also loved to use *schmaltz*. *Schmaltz,* if you don't know it, is the king of fats. *Schmaltz* makes butter look like fat-free skim milk. It was used for cooking, for frying, for putting on bread. It was the all-purpose cooking oil with a hundred uses.

As I look back now, I remember when I went to kindergarten I was rather skinny, and the school nurse sent home a report that I was suffering from malnutrition. This was a great insult to my mother, who then took corrective measures, which I'll tell you about shortly.

My older brother called me Babe. My sister called me Skinny Miriny. My father called me *Zisa Neshomah,* "sweet soul." And my mother called me *Leib*, which means "heart." Later I gave myself the middle name of Leonard. Today Leonard is on all my diplomas and certificates. I chose Leonard as the English equivalent of *Leib*. So you can see with the nicknames they gave me, I was destined to be a Mama's boy.

How did my mother handle this greatest of insults, that I was suffering from malnutrition? From that day forward, until I graduated from elementary school, I came home for lunch every day. It started, always, with about three eggs and a pound of spinach, cooked in butter. This was followed by a large lunch. The spinach and eggs were only a *forshpeiz,* an appetizer. Luckily, I had to walk back to school so I could work off that meal, but I learned to love it.

Whenever I came home for lunch, food was ready, and invariably, in those days during the Depression, someone would be knocking at the back door asking for food. We didn't have street beggars, but we did have people who were truly hungry who went from house to house. And often I was joined at lunch by one of these strangers who knocked at our door. They didn't just get a sandwich, they joined me in eating whatever I was having for lunch that day.

By now you can see that I grew up in a very interesting household.

You might even say it was exotic. In those days we never heard of dysfunctional families. I grew up learning about exotic folk medicine, exotic folk stories and exotic foods.

Let me tell you about some of these Jewish soul foods. I loved *p'shav* (also known as *kut-chu-nu*), cow's feet cooked with garlic and pepper, as well as chicken feet (a delight or a disgust depending on your taste. You could eat them or scare your neighbors with them). How would you like *gefilte helzel* (stuffed chicken or goose neck), or *varinaca* (like perogi or ravioli), or *lingen* (lung) stew, or my all-time favorite, *greven,* cooked chicken skin with onions. It was crispy and delicious. And for dessert there was *taiglach,* a candy made of honey and nuts.

Some of the foods conveyed a sense of love with their exotic qualities. The utensils were also treated with reverence. We looked upon them as *klay kodesh,* holy implements. All foods were either *milahdik,* dairy, or *flashadik,* meat. There was also *parve,* neutral, but that is not important at this point. So all plates, pots, cutlery, etc. were either *milahdik* or *flashadik,* and never, never could they mix in the pot, on the plate, on the sink, or in your stomach. This was an important prohibition. In my whole life, I witnessed only one accidental mix-up. That turned out to be an almost supernatural experience.

One day at lunch I used a *milahdik gupple* to pick up some salami. My mother saw this and it seemed that an alarm went off in heaven or on earth, I don't know which. My mother wasn't angry. She simply took the *gupple* out of my hand and ran into our back yard. She put the *gupple* into the ground, circled the area, and said some prayers. Twenty-four hours later, she dug it up and it was okay. I asked my mother what prayer she said and where she learned to do what she did. She never would agree to discuss what she did except to hint that it was to frustrate the Devil and keep him away from our house.

I'm sure you are asking, "What's a *gupple?*" Well, a *gupple* is a fork, and I didn't learn the word "fork" until I was in high school. In the cafeteria one day, I asked for a knife and a *gupple*. Someone said, "What's a *gupple?*" I reached for the tray and picked one up. A friend said, "That's a fork." I said, "What's a fork?"

I remember once, when I was about 10 years old, I saw a game in a store window. It was called Big Business, very similar to Monopoly, and it cost about a dollar and twenty-five cents. In those days men who were working were lucky to make five dollars a week, and my mother would often spend about a dollar and twenty-five cents at the grocery store and bring home two or three large bags of food. So a dollar and twenty-five cents was no small cost. I told my mother about this game, telling her how much I longed for it. But I knew it was too expensive.

One day, when no one was home, my mother told me to get dressed, because we were going for a walk. She took me first to a little restaurant around the corner, where she fed me and fed me and fed me. She apologized for the poor quality of food at the restaurant, but she didn't have time to fix lunch that day because we were going on this little excursion. Next door was the store that had the game Big Business. My mother counted out in change a dollar and twenty-five cents, (no tax in those days) and I came home and played Big Business. I remember having that game for more than twenty years. It was as precious as a jar of *schmaltz*.

Sometimes during my preteen years my mother and I would go to a Saturday matinee at the Union Theater around the corner. I remember the day it opened in 1939. It showed Don Ameche playing Alexander Graham Bell. We would go there on Saturday, where there would usually be a double or a triple feature, the news and three or four serials. All the serials were cliffhangers. My mother and I would go in at two o'clock, and often we would stay until eight or nine o'clock in the evening. It wouldn't be uncommon for my mother to leave me there for two or three hours while she went home to feed my father. She was always careful to admonish me not to leave my seat. I think it was at that time that I began to develop bladder problems.

Let me tell you what happened during those movies and all those hours of watching those wonderful serials. We'd come in after having lunch at home, and about an hour later my mother would open her large purse and take out a sandwich. An hour after that I'd get another sandwich. And then out of this magical purse came a bottle of milk, sometimes buttermilk, but often fat milk. She used to like to save the fat at the top of the milk for me. I needed it. Someone had once said I was suffering from malnutrition.

But in that movie house I don't think that one serial or one cartoon would pass without my having a banana or apple, a sandwich, and sometimes chocolate for dessert. And when my mother would return from home, there would be more food. It was really a time of great eating and great love.

Let me tell you about our home. Our kitchen was very large. There were two tables for eating. There was also a large sink, and on top of the sink there was always meat being koshered. My mother would be standing there singing *Ofen Pripichik,* salting the meat, and greeting anyone who came in with, "Sit down and eat." I have to point out that in the bathtub there was usually a fish swimming around waiting for Shabbos. My mother was a wonderful maker of gefilte fish.

Friday the house smelled clean, because we usually spent two or three days preparing for the Sabbath. But on Friday morning my mother would "cook up a storm," as she would say, and we would have the most exotic kinds of food almost every Shabbos—gefilte fish, *helzel, miltze.* Occasionally she'd make a beet or cabbage borscht, and there was usually potato blintzes and chopped liver. And always for dessert there was wonderful strudel, mandel bread or rugelah.

I should point out that everything was cooked with *schmaltz. Schmaltz,* onions and garlic, that was the style, nothing less. If you didn't have a good stomach, you couldn't survive. I remember when my mother would cook a *knobel* borscht. It was so peppery and had so much garlic in it that while it was boiling you could take a spoon and try to taste it. If the spoon didn't melt in your hands, you could try putting some in your mouth. I still have scars on my lips from those wonderful days of eating the boiling *knobel* borscht.

We also had another custom. After an hour or two, when we had finished dinner and perhaps would be sitting around listening to the radio—Jack Benny and Fred Allen were our favorites—and before my father would read to me, we would have a *glazel tay,* a glass of tea. But with the *glazel tay* we would cut off the end of a fresh loaf of rye bread or pumpernickel, put salt on a plate, rub garlic in the salt, and then rub that mixture on the bread. Then we would take a whole clove of garlic, eat it, eat a piece of onion, and then finally eat the bread. In the winter time this guaranteed that you never caught a cold. I always wondered why I began getting colds when I married and moved out of my parent's home.

My mother was the queen of her kitchen in the same way that the Sabbath queen was the queen of our home on Shabbos. When she wasn't preparing for Shabbos or cooking for a normal day, my mother would make root beer and bottle it or make *vishnic* brandy. She would make all kinds of pastries as well as her own noodles. In fact, we never had any canned food in our home until I was a senior in high school and brought something home that was revolutionary—a can of Campbell's chicken soup. Although insulted, my mother permitted that, but there were very few other cans brought in.

Food, love, sweets—I should mention that my mother developed diabetes in old age, just as I have developed clogged arteries. Following my heart attack, I had an angioplasty. The doctors were amazed that instead of plaque, they found my arteries were filled with *schmaltz*.

I remember in those days that when my father would come home after having a good day at work, he would bring us a bag full of pennies and a bag full of chocolate. My brother, sister and I would be greeted and the bags of pennies and chocolate would be opened and thrown in the air. We would scramble for the chocolate and pennies. If my father hadn't had a good day, he would not say a word. He would sit down at his table and magically, a full meal would appear before him. This could occur at any time of the day. Dinner at our house could be served morning, noon and night and often for a midnight snack.

I also remember on Hanukah we had latkes and draidles, played games, and ate and ate and ate. I remember my mother's latkes. One latke had enough *schmaltz* in it to keep the Menorah burning for all eight days.

So I learned that one of the ways to show affection for people was to feed them. After I married and moved away and got used to eating my wife's "Yankee-style" cooking, when I would return home for a Shabbos dinner, I would have a stomach ache for a week afterwards. But I loved every bite of it, and I never hesitated to eat.

Today, almost thirty years after my mother's death, I can close my eyes and enjoy the aroma of her cooking. I can also see myself, seated at our green kitchen table, enjoying one of my mother's wonderful dishes as she sits nearby, listening to me and being wise enough to rarely give advice. Just as my father was a good story teller, my mother was a good listener. While she listened she might say, "*Es past nischt*" (It is not becoming), and sometimes she would say, "*Emess*" (truth). As a good listener, she might encourage me to continue with my thoughts by saying, "Ah-ha!" with just the right tone.

Last year when I visited St. Louis, the city of my birth, I went to the cemetery to visit my parents' graves. After speaking to my father, I started to speak to my mother and said, "Mom, you're the greatest *balebosteh* in the world and the greatest cook and the greatest mom. I love you." Then I heard her say, "Sha-sha, go eat something. Everything will be all right. We'll talk later."

In my mind's eye I can still see my mother's kitchen—the meat koshering, the pots boiling, the smell of the challah baking, the freshly baked noodles and my mother singing Yiddish melodies. And at night, even now, when I get ready to go to bed, I hear my mother say, "*Gita neight, mine leib.*" And I answer, "Good night, mom."

Barbara Langsam Shuman
The Rainbow Covenant

We dashed from car to curb to roller rink entrance. On that drenching October afternoon, the roller rink beckoned as an oasis in reverse, a dry harbor for our soggy souls.

The dreary weather matched our spirits. My daughter Amanda and I were sad because of the occasion—a farewell fest for a family of dear friends.

My friendship with Francie, "the mom" of the family, began more than a dozen years ago. For at least a decade, my husband Michael and I have considered her husband Josh a close friend. Their daughters, 9-year-old Dena and 6-1/2-year-old Alena are been lifelong pals of Amanda's.

Yet our friendship would be best measured by our emotional ties to the family, strengthened by all that we've experienced together. During the past dozen years, we've shared our mutual courtships, engagements, showers, weddings, childbirths, new homes, holiday celebrations, birthdays, illnesses, mourning departed loved ones, professional triumphs and disappointments. For so many memorable moments of our lives, Francie, Josh and their girls were there.

And now they were moving, 1000 miles away to Washington, D.C. The move was prompted by a United States Army support base closing, triggered by defense cutbacks. Josh is an attorney, employed by the army.

The military industrial complex, an entity I thought would never affect us personally, was the motivating force behind Josh and Francie's exodus. Because we loved the family so much, we'd made a promise to call often and visit as much as possible.

Francie and Josh had already been feted at an adult party, so the roller rink gathering was officially a going-away party for Dena and Alena. Family friends and classmates from H.F. Epstein Hebrew Academy, their former school, and Solomon Schechter Day School, the place where they would complete their St. Louis-based education, were invited. Because so many parents chose to stay at the roller rink, the party evolved into a transgenerational event.

As a farewell party venue, the roller rink turned out to be an inspired choice. All flash and sass and glitz and glare, with disco lighting and garish decor which were ideal for camouflaging tear-stained cheeks and swollen eyes. The ear-shattering Muzak drowned out sounds of sobbing.

A barrage of impressions bombarded our senses. Skaters—both juvenile and adult—circled the rink in perpetual motion. Multi-colored lights whirled around, in sync with the cacophony. Concession stands, bold signage, and patterned carpeting added to the enclosed carnival ambiance.

Skates were squeezed on, only to be yanked off minutes later. Amid all of this were cries of "We'll miss you all so much!" and "Pleeeeasse don't go!"

Guests were preparing to leave when my husband arrived.

"Come, hurry outside!" Michael called. "There's the most beautiful rainbow in the sky!"

Amanda and I spread the word to a group of children and parents, grabbed our jackets, and followed Michael's lead. A nature lover who rarely indulges in hyperbole, my husband had been on target with his proclamation.

A fresh topaz-blue sky framed the most vivid rainbow I'd ever seen. So vivid that it spawned a spin-off, a more muted twin that also soared into the heavens and then descended to earth in a graceful arc, stretching from horizon to horizon. Amanda recited the rainbow song she'd learned in preschool, as she checked to make sure that all of the designated colors were represented.

Michael reminded me that the week's *parasha,* or Torah portion, involved the Noah story, recounting the flood and its aftermath. That *parasha* holds special meaning for us because it was also the Torah portion the week Amanda was born.

We remembered that after the flood, God "set His bow in the cloud," placing a rainbow in the sky as a sign of His promise to never again destroy the world with a flood. In return, Noah and his people would enter into a covenant with God to live by the seven commandments that God gave to Noah and his descendants.

Let's say the *bracha* for the rainbow," Michael said.

Although we were surrounded by dozens of Jewish day school students, no one could offer the appropriate Hebrew blessing.

Yet we stood there, entranced by the God-given masterpiece spanning the sky before us. We were stunned by its majestic power and exquisite symmetry. We were also achingly aware of its fragile transience.

As the rainbow began to fade, we pronounced English words that came to us instinctively, child-like and true in their simplicity. "Thank you, God, for this beautiful gift."

Attempting to capture a moment that could never be replicated on film, I pulled out my camera, which I'd brought to preserve images of our friends. I snapped a few shots, knowing as I did so that the photographic images would be pallid reproductions of the genuine vista.

And then I realized that the rainbow, with a visual echo in tow resonating its message, was a symbol for all of us who love and would miss Francie, Josh, Dena and Alena. The rainbow was there to remind us that variable distances and temporal passages mean nothing when compared to the eternal power of love and enduring human connection. Our commitment of friendship would transcend place and time.

When we returned home that evening, we found the rainbow *bracha* in our *siddur.*

Baruch atah adonai eloheinu melech ha'olam, zocher ha b'rit v'nee'eman b'vrito v'kaiyom b'ma hamaroh.

Blessed are you, Lord our God, Ruler of the universe, who has remembered the covenant, and has kept your promise faithfully.

Rabbi Lane Steinger
Mutter

As time passes, I become more and more acutely aware of the fact that the circle of the older generations of my family is shrinking, becoming smaller, ever smaller. The absence of loved ones particularly and poignantly is apparent at annual holy times (e.g., the Days of Awe, or Pesach, or Chanukah) and on special sacred occasions (such as a wedding, or *brit milah,* or a baby naming). I understand that this is a natural and normal process. I also know that Ashkenazic tradition astutely acknowledges it and provides a context for remembrance. So, for example, it is customary for us to include *Yizkor* prayers not only on Yom Kippur, but also at the three joyous festivals (Passover, Shavuot, and Sukkot), to name a child in memory of a departed dear one, and even to begin a marriage ceremony with the memorial prayer, *Eil Malei Rachamim,* if one or more of the parents of the bride and/or groom are deceased.

Nonetheless, I find that there are those who have gone from this earth whom I often recall: my father, my grandparents, aunts and uncles, and my younger brother (*'aleihem ha-shalom*). And I find myself thinking about my great-grandmother, as well.

My maternal grandmother died when my mother was an infant. My mother's father's mother raised my mom (and her older brother, too). My great-grandma thus was simply known as *Mutter* (Mother). As I was growing up first in U. City and then in Creve Coeur, *Mutter* would visit us, and when she did it was magical. She was a tiny, wizened woman who seemed to shuffle along whenever she moved and wherever she went. Her hair always was pulled back tautly into a bun. She spoke only Yiddish—on principle. She kept strictly kosher. She was devout and observant. Love and respect for others emanated from her. I have distinct recollections of her getting down on all fours to play with me when I was very young.

Mutter did not have an easy life. Born in Romania, she was "married off" at the age of sixteen to an older man who had two children who immediately became her charges. She herself gave birth to seven children, one of whom took his own life as a young adult. She sent a son off to the battlefields in World War I. She made her way to a new life in the New World, where she soon was widowed and where she suddenly became mother to two of her grandchildren.

Mutter faced her share of trials, tribulations and *tzuris,* to be sure. Yet she communicated to me her resiliency of spirit and her commitment that life is good (if not perfect), that God is good, that people are good, that Jews and Judaism are good, that learning is good, and that rabbis are good. She was, you might say, a celebrant and a champion of goodness—and of hope.

There was a time—I am ashamed to admit it—when *Mutter* was an embarrassment to me. When I was fourteen or so, she avowed that she was nearly ninety (my dad contended that she was at least four or five years older than she acknowledged), and she seemed absolutely alien and other-worldly. Full of myself and my adolescent agenda as I was, if *Mutter* happened to be at my house I didn't want my friends to come over. She seemed so very … strange.

Mutter entered Eternity when I was a senior in high school. By then I was beginning to realize that she was one of God's gifts to me, even as she had shown me that I was one for her. I have no doubt that I have become the person I am—and that I am a committed Jew and a rabbi—thanks in more than some small measure to her.

In retrospect, I now recognize that I was fortunate and privileged to have known so extraordinary a person. Through *Mutter* I was connected to a bygone realm and to another entire era. Even more, she was the embodiment of basic religious values for me, one of several positive Jewish models who luckily have been influences in my life. Will my own children (and someday their children) be so blessed?

It has been three decades since you left this world, *Mutter.* Rest in peace. I am grateful to and for you. You were an *Eishet Chayil*— a Woman of Valor. Your legacy and your memory are blessings. And they will be—so long as I live.

Daniel Suffian
Kaddish

The chants of the congregation leaked out the balcony window, drifted aimlessly down and covered the earth in a blanket of worship, warm as lamplight. Behind a cypress, concealed by dusky blue shadows of *Erev* Rosh Hashanah I wept, seized with spasms of ancient grief.

When I was a boy my father took me to *shul,* I sat next to him, in awe of him. The rabbi *davened* and dad ran his finger along with him showing me the Hebrew as it was spoken. I grabbed his hand, a finger in each fist and divined the runes of wrinkled knuckles, veins and hair that covered the back of his hand. The first time I ever went to services without him was after he died when my mother, three sisters and I went for his memorial service. We stood for the mourners' *Kaddish,* its rhythm a sewing machine stitching death's constrictive garment around my searing guts.

Yisgadal-v'yisgadash-v'yisromahn-v'yisalahl-...-v'imroo awmein

There are many *Kaddishes* but to me they are all mourners' *Kaddishes* and always they beat me into despair. The synagogue of my youth, Shaare Zedek, was full and vibrant, with young families from the county and their brash and noisy children, *babushkas* and cigar smoking *altekakers kibitzing* heatedly in thick East European accents, and Mr. Seltzer giving all the youngsters Hershey bars dug from old coat pockets whose endless inventory was as miraculous as the everlasting lamp. When dad died, that vital synagogue became silent and inanimate. The overstuffed red velveteen seats of the sanctuary, once plush and cozy like a fat aunt's lap; were now unyielding. The *bimah* before the ark, a once eloquent tongue, still. The aisles that led up and away from the altar had once gathered me up but would not again take me in their embrace. The ark was empty.

I have met my father, Moishe, many times in dreams. In dreams I have floated with him above my mother's earth, and returned with his hand; met him in the grey plains of death naked but for his *tallis,* bent and pallid wandering amidst the twisted and barren trees; told him, "You are dead." He walked away and vanished.

For one year, I am told, he sat *shiva* for his father, chanting in downtown *shiva* places with some downtown *minyan*. Does he wait for my *shiva*, for my chanting of the mourners' *Kaddish?* Can he rest before his son's *shiva* is sat and *Kaddish* is sung? How can I sit *shiva?* I have no *minyan* and my *shul* is dead. How can I sit for the dead among the dead, in the dead?

Who will be my *minyan?*

Rabbi Susan Talve
Sarika's Story

Sarika saved my life when I was a baby. I loved to ask my grandmother, "Tell me the story of when you saved my life," because she would always answer, "It was God who saved your life." Her humility and strong Jewish faith became a part of me at a very young age and shaped the life of the person that I would become.

Sarika had the most beautiful smooth olive skin one could imagine. Her first wrinkle didn't appear until after her seventieth birthday. Her granddaughters always wanted to know the secret of her beautiful skin. When she was in a serious mood, and when she knew that we were serious, she would say it was because of the waters in her town outside Salonica, near Drama. My grandmother was a Sephardic woman, and she spoke of the well in her town and the crystal-clear, pure water with which she began her life. Then she would look at us and say, "You know, all beginnings are important," as if to suggest that those waters were connected to her faith.

We would sit many hours in her apartment in Brooklyn fighting over whose turn it was to braid her long dark hair and she would tell us story after story of her life before she came to this country. One of my favorite stories took place just before the Sabbath in the small town near Drama. Sarika (a name that means "little Sara") and a bunch of her girlfriends were collecting flowers in the village square, when a handsome cavalier named Sabbatai came into town. All the girls were looking at him and he was looking at all the girls. Each young girl held out a flower for Sabbatai to smell. "Ah," she would say, and as she reenacted the scene, the room would fill with fragrance. He smelled each one, throwing them aside until, of course, he reached Sarika, who held the sweetest of them all.

She took him home, and they celebrated Shabbat together. Even though he was a Turk and she a Greek, their common Sephardic heritage linked them. They married and their families were happy. They had a beautiful child called Reina, after Sarika's mother. But this was right before World War I, and my grandfather was a merchant. He traveled around enough to know that it was time to leave, so he gathered what he could and raised the necessary fare to book passage for his young wife and their infant daughter to journey with so many others to America. With a pain in her heart that I'm sure she never lost for leaving her mother and her sisters, Sarika boarded the boat with Sabbatai and arrived like hundreds of thousands of others at Ellis Island.

In America they got off the boat with their clothes and one pair of Shabbat candlesticks that they had managed not to trade for a little more shelter for their child, or a little more clean water to bathe with. They changed their names from Sarika and Sabbatai to Sara and Sam. They birthed seven children on the kitchen table, accumulated fifteen grandchildren and fourteen (we're still counting) great-grandchildren. They were proud to be in America, but there was always that sadness in Sarika's stories because, looking back, she remembered that they were the only ones of their large extended families who survived World Wars I and II.

From Ellis Island and Eldridge Street on the Lower East Side, they made the big move to Brooklyn. My grandmother lived in the same neighborhood for sixty years and never really had to learn English because her Ladino, the Spanish language of the Sephardic Jews, was always understood at the grocery store downstairs, even as the neighborhood changed from Sephardic to Puerto Rican to Cuban. You would enter her apartment and feel like you were in a different world. The smells were different. The music was different. The movement was different. Somehow her granddaughter, this Jewish girl from the suburbs of Westchester County, felt more at home in her grandmother's apartment than anywhere else.

I don't think my grandparents ever really understood my becoming a rabbi. I was, however, the only one of all the children and grandchildren that my grandmother would call every Friday night just before the Sabbath would start. At the time I thought that this was because she knew it was also a sacred time for me, something that she and I shared. Now I think the real reason she called was to make sure that I didn't forget that it was Shabbat. I mean, I was a rabbi—wouldn't that be awful!

But the time she really tested me was when she was dying in a New York hospital. I lived across town. Every day I took the bus to bring her a kosher Sephardic meal because she wouldn't eat the hospital food: it was "poisoned." I cooked for her, brought her food, and fed her for more than a month. Then one night she was like a frail bird, so close to death. I really didn't want to leave. I stayed later than usual and then went home. Later the call came. "Come quickly, come quickly, she's asking for you." I ran all the way. I wanted to be with her. I wanted to hold her as she left this world. I wanted to say goodbye.

When I arrived she was sitting up in bed. All the doctors and nurses were standing around her with their mouths open in amazement. Sarika was putting red ribbons in her hair and giving orders just like the old "Nona" we all knew. "Ah, Suzika," (that's what she called me) "get me a rabbi."

I said, "Nona, I am a rabbi."

She laughed. You should have seen her. Red ribbons in her hair to keep the evil spirits away. Red, from the red of the earth of Lilith's hair.

She said, "Your grandfather, Sabbatai, he came to me during the night. Was he handsome! He was all dressed up. He said, 'Sara, I'm not ready for you yet. Get well. I'm having too good a time.'"

Whatever it was, my grandmother lived ten more years.

Just before my grandmother died, I brought my three-month-old daughter, Sarika, to meet her. They lay together side by side on a couch. My grandmother, losing her ability to move around but still with that glint in her eye, well past ninety, looked at this little Sarika lying next to her and said, "This is what I lived for." And then she said, "Remember Sara of the Bible? She was ninety when she had her child. This one is mine, anything is possible … "

I do all the life-cycle events in my family. It's just easier to call me for weddings, Bar/Bas Mitzvot, baby namings, whatever. They call me. I'm cheap. I do them. I know what to say, what not to say. It's easy. But when it came to my grandmother's funeral, they wanted a "'real" rabbi to say *Kaddish*. The *Kaddish* prayer is a prayer we say for the dead. Traditionally a woman does not say the *Kaddish* prayer in public. (One reason given is that she might humiliate the men. If a woman is saying the *Kaddish,* you might think it's because no man is able to.)

My father insisted that I do the eulogy because no one knew my grandmother like I did. No one loved her quite the same way, and I think everyone knew that. But when it came to the *Kaddish,* they hired an Orthodox rabbi to come and do what was really important. I gave the eulogy and stepped away for the Orthodox rabbi to come up and read the *Kaddish.* Instead, I saw that he was standing there with tears in his eyes. He nodded to me to continue. His heart had been opened by a tradition that is meant to be loving and inclusive, a tradition that is meant to open hearts and minds, not close them. And both with tears in our eyes, for this woman who had pushed our tradition to its best, perhaps just for this moment, he followed as I led the *Kaddish* for Sara Aruest Talve, the daughter of Yitshak and Reina. And we cried together for this woman, who for just that moment changed the world a little bit.

Then her children, grandchildren, and great-grandchildren—who really are more American than anything else, I must say—for that moment remembered not that they were the children of Sara and Sam but that they were the *people* of Sarika and Sabbatai. And for the very last time we all gathered around my grandmother and sang to her together her favorite lullaby ...

Duerme duerme mi alma donzella
Duerme duerme sin ansia y dolor
Duerme duerme sin ansia y dolor

Sleep, sleep my sweet soul, sleep without worry or pain. Sleep now and be at peace.

V.
FICTION

Rabbi Tsvi Blanchard
The Tale of the Garden

Reb Zvi had a fault. He arrived on time. Hasidim say that the greatest of the masters were beyond time, some even beyond space. But Reb Zvi was not. He remained rooted to the earth, and imprisoned by space. Worse, it was by his own will that he lived in time and accepted its demands. Yet it happened that Reb Zvi was tricked into transcending time.

Reb Zvi had a special room off his house where he held prayers with his Hasidim. He also gave *divrei Torahs* to his followers in a hall near his home. On days when he was to speak he rose early and walked alone before arriving at the hall. On one of these walks he passed a walled garden. The secluded garden intrigued him, and he quickly located an entrance. His first glimpse showed a garden so beautiful that he knew he would need to remain for many hours to enjoy it. He was very tempted to stay, but he remembered his *d'var Torah* of that day, and he decided to return the following day. As he was about to leave, a young woman, who seemed to be the keeper of the garden, appeared at the wall and beckoned him to enter. Nonetheless he turned and went his way.

The next day he rose earlier than before and went directly to the garden. He hoped he would have enough time to explore it, but again, the garden disclosed itself as wondrous beyond the limits of his time. Just as before, the young woman beckoned him to enter. He knew that to enter would mean being very late for his *d'var Torah*. The woman was somehow harder to resist than before, and Reb Zvi had to use all his power to turn away. This same scene was repeated many times. Reb Zvi would arise earlier, go to the garden, and find that it revealed an even deeper aspect than before, that it promised delights which demanded more time than he had to give. Each time the maiden increased her entreaties that he enter, offering him free access to the garden and all its delights. But each time Reb Zvi refused, knowing that he must go his way. Life made its demands, people were waiting.

At last Reb Zvi reached the moment when all hung in the balance. He had gone the whole night without sleep but still lacked sufficient time.

Now he stood at the entrance to the garden, facing the maiden, her face more radiant than ever before. True, others needed him; true, he was a rebbe. But he was also human, and he knew that if he were ever to enter the garden it must be now. He entered.

As he had expected, he became lost in the garden. For eons the woman guided him from flower to flower and from tree to tree. She revealed colors beyond imagination, and depths beyond his own soul. For longer than the Holy One took to create the world, Reb Zvi lived the night of his deepest dreams, holding near what before he had sensed only at a distance. Reb Zvi had often cautioned his followers about the dangers of the spiritual search. To become yourself might mean to be caught in the swirling windstorm of infinite possibilities, some of which, God forbid, might cause a man to be lost. Now he himself was lost in the swirl. He realized at last that he had slipped beyond time and was living out all his incarnations, his *gilgulim,* at once.

The maiden also pained him. He understood that she was his self facing him as a woman. He had dreamed of fulfilling the holy Zohar by finding the woman who was himself. Now, having found her, he felt entrapped in a self that was not he. The maiden offered a simple solution: "Unite with me and remain in the garden." "But what of my Hasidim," said the rebbe, "what of my wife and children?" "Here," she answered, "here, there are all the Hasidim that have ever been or will be, all the wives of all your incarnations, and all their children."

Reb Zvi remained puzzled. Then in a flash his reply came to him like a Kabbalist's magic formula, breaking the seals which barred his way. He said: "I claim *my* wife, the daughter of Rizhin, and *my* two sons, David Moshe and Yisroel, and *my* daughter who made me Yaakov Zvi."

Irving H. Breslauer
Pincus Edelman

The first time I saw Pincus Edelman I thought he was a pile of laundry. He was curled up under a huge, white bed sheet, his plumpness hidden by the folds and wrinkles. Sound asleep, in a reclining chair near the massage room door of the health club television room, he was packaged like the bundles of sheets and towels that the masseur put in that chair for the laundry man to take.

It wasn't until I put my foot up on the sheet to tie a shoe lace and heard a muffled "Get off my leg!" that I knew the space was occupied by an animate object. The sheet moved, first in this direction and then that and finally after considerable activity and several curses, a head and shoulders appeared. "What the hell do you think you're doing? Can't a man sleep in his own home? Why can't you walk on somebody else? And what time is it anyway?"

At last a question I could answer. "It's about 4:30 and I'm sorry I put my shoe on your sheet. It's pretty dark in here and I didn't realize you were under there. Usually the sleepers don't sit so close to the door because they don't want the light to wake them when people open it. Besides, that chair is where they usually put the used sheets and towels."

He shook his head in disgust. "First you almost kill me. Then when I ask you the time I get a speech. What else are you going to do?" While he talked, he stood up, letting the sheet fall at his feet. He was not an imposing man. Even in indignation. His voice squeaked and his chins wobbled like a rooster's wattle. Standing naked, his feet buried in sheeting, he tried to recover his dignity. "Other men are sleeping here. Why don't you step on them? Or have I been designated as the chosen people?" With that question he stepped out of the sheeting, swung the door to the locker room open and with head held high marched in naked triumph toward the shower room.

I didn't go to the health club for a few days and the next time I did go it was early in the morning. There weren't too many folks around. A couple of old timers were playing chess at the tables near the shower room door, regulars, who escaped retirement and their wives by retreating to the locker room on a regular basis. I nodded a hello to them, changed into my gym clothes, locked my locker and proceeded into the darkened TV room which led to the handball courts, where I had a game scheduled.

I shouldn't have been singing, but it was a fine day, I felt good, and I knew nobody would be asleep or watching television so early in the morning.

The voice jumped out of the laundry. "Hey, there's a man sleeping here. Ain't you got no respect?" An angry eye peered at me from under the folds. "Aha, it's you again. First you were a dancer, now you're a singer. Does my sleeping disturb you? Why are you doing this to me?" He must not have expected an answer because the eye disappeared and the voice dwindled to muted muttering.

I told my handball partner about my misadventure and after the game, as we passed back through the television room, we took care not to disturb the sleeping volcano that I was sure was there. We didn't see him at first but as our eyes became accustomed to the darkened room, there it was, a bundle of sheets with a bald head. We tried not to laugh until we got out of the room but, like two school boys, we exploded.

Our laughter rustled the sheets. The rustling turned into a murmur, the murmur into a roar, the roar into a torrent which followed us out the door. "Who is paying you to ruin my sleep? Who sent you here to torment me? Can't a man have privacy in his own home? Do I come to your house to wake you up?"

After that third episode with the sleeper I became more careful as I passed through the TV room. I saw him several times, or at least I presumed it was him under the pile. But I became very cautious when I entered the TV room, even during midday when the soaps were on and there was a constant babble of voices from the television set and the watchers who gossiped with each other during the commercials.

Once or twice, when I had to work late and couldn't get to the health club until 7 or 8 p.m., I noticed my bundle of laundry was gone, or at least his space was empty. But during lunch hour, early in the morning or around 5 o'clock, he would be bundled up, ignoring the TV sounds, the steady noise around him, rising only when there was a sudden change in the sound level or when some clumsy person, like me, invaded his space.

One day, when taking a massage, I asked the masseur what he knew about the man under the sheets. "Oh," he replied, "that's Pincus Edelman. He's an old timer here. He comes early in the morning, sometimes 7-8 o'clock. Usually he takes a steam and then he wraps himself in a sheet and plunks down in the corner. He don't bother anybody. Sometimes he comes in for a massage, occasionally he gets involved in a discussion with the other lounge lizards."

He responded to my raised eyebrow. "Lounge lizards, that's what I call all the old, retired guys who come to the health club and don't do anything but watch TV or play chess or sit around and solve the world's problems. But Pincus, he's ok. Just gets mad sometimes when his beauty sleep is disturbed. But you know, I wonder how a guy like that can sleep at night after all the sleeping he does during the day. And I wonder what kind of home life he must have to be here so much."

I didn't get down to the health club for a few weeks and Pincus Edelman slipped from my mind. Then one day at about 6:30 in the evening, as I was walking into the place, I met him coming out the door. He was wearing work shoes, like policemen wear, with the heavy toes. His pants didn't match his jacket and he was wearing a button sweater over his tieless shirt. His cap was puffed down to his ears. I might not have recognized him in clothes but he knew me. "Ha, I know you. You're the sleep disturber, but you're too late today. Try again tomorrow. I'll be in my office from 8 until 4:30."

The following day I made it a point to go to the health club at 4:30. The old man was mean and cantankerous and no joy to look at but somehow I wanted to know more about him. I looked for him when I went into the TV room but he was gone. I went back to my locker to change into my gym clothes and there he was. He had a locker about three away from mine. It was open and he had a pile of socks, underwear, shirts and what looked like an overcoat, shoved to the bottom. He also had a suit, draped on a clothes hanger, bent so it could fit on the locker hook.

He acknowledged me with a grunt.

I spoke first. "Hello, Pincus. Hope you got enough sleep today and since I wasn't there I'm sure you did."

He almost smiled. "Well, so you woke me up a couple of times. It wasn't really your fault. And don't think you are the only one to have that pleasure. After all, if after all these years the others don't know, how were you supposed to know?"

"What is it I'm not supposed to know?"

"I shouldn't tell you but you look like a man who can keep a secret, or at least not spread it around. My wife, God rest her soul, died about five years ago. Then the place where I lived went condo and I had to move. At my age I lost my home. When I went to look for another place I couldn't afford the rent. I didn't want to bother my children. They don't live in the city anymore and they have their own lives and troubles. So I moved into the health club here in the Jewish Community Center."

"You did what?"

"I sold the few pieces of furniture I had, packed up a few of my clothes and joined the health club. Membership costs me $450 a year, massages and whirlpool a few dollars extra, they do my laundry, my socks and underwear for a dollar a week and I don't have to pay utilities. My social security gives me enough money and besides I have a small job."

"But they close the place up at night. Where do you go at night? And what kind of a job do you have? I see you here at all hours of the day."

"That's the secret. I sleep during the day. When I get up at about 5 p.m. I go to a movie or on a nice evening go for a walk, or I stay here and *shmooz* with my friends. Then, when they close the health club at 10, or when I get out of the movies, I have something to eat and then I go to work. I work as a clean up man in an all night supermarket. I get through at about 6, eat something, then I come here, take a shower or a steam and then go to sleep in my corner. I've been doing it for 3 years now."

"But what do you do on holidays when the club is closed? How do you get your mail? What do you do for entertainment?"

"I told you. I have a job and I get social security, so I have a few dollars. When the health club is closed I take my suit which I got hanging here and get dressed up and go to a hotel for a couple of days. I sometimes go to a ball game, or maybe even take a bus ride. And I enjoy just walking around. I don't need much."

"And as for mail, I have a post office box for my social security and the little bit of mail I get. So you see I really live in the health club, so when you bump me or tie your shoe on my chair while I'm asleep, you're doing more than disturbing my sleep. You're trespassing."

Stanley Elkin
Criers and Kibitzers, Kibitzers and Criers

Greenspahn cursed the steering wheel shoved like the hard edge of someone's hand against his stomach. Goddamn lousy cars, he thought. Forty-five hundred dollars and there's not room to breathe. He thought sourly of the smiling salesman who had sold it to him, calling him Jake all the time he had been in the showroom: Lousy *podler*. He slid across the seat, moving carefully as though he carried something fragile, and eased his big body out of the car. Seeing the parking meter, he experienced a dark rage. They don't let you live, he thought. *I'll put your nickels in the meter for you, Mr. Greenspahn,* he mimicked the Irish cop. Two dollars a week for the lousy grubber. Plus the nickels that were supposed to go into the meter. And they talked about the Jews. He saw the cop across the street writing out a ticket. He went around his car, carefully pulling at the handle of each door, and he started toward his store.

"Hey there, Mr. Greenspahn," the cop called.

He turned to look at him. "Yeah?"

"Good morning."

"Yeah. Yeah. Good morning."

The grubber came toward him from across the street. Uniforms, Greenspahn thought, only a fool wears a uniform.

"Fine day, Mr. Greenspahn," the cop said.

Greenspahn nodded grudgingly.

"I was sorry to hear about your trouble, Mr. Greenspahn. Did you get my card?"

"Yeah, I got it. Thanks." He remembered something with flowers on it and rays going up to a pink Heaven. A picture of a cross yet.

"I wanted to come out to the chapel but the brother-in-law was up from Cleveland. I couldn't make it."

"Yeah," Greenspahn said. "Maybe next time."

The cop looked stupidly at him, and Greenspahn reached into his pocket.

"No. No. Don't worry about that, Mr. Greenspahn. I'll take care of it for now. Please, Mr. Greenspahn, forget it this time. It's okay."

Greenspahn felt like giving him the money anyway. Don't mourn for me, *podler,* he thought. Keep your two dollars' worth of grief.

The cop turned to go. "Well, Mr. Greenspahn, there's nothing anybody can say at times like this, but you know how I feel. You got to go on living, don't you know."

"Sure," Greenspahn said. "That's right, Officer." The cop crossed the street and finished writing the ticket. Greenspahn looked after him angrily, watching the gun swinging in the holster at his hip, the sun flashing brightly on the shiny handcuffs. *Podler,* he thought, afraid for his lousy nickels. There'll be an extra parking space sooner than he thinks.

He walked toward his store. He could have parked by his own place but out of habit he left his car in front of a rival grocer's. It was an old and senseless spite. Tomorrow he would change. What difference did it make, one less parking space? Why should he walk?

He felt bloated, heavy. The bowels, he thought. I got to move them soon or I'll bust. He looked at the street vacantly, feeling none of the old excitement. What did he come back for, he wondered suddenly, sadly. He missed Harold. Oh my God. Poor Harold, he thought. I'll never see him again. I'll never see my son again. He was choking, a big pale man beating his fist against his chest in grief. He pulled a handkerchief from his pocket and blew his nose. That was the way it was, he thought. He would go along flat and empty and dull, and all of a sudden he would dissolve in a heavy, choking grief. The street was no place for him. His wife was crazy, he thought, swiftly angry. "Be busy. Be busy," she said. What was he, a kid, that because he was making up somebody's lousy order everything would fly out of his mind? The bottom dropped out of his life and he was supposed to go along as though nothing had happened. His wife and the cop, they had the same psychology. Like in the movies after the horse kicks your head in you're supposed to get up and ride him so he can throw you off and finish the job. If he could get a buyer he would sell, and that was the truth.

Mechanically he looked into the windows he passed. The displays seemed foolish to him now, petty. He resented the wooden wedding cakes, the hollow watches. The manikins were grotesque, giant dolls. Toys, he thought bitterly. Toys. That he used to enjoy the displays himself, had even taken a peculiar pleasure in the complicated tiers of cans, in the amazing pyramids of apples and oranges in his own window, seemed incredible to him. He remembered he had liked to look at the little living rooms in the window of the furniture store, the wax models sitting on the couches offering each other tea. He used to look at the expensive furniture and think, *Merchandise*. The word had sounded rich to him, and mysterious. He used to think of camels on a desert, their bellies slung with heavy ropes. On their backs they carried *merchandise*. What did it mean, any of it? Nothing. It meant nothing.

He was conscious of someone watching him.

"Hello, Jake."

It was Margolis from the television shop.

"Hello, Margolis. How are you?"

"Business is terrible. You picked a hell of a time to come back."

A man's son dies and Margolis says business is terrible. Margolis, he thought, jerk, son of a bitch.

"You can't close up in a minute. You don't know when somebody might come in. I didn't take coffee since you left," Margolis said.

"You had it rough, Margolis. You should have said something, I would have sent some over."

Margolis smiled helplessly, remembering the death of Greenspahn's son.

"It's okay, Margolis." He felt his anger tug at him again. It was something he would have to watch, a new thing with him but already familiar, easily released, like something on springs.

"Jake," Margolis whined.

"Not now, Margolis," he said angrily. He had to get away from him. He was like a little kid, Greenspahn thought. His face was puffy, swollen, like a kid about to cry. He looked so meek. He should be holding a hat in his hand. He couldn't stand to look at him. He was afraid Margolis was going to make a speech. He didn't want to hear it. What did he need a speech? His son was in the ground. Under all that earth. Under all that dirt. In a metal box. Airtight, the funeral director told him. Oh my God, *airtight*. *Vacuum-sealed*. Like a can of coffee. His son was in the ground and on the street the models in the windows had on next season's dresses. He would hit Margolis in his face if he said one word.

Margolis looked at him and nodded sadly, turning his palms out as if to say, "I know." Margolis continued to look at him and Greenspahn thought, He's taking into account, that's what he's doing. He's taking into account the fact that my son has died. He's figuring it in and making apologies for me, making an allowance, like he was doing an estimate in his head what to charge a customer.

"I got to go, Margolis."

"Sure, me too," Margolis said, relieved. "I'll see you, Jake. The man from R.C.A. is around back with a shipment. What do I need it?"

Greenspahn walked to the end of the block and crossed the street. He looked down the side street where he saw the *shul* where that evening he would say prayers for his son.

He came to his store, seeing it with distaste. He looked at the signs, like the balloons in comic strips where they put the words, stuck inside against the glass, the letters big and red like it was the end of the world, the big whitewash numbers on the glass thickly. A billboard, he thought.

He stepped up to the glass door and looked in. Frank, his produce man, stood by the fruit and vegetable bins taking the tissue paper off the oranges. His butcher, Arnold, was at the register talking to Shirley, the cashier. Arnold saw him through the glass and waved extravagantly. Shirley came to the door and opened it. "Good morning there, Mr. Greenspahn," she said.

"Hey, Jake, how are you?" Frank said.

"How's it going, Jake?" Arnold said.

"Was Siggie in yet? Did you tell him about the cheese?"

"He ain't yet been in this morning, Jake," Frank said.

"How about the meat? Did you place the order?"

"Sure, Jake," Arnold said. "I called the guy Thursday."

"Where are the receipts?" he asked Shirley.

"I'll get them for you, Mr. Greenspahn. You already seen them for the first two weeks you were gone. I'll get last week's."

She handed him a slip of paper. It was four hundred and seventy dollars off last week's low figure. They must have had a picnic, Greenspahn thought. No more though. He looked at them, and they watched him with interest. "So," he said. "So."

"Nice to have you back, Mr. Greenspahn," Shirley told him, smiling.

"Yeah," he said, "yeah."

"We got a shipment yesterday, Jake, but the *schvartze* showed up drunk. We couldn't get it all put up," Frank said.

Greenspahn nodded. "The figures are low," he said.

"It's business. Business has been terrible. I figure it's the strike," Frank said.

"In West Virginia the miners are out and you figure that's why my business is bad in this neighborhood?"

"There are repercussions," Frank said. "All industries are affected."

"Yeah," Greenspahn said, "yeah. The pretzel industry. The canned chicken noodle soup industry."

"Well, business has been lousy, Jake," Arnold said testily.

"I guess maybe it's so bad, now might be a good time to sell. What do you think?" Greenspahn said.

"Are you really thinking of selling, Jake?" Frank asked.

"You want to buy my place, Frank?"

"You know I don't have that kind of money, Jake," Frank said uneasily.

"Yeah," Greenspahn said, "yeah."

Frank looked at him, and Greenspahn waited for him to say something else, but in a moment he turned and went back to the oranges. Some thief, Greenspahn thought. Big shot. I insulted him.

"I got to change," he said to Shirley. "Call me if Siggie comes in."

He went into the toilet off the small room at the rear of the store. He reached for the clothes he kept there on a hook on the back of the door and saw, hanging over his own clothes, a woman's undergarments. A brassiere hung by one cup over his trousers. What is it here, a locker room? Does she take baths in the sink? he thought. Fastidiously he tried to remove his own clothes without touching the other garments, but he was clumsy, and the underwear, together with his trousers, tumbled in a heap to the floor. They looked, lying there, strangely obscene to him, as though two people, desperately in a hurry, had dropped them quickly and were somewhere near him even now, perhaps behind the very door, making love. He picked up his trousers and changed his clothes. Taking a hanger from a pipe under the sink, he hung the clothes he had worn to work and put the hanger on the hook. He stooped to pick up Shirley's underwear. Placing it on the hook, his hand rested for a moment on the brassiere. He was immediately ashamed. He was terribly tired. He put his head through the loop of his apron and tied the apron behind the back of the old blue sweater he wore even in summer. He turned the sink's single tap and rubbed his eyes with water. Bums, he thought. Bums. You put up mirrors to watch customers so they shouldn't get away with a stick of gum, and in the meanwhile Frank and Arnold walk off with the whole store. He sat down to try to move his bowels and the apron hung down from his chest like a barber's sheet. He spread it across his knees. I must look like I'm getting a haircut, he thought irrelevantly. He looked suspiciously at Shirley's underwear. My movie star. He wondered if it was true what Arnold told him, that she used to be a 26-girl. Something was going on between her and that Arnold. Two bums, he thought. He knew they drank together after work. That was one thing, bad enough, but were they screwing around in the back of the store? Arnold had a family. You couldn't trust a young butcher. It was too much for him. Why didn't he just sell and get the hell out? Did he have to look for grief? Was he making a fortune that he had to put up with it? It was crazy. All right, he thought, a man in business, there were things a man in business put up with. But this? It was crazy. Everywhere he was beset by thieves and cheats. They kept pushing him, pushing him. What did it mean? Why did they do it? All right, he thought, when Harold was alive was it any different? No, of course not, he knew plenty then too. But it didn't make as much difference. Death is an education, he thought. Now there wasn't any reason to put up with it. What did he need it? On the street, in the store, he saw everything. Everything. It was as if everybody else were made out of glass. Why all of a sudden was he like that?

Why? he thought. Jerk, because they're hurting *you*, that's why.

He stood up and looked absently into the toilet. "Maybe I need a laxative," he said aloud. Troubled, he left the toilet.

In the back room, his "office," he stood by the door to the toilet and looked around. Stacked against one wall he saw four or five cases of soups and canned vegetables. Against the meat locker he had pushed a small table, his desk. He went to it to pick up a pencil. Underneath the telephone was a pad of note paper. Something about it caught his eye and he picked up the pad. On the top sheet was writing, his son's. He used to come down on Saturdays sometimes when they were busy; evidently this was an order he had taken down over the phone. He looked at the familiar writing and thought his heart would break. Harold, Harold, he thought. My God, Harold, you're dead. He touched the sprawling, hastily written letters, the carelessly spelled words, and thought absently, He must have been busy. I can hardly read it. He looked at it more closely. "He was in a hurry," he said, starting to sob. "My God, *he* was in a hurry." He tore the sheet from the pad, and folding it, put it into his pocket. In a minute he was able to walk back out into the store.

In the front Shirley was talking to Siggie, the cheese man. Seeing him up there leaning casually on the counter, Greenspahn felt a quick anger. He walked up the aisle toward him.

Siggie saw him coming. "*Shalom,* Jake," he called.

"I want to talk to you."

"Is it important, Jake, because I'm in some terrific hurry. I still got deliveries."

"What did you leave me?"

"The same, Jake. The same. A couple pounds blue. Some Swiss. Delicious," he said, smacking his lips.

"I been getting complaints, Siggie."

"From the Americans, right? Your average American don't know from cheese. It don't mean nothing." He turned to go.

"Siggie, where you running?"

"Jake, I'll be back tomorrow. You can talk to me about it."

"Now."

He turned reluctantly. "What's the matter?"

"You're leaving old stuff. Who's your wholesaler?"

"Jake, Jake," he said. "We already been over this. I pick up the returns, don't I?"

"That's not the point."

"Have you ever lost a penny on account of me?"

"Siggie, who's your wholesaler? Where do you get the stuff?"

"I'm cheaper than the dairy, right? Ain't I cheaper than the dairy? Come on, Jake. What do you want?"

"Siggie, don't be a jerk. Who are you talking to? Don't be a jerk. You leave me cheap, crummy cheese, the dairies are ready to throw it away. I get everybody else's returns. It's old when I get it. Do you think a customer wants a cheese it goes off like a bomb two days after she gets it home? And what about the customers who don't return it? They think I'm gypping them and they don't come back. I don't want the *schlak* stuff. Give me fresh or I'll take from somebody else."

"I couldn't give you fresh for the same price, Jake. You know that."

"The same price."

"Jake," he said, amazed.

"The same price. Come on Siggie, don't screw around with me."

"Talk to me tomorrow. We'll work something out." He turned to go.

"Siggie," Greenspahn called after him. "Siggie." He was already out of the store. Greenspahn clenched his fists. "The bum," he said.

"He's always in a hurry, that guy," Shirley said.

"Yeah, yeah," Greenspahn said. He started to cross to the cheese locker to see what Siggie had left him.

"Say, Mr. Greenspahn," Shirley said, "I don't think I have enough change."

"Where's the *schvartze?* Send him to the bank."

"He ain't come in yet. Shall I run over?"

Greenspahn poked his fingers in the cash drawer. "You got till he comes," he said.

"Well," she said, "if you think so."

"What do we do, a big business in change? I don't see customers stumbling over each other in the aisles."

"I told you, Jake," Arnold said, coming up behind him. "It's business.

Business is lousy. People ain't eating."

"Here," Greenspahn said, "give me ten dollars. I'll go myself." He turned to Arnold. "I seen some stock in the back. Put it up, Arnold."

"I should put up the stock?" Arnold said.

"You told me yourself, business is lousy. Are you here to keep off the streets or something? What is it?"

"What do you pay the *schvartze* for?"

"He ain't here," Greenspahn said. "When he comes in I'll have him cut up some meat, you'll be even."

He took the money and went out into the street. It was lousy, he thought. You had to be able to trust them or you could go crazy. Every retailer had the same problem; he winked his eye and figured, All right, so I'll allow a certain percentage for shrinkage. You made it up on the register. But in his place it was ridiculous. They were professionals. Like the Mafia or something. What did it pay to aggravate himself, his wife would say. Now he was back and he could *watch* them. Watch them. He couldn't stand even to be in the place. They thought they were getting away with something, the *podlers*.

He went into the bank. He saw the ferns. The marble tables where the depositors made out their slips. The calendars, carefully changed each day. The guard, a gun on his hip and a white carnation in his uniform. The big safe, thicker than a wall, shiny and open, in the back behind the sturdy iron gate. The tellers behind their cages, small and quiet, as though they went about barefooted. The bank officers, gray-haired and well dressed, comfortable at their big desks, solidly official behind their engraved name-plates. That was something, he thought. A bank. A bank was something. And no shrinkage.

He gave his ten-dollar bill to a teller to be changed.

"Hello there, Mr. Greenspahn. How are you this morning? We haven't seen you lately," the teller said.

"I haven't been in my place for three weeks," Greenspahn said.

"Say," the teller said, "that's quite a vacation."

"My son passed away."

"I didn't know," the teller said. "I'm very sorry, sir."

He took the rolls the teller handed him and stuffed them into his pocket. "Thank you," he said.

The street was quiet. It looks like a Sunday, he thought. There would be no one in the store. He saw his reflection in a window he passed and realized he had forgotten to take his apron off. It occurred to him that the apron somehow gave him the appearance of being very busy. An apron did that, he thought. Not a business suit so much. Unless there was a briefcase. A briefcase and an apron, they made you look busy. A uniform wouldn't. Soldiers didn't look busy, policemen didn't. A fireman did, but he had to have that big hat on. Schmo, he thought, a man your age walking in the street in an apron. He wondered if the vice-presidents at the bank had noticed his apron. He felt the heaviness again.

He was restless, nervous, disappointed in things.

He passed the big plate window of "The Cookery," the restaurant where he ate his lunch, and the cashier waved at him, gesturing that he should come in. He shook his head. For a moment when he saw her hand go up he thought he might go in. The men would be there, the other business people, drinking cups of coffee, cigarettes smearing the saucers, their sweet rolls cut into small, precise sections. Even without going inside he knew what it would be like. The criers and the kibitzers. The criers, earnest, complaining with a peculiar vigor about their businesses, their gas mileage, their health; their despair articulate, dependably lamenting there lives, vaguely mourning conditions, their sorrow something they could expect no one to understand. The kibitzers, deaf to grief, winking confidentially at the others, their voices high-pitched in kidding or lowered in conspiracy to tell of triumphs, of men they knew downtown, of tickets fixed, or languishing goods moved suddenly and unexpectedly, of the windfall that was life; their fingers sticky, smeared with the sugar from their rolls.

What did he need them, he thought. Big shots. What did they know about anything? Did they lose sons?

He went back to his place and gave Shirley the silver.

"Is the *schvartze* in yet?" he asked.

"No, Mr. Greenspahn."

I'll dock him, he thought. I'll dock him.

He looked around and saw that there were several people in the store. It wasn't busy, but there was more activity than he had expected. Young housewives from the university. Good shoppers, he thought. Good customers. They knew what they could spend and that was it. There was no monkey business about prices. He wished his older customers would take lessons from them. The ones who came in wearing their fur coats and who thought because they knew him from his old place that entitled them to special privileges. In a supermarket. Privileges. Did A&P give discounts? The National? What did they want from him?

He walked around straightening the shelves. Well, he thought, at least it wasn't totally dead. If they came in like this all day he might make a few pennies. A few pennies, he thought. A few dollars. What difference does it make.

A salesman was talking to him when he saw her. The man was trying to tell him something about a new product, some detergent, ten cents off on the box, something, but Greenspahn couldn't take his eyes off her.

"Can I put you down for a few trial cases, Mr. Greenspahn? In Detroit when the stores put it on the shelves..."

"No," Greenspahn interrupted him. "Not now. It don't sell. I don't want it."

"But, Mr. Greenspahn, I'm trying to tell you. This is something new. It hasn't been on the market more than three weeks."

"Later, later," Greenspahn said. "Talk to Frank, don't bother me."

He left the salesman and followed the woman up the aisle, stopping when she stopped, turning to the shelves, pretending to adjust them. One egg, he thought. She touches one egg, I'll throw her out.

It was Mrs. Frimkin, the doctor's wife. An old customer and a chiseler. An expert. For a long time she hadn't been in because of a fight they'd had over a thirty-five-cent delivery charge. He had to watch her. She had a million tricks. Sometimes she would sneak over to the eggs and push her finger through two or three of them. Then she would smear a little egg on the front of her dress and come over to him complaining that he'd ruined her dress, that she'd picked up the eggs "in good faith," thinking they were whole. "In good faith," she'd say. He'd have to give her the whole box and charge her for a half dozen just to shut her up. An expert.

He went up to her. He was somewhat relieved to see that she wore a good dress. She risked the egg trick only in a housecoat.

"Jake," she said, smiling at him.

He nodded.

"I heard about Harold," she said sadly. "The doctor told me. I almost had a heart attack when I heard." She touched his arm. "Listen," she said. "We don't know. We just don't know. Mrs. Baron, my neighbor from when we lived on Drexel, didn't she fall down dead in the street? Her daughter was getting married in a month. How's your wife?"

Greenspahn shrugged. "Something I can do for you, Mrs. Frimkin?"

"What am I, a stranger? I don't need help. Fix, fix your shelves. I can take what I need."

"Yeah," he said, "yeah. Take." She had another trick. She came into a place, his place, the A&P, it didn't make any difference, and she priced everything. She even took notes. He knew she didn't buy a thing until she was absolutely convinced she couldn't get it a penny cheaper some place else.

"I only want a few items. Don't worry about me," she said.

"Yeah," Greenspahn said. He could wring her neck, the lousy *podler.*

"How's the fruit?" she asked.

"You mean confidentially?"

"What else?"

"I'll tell you the truth," Greenspahn said. "It's so good I don't like to see it get out of the store."

"Maybe I'll buy a banana."

"You couldn't go wrong," Greenspahn said.

"You got a nice place, Jake. I always said it."

"So buy something," he said.

"We'll see," she said mysteriously. "We'll see."

They were standing by the canned vegetables and she reached out her hand to lift a can of peas from the shelf. With her palm she made a big thing of wiping the dust from the top of the can and then stared at the price stamped there. "Twenty-seven?" she asked, surprised.

"Yeah," Greenspahn said. "It's too much?"

"Well," she said.

"I'll be damned," he said. "I been in the business twenty-two years and I never did know what to charge for a tin of peas."

She looked at him suspiciously, and with a tight smile gently replaced the peas. Greenspahn glared at her, and then, seeing Frank walk by, caught at his sleeve, pretending he had business with him. He walked up the aisle holding Frank's elbow, conscious that Mrs. Frimkin was looking after them.

"The lousy *podler*," he whispered.

"Take it easy, Jake," Frank said. "She could be a good customer again. So what if she chisels a little? I was happy to see her come in."

"Yeah," Greenspahn said, "happy." He left Frank and went toward the meat counter. "Any phone orders?" he asked Arnold.

"A few, Jake. I can put them up."

"Never mind," Greenspahn said. "Give me." He took the slips Arnold handed him. "While it's quiet I'll do them."

He read over the orders quickly and in the back of the store selected four cardboard boxes with great care. He picked the stock from the shelves and fit it neatly into the boxes, taking a kind of pleasure in the diminution of the stacks. Each time he put something in a box he had the feeling that there was that much less to sell. At the thick butcher's block behind the meat counter, bloodstains so deep in the wood they seemed almost a part of its grain, he trimmed fat from a thick roast. Arnold, beside him, leaned heavily against the paper roll. Greenspahn was conscious that Arnold watched him.

"Bernstein's order?" Arnold asked.

"Yeah," Greenspahn said.

"She's giving a party. She told me. Her husband's birthday."

"Happy birthday."

"Yeah," Arnold said. "Say, Jake, maybe I'll go eat."

Greenspahn trimmed the last piece of fat from the roast before he looked up at him. "So go eat," he said.

"I think so," Arnold said. "It's slow today. You know?"

Greenspahn nodded.

"Well, I'll grab some lunch. Maybe it'll pick up in the afternoon."

He took a box and began filling another order. He went to the canned goods in high, narrow, canted towers. That much less to sell, he thought bitterly. It was endless. You could never liquidate. There were no big deals in the grocery business. He thought hopelessly of the hundreds of items in his store, of all the different brands, the different sizes. He was terribly aware of each shopper, conscious of what each put into the shopping cart. It was awful, he thought. He wasn't selling diamonds. He wasn't selling pianos. He sold bread, milk, eggs. You had to have volume or you were dead. He was losing money. On his electric, his refrigeration, the signs in his window, his payroll, his specials, his stock. It was the chain stores. They had the parking. They advertised. They gave stamps. Two percent right out of the profits— it made no difference to them. They had the tie-ins. Fantastic. Their own farms, their own dairies, their own bakeries, their own canneries. Everything. The bastards. He was committing suicide to fight them.

In a little while Shirley came up to him. "Is it all right if I get my lunch now, Mr. Greenspahn?"

Why did they ask him? Was he a tyrant? "Yeah, yeah. Go eat. I'll watch the register."

She went out, and Greenspahn, looking after her, thought, Something's going on. First one, then the other. They meet each other. What do they do, hold hands? He fit a carton of eggs carefully into a box. What difference does it make? A slut and a bum.

He stood at the checkout counter, and pressing the orange key, watched the *No Sale* flag shoot up into the window of the register. He counted the money sadly.

Frank was at the bins trimming lettuce. "Jake, you want to go eat I'll watch things," he said.

"Not yet," Greenspahn said.

An old woman came into the store and Greenspahn recognized her. She had been in twice before that morning and both times had bought two tins of the coffee Greenspahn was running on a special. She hadn't bought anything else. Already he had lost twelve cents on her. He watched her carefully and saw with a quick rage that she went again to the coffee. She picked up another two tins and came toward the checkout counter. She wore a bright red wig which next to her very white, ancient skin gave her the appearance of a clown. She put the coffee down on the counter and looked up at Greenspahn timidly. He made no effort to ring up the sale. She stood for a moment and then pushed the coffee toward him.

"Sixty-nine cents a pound," she said. "Two pounds is a dollar thirty-eight. Six cents tax is a dollar forty-four."

"Lady," Greenspahn said, "don't you ever eat? Is that all you do is drink coffee?" He stared at her.

Her lips began to tremble and her body shook. "A dollar forty-four," she said. "I have it right here."

"This is your sixth can, lady. I lose money on it. Do you know that?"

The woman continued to tremble. It was as though she were very cold.

"What do you do, lady? Sell this stuff door-to-door? Am I your wholesaler?"

Her body continued to shake, and she looked out at him from behind faded eyes as though she were unaware of the terrible movements of her body, as though they had, ultimately, nothing to do with her, that really she existed, hiding, crouched, somewhere behind the eyes. He had the impression that, frictionless, her old bald head bobbed beneath the wig. "All right," he said finally, "a dollar forty-four. I hope you have more luck with the item than I had." He took the money from her and watched her as she accepted her package wordlessly and walked out of the store. He shook his head. It was all a pile of crap, he thought. He had a vision of the woman on back porches, standing silently at back doors open on their chains, sadly extending the coffee.

He wanted to get out. Frank could watch the store. If he stole, he stole.

"Frank," he said, "it ain't busy. Watch things. I'll eat."

"Go on, Jake. Go ahead. I'm not hungry, I got a cramp. Go ahead."

"Yeah."

He walked toward the restaurant. On his way he had to pass a

National; seeing the crowded parking lot, he felt his stomach tighten. He paused at the window and pressed his face against the glass and looked in at the full aisles. Through the thick glass he saw women moving silently through the store. He stepped back and read the advertisements on the window. My fruit is cheaper, he thought. My meat's the same, practically the same.

He moved on. Passing the familiar shops, he crossed the street and went into "The Cookery." Pushing open the heavy glass door, he heard the babble of the lunchers, the sound rushing to his ears like the noise of a suddenly unmuted trumpet. Criers and kibitzers, he thought. Kibitzers and criers.

The cashier smiled at him. "We haven't seen you, Mr. G. Somebody told me you were on a diet," she said.

Her too, he thought. A kibitzer that makes change.

He went toward the back. "Hey, Jake, how are you?" a man in a booth called. "Sit by us."

He nodded at the men who greeted him, and pulling a chair from another table, placed it in the aisle facing the booth. He sat down and leaned forward, pulling the chair's rear legs into the air so that the waitress could get by. Sitting there in the aisle, he felt peculiarly like a visitor, like one there only temporarily, as though he had rushed up to the table merely to say hello or to tell a joke. He knew what it was. It was the way kibitzers sat. The others, cramped in the booth but despite this giving the appearance of lounging there, their lunches begun or already half eaten, somehow gave him the impression that they had been there all day.

"You missed it, Jake," one of the men said. "We almost got Traub here to reach for a check last Friday. Am I lying, Margolis?"

"He almost did, Jake. He really almost did."

"At the last minute he jumped up and down on his own arm and broke it."

The men at the table laughed, and Greenspahn looked at Traub sitting little and helpless between two big men. Traub looked down shame-faced into his Coca-Cola.

"It's okay, Traub," the first man said. "We know. You got all these daughters getting married and having big weddings at the same time. It's terrible. Traub's only got one son. And do you think he'd have the decency to get married so Traub could one time go to a wedding and just enjoy himself? No, *he's* not *old* enough. But he's old enough to turn around and get himself bar mitzvah'd, right, Traub? The lousy kid."

Greenspahn looked at the men in the booth and at many-daughtered Traub, who seemed as if he were about to cry. Kibitzers and criers, he thought. Everywhere it was the same. At every table. The two kinds of people like two different sexes that had sought each other out. Sure, Greenspahn thought, would a crier listen to another man's complaints? Could a kibitzer kid a kidder? But it didn't mean anything, he thought. Not the jokes, not the grief. It didn't mean anything. They were like birds making noises in a tree. But try to catch them in a deal. They'd murder you. Every day they came to eat their lunch and make their noises. Like cowboys on television hanging up their gun belts to go to a dance.

But even so, he thought, they were the way they pretended to be. Nothing made any difference to them. Did they lose sons? Not even the money they earned made any difference to them finally.

"So I was telling you," Margolis said, "the guy from the Chamber of Commerce came around again today."

"He came to me too," Paul Gold said.

"Did you give?" Margolis asked.

"No, of course not."

"Did he hit you yet, Jake? Throw him out. He wants contributions for decorations. Listen, those guys are on the take from the paper-flower people. It's fantastic what they get for organizing big stores downtown. My cousin on State Street told me about it. I told him, I said, 'Who needs the Chamber of Commerce? Who needs Easter baskets and colored eggs hanging from the lamppost?'"

"Not when the ring trick still works, right, Margolis?" Joe Fisher said.

Margolis looked at his lapel and shrugged lightly. It was the most modest gesture Greenspahn had ever seen him make. The men laughed. The ring trick was Margolis' invention. "A business promotion," he had told Greenspahn. "Better than Green Stamps." He had seen him work it.

Margolis would stand at the front of his store and signal to some guy who stopped for a minute to look at the TV sets in his window. He would rap on the glass with his ring to catch his attention. He would smile and say something to him, anything. It didn't make any difference; the guy in the street couldn't hear him. As Greenspahn watched, Margolis had turned to him and winked slyly as if to say, "Watch this. Watch how I get this guy." Then he had looked back at the customer outside, and still smiling broadly had said, "Hello, schmuck. Come on in, I'll sell you something. That's right, jerk, press your greasy nose against the glass to see who's talking to you. Shade your eyes. That-a-jerk. Come on in, I'll sell you something." Always the guy outside would come into the store to find out what Margolis had been saying to him. "Hello there, sir," Margolis would say, grinning. "I was trying to tell you that the model you were looking at out there is worthless. Way overpriced. If the boss knew I was talking to you like this I'd be canned, but what the hell? We're all working people. Come on back here and look at a real set."

Margolis was right. Who needed the Chamber of Commerce? Not the kibitzers and criers. Not even the Gold boys. Criers. Greenspahn saw the other one at another table. Twins, but they didn't even look like brothers. Not even they needed the paper flowers hanging from the lamppost. Paul Gold shouting to his brother in the back, "Mr. Gold, please show this gentleman something stylish." And they'd go into the act, putting on a thick Yiddish accent for some white-haired old man with a lodge button in his lapel, giving him the business. Greenspahn could almost hear the old man telling the others at the Knights of Columbus Hall, "I picked this suit up from a couple of Yids on Fifty-third, real greenhorns. But you've got to hand it to them. Those people really know material."

Business was a kind of game with them, Greenspahn thought. Not even the money made any difference.

"Did I tell you about these two kids who came in to look at rings?" Joe Fisher said. "Sure," he went on, "two kids. Dressed up. The boy's a regular *mensch*. I figure they've been downtown at Peacock's and Field's. I think I recognized the girl from the neighborhood. I say to her boy friend—a nice kid, a college kid, you know, he looks like he ain't been bar mitzvah'd yet—'I got a ring here I won't show you the price. Will you give me your check for three hundred dollars right now? No appraisal? No bringing it to Papa for approval? No nothing?'

"'I'd have to see the ring,' he tells me.

"Get this. I put my finger over the tag on a ring *I* paid eleven hundred for. A *big ring.* You got to wear smoked glasses just to look at it. Paul, I mean it, this is some ring. I'll give you a price for your wife's anniversary. No kidding, this is some ring. Think seriously about it. We could make it up into a beautiful cocktail ring. Anyway, this kid stares like a big dummy, I think he's turned to stone. He's scared. He figures something's wrong a big ring like that for only three hundred bucks. His girl friend is getting edgy, she thinks the kid's going to make a mistake, and she starts shaking her head. Finally he says to me, listen to this, he says, 'I wasn't looking for anything that large. Anyway, it's not a blue stone.' Can you imagine? Don't tell me about shoppers. I get prizes."

"What would you have done if he said he wanted the ring?" Traub asked.

"What are you, crazy? He was strictly from wholesale. It was like he had a sign on his suit. Don't you think I can tell a guy who's trying to get a price idea from a real customer?"

"Say, Jake," Margolis said, "ain't that your cashier over there with your butcher?"

Greenspahn looked around. It was Shirley and Arnold. He hadn't seen them when he came in. They were sitting across the table from each other—evidently they had not seen him either—and Shirley was leaning forward, her chin on her palms. Sitting there, she looked like a young girl. It annoyed him. It was ridiculous. He knew they met each other. What did he care? It wasn't his business. But to let themselves be seen. He thought of Shirley's brassiere hanging in his toilet. It was reckless. They were reckless people. All of them, Arnold and Shirley and the men in the restaurant. Reckless people.

"They're pretty thick with each other, ain't they?" Margolis said.

"How should I know?" Greenspahn said.

"What do you run over there at that place of yours, a lonely hearts club?"

"It's not my business. They do their work."

"Some work," Paul Gold said.

"I'd like a job like that," Joe Fisher said.

"Ain't he married?" Paul Gold said.

"Jake's jealous because he's not getting any," Joe Fisher said.

"Loudmouth," Greenspahn said, "I'm a man in mourning."

The others at the table were silent. "Joe was kidding," Traub, the crier, said.

"Sure, Jake," Joe Fisher said.

"Okay," Greenspahn said. "Okay."

For the rest of the lunch he was conscious of Shirley and Arnold. He hoped they would not see him, or if they did that they would make no sign to him. He stopped listening to the stories the men told. He chewed on his hamburger wordlessly. He heard someone mention George Stein, and he looked up for a moment. Stein had a grocery in a neighborhood that was changing. He had said that he wanted to get out. He was looking for a setup like Greenspahn's. He could speak to him. Sure, he thought. Why not? What did he need the aggravation? What did he need it? He owned the building the store was in. He could live on the rents. Even Joe Fisher was a tenant of his. He could speak to Stein, he thought, feeling he had made up his mind about something. He waited until Arnold and Shirley had finished their lunch and then went back to his store.

In the afternoon Greenspahn thought he might be able to move his bowels. He went into the toilet off the small room at the back of the store. He sat, looking up at the high ceiling. In the smoky darkness above his head he could just make out the small, square tin-ceiling plates. They seemed pitted, soiled, like patches of war-ruined armor. Agh, he thought, the place is a pigpen. The sink bowl was stained dark, the enamel chipped, long fissures radiating like lines on the map of some wasted country. The single faucet dripped steadily. Greenspahn thought sadly of his water bill. On the knob of the faucet he saw again a faded blue S. S, he thought, what the hell does S stand for? H hot, C cold. What the hell kind of faucet is S? Old clothes hung on a hook on the back of the door. A man's blue wash pants hung inside out, the zipper split like a peeled banana, the crowded concourse of seams at the crotch like carelessly sewn patches.

He heard Arnold in the store, his voice raised exaggeratedly. He strained to listen.

"*Forty-five,*" he heard Arnold say.

"*Forty-five, Pop.*" He was talking to the old man. Deaf, he came in each afternoon for a piece of liver for his supper. "*I can't give you two ounces. I told you. I can't break the set.*" He heard a woman laugh. Shirley? Was Shirley back there with him? What the hell, he thought. It was one thing for them to screw around with each other at lunch, but they didn't have to bring it into the store. "*Take eight ounces. Invite someone over for dinner. Take eight ounces. You'll have for four days. You won't have to come back.*" He was a wise guy, that Arnold. What did he want to do, drive the old man crazy? What could you do? The old man liked a small slice of liver. He thought it kept him alive.

He heard footsteps coming toward the back room and voices raised in argument.

"I'm sorry," a woman said, "I don't know how it got there. Honest. Look, I'll pay you for it."

"You bet, lady," Frank's voice said.

"What do you want me to do?" the woman pleaded.

"I'm calling the cops," Frank said.

"For a lousy can of salmon?"

"It's the principle. You're a crook. You're a lousy thief, you know that? I'm calling the cops. We'll see what jail does for you."

"Please," the woman said. "Mister, please. This whole thing is crazy. I never did anything like this before. I haven't got any excuse, but please, can't you give me a chance?" The woman was crying.

"No chances," Frank said. "I'm calling the cops. You ought to be ashamed, lady. A woman dressed nice like you are. What are you, sick or something? I'm calling the cops." He heard Frank lift the receiver.

"Please," the woman sobbed. "My husband will kill me. I have a little kid, for Christ's sake."

Frank replaced the phone.

"Ten bucks," he said quietly.

"What's that?"

"Ten bucks and you don't come in here no more."

"I haven't got it," she said.

"All right lady. The hell with you. I'm calling the cops."

"You bastard," she said.

"Watch your mouth," he said. "Ten bucks."

"I'll write you a check."

"Cash," Frank said.

"Okay, okay," she said. "Here."

"Now get out of here, lady." Greenspahn heard the woman's footsteps going away. Frank would be fumbling now with his apron trying to get the big wallet out of his front pocket. Greenspahn flushed the toilet and waited.

"Jake?" Frank asked, frightened.

"Who was she?"

"Jake, I never saw her before, honest. Just a tramp. She gave me ten bucks. She was just a tramp, Jake."

"I told you before. I don't want trouble," Greenspahn said angrily. He came out of the toilet. "What is this, a game with you?"

"Look, I caught her with the salmon. Would you want me to call the cops for a can of salmon? She's got a kid."

"Yeah, you got a big heart, Frank."

"I would have let you handle it if I'd seen you. I looked for you, Jake."

"You shook her down. I told you before about that."

"Jake, it's ten bucks for the store. I get so damned mad when somebody like that tries to get away with something."

"*Podler,*" Greenspahn shouted. "You're through here."

"Jake," Frank said. "She was a tramp." He held the can of salmon in his hand and offered it to Greenspahn as though it were evidence.

Greenspahn pushed his hand aside. "Get out of my store. I don't need you. Get out. I don't want a crook in here."

"Who are you calling names, Jake?"

Greenspahn felt his rage, immense, final. It was on him at once, like an animal that had leaped upon him in the dark. His body shook with it.

Frightened, he warned himself uselessly that he must be calm. A *podler* like that, he thought. He wanted to hit him in the face.

"Please, Frank. Get out of here," Greenspahn said.

"Sure," Frank screamed. "Sure, sure," he shouted. Greenspahn, startled, looked at him. He seemed angrier than even himself. Greenspahn thought of the customers. They would hear him. What kind of a place, he thought. What kind of a place? "Sure," Frank yelled, "fire me, go ahead. A regular holy man. A saint! What are you, God? He smells everybody's rottenness but his own. Only when your own son—may he rest—when your own son slips five bucks out of the cash drawer, that you don't see."

Greenspahn could have killed him. "Who says that?"

Frank caught his breath.

"Who says that?" Greenspahn repeated.

"Nothing, Jake. It was nothing. He was going on a date probably. That's all. It didn't mean nothing."

"Who calls him a thief?"

"Nobody. I'm sorry."

"My dead son? You call my dead son a thief?"

"Nobody called anybody a thief. I didn't know what I was saying."

"In the ground. Twenty-three years old and in the ground. Not even a wife, not even a business. Nothing. He had nothing. He wouldn't take. Harold wouldn't take. Don't call him what you are. He should be alive today. You should be dead. You should be in the ground where he is. *Podler. Mumser,*" he shouted. "*I saw the lousy receipts, liar,*" he screamed.

In a minute Arnold was there and was putting his arm around him. "Calm down, Jake. Come on now, take it easy. What happened back here?" he asked Frank.

Frank shrugged.

"Get him away," Greenspahn pleaded. Arnold signaled Frank to get out and led Greenspahn to the chair near the table he used as a desk.

"You all right now, Jake? You okay now?"

Greenspahn was sobbing heavily. In a few moments he looked up. "All right," he said. "The customers. Arnold, please. The customers."

"Okay, Jake. Just stay back here and wait till you feel better."

Greenspahn nodded. When Arnold left him he sat for a few minutes and then went back into the toilet to wash his face. He turned the tap and watched the dirty basin fill with water. It's not even cold, he thought sadly. He plunged his hands into the sink and scooped up warm water, which he rubbed into his eyes. He took a handkerchief from his back pocket and unfolded it and patted his face carefully. He was conscious of laughter outside the door. It seemed old, brittle. For a moment he thought of the woman with the coffee. Then he remembered. The porter, he thought. He called his name. He heard footsteps coming up to the door.

"That's right, Mr. Greenspahn," the voice said, still laughing.

Greenspahn opened the door. His porter stood before him in torn clothes. His eyes, red, wet, looked as though they were bleeding. "You sure told that Frank," he said.

"You're late," Greenspahn said. "What do you mean coming in so late?"

"I been to Harold's grave," he said.

"What's that?"

"I been to Harold's grave," he repeated. "I didn't get to the funeral. I been to his grave cause of my dream."

"Put the stock away," Greenspahn said. "Some more came in this afternoon."

"I will," he said. "I surely will." he was an old man. He had no teeth and his gums lay smooth and very pink in his mouth. He was thin. His clothes hung on him, the sleeves of the jacket rounded, puffed from absent flesh. Through the rents in shirt and trousers Greenspahn could see the grayish skin, hairless, creased, the texture like the pit of a peach. Yet he had a strength Greenspahn could only wonder at, and could still lift more stock than Arnold or Frank or even Greenspahn himself.

"You'd better start now," Greenspahn said uncomfortably.

"I tell you about my dream, Mr. Greenspahn?"

"No dreams. Don't tell me your dreams."

"It was about Mr. Harold. Yes, sir, about him. Your boy that's dead, Mr. Greenspahn."

"I don't want to hear. See if Arnold needs anything up front."

"I dreamed it twice. That means it's true. You don't count on a dream less you dream it twice."

"Get away with your crazy stories. I don't pay you to dream."

"That time on Halsted I dreamed the fire. I dreamed that twice."

"Yeah," Greenspahn said, "the fire. Yeah."

"I dreamed that dream twice. Them police wanted to question me. Same names, Mr. Greenspahn, me and your boy we got the same names."

"Yeah. I named him after you."

"I tell you that dream, Mr. Greenspahn? It was a mistake. Frank was supposed to die. Just like you said. Just like I heard you say it just now. And he will. Mr. Harold told me in the dream. Frank he's going to sicken and die his own self." The porter looked at Greenspahn, the red eyes filling with blood. "If you want it," he said. "That's what I dreamed, and I dreamed about the fire on Halsted the same way. Twice."

"You're crazy. Get away from me."

"That's a true dream. It happened just that very way."

"Get away. Get away," Greenspahn shouted.

"My name's Harold, too."

"You're crazy. Crazy."

The porter went off. He was laughing. What kind of a madhouse? Were they all doing it on purpose? Everything to aggravate him? For a moment he had the impression that this was what it was. A big joke, and everybody was in on it but himself. He was being *kibitzed* to death. Everything. The cop. The receipts. His cheese man. Arnold and Shirley. The men in the restaurant. Frank and the woman. The *schvartze*. Everything. He wouldn't let it happen. What was he, crazy or something? He reached into his pocket for his handkerchief, but pulled out a piece of paper. It was the order Harold had taken down over the phone and left on the pad. Absently he unfolded it and read it again. Something occurred to him. As soon as he had the idea he knew it was true. The order had never been delivered. His son had forgotten about it. It couldn't be anything else. Otherwise would it still have been on the message pad? Sure, he thought, what else could it be? Even his son. What did he care? What the hell did he care about the business? Greenspahn was ashamed. It was a terrible thought to have about a dead boy. Oh God, he thought. Let him rest. He was a boy, he thought. Twenty-three years old and he was only a boy. No wife. No business. Nothing. Was the five dollars so important? In helpless disgust he could see Harold's sly wink to Frank as he slipped the money out of the register. Five dollars, Harold, *five dollars,* he thought, as though he were admonishing him. "Why didn't you come to me, Harold?" he sobbed. "Why didn't you come to your father?"

He blew his nose. It's crazy, he thought. Nothing pleases me. Frank called him God. Some God, he thought. I sit weeping in the back of my store. The hell with it. The hell with everything. Clear the shelves, that's what he had to do. Sell the groceries. Get rid of the meats. Watch the money pile up. Sell, sell, he thought. That would be something. Sell everything. He thought of the items listed on the order his son had taken down. Were they delivered? He felt restless. He hoped they were delivered. If they weren't they would have to be sold again. He was very weary. He went to the front of the store.

It was almost closing time. Another half hour. He couldn't stay to close up. He had to be in *shul* before sundown. He had to get to the *minyan.* They would have to close up for him. For a year. If he couldn't sell the store, for a year he wouldn't be in his own store at sundown. He would have to trust them to close up for him. Trust who? he thought. My Romeo, Arnold? Shirley? The crazy *schvartze?* Only Frank could do it. How could he have fired him? He looked for him in the store. He was talking to Shirley at the register. He would go up and talk to him. What difference did it make? He would have had to fire all of them. Eventually he would have to fire everybody who ever came to work for him. He would have to throw out his tenants, even the old ones, and finally whoever rented the store from him. He would have to keep on firing and throwing out as long as anybody was left. What difference would one more make?

"Frank," he said. "I want to forget what we talked about before."

Frank looked at him suspiciously. "It's all right," Greenspahn reassured him. He led him by the elbow away from Shirley. "Listen," he said, "we were both excited before. I didn't mean it what I said."

Frank continued to look at him. "Sure, Jake," he said finally. "No hard feelings." He extended his hand.

Greenspahn took it reluctantly. "Yeah," he said.

"Frank," he said, "do me a favor and close up the place for me. I got to get to the *shul* for the *minyan*."

"I got you, Jake."

Greenspahn went to the back to change his clothes. He washed his face and hands and combed his hair. Carefully he removed his working clothes and put on the suit jacket, shirt and tie he had worn in the morning. He walked back into the store.

He was about to leave when he saw that Mrs. Frimkin had come into the store again. That's all right, he told himself, she can be a good customer. He needed some of the old customers now. They could drive you crazy, but when they bought, they bought. He watched as she took a cart from the front and pushed it through the aisles. She put things in the cart as though she were in a hurry. She barely glanced at the prices. That was the way to shop, he thought. It was a pleasure to watch her. She reached into the frozen-food locker and took out about a half-dozen packages. From the towers of canned goods on his shelves she seemed to take down only the largest cans. In minutes her shopping cart was overflowing. That's some order, Greenspahn thought. Then he watched as she went to the stacks of bread at the bread counter. She picked up a packaged white bread, and first looking around to see if anyone was watching her, bent down quickly over the loaf, cradling it to her chest as though it were a football. As she stood, Greenspahn saw her brush crumbs from her dress, then put the torn package into her cart with the rest of her purchases.

She came up to the counter where Greenspahn stood and unloaded the cart, pushing the groceries toward Shirley to be checked out. The last item she put on the counter was the wounded bread. Shirley punched the keys quickly. As she reached for the bread, Mrs. Frimkin put out her hand to stop her. "Look," she said, "what are you going to charge me for the bread? It's damaged. Can I have it for ten cents?"

Shirley turned to look at Greenspahn.

"Out," he said. "Get out, you *podler.* I don't want you coming in here any more. You're a thief," he shouted. "A thief."

Frank came rushing up. "Jake, what is it? What is it?"

"Her. That one. A crook. She tore the bread. I seen her."

The woman looked at him defiantly. "I don't have to take that," she said. "I can make plenty of trouble for you. You're crazy. I'm not going to be insulted by somebody like you."

"Get out of here," Greenspahn shouted, "before I have you locked up."

The woman backed away from him, and when he stepped forward she turned and fled.

"Jake," Frank said, putting his hand on Greenspahn's shoulder. "That was a big order. So she tried to get away with a few pennies. What does it mean? You want me to find her and apologize?"

"Look," Greenspahn said, "she comes in again I want to know about it. I don't care what I'm doing. I want to know about it. She's going to pay me for that bread."

"Jake," Frank said.

"No," he said. "I mean it."

"Jake, it's ten cents."

"*My ten cents.* No more," he said. "I'm going to *shul.*"

He waved Frank away and went into the street. Already the sun was going down. He felt urgency. He had to get there before the sun went down.

That night Greenspahn had the dream for the first time.

He was in the synagogue waiting to say prayers for his son. Around him were the old men, the *minyan,* their faces brittle and pale. He recognized them from his youth. They had been old even then. One man stood by the window and watched the sun. At a signal from him the others would begin. There was always some place in the world where the prayers were being said, he thought, some place where the sun had just come up or just gone down, and he supposed there was always a *minyan* to watch it and to mark its progress, the prayers following God's bright bird, going up in sunlight or in darkness, always, everywhere. He knew the men never left the *shul.* It was the way they kept from dying. They didn't even eat, but there was about the room the foul lemony smell of urine. Sure,

Greenspahn thought in the dream, stay in the *shul*. That's right. Give the *podlers* a wide berth. All they have to worry about is God. Some worry, Greenspahn thought. The man at the window gave the signal and they all started to mourn for Greenspahn's son, their ancient voices betraying the queer melody of the prayers. The rabbi looked at Greenspahn and Greenspahn, imitating the old men, began to rock back and forth on his heels. He tried to sway faster than they did. I'm younger, he thought. When he was swaying so quickly that he thought he would be sick were he to go any faster, the rabbi smiled at him approvingly. The man at the window shouted that the sun was approaching the danger point in the sky and that Greenspahn had better begin as soon as he was ready.

He looked at the strange thick letters in the prayer book. "Go ahead," the rabbi said, "think of Harold and tell God."

He tried then to think of his son, but he could recall him only as he was when he was a baby standing in his crib. It was unreal, like a photograph. The others knew what he was thinking and frowned. "Go ahead," the rabbi said.

Then he saw him as a boy on a bicycle, as once he had seen him at dusk as he looked out from his apartment, riding the gray sidewalks, slapping his buttocks as though he were on a horse. The others were not satisfied.

He tried to imagine him older but nothing came of it. The rabbi said, "Please, Greenspahn, the sun is almost down. You're wasting time. Faster. Faster."

All right, Greenspahn thought. All right. Only let me think. The others stopped their chanting.

Desperately he thought of the store. He thought of the woman with the coffee, incredibly old, older than the old men who prayed with him, her wig fatuously red, the head beneath it shaking crazily as though even the weight and painted fire of the thick, bright hair were not enough to warm it.

The rabbi grinned.

He thought of the *schvartze,* imagining him on an old cot, on a damp and sheetless mattress, twisting in a fearful dream. He saw him bent under the huge side of red, raw meat he carried to Arnold.

The others were still grinning, but the rabbi was beginning to look a little bored. He thought of Arnold, seeming to watch him through the *schwartze's* own red, mad eyes, as Arnold chopped at the fresh flesh with his butcher's axe.

He saw the men in the restaurant. The criers, ignorant of hope, the *kibitzers,* ignorant of despair. Each with his pitiful piece broken from the whole of life, confidently extending only half of what there was to give.

He saw the cheats with their ten dollars and their stolen nickels and their luncheon lusts and their torn breads.

All right, Greenspahn thought. He saw Shirley naked but for her brassiere. It was evening and the store was closed. She lay with Arnold on the butcher's block.

"The boy," the rabbi said impatiently, "*the boy.*"

He concentrated for a long moment while all of them stood by silently. Gradually, with difficulty, he began to make something out. It was Harold's face in the coffin, his expression at the moment of death itself, before the undertakers had had time to tamper with it. He saw it clearly. It was soft, puffy with grief; a sneer curled the lips. It was Harold, twenty-three years old, wifeless, jobless, sacrificing nothing even in the act of death, leaving the world with his life not started.

The rabbi smiled at Greenspahn and turned away as though he now had other business.

"No," Greenspahn called, "wait. Wait."

The rabbi turned and with the others looked at him.

He saw it now. They all saw it. The helpless face, the sly wink, the embarrassed, slow smug smile of guilt that must, volitionless as the palpitation of a nerve, have crossed Harold's face when he had turned, his hand in the register, to see Frank watching him.

Shelly R. Fredman
One, Up in the Sky

It is Friday, late afternoon, a brittle and dry autumn day just before winter arrives for good. Lisa, Michael and I walk toward our grandparents' house, our footsteps irregularly smacking the pavement, the only sound. I see shadows moving inside the other houses, and the smells of chicken roasting and something sweet—candied potatoes—drift toward me.

Perhaps those people are dreaming or singing or laughing and we walk together, not talking, hastening to get there and wanting never to arrive. In that house, at 7875 Russell, my brother once took a buzz saw to the unruly bushes in front, carved them to bare stumps because he was tired of Pearl asking him to prune, to shape, to cut, this week, next week, next, and my sister and I used to throw a red rubber ball against the brick wall of the house next door endlessly—one, up in the sky, two, behind my back, three, around and around.

"It's strange to be with you both," Michael says, walking between us. He is eight years younger than me, six years younger than my sister and alludes to the fact that his relationship with her spans years when I was gone, away at college, and his newer alliance with me traverses these later years, when she has moved to New York. But his comment touches on something bigger—replacement and loss, the trading in of one for another. He is unsure of where to walk, as if that will reveal where his allegiance lies. He carefully places himself halfway between the two of us.

We could be going to two different places, my sister and I, given the deliberate way she places one foot behind the other and the zigzaggy bends and turns I take. She is forceful; I float and glide.

Michael puts his arm around her and reaches out for me, awkwardly pulling us in closer. Now we bump and step, but at least he has closed the distance.

We knock and bang on the door and front window. Ben and Pearl have been almost deaf for a long time. With each visit their two-bedroom house seems to stretch longer, loom further from its doorframe. It is a channel, a tunnel, a pipeline; they are small figures, receding.

Lisa's head is bent sideways. She peers between the white blinds scanning for signs of life. "I think I see someone."

"O.k. o.k." Pearl's voice, threadbare and naked, moves toward us.

She opens the door, one hand clutching her unbuttoned pajama top, a thin white t-shirt beneath it. I recognize the pajamas—flannel with tiny pink roses, the same style my sister and I wore when we were eight and ten. Ben must have bought boxes and boxes of them on closeout to sell in his dry goods store in East St. Louis, now boarded up and abandoned. Up in their attic I have seen still more boxes of pajamas—they seem to multiply with the years and Pearl will never wear them all.

"Grandpa's in the kitchen. Come on."

"Ben. Ben," she calls, "look who's here." Her powder blue house slippers shuffle and we follow.

Ben sits at the kitchen table tearing a napkin into a small square shape. After he tears it, he folds it in half, places it at the top of a pile to his right, and picks up another.

"Stop with that, Ben. The children are here. They want to talk to you." He keeps folding.

The lamp on the windowsill behind him is familiar. I remember the lamp, with its mottled base and orange plastic flower glued at its center, from my childhood, a lost object which once held a prominent place.

Before Pearl had cancer we ate in the dining room and they waited on us, slowly, drawing each gesture out, as if we were inside a movie and the frame was sticking. If Pearl forgot something—the soda, the green beans, the salmon croquettes—we had to wait while she shuffled off to get it. She cooked everything in orange juice: chicken in orange juice, potatoes in orange juice, jello, everything. "Orange juice," she would say, leaning forward as if revealing the world in all its mystery, "It's the secret ingredient."

We have not been over for dinner in months. They take their meals in the kitchen. Here the T.V. sits on the table before us, a row of pill bottles lined up on top of it. "It's bad enough me being sick without your grandpa getting sick too," Pearl says. "He's supposed to be taking care of me. Now I have to take care of him." Five small pots of ivy are scattered along the windowsill, but the variegated leaves tangle and tumble as if they are one.

"And the lady didn't show up to give me my bath," she continues, "She's supposed to give me my bath on Fridays."

She says it a few times.

Michael shifts in his chair. Lisa bites at her cuticle and studies where she just bit. I'm trying to look anywhere except at my grandmother's face.

"I really wish I could have a bath," she says once more.

I pause, hesitate, because I am afraid - afraid she will slip or fall, break something even, afraid of the responsibility, but most of all, afraid of facing her 84-year-old body, of facing my dark and inescapable future.

Finally, just when I am about to say it, Lisa says, "Grandma, we'll give you a bath."

Pearl's face lights up. "Oh that would be so good. It would feel so nice to have a bath. "Ben," she says, loudly now, leaning toward his one good ear, "Sarah and Lisa are gonna give me a bath."

"Michael, play a game of cards with your grandpa," she says, as we leave.

Lisa and I follow her into the bathroom. "We have to make this fast," I whisper to Lisa, "Those people are coming over at 5:30."

The fluorescent bulb flickers and then blinks on. Pearl begins gathering her things—robe, towels, bubble bath. She runs the water. There is a heaviness in these small acts, everything shaded by the fact that she is dying. Her balding head with white wisps of hair tells me, there is a world beyond this one, a largeness, and what's here is only a whisper of what's to come.

She takes a washcloth from the shelf, drops it into the water and I watch it grow darker, sink and fold in upon itself. Her slow deliberate movements, each singular and compressed in time, make me think of ritual.

Lisa and I mostly stand and watch. Trying to appear useful, I pour some bubblebath into the stream of running water. The bubbles build and connect, clustering like cells. Lisa places the towels on the laundry hamper. The room is steaming. I am sweating in my wool turtleneck.

Pearl undresses slowly at one end of the tiny room. Her breasts are clearly defined beneath the white t-shirt. The t-shirt is ragged, thin, as if it has been laundered to its softest, finest hour. It is the last to go.

I try to look at her body and appear as if I'm looking away, all at the same time. I am curious to see what I'll look like and I am surprised, relieved. She is very beautiful lying in the water with her head resting against the tiled wall. Her skin is a light copper, still tanned from the Miami sun she misses now. Her breasts are full and although they are not firm, the nipples are a wondrous pink, innocent as the pinkish flesh of a cat's ear. In her slow acts there is profound joy. She runs the washcloth over her breasts and down her rounded white belly.

"Does it feel good, Grandma?" Lisa says. "I love to take a bath." She is trying to make conversation, to establish a normalcy in the abnormal situation, to make some reason for our being there, other than the fact that Pearl has cancer and is dying.

I squirt a glob of shampoo into Lisa's outstretched palm and Lisa washes Pearl's hair.

"She's so soft," Lisa whispers, leaning toward me, "Her skin and hair are like a baby's."

Pearl's eyes are closed and she is smiling.

After a while, Pearl sits up and rinses the soap off. Lisa and I help her out of the tub. "I have to get to my knees first," she says, balancing herself at a metal bar and then rising.

Lisa offers her a towel. "Wrap it around my shoulders," Pearl says. She bends her head and gathers what's left of her hair into a towel. "I need my lotion," she says. I squeeze some into my palm, hesitate for a moment.

Although I had always thought of my grandfather as an ancient version of myself, Pearl and I were like two old goats staring each other down from opposite sides of the mountain. There had been years of conflict and storm, years of demands I could not fulfill, years when she waved my sister's filigreed Hallmarks inches from my eyes, "Look what your sister Lisa sent me for Mother's Day. Read what she wrote. Read it out loud."

In these past few months, as I watched her radiated body weaken, the years and the cards have faded. They have been diluted by Pearl's pain, by the slow, falling loss of her hair. It is as if the radiation has taken red and white blood cells from her and something from me, also.

I begin rubbing the lotion onto Pearl's back. I want to do something helpful, to be kind. Her shoulders are slightly rounded and freckled, the skin warm beneath my palm.

Pearl spreads lotion on her arms and legs. The floor is filthy and dust coats the window ledge, but the room is beginning to smell like a garden.

Lisa turns and whispers, "We're gonna be like this someday."

Mom is gonna be like this someday, sooner, is what I am thinking. Lisa looks at me and together we mouth the words, "Mom is gonna be like this."

"And you won't be here to share it with me," I add. "It's not so bad doing this together. I could never have done it by myself."

Lisa places Pearl's robe around her shoulders. I wipe at the dirt and water soaking the floor and hand Lisa the wet towel to put in the hamper. She runs water into the tub and I wipe my hand around, chasing bubbles down the drain.

In the kitchen, Ben is hunched over his cards, studying them, his eyes squinting to make out a Jack from a Queen. His yellowed fingernail pushes one card out of the way so he can see another.

Ben used to entertain us with games of Gin Rummy when we were children. Or Pearl built complicated palaces of cards, spades and hearts leaning in upon each other, mushrooming out from the center. Hush, she used to tell Michael, one breath can knock them down.

Now Michael scribbles upon a small white pad. Michael, 10. Ben, 35.

Ben looks at Michael and spreads his cards upon the table. "You beat me?" Michael asks. "You ginned again?" He slaps his cards down. "How many points did you get?"

Ben stares at the cards, raises an eyebrow at Michael. "Twenty-one?"

"You're right."

"Of course I'm right. You know when that fella asked me what's thirty-three and a half times thirty-three and a half, I was only six but I got it right."

Ben is telling stories again, stories we've heard hundreds of times, so often in fact that we can now fill in the missing spaces, the forgotten bits and pieces. He begins folding squares of napkin in half again. The pile grows. He coughs and spits into one of the folded squares. He crumples that one and begins folding again.

"It helps me pass the time," Ben says, "Too many hours in the day. Everything hurts. The only peace I have is when I can sleep."

He looks at his watch. "It's 5:30," he says. "Isn't it dark out? It's time to *bench lecht*." He wants us to light the Sabbath candles. He hasn't been out of the house in weeks —the only time he leaves is to get a hair cut or visit the doctor. He is cut off from everything else in the world and yet in that fogged and floating Chagall-like world of his—remembrances of a Russian childhood, Belarutka, a forgotten train, games of gin, jars of medicine, a *Reader's Digest* in large print—he knows the Sabbath has come.

Pearl places the candles in their holders, hovering at the stove. She lights. Her head is bent, her eyes are closed. Her hands wing the air silently, circling above the flames, once, twice, again, drawing in all that has flown from us.

She turns from the stove and wishes us a good Shabbat. I get up and kiss her.

I can feel the presence of the Sabbath Queen in this small kitchen, with its television set and rows of medicines and two bowls on the counter, waiting for soup.

We must leave. I remember there are people gathering now at my house to eat leftovers from Thanksgiving dinner.

"We have to go," Lisa whispers. "We're really late." She says it, but we linger still.

"You should eat dinner," I finally say.

At the door Michael hugs Ben too tightly and Ben moans. He is brittle and dry, too old for embracing.

We step outside into blackness. It is as if we entered from one world, but came out into another.

We walk together, the sounds of our feet in synchrony now, and yet it is a hollow sound, as if everything else has been drained from us and that one sound is all that's left.

"Grandma's so different," Lisa says.

It's true. I had noticed it weeks ago. Pearl is regal, almost queenlike—

the hard and tactless edge is gone. The vanity is a bare remembrance.

"She was so dignified," Lisa says, "You know what she told me? She said, 'You know Lisa, my hair used to be the most important thing to me, but now I don't even care that it's gone. I was so sick it doesn't even matter.'"

The branches of the trees are silver at their edges, reaching into the night.

"I was so scared," I say.

"Me too," Lisa adds.

Across Michael, our eyes meet and recognition leaps there, if only for an instant.

"I can't believe you guys did it," Michael says.

We tell him it wasn't bad at all, tell him how beautiful she is.

As we approach my house, I can see the cars lined up in front. I have done nothing to prepare. I didn't set the table, put the food in to warm or turn on the coffee. The guests are inside. I begin to run up the front walk and hear a loud boom from above. I turn to look as the last streak of a white flame wings across the sky. I can just see it through the space between the two houses across the street. Fireworks. Fireworks in November.

I should go in, at least run and get my son Joshua. Look Joshua, I will say, look up into the sky. I turn back toward the house, the bay window washed in a golden light, dark figures moving around inside.

But I can't. There is something out there, pulling me, making me feel at home in the darkness and cold. I rejoin my sister and brother and we stand and watch, in our down coats and gloves. We are three figures etched against the night, amazed, wondrous at the play of light in the sky.

Purple, red, white, the fireworks ignite and boom, breaking the world open with their sound. We stare and stare.

"Isn't this poetic or something?" Michael asks.

I am thinking the same. It is more than pure coincidence.

Oh yes, it can be explained. There is a university nearby and some students who couldn't get home for the weekend are celebrating Friday night. They've done it before.

But for me, these fireworks are my exploding heart, a last paragraph, a coda, the story's end. They mark the end of this day, the sharing of one generation in another's swan song, dying fugue, last wishes and dreams. We will carry their lives forward as we carry this—a Sabbath flame, a purple star bursting in a quiet sky, a light of love burning within, on and on.

Love Like Coriander

I found Laura's diary one day when I was snooping around in Michael's drawers. Michael and I had been together for less than a year— he was a vast uncharted territory then, and I, a modern day Magellan set sail for essential terrain. The diary was a small, leather-bound book the color of crushed leaves. It lay buried beneath Michael's old t-shirts, in a bottom bureau drawer, and after retrieving it, the first thing I did was to cover it back up again and slam the drawer shut, as if in sealing it off that way, I could seal her off from him, too.

Laura was present in bits and pieces throughout the house. Opening an odd drawer or closet, I often came upon her things—a recipe she'd scribbled upon in a cookbook, a blue paisley scarf in Michael's sock drawer, a musty-smelling black velvet box filled with beads and chains, a small gold hoop earring on the bathroom closet shelf. These things always brought me up short, but after I got past the initial surprise, I held the scarf in my hand, studied it with my fingers like a blind person, felt the bumpy edge of it, the seam folded back into itself.

Laura and Michael met in high school and married just after college. The plane crash that ended her life could not end that image I carried with me of the two of them lying down together for the first time. They had been teenagers, discovering desire and their bodies at the exact same moment. I imagined the white sheets their playground, kept seeing their young faces turning toward each other—expressions darkening from innocence to knowledge.

Although Michael had assured me his mourning was over, there were times, still, on Sunday drives, skirting the long, slow bluffs of the Great River Road, the Mississippi gathering strength beneath us, when he would stare out absently toward the muddy brown water and I was certain it was

Laura's face he saw out there.

That first time, I buried the diary for weeks but it haunted me. Its torn pages flew, scattered throughout my dreams. I came back to it again on a brilliant November day when Michael was away at work, the sun breaking through the dusty windowpanes of his bedroom, challenging the notion that winter was almost upon us.

I sought the book out as if some inexplicable force guided my hands, willing me to push the faded t-shirts aside.

My English teachers had always urged me to keep journals. Sometimes I grabbed pieces of scrap paper, rushing thoughts and experiences onto the page, the words spilling from me faster than I could put them down. But I always ended up misplacing them, and was forever failing to maintain the coherent wholeness of a journal.

I opened Laura's book slowly, half-expecting her to jump out at me, springing to life from between the thin white pages, the way genies do from magic lanterns.

I'm not sure what I was looking for, except perhaps some clue that would lead through her, and back to Michael.

Before reading, I ran my fingers across the pages, certain some residue of her remained.

Most of Michael's friends and family never spoke of Laura. I sometimes thought this was because of me, and sometimes thought it was not. It was as if they believed by not speaking about her, they could protect us all from the knowledge of her dying. Ridiculous as it was, we were all caught in a great game of Let's Pretend, children still, no one rising to the status of adulthood, no one willing to call the nonsense off, tell us it was time to put away the dress-up clothes and head for home.

I wanted reality. I plopped down upon the beige carpet, drinking in her written life, reading word after word after word, adding them together to make the equation, assembling them like puzzle pieces, hoping to compile her whole self here and now, to apprehend her between the faint blue lines that ran the width of every page.

I wanted to hear she was stubborn and single-minded, like me. I admit, I was looking for the darkness, seeking to lay her out bare, naked, someone

I could relate to, and begin to understand.

Laura had been a nurse, and was training to become a midwife. She loved gardening and cooking and spent much of her free time trekking to the Hill to gather ingredients at the small Italian markets. Reading about her, the squares of mint and calendulas, sweet marjoram and chervil out in the backyard suddenly made sense. So did the vanilla beans soaking in brandy on a dark kitchen shelf, and the dated jars of bay leaves from Turkey, cloves from Madagascar, cinnamon from Ceylon.

I read the entire diary, front to back, stopping only once, when the old bureau door creaked open of its own accord. I stared up at it from my post, and told myself it had broken ages ago and often did that. Still, I couldn't help thinking of how Michael once said the mystics of Sefad believed the soul hovers for a whole year after a person dies, reluctant to leave the physical realm it once inhabited, the place it once called home. Of course Michael didn't believe a word of it.

Even though it was way past lunchtime, and my stomach rumbled in protest, I read on. There were entries documenting Laura's culinary experiments, her Bernaise sauces, her rising and falling soufflÈs. There were entries on God, some written directly to Him, and entries about how lonely she felt when Michael retreated from her sadness. I read those passages over twice.

The last twenty pages of the book were empty, and I was left to ponder all that blank white space as I shut it, hands trembling. I quickly hid it beneath the t-shirts, as if it were an explosive that would detonate if exposed again to air. I hoped those thin layers of cotton would be enough to hold the book down. It had taken on wings.

I suddenly realized I had been holding my breath at the end there, as a long burst escaped my lips. I breathed in, starving for air, as if all this time, as the sun had tumbled on toward the western side of the house, I had been submerged under water, and had only now surfaced to oxygen.

When Michael came home that evening, he was barely in the front door before I told him I had found the diary and read it. He stared at me, as if I were a phantom.

I shrank back from his gaze. "Sorry," I said, "I didn't realize you would mind, I..."

"No, no that's not it. Julia, do you know what day it is?"

There were no calendars in my drifting world, no dates or times I needed to be aware of so I could show up at work or at school. I had graduated college months ago, a Theatre major with a minor in English Lit without a job. I had no marketable skills. Oh, I could tear apart a poem by William Carlos Williams, and I knew Stanislavski's Method of Acting as well as some people knew the patterns of the stock market. Nothing anyone cared about.

"No," I said, "I have no idea what day it is. November something."

"It's Laura's *yahrtzeit.*" His eyes sank into mine. "Do you know what a *yahrtzeit* is?" My utter lack of a Jewish education rolled on, boundary-less to him.

Even in my mother's ritual-free home, *yahrtzeit* candles had burned for her mother and father once each year. A small glowing glass cup sitting on the olive green formica counter. Aluminum foil underneath, for protection, reflecting the kitchen back upon itself.

"Oh my God," I said. "Oh my God." My whole body began to tremble, as if a giant hand had reached into this world, snatching me from some solid summer heat, setting me down amidst the snowdrifts of December. I sank onto the living room couch, grateful for the broad cushions beneath me, the thick armrest at my side. We didn't say anything for awhile. Michael glanced up at me now and again, but mostly he stared into the blue tiles at the base of the fireplace, as if further instructions might be written there.

"My mother had this expression she used once in a while when things happened that stretched beyond the range of coincidence. *Bashert,* she would say. It's *bashert.* I think she got it from her mother. She never spoke of God, but to me that word seemed to imply there might be something beyond the random jumble of events, some suggestion of an ultimate plan or design."

"Julia, I know *bashert.* Are you saying you were destined to read Laura's diary today?"

"I don't know if I'd put it exactly that way. But yes. Yes I was."

"Oh come on," he said.

"What do you mean, come on. Why on this day did I..."

"So. It's this day. What difference does it make?"

"It makes a big difference." I stood up. I couldn't believe what he was saying, couldn't believe he had been raised in a house of faith. He seemed to have no awareness of the whisperings of other worlds beyond this one, of parallel universes unfolding in time. No awareness beyond the things he could see and know, objects like floor plans and architectural details he could manipulate with his hands. C followed B as B followed A. No questions asked, no mystery.

I, on the other hand, the one who had not been raised in the tradition, had always sensed something out there, read messages in clouds. I just knew wisdom was being passed down, breathed on. Incidents like this, once you got over the shock, only confirmed that.

"You read the diary," he said. "Okay. Okay."

I got up, began pacing back and forth, thinking. I couldn't even look at him.

"I told you it existed and today you decided to read it. It's a little strange that it happens to be November 16, but it's just what you said. A coincidence."

"It's so much more than that." I stopped my frenzied movements and turned to him. "Can't you see it implies a connection. It suggests..." I could tell from the confused look on his face that there was no point in going on. I stormed off, into the hall.

"Some yeshiva boy you are." This last I threw back at him as I ducked into the kitchen. I began gathering mushrooms and onions from the refrigerator. I laid them on the counter and turned on the faucet. I was thinking of all the times I had sensed Laura's ghost, still wandering the house. Candles on his nightstand flickered when he reached for me, but there was no breeze, not a hint of wind in the room. Doors creaked open of their own accord and a book about challah baking was always tumbling from the kitchen shelf. And one strange Sunday my grandfather had revealed Laura and I were in fact distant relatives, that we might have played together as children at the annual cousin club gatherings at Heman

Park. I had thought backward then, seeking her face among the swings and
monkey bars, but I could not find it.

"I think you have a romantic idea of what yeshiva is," Michael said,
coming up behind me. "Mostly it was setting off smoke bombs in the
library, egging the Rabbi's car and seeing how many classes I could skip
and still manage to pass the Hebrew tests."

"Sounds like public school," I said, running warm water over the
sponge-like surface of one last white mushroom and rubbing at it with
my finger.

"I'm sure they're not that different. We were kids."

"I know. I just thought if you were raised with a religious world-view,
it might somehow penetrate your thinking." I began slicing the onions,
leaving the water running because that's what my mother always did when
she cut onions. It was supposed to help with the tears. It didn't, but I
continued to run the water nonetheless.

"You're crying."

"I'm crying because of the onions." He reached into his shirt pocket
and took out a crumpled ball of kleenex. "It's a little used," he said.

"Thanks." I wiped at my eyes and running nose and gave the kleenex
back to him.

"Can you just tell me how you can keep all these commandments—
keep kosher, keep Shabbat, go to synagogue—if you don't believe."

"It's not about belief. It's a way of life."

"Aren't the two things connected?"

"Yes. I mean, they're supposed to be. But I'm having a lot of trouble
with God right now." He looked out the kitchen window at some point
way beyond the neighbor's backyard and fence posts. "That doesn't mean
you stop, though. The rabbis teach 'Naaseh v'nishma.' Do and then believe."

This made no sense to me whatever. Throughout my education I had
been taught to think critically, to examine and analyze each situation, each
new theory, to turn it on its ear and then, and only then could you possibly
think of putting it into practice within the framework of your life.

"I don't get it."

"The idea is that by acting, by trying to be a holy person, which to me translates as being a good person, by doing the acts over and over, eventually you become that. And the belief inevitably follows, almost without your realizing it."

"That is so backwards. It goes against everything I've ever learned. 'The unexamined life is not worth living.' My philosophy professor repeated that one like a mantra."

"Your problem is you examine everything—you analyze things to pieces."

"And nothing matters to you at all." I banged the saucepan onto the burner and turned up the flame. "You just drift through your life letting it all happen to you." If this hurt, he didn't show it. Michael's character was such that he seemed to always be standing on some firm length of granite, whereas the rest of us were busy plodding through layers of clay, our feet sinking and slipping, our toes half buried in mud.

He filled a big pot with water and set it to boil for the spaghetti. Then he began gathering dishes, forks, knives. "I think you have too much time on your hands. You really need to get a job."

"What am I going to do? I haven't been trained to do anything reasonable."

"Take that job with the public relations firm. Teach dance or theatre classes. Something. Anything."

I stirred the mushrooms and onions into the spaghetti sauce, watching the bubbles surface and dive. Michael came and stood an inch away from me, his breath warm upon the back of my neck. He pulled my hair aside, and kissed me, his mouth tender but insistent.

"Stop it. I'm mad at you."

"Ummhmm," was all he said, continuing to suckle that hollow place where neck met shoulder, feeling my body slacken. He pulled me against him, and although I was wondering how I had come to love someone whose world view was so at odds with my own, I dropped the spoon and turned towards him, leaving the tomato sauce simmering, the smells of oregano and basil and thyme enveloping us in a vapid warmth.

In February, I tried out for Ansky's play, *The Dybbuk,* to be performed at Washington University in the Spring, and was cast as Leah. It didn't pay anything, but at least it kept me busy.

We were an odd theatrical troupe. Our director had overseen repertory productions throughout St. Louis, but he was a lapsed Catholic who had never set foot in a synagogue. A philosophy professor was playing Rabbi Azrael.

Shirley Yankowitz, who had made a name for herself at the Jewish Community Center playing all the major roles, was cast as Frade, Leah's old nurse. Onstage and off, Shirley spoke in an exaggerated theatrical voice, so that at first, it was hard for me to tell whether she was addressing me or simply rehearsing her lines. Dena Jacobs played Leah's friend, Gittel. Dena dressed in lush, multi-colored layers of clothing and always wore a scarf that soared, like some long forgotten wing, behind her. We immediately became friends.

The play centered on Channon, a poor student of mysticism who had been betrothed to Leah since forty days before birth. Prevented by Leah's father from marrying her, Channon eventually dies of a broken heart, only to return in spirit to inhabit Leah's body as a *dybbuk*. Although Rabbi Azrael succeeds in exorcising the *dybbuk*, Leah ends up dying shortly after, and thereby triumphantly joins her lover in death.

In rehearsals, our director was constantly talking about the strange elements of the play—the taking over of Leah's body by her lover, the graveyard scene, the exorcism the rabbi must perform at the end. He told us that Ansky was exploring the connection between our world and the hereafter, that we needed to reach toward that extra dimension throughout the play.

He made it sound daunting. I couldn't imagine convincing an audience that all this strange stuff was actually happening, but I'd been in enough plays to know a kind of magic happens when those lights come up and the costumes are on. And I liked Leah very much. She seemed younger than me, although our ages were the same, but she was searching for answers, too.

It was already April, the earth not quite ready to decide whether to plunge toward Spring or linger with Winter. We had been rehearsing for weeks and although the exorcism scene was the one that had initially worried me the most because it would be difficult to make it believable, that scene turned out to be manageable.

It was the scene in the courtyard, the scene in which Leah says that souls who die prematurely are "here in our midst, unheard and invisible," that still unnerved me. Tech rehearsal was only three days away. The playwright's certainty about the connections between this life and the next one was so powerful it frightened me.

In preparation, I had read Stanislavski over again, and I could hear Professor Baldwin telling me to seek my own life within the circumstances of my character's.

There was only Laura. Even though it had now been over a year since, as the rabbis put it, her soul had departed this world, I sensed her all around me. She still hovered in my thoughts, and seemed to be more present in my life than in Michael's. He had apparently tucked her memory away somewhere, whereas I kept coming upon her spices on the shelf as I tried a new recipe. I couldn't help dwelling on the fact that they were her spices, as if some part of her was being poured into my Gypsy Soup, my Pasta Primavera, my Apple Almond Rice. But I hadn't known her. How can you reach back to, seek out, miss someone you have never known?

Tech rehearsals turned out to be awful. The lights came up too fast or not at all; sound effects bumped two beats behind their appropriate places, and everyone kept missing their cues. We considered ourselves lucky. Botched technical rehearsals guarantee a great opening night. This was a thespian tradition, and like all actors, we honored our traditions, welcomed our theatre ghosts with open arms.

On opening night, in a large closet that had been converted to a dressing room, Dena and Shirley scurried around me. They lifted dresses and petticoats over their heads and emerged, turtlelike, from between the cloth. Dena gathered her unruly locks into a kerchief, knotting it tightly in back. I stared into the mirror our stagehand had rigged, trying to escape the frenzied movements all around me.

"The house is full," our director called.

My heart bumped. I dipped my finger into the makeup tin, and applied much too much rouge across my cheekbones. I did the same thing with the lipstick. I suddenly wished I was back in high school, playing Eliza Doolittle in "My Fair Lady." That sort of transformation at least seemed possible. I bit at my cuticle, an old habit, staining my whole finger red.

"You look terrible," Dena said. She had come up behind me to check her makeup in the mirror and had lit upon my face instead.

I looked back into the mirror, began applying more eyeliner. My eyes were already heavily rimmed and this only made them look less human, like a raccoon's.

"I don't think that's helping," Dena whispered.

"In high school, whenever my boyfriend broke up with me and I was falling apart, my mother always told me to put on my best outfit and lots of makeup and then I would feel better."

"Did it work?"

"I don't know. But it's like a reflex now."

"Two minutes," our director called.

"C'mon," Dena said, hustling me out of my chair and toward the door. "It's always worse back here. You'll be fine once you get out there."

"Do you promise?"

"I promise."

Shirley was right behind us, going through her scales as if she were about to perform an aria, instead of a speaking role. Then she started making these gurgling sounds, like she was gargling without any water.

The yeshiva boys all skimmed past us, feeling their way in the darkness like blind men, moving to take their places for the first scene.

As the lights began to come up, Dena whispered, "Shirley, stop gurgling."

"I'm not gurgling. I'm warming my voice."

"Well you sound like the *dybbuk*. And the play hasn't even started."

We were in the wings. I watched as the curtain came up and the men who were gathered at the tables said their lines, just as they had a hundred times before in rehearsal. It was hard to see the darkness beyond the glaring stage lights and you could almost pretend there was nobody out there. I thought of F. Scott Fitzgerald saying that genius is the ability to hold two opposing ideas at exactly the same time. While I could choose to believe there was no one out there in the audience, I also knew there were many waiting, a great "we," and I needed to gather courage, strength, insanity, whatever and venture out to them.

I looked back at Dena one last time, and then Shirley and I walked out onto the stage. She said her first lines and I found myself answering her. My body was trembling and I prayed no one in the audience could see the way my fingers shook, looped as they were around Shirley's arm. I was glad for all the times I had paced the sunroom at home, learning my lines. Now they were in me and they just came. It was like moving in a dream, like being back in Miss Alexandra's ballet class in fourth grade. Sometimes Miss Alexandra put so many steps together for our routine, you just had to let go of your brain, let it float away somewhere while your feet took over.

It was like that now, except I could feel the stage lights, hot and white, burning my skin, and Shirley's arm, experienced as she was, shaking a bit, too.

The rest of Act I went smoothly. In Act II, when it was finally time for my monologue, Shirley moved away from me and it seemed as if I was out there alone.

I began speaking, addressing my old nurse, and about three lines into the speech, something happened. At the edge of that blurry line where the stage lights gave way to the audience, someone stood. At first she was a bare presence, little more than a shadow. But as I continued speaking my lines, she took on weight and mass. She shimmered in her own smoky haze, there just beyond the footlights.

If I could have stepped out of my role, stopped the performance, stopped being Leah, I would have seen the edges of people's shoes, the thin, silver legs of their chairs barely lit, the wash of the lights spreading out just beyond the stage. But I was Leah, completely at one with her, and just beyond that darkness, someone was waiting, listening to every line. I knew she was there, impossible as it was, among the rows. Quiet, but as real as the silver legs of the chairs, and listening to me. A heart feels a heart, my grandpa had once told me, and there was mine, beating, and hers there, too, like an echo.

Leah was trying to tell her nurse that the soul lives on, that it is eternal, but she knew the old woman did not believe her. Her cauliflower ears had been too long in this world, with its doubts and rules, ladders and hierarchies. My blind fingers reached into air, spinning phrases, and as I did, as I spoke with Laura, I sealed my part of the bargain. I would acknowledge her. I would refuse to let her die. I would take her soul into mine and carry it on. In turn, she would give Michael to me, set him free. These are the things we said to each other, speaking in breaths and sighs and whispers. Our language is not transcribable, it was a silent murmuring, an exchange of heart beats and pauses. I could hear her voice—resonant, singular, the same voice of the diary, but speaking to me now of time never ending, of eternity. All of this ran beneath the lines of the play, the words Leah was supposed to be saying. The script.

After the monologue was over, I drew back a few feet. I could hear Shirley shuffling across the stage, coming to my side. My arms felt as if the blood was coursing through them at twice its normal speed. I was glad that clasping Shirley's arm was part of the stage business our director had insisted upon. The gesture had never felt right before, and suddenly I couldn't imagine doing it any other way.

As we made our way offstage, I was hoping no one had noticed I had been addressing my lines to someone not even remotely connected to the play. I knew I could never explain what had happened out there. The rest of the performance was fine, except for the last scene when the philosophy professor turned rabbi got carried away shaking his walking stick at the *dybbuk*. It flew through the air, shaved one of the yeshiva student's heads and landed just beyond him. The play was so rich with ghosts and demons that I doubt anyone in the audience guessed that this was not part of the performance.

When applause erupted at the final curtain, Dena and I, backstage with everyone else, squeezed each other's hands. Shirley's face was tear-stained, and so was mine.

The curtain rose, and at the edge of the stage, I could finally see beyond that invisible wall. I searched among the rows of faces, but she was gone. Instead I saw the audience, clapping. We had not been dream walking, after all. It was real.

After a certain amount of backstage frenzy, we went out to the lobby. Michael was smiling. He hugged me and told me how good the play was.

"Did you really think so?" I asked.

"Yes," he said, "It was very...convincing." In the pause, I thought I heard something else, the beginnings of an acknowledgment. But I wasn't sure. And I didn't know how to tell him what had happened. I could barely make sense of it myself.

"Really," I said, "You really liked it?" The crowd began to press against us.

"Yes. I said yes."

"But do you think..."

"Julia," he said, "It was great, o.k. I told you already."

"Michael, something happened out there, something..." Friends came up, the crowd swirled around us, and we were separated by a stream of well-wishers.

The cast party that night stretched on until three in the morning, and when I got home, Michael was deep in slumber.

The next day, while he was off at work, I gathered all of Laura's cookbooks and sat down with them at the kitchen table. Outside the window, a wash of grey clouds spilled across the sky. The world seemed to be bathed in a state of lackluster, that greyness leaking down from the sky to the dark bare trees, to the dead wet grass.

I found a recipe for Curried Chicken and Rice and held my finger at that spot as I flipped through the book. I was thinking of the labelled jar of curry Laura must have made up herself, still sitting among the dark row of spices, unused. I found a recipe for Salmon with Sweet Marjoram and Chervil that Laura had marked up, but it said to make a "good, smooth veloute" to accompany it, and I had no idea what a veloute was, let alone a good and smooth one.

I went through all the books that morning, caught in the task, gripped by my new mission, an emerging sense of purpose. The play was over, and I knew I was not quite ready to go back to my life. I glanced up once when a flock of crows called out to me. They had lit on the branches of the sycamore, filling its arms like a great black cloud. The house was quiet, though I listened for Laura's ghost, even began to long for her. There was only silence, the sound of flipping pages.

Midday, and there I was chopping onions and garlic, apples and carrots. I set the oven to 350 degrees and began on my challah. I was thinking of the Israelites, the layers of dew and manna that had fallen for them in the desert, the bread of the angels.

According to the mystics, the manna fell in the form of coriander seeds. It continues to be milled by the angels and manna rivers continue to flow, reserved for righteous souls. As I mixed water and yeast and flour, I wondered if Laura was up there, just beyond those grey velvet clouds, enjoying the stillness of the river bank.

I began to knead the dough, pounding and turning, circle after circle, my hands following a rhythm that seemed to have been lodged in them forever. I pressed and turned, pressed and turned, feeling the warmth of the dough beneath my palms, powdery clouds of flour floating down upon the counter. Other hands worked alongside me, within me, the dough becoming smooth and elastic until at last I knew it was ready. I formed it into a round ball and placed it in the warm oven to rise.

By the time Michael came home, the whole house was alive with the smells of coriander and cardamom, tamarind and pomegranate.

"Smells great," he said, standing in the kitchen doorway, staring.

It was then I realized I hadn't even bothered combing my hair that day, was still in a slight state of disarray, as if I had just awoken.

"Geez, I guess I got caught up in this recipe."

"What are you doing?" I thought he might recognize the smells, but he didn't say anything. I took his hand and led him to the table.

"Sit."

He recited the blessings. Outside the window, the crows were gone, but I could still see them, suspended in the sycamore, my witnesses. Michael and I sat and ate quietly, our eyes playing upon each other's faces, a search and rescue fueled by desire.

I still wanted to tell him what had happened, but I couldn't. After he finished his last bite, though, he held his fork suspended in mid-air. "This is Laura's recipe, isn't it?"

"Ummhmm."

"She was there last night, wasn't she?"

"Yes, Michael. Yes. She was."

We stared at each other for what seemed a long time. "I can't explain this, but she was there. I just know she was. We had a long conversation about you," I said, half-smiling.

"All good I hope," he laughed.

"Not at all. It was a long conversation. We said everything." He looked disappointed. There was this sad thing he did with his chestnut eyes that never failed to move me.

"Some of it was good," I said.

We began to clear the table. I had managed to destroy the kitchen and it took him a long time to put it back together. I went and laid in his bed, taking the Sabbath candles with me and placing them on the nightstand. They didn't move even a little bit, although I kept my eyes on them for a long time.

There was more I wanted to tell him—about how I was going to carry Laura's soul along with me, like an accompanying angel the rabbis say we acquire on Shabbat. Only Laura was not going to arrive on Friday night and depart on Saturday night, as the other angels did. She would be with me always, somewhere inside, our lives merging and blending until some time in the future, when it would be impossible to say where her life ended and mine began.

I wanted to tell him he did not have to choose anymore, play that silly game of telling me I was the best. We were as one. But I couldn't say any of this. It was all too much for words, too fine to be breathed into air. It would have to remain like this, a thin distance between us, a layer of dew, a cloud—love like coriander, intoxicating, silent, remarkable.

I couldn't fall asleep that night, though he hit the pillow with his usual thud. How I envied him that ability, to relinquish his troubles to the dreaming, to ride so willingly into the night.

After a good deal of tossing and turning, I tiptoed over to his bureau and opened the bottom drawer ever so slowly, being careful not to wake him. His regular breathing ebbed into the room. I fished blindly through the t-shirts. My fingers closed around the diary. I padded into the bathroom, clutching the brown leather. I stationed myself upon the bath mat, leaned against the cold, hard tub.

I opened the book to the very last written page, and at the top of the next page, I began to write. "Today I made challah and Curried Chicken with Rice. The cooking filled our house with the smells of coriander and cardamom."

I closed the book, having written only two sentences. It was a good beginning. Just before I got back in bed, I went to the window and looked outside. The finest dusting of snow was falling, covering trees, fences, rooftops, telephone wires, everything. I felt newborn to it. Naked. I held my fingers against the glass and let my head fall back, feeling it alight upon me, like dew. It kept falling and falling, a silent white wonder, born from the April sky.

Robert Friedman
The Legend of Zeml the Wise

Be it known, there was a small village called Obrom which lay in a cleft between three mountains. Whatever names the ancients had given these mountains had long been forgotten, so the elders of Obrom called them "The Mountain of Yesterday," "The Mountain of Now," and "The Mountain of all the Days to Come."

Now the people of Obrom were a contentious lot, much given to bitter quarrels in which stones were cast, evil spells were visited upon enemies and, on days other than the Sabbath, blood was spilled. At times of such controversy, everyone would march in warlike manner beside their allies, and conflict would follow. The weakest would fall like leaves from a dead sapling. Finally, even the children knew the numbers of Obrom had diminished.

There was only one person in all the land held in respect and admiration by everyone, and that person was Zeml the Wise. He was a giant man ten hand-spans tall. His beard was the color of a white Spring bird. His eyes glistened like fine gold and his words burned like a flame from the mid-day sun.

Finally, there came a day when not one, but three, angry disputes arose by early sun-up. Two shepherds claimed the same ram. Two landowners claimed a fig tree which rose exactly where their fields came together. And two young men demanded the hand of the only maiden in all of Obrom that had wifely bearing.

On that very morning, certain persons testified that the mountains had begun to shake. And all could see the sky was uncommonly dark. So the hearts of the people filled with fear and foreboding. In great distress, they gathered at the tent of Zeml the Wise, hoping his judgment would settle their discord and appease the Lord and his Angels.

And, to Zeml, they related all three disputes. The Wise Man listened with great attention. He stroked his beard at length and fell into a state of contemplation. Finally, a look of profound enlightenment crossed his countenance. He stretched out his arms to those assembled and spake thusly:

"I have arrived at just resolution for all three claims. The ram shall be immolated, its bones ground by mortar and pestle and the grains cast to the four winds. The fig tree shall be cut down, its wood shredded and cast aside and its fruit left to rot in the sun. The maiden shall be sent to the farthest field to live alone and bear no children in all her days. Thus shall the justice of Zeml the Wise be visited upon malcontents."

The people were surprised by Zeml's words but determined to obey the commands of this great man. But, suddenly, as they rose to their feet, a fierce wind swept across all of Obrom. The birds took flight in great distress and the sun vanished. "The Mountain of Yesterday" was seen to split asunder and "The Mountain of Now" began to crumble. Only "The Mountain of All the Days to Come" stood brave and unshaken. And an angry voice thundered forth from the black sky:

"Now, as the people of Obrom continue to fight with one another, knowing neither patience nor mercy, it is decreed that they and their descendants, henceforth and forever, shall know only dissension and distrust, wheresoever their seed may travel, and however much they may multiply. And, for his arrogance, Zeml shall know justice such as he would pass upon others. He shall become a misshapen rock on the slope of 'The Mountain of All the Days to Come.' This shall be a sign for all to witness. Lay not waste to the beasts I have created, nor the green foliage I have designed, nor those few decent souls who dwell among you."

Which is why, to this very day, should you visit the Land of Obrom, only one mountain remains and on its slope there is a misshapen rock which resembles a tall figure with a long beard, and a look of great astonishment upon its countenance.

Naama Goldstein
The Follower

It was a new tune they learned today, special for Hanukkah. She played it good, she knew. When Mr. Berko said nothing to you, it was good. Stood by you with his big brown pants all folds and bags and was quiet and then walked on, that meant good. And it was not an easy one, either. Some high up notes where you press only half your little fingertip cushion over the holes and blow not too soft, not too hard, otherwise it spits and screeches. But she did it good. Ta-teh ta-teh, with the tip of the tongue. That's how you did it.

She could hear the recorder swishing against the music sheets in the blue plastic case she swung beside her. She hopped across a tile in the sidewalk and her lunch bag, hanging by its strap around her neck, swung up and flopped back against her stomach. Her briefcase, stretched out with books like an accordion against her back, lurched down an instant after her feet struck the concrete, nearly upsetting her balance. She smiled, and played the sequence again.

One block beyond the school, she paused at a crosswalk. This was a big street. Look one way until the cars don't come, then you look the other way and they start coming from there. Her heart sounded loudly. At this time the big kids with their signs on long wooden sticks and their yellow vests weren't here anymore to show you over. So many fast cars. When her friend Shiri came over for a visit, the two of them had gone for a walk so Shiri could see the school. Oysh, soon there's a big street to cross, she'd told Shiri. More than one time she told her this while they walked. When finally they reached the street, Shiri, who lived in Tel Aviv, laughed and said, this isn't big.

More cars, and the faces inside you couldn't see. Facing her across the street was the dark corner restaurant where men sat, sometimes smiling and winking over their glasses when she peeked through the brown windows. She swung her case a few times, then stomped, pivoted, and started away, looking once towards the stretch of shops beyond the busy road. Today she wouldn't get to walk by all the places. What could she do? There would be tomorrow.

Tomorrow maybe Imma would give her money and on the way home she'd stop by the kiosk, reach up with her coin and say gumball, please. She would try to make her voice loud and tall, other children sometimes teasing her because she whispered, they said. The kiosker would put out his hand with the big gumball, and sometimes she got the blue one, like she wanted. You had to chew with your lips tight together, these great big gumballs, otherwise blue or green or red spit would come dripping down your chin, they were so big.

Now the kiosk would be closed. Even so, she liked walking by it, shutters down and nothing but the smell of old creamsicles melted into the sidewalk. Soon the smell would be the sweet heaven smell of *sufganiot,* cartons of them for Hanukkah, round and spongy and thickly coated in sweet powder. Sometimes you'd get a big warm slop of jam in the middle when you bit in, sometimes only a little. Always the powder would melt cool on your tongue and puff out between your teeth; careful not to breath it in because of coughing.

Thinking of the *sufganiot* made her wonder had the *dreidls* come to Goldvasser's already. In Goldvasser's window, across the street from the kiosk and past the knife-sharpener man, were the *dreidls* waiting on beds of cellophane? Every year the ones in the window came in candy colors brighter and brighter. The best ones, though, never changed. Small and heavy, steady spinners of plain gray lead, Goldvasser would keep in his case inside.

Inside Goldvasser's it was dark and piled to the ceiling with games and books and sheets of paper with one side shiny. Behind the counter always was Goldvasser, quietly, and on the counter trays of lovely erasers in the colors and shapes of all things, and some even came with a smell in them. There were girls in her class who liked to spend their recess rubbing erasers like those on their desks, back and forth with serious faces and one hand holding onto the desk. When they stopped, they'd stretch a plastic bag to the edge of the desk and carefully brush in every shred, and whoever had the largest bag was proudest. The teacher when she saw would say, a waste of time. But later she would say, good, everyone should keep their desks so nice and clean.

Goldvasser's, though he had trays and trays of these erasers, smelled not of the eraser fruit and flowers and houses but of the holy books that Goldvasser had, with leathery dark covers and designs pressed into them of gates with vines and flowers climbing. When you opened the cover of these books, carefully because of the thin pages, there was the smell of the old *Shul* down the street from Goldvasser's. In the old *Shul* old men prayed and there were plain wooden benches and diamond chandeliers and a smell of be quiet and look. Of course Goldvasser himself prayed there, only instead of his week clothes he'd wear a glistening capota, and no pencil behind the ear.

But today, no Goldvasser. Today no stores at all, only sidewalk and more sidewalk. After she checked carefully both ways and crossed an alley, she picked up her hopping game for a little while, stopping when ahead she noticed a few figures perched on a curb railing. She trudged by the small group of young men who were spitting sunflower seed shells into a thick bed of grayish hulls on the stained sidewalk. She eyed them discreetly, face turned to the pavement and fingers gripping tightly the music case handle. One of the men said something to another who, in turn, shoved his friend's elbow with a palm that remained suspended as little seeds sharp as teeth came hailing down. She brisked up her pace, her baggage pummeling her from every direction.

"Ahh, piece of *dreck,* you scared the child," someone scolded, then laughed.

A rush of pavement away, when the green man lit up, she made her way to the other side. Now there was a long straight street ahead, on each side nothing but rows of the same-looking tall white buildings with bumpy outsides like whipped frosting and tile collages down the edges. Someone had chalked hopscotch numbers onto the sidewalk. She hopped through. Where she lived the buildings were also a family, all in a row, but shorter and already not so white, though not yet brown like the ones over Goldvasser's and the kiosk. In the shadow of the great pillars that held up each of her neighborhood buildings was a small playground: blue and yellow seesaw, blue and yellow slide and a stone sandbox. In the sandboxes you couldn't play because the cats filled them up, but she and the others would catch themselves on the slide just before they'd touch the lumpy sand.

A long dark stripe of clipped hedge marked the distance ahead of her before she could turn. She put out her hand and let it brush against the small waxy leaves. Many of them were severed, punctuated by borders of whitish scab. They scraped against the pads of her fingers. She pulled back and scrutinized the hedge. The same bush lined her street. In the spring, small, stiff white flowers sprang out on these bushes, and later red bulbs like tiny plums. The fruit would be rich with the hedge's milky blood, but never would you touch it to your lips, she knew, anymore than the beautiful pink blooms of the great oleander behind her building. Now she searched the hedge for the last surviving fruit, but could see none. Instead she plucked herself a perfectly oval leaf. From the wound of its stem she squeezed a small bead of white sap.

"Tsk tsk, tsktsk."

Like someone calling a cat, the clucking came from behind her. The leaf fell to the pavement. She turned and faced a dark-haired man, who looked back at her. He wagged his finger two or three times, laying claim to the sound. They looked at each other, both faces still and grave, both pairs of eyes dark and wondering. She felt a smallness, and moved a step back. The man was silent and still. He was older than the men on the curb railing, but not old. His hair was smooth and all one dark color. He wore a clean, collared shirt and clean blue pants. He did not look angry. She turned her back to him and on weak legs started again on her way.

She kept her arms at her sides and did not look at the hedges. Only at the sidewalk she looked. Did the man see her hopping before? That was allowed, but she wouldn't have if someone was watching. Quietness behind. The man didn't yell at her, but she was breathing too-small breaths.

Now she could feel her bags bumping against her even when she did not hop. She felt clumsy. She looked at the sidewalk. Only the flat stone steps leading up to each building interrupted the long dark hedge alongside her.

At the end of the block she felt tired and could not wait for the walk to be finished. She turned, now passing smaller houses, old and chipped, with pale gardens spilling over walls and crawling through fence links onto the pavement. She thought the man would go a different way at the end of the tall buildings, but now, though she did not turn and look, she knew he hadn't. She felt his stillness and quietness behind her, like a heavy tent sheet on a hot day. She kept her arms close by her sides. If she would not pick from gardens he would go.

One small leaf when the hedge had so many was not so bad, maybe. She knew it wasn't allowed. When the red fruit came out on the hedges on her street they would pick them when no grown ups were around and squeeze out the goo. Then they'd go out back by the garbage room, send the cats running into the oleander. They'd hold their breath for the stink, and wash their hands in the garbage room basin in case they would later forget and lick them and be poisoned, and then it would be known they had picked off the hedges.

The man knew it wasn't allowed. Like a thick wool blanket waiting to fall over her, he followed. It was not yet the weather for such blankets. She thought of the worn pink blanket she used to finger to feel quiet. For a long time now she had not used her pink blanket. She'd even stopped sucking her thumb in the summer. One night Imma had smoothed on the cool, clear liquid to keep the mosquitoes away and had forgotten about the thumb and covered it, too. Get it in the ears, get it in the ears, she had told Imma that night, like every night, because the sound of the mosquitoes whining, whining by her temples was a terrible sound. She had not noticed that Imma had forgotten to leave the thumb sweet. Since then she did not suck her thumb. Imma and Abba were proud, because big girls didn't suck their thumb. Big girls also knew not to take from people's hedges.

Such a long way she had walked since the leaf from the hedge. He would know now she would pick no more. Maybe he knew, but still followed. When she'd looked in his eyes they were like hers, looking to be shown, not a grown-up's eyes, though he shook his finger like one. He hadn't looked angry. Maybe he didn't mind so much about the leaf.

Maybe he wanted her with him. She wanted suddenly to sit down on the sidewalk and cry. From here on she would usually start seeing only faces she knew. Today the streets were quiet for supper time. The man she had never seen before. Where did the man live? She didn't want a new home. It would be quiet with no children and at night she would stare at the light swimming across the ceiling for each car that passed, and would not sleep. Day after day she would look to the man who was looking to be shown, and who would show him? She wanted to sit down. She could not imagine the man's table, his chairs, his stove, his bed. Only the stillness could she see, and the light passing over the ceiling at night. She blinked again and again to push the crying back inside.

Each step on the hard pavement pounded through her back. Once in a while her recorder case would scrape painfully against the soft skin of her calf, but if she turned her thoughts away from her legs, they would stop moving. She would not even listen for the man's footsteps. She would march, only march. If she stopped, he would set his great brown eyes on her and never let go.

The sound of a donkey's bray told her the way was not long. It was the watermelon man's donkey who cried every morning and every night, the last donkey in town. In a moment, she would turn the corner and be on her street.

The donkey heaved a final, fading groan just as she saw the first in the row of yellowing stucco buildings. Her home was the farthest down the block. She thought she heard a soft footfall behind her, and her shoe caught on a skewed pavement tile. Every muscle in her neck, her back, her legs, struggled to counter the pull of her briefcase. She wanted to fall down, but if she fell, he would set his great eyes on her, reach out, and never let go. She tipped her head down, closing her eyes, and regained her balance. When she opened her eyes she could see nothing but her building up ahead, but she would not run. She could not show she knew he followed, or else she could not show she was afraid. Which it was, she didn't know. But this she knew: no running.

When she reached the three stone steps leading to her building, she felt as tired and as weepy as if kept up long past her bedtime. She wanted to fall down more than before. She was home. He would know this, too. He would stop her leaving him. She walked the path to the buzzer, slowly, knowing he would take her away before she could let Imma know she was home. She lifted a heavy finger to a small black button on the intercom.

Her mother's voice, tinny-strange, familiar, sifted through the slotted metal. Her hand clenched over the door handle, the child waited for the lock to release. A shrill, raspy ring, and the lobby door clicked open. She pushed her way in and shoved the heavy door behind her. The comforting gumminess of linoleum beneath her feet, she pressed her face against the thick glass pane. He stood at the foot of the stone steps, as still and as placid as an old sentry.

It was several weeks later when the follower came for her. She was dressed in blue and white for the holiday, the colors of the flag, and he came for her again. The morning streets rang with the shouts and laughter of school children, and many other blue and white figures bounced past her as she turned the corner after the last of the buildings in her row. The man was there. One foot on the pedal of a great, rickety black bicycle, the other firm against the gray road, he fixed his still eyes on her, and spoke.

"Come."

She stood and stared at the man with eyes as still. His voice was soft. There were many children around, and they did not look afraid.

"I'll take you to school," he said.

She had never been on a bicycle so big or so old. How would it be to fly rattling and lurching over the streets all the way to school? She stared at the man. His bike loomed high. She would have to clasp her hands over the man's belly, or she would fall. She lowered her eyes then and scuffed the sidewalk with her buckled holiday shoes. When the shyness iced through her, she could do nothing to stop it. She tried to whisper an answer, but even a whisper wouldn't come. She turned and followed the other children. The man cycled off a moment later, turning his empty face towards her once as he streamed by. She looked back with timid eyes. The wind did not ruffle his hair.

In school that day the teacher gave each of them a small blue carton of twisted Hanukkah candles to take home. The entire school, in blue skirts and white blouses, gathered in the sandy yard and sang songs and danced some dances. She went on stage with other girls from Mr. Berko's class, and they played the tune they had learned and practiced well. Everyone sang along the words about the brave Maccabees banishing all the Greeks, who were one of the dangers, but they'd shown them. Later they ate sufganiot, which were as soft and sweet-smelling as the year before. By the end of the day, with the smell of vanillin sugar and candle-wax at her fingertips, she had forgotten the follower, and did not think of him when she walked home.

Rabbi James Stone Goodman
Basketball With the Ancestors
A dream fragment from Rosh Hashanah 5753

Near Rosh Hashana, 5753, I had a dream. God was sitting in front of the Big Book, gazing into my life, chewing on the end of a pencil. What did God look like? I couldn't see; I did, however, hear a voice. It was a specially created voice, unlike other voices yet the words were clear. God asked me one and only one question: What are you going to do?

"What can I do?" I said. In my dream, I am laying on my couch in front of the television. I switch on the tube, remote control so I don't have to move (America is so great.) Thank God it's time for Ted Koppel, I think. I am expecting Ted Koppel, but he is Rabbi Tarphon now, in robes and sandals. He is standing behind Ted Koppel's desk and he explains to me from out of the tube: you do not have to do everything, but you do have to do something. His more precise words are "it is not your duty to complete the work, but neither are you free to desist from it."

I roll over on the couch, pop another fat free fig newton into my mouth, change the channel to something safe like Jay Leno and think, "what can I possibly do by myself?"

The great Hillel is now staring at me from channel five; he is nineteen inches long and he answers me from out of the tube, "in a place where there are no human beings, strive to be a human being." I pick up the remote control and shut him off but his words linger in the air, they are written in the space between the television and the couch, like a ribbon of light they drift lazily through the air space of my living room, "in a place where there are no human beings, strive to be a human being."

In an act of defiance, I turn off the tube altogether. "Leave me alone," I mutter, and I head for my favorite city of refuge, Schnucks Supermarket, for a little late night shop. I pull into the west lot at Schnucks, corner of Hanley and Clayton, and park in the same lot I always park in. The lot is almost full, as usual, only this time the doors do not open. Schnucks is closed. Schnucks is never closed I think.

I begin to panic. I depend on Schnucks for a lot more than food, and I return to my car. In the parking lot I notice the other cars now. I wonder

what all these cars are doing here if Schnucks is closed. In the cars I see
them all, Hillel, Rabbi Tarphon, Moshe Heifetz, the Ramban, Maimonides,
Yosef Caro, sitting behind the wheels of shiny new Mustangs and Chevys.
Yochanan ben Zakkai looms over the others in a Dodge pick-up truck,
like it's a drive-in and I am the show. They are all looking at me, smiling
and waving.

"All right, already," I say to them. "So what am I supposed to do?"
Hillel gets out of a tan Mitsubishi and says," love peace, pursue peace. Love
human beings, and draw them near to the Torah." He is holding a
basketball and wearing pump Nikes. Rabbi Tarphon sticks his head out of
a Ford 4 X 4 and says, "the day is short, the work is great, the laborers are
sluggish, the reward is much, and the Master is pressing. It is not your duty
to complete the work, but neither are you free to desist from it." "*Yella,*"
he says, which means "get on with it" in Arabic street slang.

"Yeah, but, the days are long, longer, it seems, every vision fails.

There is no more any prophet, and everything is shut up before us,
shut up and sealed."

I am quoting a poem.

"Sha!" Hillel says. He looks so funny holding a basketball. "Sha! Don't
separate yourself from your community...and how dare you judge another
human being until you stand in that person's place?" Rabbi Tarphon
stretches his arms out towards me and asks, "How long will you rake words
together and use them against us?"

Sitting in the car with Maimonides is my daughter, Adina. She gets out
of a Jeep Cherokee and Maimonides gently helps her to the ground. She
comes over to me. She is holding a turquoise blue bubble gum cigar that
has written on it "it's a boy." The cigar is the color of good fortune and joy
in the Middle East. "Where did you get that cigar?" I ask Adina.

"One of the guys gave it to me. He wanted to share his happiness with
us," she says.

"All my life I've been wondering what happiness is," I say, feeling very
philosophical, no doubt due to the company.

"Me, too," Adina says. She is five years old—how I love the way she
talks. "He had a baby," Adina says. "He's passing out cigars. The Talmud says

a person should do three things in their life: plant a tree, make a baby, write a book. If you can't do all, do one of them. They're all about leaving something behind, so even if you don't have a baby, you can make something that stays."

"How do you know this?" I ask her.

"That guy over there told me." She points to the Jeep where Maimonides is behind the wheel. "*Yella,*" she says, "do you know what that means Daddy?" "Yes," I say. They've all started their engines like it's a road race and the next thing I know they're gone down Hanley Road.

I recall what a dangerous place Schnucks is for me at night, and we are going home. I remember that it is 500 years since my people's exile from Spain, and I feel the joy to mark out a small territory and claim it for the future, and the conviction that it is worth building because we believe in it.

"Daddy, are you afraid of the future?" Adina asks me.

"No."

"Then, *Yella,* let's get on with it."

Five years old, having picked up a little street Arabic from Maimonides, she teaches me the last link and I have what I need to get on with it. *Yella.* I awoke with a feeling of clarity and complete recall, knowing that if I had come into the world only to have had this dream, it would have been enough.

Gene Holtzman
The Professor's Work

The Professor hunched over his orderly desk and opened his worn and creased leather briefcase. He pulled out a thick stack of papers held loosely together by a brittle rubberband that had already snapped and been knotted in several places.

Everybody knew of this manuscript he had been lugging around through the years, never mentioning it and evading any inquiries. There were endless murmurs and theories as to its content, but the consensus was that this was his "big" book in the making and the Professor's possessive secrecy only heightened the curiosity and the assumption that this was his magnum opus in progress.

The Professor settled into his overstuffed vaguely mildewy chair, its hollows and sags perfectly embracing his shape. As he stuffed, tamped, and lit his pipe, he briefly felt the mixed sensations, the abstracts of memory, of the years of reflection and relaxation; the restless times of ambition, frustration, cerebral labor over a lecture or a paper or a thought refusing to gel; and then the later years ... despondency, repudiation of his work, his profession, the academic political shenanigans; the seizures of defeat and belief that none of it was worth the effort, none of it amounted to anything—100's of papers, a dozen or so books (he forgot exactly how many), lectures, speeches, symposia, colloquial advising on master's and doctoral theses—all the emblems of academic profundity, or—when he was in one of the funks—the stasis of scholarly thought like wheels free-spinning and each new contribution to the body of knowledge just another wheel spinning in air and getting nobody anywhere, redemption or enlightenment nowhere in sight. He felt tired.

He drew on his pipe but it had already died out and instead of smoke he exhaled a deep sigh that amplified would have more closely resembled a groan or a growl. As he coughed dryly, the Professor pulled off the rubberband from the papers. It cracked and fell limply on his lap prompting a momentary swell of self-disgust. He bit down hard on his pipe, feeling it slip through the gaps between his teeth and rubbed his hand over his scalp across the few feathery strands of hair. Eighty-three years old, not so much tired as bored, not so much used up as just plain empty; the old philosopher, emeritus of one of the best philosophy departments in one of the most prestigious institutions in the country; multiple committee ex officio; a respected and even revered ... awed member of the thinktank: How could even other revered and awed associates not be impressed by the scope of his knowledge, his publications, his seeming command of and ease with multiple academic disciplines. He had proclaimed in his younger days, when he was given to lofty proclamations—when he thought, wrote, talked, strode with confidence and authority—that all areas of knowledge were really about the same thing, just different frameworks—all about all he used to think in moments of intellectual elation; and all about nothing, nothing about nothing, as he thought more and more in recent years as he started forgetting his students' and colleagues' names, as his work and gait both grew unsteady.

The Professor removed his pipe, placed it on the side table and slowly brought his thumb—tremoring slightly, not so badly for a man of his years—to his dry lips and rubbed it several times until it moistened. He thumbed through the pages—musty, saturated with odors of tobacco and years; worn out, faded, stained, smeared, and smudged—looking for the section he wanted to work on now. He came to the chapter he was after, scribbles, additions, notes obscuring the original type. His posture improved like a deflated ball becoming taut with an infusion of air. He curved his thumb and forefinger to the side of his nose and mouth, studying the problem, summoning a solution. His eyes, moist and clouded behind thick glasses, cleared and gleamed as a sneer turned to a snarl and resolved into a self-satisfied smile.

He began to write in the margin of the manuscript in a scrawl that seemed almost adolescent, disregarding, as he had many times before, that the thinktank was about to get underway with all its postulations and protestations, pretenses and pontifications. He noted in the margin: "revisions—3/2/86 on reverse side." Then turned the page over and began writing:

Nick Stone rolled a cigarette, plugged it into his mouth, lighted it, inhaled and let out a jet of smoke along with a rasping cough thickened by years of straight bourbon. He had that familiar feeling that this case would be his last, but this time it felt real. The feeling had gnawed at him since the day Grace first came into his office. It took a deep bite into him the night he got bushwacked and dragged into an alley by four burly thugs to be reminded of the precise location of his kidneys and that even a tough hack like Stone sees stars after the seventh or so blow to the head. And now it ate at him.

He didn't have a clue of what the next step should be, if Grace's name was a malicious irony, if her passion for his help and heat were a hooker's theatrics or the real thing. He couldn't make heads or tales out of why someone had ransacked and chopped up his office. As he sat looking over the mess that once was an office, where he once felt confidence and hardnosed cynicism he now felt a vacancy where a whole community of foreboding was claiming squatter's rights.

He heard a faint rustle in the outer office and nimbly reached into his top drawer, withdrawing extra confidence and resting his filled hand in his lap. The door opened and a short slime oozed into the room with a twisted hooked nose pointing to the floor and the long straight-nosed barrel of a forty-five pointing at Stone.

He took a second to congratulate himself that his instincts weren't shot yet, then quickly sized up the short menace standing in front of him, deciding the squirt meant business and to wait for him to state it would be to wait too long. Without a twitch or a blink, he aimed and shot his thirty-eight through the knee opening in the center of the desk, and as the short slime dissolved into a puddle on the floor, a slug in his thigh, Stone stood upright and aimed his gun at the groaning man's head and said, "Always gets me mad when customers barge in without knocking ... damned impolite..."

There was a knock at the Professor's door and he flinched like it was a shot. Amused by his reaction then disgruntled by the intrusion, he answered gruffly, "What? What is it?" The timid, deferential voice of a student responded. "Sorry to interrupt, Professor, but Dr. Uslavsky asked me to come down to see if you were going to be coming to the meeting today. It's about to begin." The Professor answered abruptly, distractedly, "No. Can't make it today. I'm in the middle of some important work." "Ok, Professor, they figured you were working on your, ah ... your work. Sorry to bother you."

And the Professor, an absent-minded sneer, snarl, and smile intermingling in his expression, returned to the manuscript, hoping in the back of his mind that he'd manage to finish this book, his magnum opus, his "work" in his lifetime.

Irving Litvag

Commodore Levy

*Commodore Levy is a biographical novel based on the life of Uriah Phillips
Levy, an American Jewish naval officer who rose to the Navy's highest rank
despite pervasive anti-Semitism. It also is a saga of the small Jewish community
in the United States during the period between the Revolutionary War and the
Civil War. The following is an excerpt from the novel.*

It is now 1802. Uriah Phillips Levy, ten years old and obsessed with
sailing ships and the sailor's life, has run away from his Philadelphia home
to ship out as a cabin boy. His ship is The New Jerusalem, a coaster that
plies the Atlantic seaboard, carrying cargo from ports in the Northeast to
those in Georgia and Florida. Now the ship has stopped at Savannah, home
port of its captain James Wilkins, for an overhaul and provisioning.

It was Shabbat morn and Uriah set out in search of a synagogue in
which to pray. He thought that all synagogues were named *Mikveh Israel*
and so he inquired of Mrs. Wilkins as to whether Savannah had a *Mikveh
Israel* and if so, where it might be found. It was the Israelite Sabbath, he told
her, and he had not been in a synagogue since he had left Philadelphia. He
knew that his mother and father and especially his grandfather would want
him to be in a synagogue this morning to say the Sabbath prayers.

The Captain's wife of course had no idea if Savannah had a Jews'
church: she never had seen such. But there were some Jews in the city and
surely they would know. She started to direct the boy to a printer's shop
which she believed to be owned by a Hebrew, but he quickly assured her
that if the man was indeed one of his people, he would not be found in
his shop on the Sabbath.

Elizabeth Wilkins sought out her husband to ask his counsel and he
nodded approvingly at the boy's desire to worship on his holy day. There
was, he told her, a Jew called Levi de Lyon, who lived in the small white
house where the Augusta road enters the market square. Surely this man
would know if Savannah had a "Mikke" or whatever the boy had called it.
He would take him there, the Captain said, except that he had to finish
repairing the back fence.

Guided by Mrs. Wilkins' careful directions, Uriah arrived within a few minutes at the white house of Levi de Lyon. A low picket fence guarded the tiny, well-kept yard and the boy was about to open the gate when a plump man dressed in a black frock coat and gray pantaloons, a handsome beaver hat on his head, came out the front door. He walked to the fence and inquired as to what Uriah wanted.

"Sir, I seek a Mr.—" he glanced quickly at the paper in his hand, "a Mr. de Lyon."

"I am Levi Isaac de Lyon," the man said. "What is your business?"

"Sir, I was told you could tell me: does this city have a *Mikveh Israel?*"

De Lyon's brow furrowed at the unexpected question. "Who are you, boy, and why would you ask of that?"

"My name is Uriah Phillips Levy and I am a sailor off the ship New Jerusalem, provisioning now at Savannah. If there be a Mikveh Israel in this place, I would like to say Shabbat prayers there."

De Lyon noticeably relaxed. "You are a Hebrew boy, then?"

"Aye, Sir. Of Philadelphia. And away from home these months aboard my ship.

Suspicion came again to de Lyon's mind and his eyes narrowed. "If you are of Philadelphia, how then did you know that our *esnoga* is called *Mikveh Israel?*"

The boy paused, confused. "Every city that has Jews living in it has a Mikveh Israel, does it not?"

De Lyon's face went completely blank for a moment and he stroked his cheek in puzzlement. Then he understood and laughed aloud. "You thought that, because your own *esnoga* in Philadelphia is named *Mikveh Israel*, that every *esnoga* in the world has the same name, eh? Is that what you thought? Not at all, not at all. Why, New York City has its *Shearith Israel* and the Jews of Charleston have their *Beth Elohim*. And London has the *Shaar Hashamayim* and the *Great Synagogue*. Why...why, I hear that even your home city now has another synagogue. The Tedescoes of Philadelphia have started a synagogue of their own called—I believe—*Rodeph Shalom*." He laughed again and patted Uriah on the shoulder. "No, no, my boy, synagogues bear all sorts of names. It just happens by coincidence, you see, that our little *esnoga* here in Savannah bears the same name as yours in Philadelphia. Though the names are spelled slightly different in English. I am bound there now for Shabbat worship. If you would like to be our guest, I would be happy to guide you there."

The boy nodded and the two walked together across the market square.

"When you gave your name to me," de Lyon said, "your middle name was Phillips. Are you then kin of Jonas Phillips?"

Uriah smiled and nodded vigorously. "Yes, sir, he is my grandfather!"

"Ah, I know him. Or at least I have met him. He is much respected, your grandfather, as a courageous man who speaks up loudly to right a wrong. I know that the Israelites of Philadelphia have great honor for him. Is he well, your grandfather?"

"I have not seen him in more than six months," the boy answered. "And it will be another year and a half until I do again. But I hope he is well, and my parents and brothers and sisters."

"You do not communicate with them by the mail riders?"

"I have posted them some letters when we have dropped anchor at a port, but they do not know where to write me and so I have no news. I'm sure, though, that they're well."

They had come by now to a handsome three-story clapboard house anchored sturdily on a brick foundation. The outside was painted a restful pale green. Two other men preceded them up the walk and nodded silently to de Lyon. They cast curious glances at Uriah.

"Well," de Lyon said, "here we are."

"This is your *Mikveh Israel?*" Uriah was puzzled. This looked nothing like a synagogue. Certainly nothing like the only synagogue he knew.

"This is the house of Benjamin Sheftall," de Lyon explained. "This is where our *esnoga* holds its services. We are too few Israelites in Savannah to have a separate *esnoga* building. *Mikveh Israel*—our *Mikveh Israel* has been meeting in the homes of our people ever since it was founded about 70 years ago."

"Have you a Torah?" asked Uriah innocently.

De Lyon almost angered at the question, but he realized the boy's sincerity and naivetÈ. He smiled. "Of course. Two of them, in fact. One owned by Isaac Minis and one by myself. And, believe it or not, we even have a *hazzan*. Not too bad for a town in the wilderness, eh, my Philadelphia friend?"

They walked into the vestibule and de Lyon took Uriah to a small group of men standing together, enjoying a moment or two of talk before entering the sitting room for the service.

"Gentlemen, we have a Shabbat guest with us," exclaimed de Lyon. "Meet Master Uriah Phillips Levy, grandson of our honored friend Jonas Phillips of Philadelphia. Master Levy has gone to sea and finds himself now in Savannah with his ship. He requests the privilege of joining our Shabbat worship and I have told him we are honored. Master Levy, shake hands with Dr. Moses Sheftall, Mr. Levi Sheftall, and Mr. Moses Mordecai Myers."

Uriah gravely shook hands with the men and wondered how many of the Hebrew in this city were called Sheftall.

"We may not have a service unless the *minyan* is complete," growled Dr. Moses Sheftall. "It's growing late. Too bad the boy is too young to be counted."

"They'll be here, Moses," de Lyon assured him. "We have failed to have a *minyan* only twice this year. Our men are faithful. They'll be here." He took Uriah by the arm and walked with him to a wall near the door, on which hung a large wooden frame with a document under glass.

"Look, Uriah. Do you know that signature? It is the hand of General Washington himself. It is the proudest possession of our *esnoga*." He explained that Levi Sheftall as president of the synagogue, had sent a congratulatory message to the General on his assumption of the presidency in 1789. In response, Washington had sent the synagogue a long message of his appreciation. "It is a fine, noble proclamation," de Lyon said. "A great expression that will pride each of us until we die. Here, look at how he concluded..." de Lyon bent close to the framed letter and read the words in a soft, yet precisely enunciated tone: "May the same wonder-working Deity, who long since delivered the Hebrews from their Egyptian oppressors, planted them in a promised land, whose providential agency has

lately been conspicuous in establishing these United States as an
independent nation, still continue to water them with the dews of heaven
and make the inhabitants of every denomination participants in the
temporal and spiritual blessings of that people whose God is Jehovah."

He stood up straight again and took a deep breath. Uriah saw that his
eyes glistened with tears.

The door of the Sheftall house opened again and several more men
arrived. The *minyan* was complete and the Israelites walked into the sitting
room and sat in the chairs placed there in two rows.

De Lyon produced a prayer book and handed it to Uriah, who saw
with relief that it was the familiar book from his synagogue at home. He
had worried that somehow the book here would be unreadable for him or
even would be written in some foreign kind of Hebrew that he could not
make out. He relaxed when he saw the familiar words.

Hazzan de la Motta began to chant the opening prayer. Uriah joined
in the response, his high-pitched voice sounding a treble among the deeper
sing-song reading of the elders around him.

He looked up and saw the Torah scrolls in their red vestments, resting
in a shiny mahogany case. The sun streamed through the front windows
and the rich wood of the case glowed and sang with light.

Uriah couldn't help smiling as he chanted the blessings. It was good to
be a Jew, once again.

Edward M. Londe
The Legend of the Gypsy Cantor

Long ago, in the old country, there was an old man known as the Gypsy Cantor. No one knew where he came from or where he lived, and if anyone asked him, he would smile and point to his head and his heart. It was the custom of the Gypsy Cantor to seek out synagogues off the beaten path, devout congregations that were hard-pressed to find a minyan as their numbers dwindled.

Wherever the Gypsy Cantor went, he was accompanied by his son, Gershon. It was Gershon's job to tend to the cart that they brought with them everywhere, which held a chest. That chest was covered with a purple velvet robe, which depicted, in vivid detail, the history of the Jewish people. Everyone would gather around the chest, marveling at the many illustrations and the beautiful needlework. And whenever the Gypsy Cantor was asked who had done such magnificent work, he would always reply, "An angel."

Once the Gypsy Cantor arrived in a tiny village just before dusk on the eve of Rosh Hashanah. He found five old men huddled inside the tiny House of Prayer, bemoaning their fate. For they were the only Jews left in that village, and what hope did they have of gathering a minyan on that holy night? Of course they were pleased to welcome the Gypsy Cantor and his son, but still they were three men short of comprising a *minyan*.

This dilemma did not seem to disturb the Gypsy Cantor in the least, however, and he and his son went outside and carried in the chest from the cart. The old men gathered around and marveled at the beauty of the cloth that covered the chest, but the Gypsy Cantor told them to be seated and prepare to pray. This confused the old men, but they did as he said, and from their seats they watched in amazement as he pulled the cover aside, revealing a chest made of cedars from Lebanon. That chest was without blemish, without the scars of tools, and was joined by wooden pegs, without a piece of metal in its construction.

Then, in a sweeping gesture, the Gypsy Cantor raised his hands high and then let them descend to the chest, raising the lid. The old men of the congregation all watched very closely, and at first it appeared to them that the chest contained three Torahs. But imagine their surprise when three *Tzaddikim,* each dressed in a white ceremonial robe and wearing a purple mitre, emerged from the chest, one after the other. They each stepped forward, raised their hands high, and began to chant the Rosh Hashanah prayers, and the Gypsy Cantor and his son and the old men of the congregation all followed. And as they prayed, tears ran down the checks of the old men, for they knew that the Gypsy Cantor had brought them a very great blessing.

So it was that the Gypsy Cantor and his son and the three *Tzaddikim* all remained in that village during all of that holy week, and made it possible for the old men to complete their prayers. And when the last prayers had been said at the end of Yom Kippur, they watched as the Gypsy Cantor opened the chest and the *Tzaddikim* climbed inside. And it seemed to the old men that just before he closed the chest, they saw three holy scrolls gathered there, each wrapped in a white cover, with a purple mitre. Then the Gypsy Cantor and his son carried the chest out to the cart, took their leave of the old men with many tears, and set off again in their wandering.

If the Suit Fits, Wear It

For Gershon Simon Londe

Rabbi Leib had a son, and his fondest dream was of the day when his son, Simon, would follow in his footsteps and become a rabbi. And Simon did become a rabbi, and a good one, but his heart was elsewhere. His father sensed his restlessness, but assured him he would eventually become reconciled to his fate.

Then one day a traveling circus of Romanian gypsies, with some Jews among them, came to their small Russian town. After visiting the circus, Rabbi Simon was so enthralled that he decided to run away and join them—as a clown. When his father found out, it was as though his son had died and he said *Kaddish* for him in his heart.

Now Simon was very comfortable as a clown, and loved making the children laugh and feeling so free. Still, he never failed to put on his *tallis* and *tefillin* and to pray in the morning and evening. Before long he discovered that the circus was a world in itself, and he came to know each performer and worker, and to know their dreams and their heartaches.

There was Mishka, the trapeze artist, who confided in Simon and told him of his deep melancholy and guilt over the death of his son, Gershon. His son had performed with him on the trapeze, and he had constantly urged him to do ever more daring feats. First there was a twist, a double somersault, and then he would catch Gershon, to thunderous applause. At last he coaxed him to attempt what had never been done before, a triple twist. And it was while attempting this that Gershon slipped through his father's waiting arms and fell to his death.

Using all the wisdom he had learned, Simon recounted to Mishka how King David had lost his beloved son, and how he must carry on. He also taught him the *Kaddish,* and helped him to heal his broken heart.

Before long everyone turned to Simon, and he assisted all those in need of help. Even when the trained bear became lethargic and would not eat and was very surly, Simon knew just what to do. He took the bear for a walk in the forest near the town, where the bear nuzzled the earth and smelled the forest air, for which he had longed so much. And when the bear came back, he once more danced to the delight of the children.

One day word came to Simon that his father, Rabbi Leib, was dying, and he hurried home to be with him. When he came to his father's side he was still wearing his clown's costume, so quickly had he come. He asked his father's forgiveness, but his father silenced him with a raised hand. For the old rabbi had received word of his son's many noble acts, and he said: "You found a suit that fits you, and you wore it. You filled all the duties of a rabbi and were compassionate to all, even to a dumb animal. For this I bless you."

After his father's death, when the high holidays came, Simon put on his father's vestments, and for the first time the garments felt comfortable, for he had grown into them.

Fathers—don't make your sons wear suits that don't fit them. Don't demand that they soar higher and higher into the top of the tent. They may slip through your fingers and you will hold only air.

The Tallis Weaver

For Milford Gilbert

There once was a man who was a master craftsman, the finest tailor in Poland. This tailor was a devout man, who was never missing from the Minyan. It was his dream to make a *tallis* like one of those worn by the ancient rabbis. To do so he would have to find the dye known as *tekhelet,* which was used to dye a thread of the fringers of the tallis. This was said to be the shade of sky blue, but no one knew for sure what exactly the color was, or how it was made. The tailor searched in every text, but he could not find out the secret of how to make that dye, and without it he could not weave the *tallis* of his dreams.

At last the tailor decided to travel to the land of Israel, for if the secret of the dye could be found anywhere, it would be there. And so he uprooted himself late in life, and traveled alone to the Holy Land. When he was settled there, he began to search for the missing dye, but not even the greatest rabbis knew the secret of how it had been made.

Then it happened that the tailor had a dream in which he was riding in a boat with an old man who was fishing, while the tailor was weaving the tallis of his dreams. All at once the old man pulled a bottle out of the sea. That bottle glowed as if there was a blue light in it. Then the old man handed the bottle to the tailor, but before he could accept it, he woke up. Now the tailor was certain that this was a prophetic dream, and he decided to go to the sea, to see if perhaps he could find that old fisherman.

And one day, in the port of Jaffa, the tailor saw an old man who looked exactly like the old man of his dream. He went up to him and introduced himself and asked him if he had ever pulled a bottle out of the sea. The old man seemed very surprised, and told him that many years before he had found a bottle of blue ink in his net, and he had kept it at home, but no one knew about it. And when the tailor told the old fisherman his dream, the old man went to his house and came back with a small crystal bottle, filled with a blue substance. He told the tailor that it was surely intended for him, and he gave it to him. The tailor held the bottle up to the light and saw it was unlike any blue he had ever seen. And he knew that this must be the lost dye for which he had searched so long. And the tailor turned to the old man to thank him, but the old man was gone. And only then did the tailor realize that he must have been none other than Elijah himself, who had brought him that precious gift.

So it was that in his seventieth year the tailor at last started to create the *tallis* he had dreamed about for so long. He selected the finest merino wool, and silk, and created his own dyes, made in the ancient ways. And at last he opened the bottle of the blue dye and dyed the threads of the corner fringes of that *tallis*. And when the dye had dried, he put on that *tallis* for the first time, and he felt himself surrounded by a holy presence.

So it was that every time the tailor wore that *tallis,* he was filled with holiness and awe, and saw the world through the eyes of a mystic. Then nothing was withheld from him and he could read the letters on every man's forehead that are invisible to everyone else. So too did the words of the Torah reveal themselves to him as never before. And only when he took the *tallis* off did he lose that extra soul and become a simple man once more.

Now the tailor could have been buried in that *tallis,* for surely it would have protected his soul against all evil. But as he lay on his deathbed, the tailor's last request was that the *tallis* be given to a poor student in a Yeshivah in Jerusalem. The rabbi to whom he made this request saw that it was fulfilled. And the student who received that *tallis* found from the first time he wrapped it around himself that a kind spirit seemed to fuse with his own, which strengthened and inspired him. And that was none other than the spirit of the old tailor, who in this way was rewarded for his pious ways.

The Tefillin That Cried

For my father, Simon

About four in the morning he awoke with a start. He heard something, like a sobbing. Not loud, as at a funeral, but gentle and low. It seemed to be coming from the basement. He thought he must be losing his mind, hearing things. If this continued, soon he would start seeing things that were not there.

After the sobs subsided, he fell back to sleep, intending to look around the basement the next day. But when he did, there was nothing out of the ordinary. The windows were intact. Everything was in its place.

The next few nights he slept soundly, but on the fourth night he was again awakened by a strange sound. He sat up in bed and listened carefully. It seemed to him that he could hear a voice whispering, but try as he might, he could not make out the words.

That is when he decided it was time to see the doctor for his annual checkup, even though it was not due for another few months. The doctor identified it as a case of auditory hallucinations, and prescribed a sedative to be taken before going to sleep. Yet despite the medication, the sounds continued, and he decided to make a thorough examination of the basement.

There, in one of the boxes, he found his father's *Tefillin* bag, embroidered by his grandmother, Pearl, for his father. He had put it in the basement years before and had forgotten it. But when he lifted the bag, he found that it was wet, although everything else in the box was dry. Then, all at once, he realized that the sobbing he had heard had come from the bag, and that it was wet from tears for having been abandoned. Now tears came to his eyes as he remembered his father and recognized that a miracle had taken place.

He carried the bag upstairs, dried and brushed it, and placed it in a prominent spot on the library shelf. The next morning he took out the *Tefillin* and put them on and prayed for the first time in many years. And from the moment he put on the Tefillin, he felt the presence of his father, as if he were in that room with him. And this presence remained with him as long as he wore the *Tefillin*.

After that he put on the *Tefillin* every morning, and prayed in the presence of his father's spirit. And never again did he hear any strange sounds from the basement.

The Ten Hidden Tzaddikim

For ten many years, Rabbi Simon ben Loeb worked alongside his *shamash,* whose name was Scissors, but never did he realize how holy he was, for the *shamash* kept his holiness hidden. Then one night Rabbi Simon had a dream in which he visited Paradise, and there he saw Scissors in the company of the patriarchs and sages, and they honored him as one of their own. And when he awoke, Rabbi Simon realized that the shamash must be one of the *Lamed Vav Tzaddikim,* the thirty-six hidden saints whose very existence preserves the world.

Rabbi Simon thought on this matter night and day, and at last he perceived heaven's purpose in revealing this secret to him. He saw it as a sign that if he could convene a *minyan* of these hidden saints in Jerusalem, in their little synagogue, it would herald the start of the Messianic Age.

But now that Rabbi Simon knew the identity of one of these hidden saints, how was he to find the others? He considered approaching the *shamash* directly, but he was hesitant to do so, for he was certain that he would not want his secret to be known. Instead, Rabbi Simon began to watch the *shamash* very closely. Little in his actions betrayed his holiness. True, he lovingly cared for the synagogue and those that worshipped there. But he rarely offered a comment during the time of *shiur,* when they studied between services. Nor did the *shamash* seem to spend a lot of time in the study of the sacred texts.

Then Rabbi Simon noticed something unusual. On several occasions when one man was missing from the *minyan,* the *shamash* went outside, even when he had to face strong winds, and before long he would return with a man who was a stranger. How did it happen that he was able to find so many strangers at the last minute? And Rabbi Simon realized that those strangers must also be hidden saints, and that the *shamash* must have beckoned them by some kind of magic. That is how Rabbi Simon learned that the *shamash* could call upon the other hidden saints anytime he wanted to.

Now Rabbi Simon struggled with himself to decide if he should share his plan with the *shamash.* For if the *shamash* agreed to help, then surely it would be possible for him to beckon the nine hidden saints whose presence in such a holy *minyan* would surely initiate the End of Days. But what if the *shamash* refused to gather that *minyan* , for the very reason of not wanting to hasten the End of Days? Then all would be lost, for surely he could not overcome the opposition of one of the *Lamed Vav Tzaddikim.*

This struggle went on for forty days and nights. During all this time Rabbi Simon observed the *shamash* closely, and noticed that whenever he went outside to find the tenth man for the *minyan,* he always took his Siddur with him. This seemed strange to him. So Rabbi Simon spied on the *shamash* through the window when he went outside one night in the depths of winter. He saw that the *shamash* opened the *siddur* and seemed to daven there in the dark, when all at once a light seemed to rise up from the pages of the siddur. Just then a man appeared out of nowhere, and accompanied the *shamash* into the synagogue. And when he saw this, Rabbi Simon understood that the *shamash* had said some kind of prayer or spell that had both invoked that light and beckoned the stranger who had joined them.

At last, after a long struggle, Rabbi Simon decided to reveal his plan to the shamash. For, he reasoned, if one of the hidden saints turned him down, surely the others would as well. Therefore, what he planned to do had to be sanctioned by heaven, or it would not succeed in any case. And had heaven not shown him the dream that revealed the true identity of the *shamash?*

The next morning Rabbi Simon arrived at the synagogue very early, while the *shamash* was still setting up. He called the *shamash* over to him and, even though no one else was there, whispered to him all that he had learned. In reply, the *shamash* did not deny that what Rabbi Simon had said was true. And, much to his amazement, he agreed to call upon the other hidden saints on the day Rabbi Simon had selected.

On that day Rabbi Simon entered the synagogue to find that the *shamash* had been joined by eight others, every one of whom Rabbi Simon recognized as one of the strangers that had once served as the tenth man. But one of the hidden saints was still missing. Rabbi Simon went over to the *shamash* and asked about the tenth man, who was missing. And in reply the *shamash* said: "It is you that we have been waiting for."

Rabbi James L. Sagarin
Avrom's Light

A blind man, named Avrom, lived in a small village on what was then the border of Russia and Poland. He was born in that village and despite his blindness knew its every corner with the touch of his hand, or the end of his stick. Avrom was very independent and felt good about his ability to get around.

His blindness seemed not to hinder him in the slightest, going about his daily business with a sense of confidence and joy. Until that one day.

He never just stayed in the village. On occasion he would wander into the nearby forest to smell the beautiful summer flowers or sit on the damp moss and listen to the sounds of nature.

One day Avrom got up yearning to take steps beyond his well known, secure "borders." He knew the sun would be setting soon so he'd have to get back to the village quickly for his own well-being. But just a little more time in the forest.

He went on, but soon on that particular day the ground upon which he walked seemed strangely unfamiliar. As he walked deeper and deeper into the forest he cried for help, but no one responded. He felt terribly alone.

He continued on despite his fear, until by chance a young traveler spotted him in a clearing deep within the woods.

The traveler approached him, sensing he was blind, asking him if he needed help in getting out of the forest. Too tired to speak, Avrom gratefully nodded.

Finally, Avrom regaining his strength, told the traveler of his village and where it could be found. Gently guiding him home, the traveler felt good within. Avrom wished to do something special for the traveler in return for his kindness.

When they arrived at Avrom's home, Avrom lit the rarely lit torch next to the door so that the traveler could see, an act which now enabled the blind man to help his new-found friend. For you see, the blind know the importance of bringing light into others lives, that all may benefit from what they have learned from their own experience of darkness.

Beverly Schneider
The Four Leaf Clover Story

We were still four blocks from the cemetery, waiting for the left turn arrow onto North and South Road, when Aunt Bertha began apprising us of the local IT victims: Mr. Gumpfer, from the dry cleaners, had IT; Label's son was taking radiation treatments (you know what that means); and a TV soap opera star had IT (I don't know whether she had IT in real life or only on stage; Aunt Bertha was unclear). Three years earlier, my mother had died from cancer and it was since then that Aunt Bertha had refused to let the dreaded word fall from her lips, as though the name itself evoked the disease's destruction. Protected in this manner, she was free to talk about IT as frequently as possible. My other aunts were not quite ready to play the IT game. They were reading the laundry label of Aunt Lottie's half-priced raincoat. I was confident that Aunt Bertha would be but momentarily thwarted. Having sheltered my own vulnerabilities within a cynical, condescending anticipation of another Kaplan sisters' play of fools, I listened, half-humored, to Aunt Bertha's horror stories as I drove the car down North and South Road, past the house in which I had lived with my family, and pulled into the B'nai Amoona cemetery where my mother was buried.

This visit had started as inauspiciously as the other five visits we had made together these past three years. Exactly one week earlier, Aunt Bertha's daily phone calls had begun. "Becky, I'm going with you. With Aunt Sissy and Aunt Lottie." She was always afraid of being excluded. "We'll go to Ida's grave, I mean Mama's, I mean your mother's grave, first. Then you'll drive us to the other cemetery, Cheser Shamos, uh, no Chaim, no. You know where it is. To see Grandma and Grandpa. You remember them." It was futile to again remind her that her parents had died long before I was born.

I always called my father at the nursing home before I left on these visits. By tacit agreement, we never spoke of my mother's death, which had coincided with his first stroke, but I liked to hear his voice anyway. The phone was busy all morning so I called my sister in Chicago instead. She was bored by these visits, but I felt obliged to tell her in spite of her condescension. "Why don't you just drop off the three Fates at the cemetery and wait in the car while they have a good cry?" she snickered. We chatted briefly about the baby and her new kitchen wallpaper, but she was in a hurry to go bowling. "You don't have anything in particular you want, do you? I've got to be running. I'm late as it is." I hung up, hoping that somewhere between Aunt Bertha's fixations and my sister's denial, there was some room for me.

Nothing seemed to alter these visits. They unfolded like some inexorable ritual upon which I exercised no control. So, the production continued as we parked the car a short distance from my mother's gravesite. "Did you bring enough Kleenex, Becky, should we roll up the windows, it'll get hot, it may rain, are you bringing a purse, Bertha, we won't have to roll up the windows." Eventually, they removed themselves clumsily from the car, with three purses, two umbrellas, and Kleenex for an army.

Aunt Bertha jabbered incessantly.

"Look, isn't it nice how they keep this cemetery," she said, remarking on the black man mowing the grass in the distance. "Not like that awful place where Mama is. Wait till we get to Ida's grave. I'll bet it's clean and neat.

"Quiet, Bertha. You shouldn't say that about Mama's grave. There weren't any weeds on it last year." Aunt Sissy could not tolerate ugliness. It was not respectful and threatened her vanity.

So, this year's theme is Cemetery Upkeep. I sneered silently and began to muse about my grandparents' cemetery with its trees spreading shade and leaves over crowded tombstones and its shabby old men with beards who hovered about with charity boxes, insinuating eyes, and mumbled Yiddish prayers. There, death was really Death and any form of life, even weeds, was counted as victory. I didn't want some hired hand mowing my produce when I died. Manicured cemeteries. Humpf. My poor aunts were certainly of the Depression generation.

"Oh, it was horrible! What do you mean you don't remember? Would you want to lie in a place like that? Forever?" Aunt Bertha baited her.

"When I die, I want to be buried here. Near Ida," Aunt Sissy responded.

"Do you hear that, Lottie? She doesn't want to be buried near Mama and Papa."

"Bertha!" Aunt Sissy was angry but felt obliged to offer an explanation; "I knew Ida longer."

"Oh," Aunt Bertha was stopped by the logic. So was I.

Aunt Bertha had difficulty keeping up with us. Her legs were shorter and she had to read the complete inscription on almost every gravestone. "*Jennie Greenspan,*" she whimpered. "Remember her? *Died 1952.* Lottie, what was her boyfriend's name? You know, the one with the limp...*Sadie Schwartz.*Wasn't that a shame! She's buried near Izzy Yawitz, from the South Broadway dairy. How they used to fight!"

Curiosity overcame Aunt Sissy, who dropped back to join her older sister. They continued their banter, arguing now over biographic details. Aunt Lottie, as usual, walked close behind me. I tried to believe that she identified my silence with quiet dignity, but more often I feared she was simply guarding over me, watching, worrying about my secrecy. I was relieved when she too would stop to glance at the names and dates on the tombstones. Periodically, when she would release a quiet sigh, I would peer at her from out of the corners of my eyes.

This year, the completion of another row of graves and the healthy thickness of ivy that now covered my mother's gravesite gave the illusion of change. It was the same grave, the double tombstone, as yet half-inscribed: *IDA SCHREIBER*, no middle name, *1908-1963.* The four of us formed an automatic semicircle around it. My aunts quieted abruptly and appeared to lose themselves in thought. This was the very moment I dreaded. I never knew what to do, never was in the right frame of mind, never had the right feelings. I resorted to an old exercise, closed my eyes, imagined the white bones, the lost flesh that was now my mother, trying to remember, to feel something, anything. I pictured her skeleton deep beneath the green ivy. "This was my mother. This was my mother," I repeated silently over and over again. But without conviction. I could not bridge the gap between my mother and those bones. I grew irritated with my aunts whose shadows seemed to have returned to haunt me. They took my feelings, they felt more, loved more, missed more. They cried. I didn't. They cried in descending order. Aunt Bertha with a red nose and real tears. Aunt Sissy with pink eyes and sniffling. Aunt Lottie teary-eyed. They always cried in that order. Maybe, if they weren't here, maybe I would dare explode, dare cry. But they were here, watching me, waiting. Thank God my sister wasn't here too. She would mock everything. Even me. Once again I tried to imagine my mother, but even the white bones had been snatched away by these images of my aunts' tears and my sister's sarcasm.

Irritated and dry-eyed, I ended the silence with a signal that I was about to read the *Kaddish,* the traditional Jewish prayer of mourning. I never told them that this recitation with four women was not proper. They would have condemned the religion, would have insisted that the rightful way for a Jewish woman to mourn is to recite the *Kaddish* from her Jewish heart at the cemetery. I did not want to persuade them otherwise for I too liked to hear the incantation of that prayer. Relieved to have a prepared script before me, I read in a rolling rumbling monotone the practiced syllables of generations, until the last cadence was maintained and the silence held for them, a sufficient time to allow for respect. They all stared, motionless, a bit teary. Three sisters, with slightly stooped shoulders, scarves carefully covering their heads, arms forming a "V" at their pocketbooks. I always repented of my anger when I saw them like this.

After a moment or two I bent down, tore up some grass, and solemnly spread it over the ivy-colored grave according to the custom in my family. Moving slowly, significantly, my aunts followed suit. I loved this form, although I never learned its source. It was sweet and simple. Final. Another visit was completed. Thank God, I made it without...

"A four leaf clover!" Aunt Sissy exclaimed, startling our solemnity. We stared in bewilderment as she separated a four leaf clover from the tuft of grass she had uprooted and displayed it to us.

"What're you going to do with that?" Aunt Bertha demanded.

Aunt Sissy spread the grass over my mother's grave with care and delicacy—she loved ceremony; and then, with as noble a gesture as she could manage, she bestowed the single clover upon me.

"Here, Becky. This is yours. From your mother. Now you can have everything you ever wanted."

"Thank you, Aunt Sissy. Thank you." I started to put the four leaf clover into my prayer book with borrowed pomp while Aunt Bertha, so touched by this gesture, began hunting for a clover of her own discovery, "so I can give good luck to Becky, too."

Trying to understand, I stared blankly at her fragile gift. Is this all it takes to stop the writhing and suffering: this delicate, green clover I cradled in my palm? It seemed so easy, and yet such a betrayal. I did not know why my mother died, only that I needed something more to explain her death than this petite symmetry, mute to eternity.

Aunt Lottie stood by me with a puzzled look as though she were trying to understand a naughty game her sisters played. When I turned to her, she urged Aunt Bertha to get up and reminded Aunt Sissy that we still had to stop at Rabbi Halpern's grave before we could leave the cemetery.

I guided them to his grave at the very front of the cemetery. We always stopped there. Nothing spoiled our routine, although Aunt Bertha availed herself of various clover patches surrounding his large, simple tombstone and interrupted our meditation more than once with premature victory cries of discoveries. Aunt Sissy and Aunt Lottie remained solemn, until one of them finally sighed, "Remember how Ida used to say, 'If only Rabbi Halpern were alive now?'" Yes, my mother believed in miracles, too—not in four leaf clover miracles, she was too practical for such flimsy promises—but in Rabbi Halpern. If only he had been alive, her cancer would have gone away.

After corralling Aunt Bertha, we returned to the car and began the short trip to my grandparents' cemetery, a trip which was always a relief to me. Somewhere between the two cemeteries, Aunt Bertha, as usual, started calling her sisters by the Yiddish diminutives used when they were children. The names were soft and enchanting, "Liba" and "Lehya." From the moment I turned left from Olive Street Road into the Chesed Shel Emeth Cemetery, the sisters would argue regarding the location of the grave. It was lane no. 113b or no. 117b, across path no. 7 or no. 3. The argument continued even as we walked. I never minded. Here were the noble dead of a generation I never knew. I imagined myself immersed in that immigrant culture. Many of the graves had faded oval pictures of the dead permanently attached to the tombstones. I was intrigued by the faces. Aunt Bertha's cemetery geography fascinated me. And even though we walked for awhile, we were never lost. She seemed to know everyone on the block.

I forget which aunt was right—they probably each claimed to be— but we finally found the gravesite. "Oh, I knew it all the time. Right across from Minnie Klein. They used to walk to Soulard Market together."

Once again I waited for an appropriate length of time for silent meditation. I looked at my aunts. They did not seem so old. I tried to make them even younger, tried to imagine their bereavement when their mother died. Did they remember her kiss, her face, her voice after all these years? What she wore when she died? Did they try to communicate with her now? "Mama, I've been good, Mama. Honest, Mama. I still learn things the hard way, Mama; I'm learning only now what you meant to me. I never really knew you, Mama." Did they think that she understood her children better now that she was dead? My mother used to make these visits with them. I could not imagine her having had these thoughts and then coming home to us as she did to iron and fry liver. The thought almost made me cry.

Aunt Sissy signaled me to begin the performance of the *Kaddish*. Slow, mournful, illegitimate, I tried to read as correctly as possible, substituting the European pronunciation familiar to the modern Israeli for the one I commonly used. I felt the moment transformed. The sun withdrew respectfully behind a dark cloud, erasing all shadows. An orchestra of birds and spring breezes played an accompaniment in the trees above. My voice chronicled the death of generations.

I was sure I heard my aunts whimpering and slowed my reading to prolong the soulful mood. It seemed the birds honored the changed tempo. The leaves lay still. Only my breathing, somehow, was not completely right; the short gasps incorrectly punctuated the rhythm.

"Oh, I see one. Over there." Aunt Bertha stood next to me with her head bent downwards, eyes studying the weeds. I pretended to ignore her but raised my voice and read in a deliberate style, hoping this gentle reprimand would silence her. It did. Soon after, though, I noticed Aunt Sissy, on my left side, buckling slightly. I cast a reproving glance at her during an awkward breath stop and she straightened guiltily, but momentarily. Soon my peripheral vision became a seesaw. Right side up respectfully; left side down irresistibly until the two sisters succumbed completely.

I continued to read falteringly. The birds and breezes seemed to have deserted me. Only Aunt Lottie stood by me, a faithful attendant to my *Kaddish*. Eventually, when her knees began to bend and then straighten alternately, I knew that in a moment I would remain alone. I read on, compulsively, to silence my fears. Aunt Lottie, don't leave me. Don't leave me unprotected from that wild wind that weaves through these stones, from the vultures that eye my flesh.

"Lehya, look. Here's one. Just look." Her eldest sister bid her join the search. Aunt Lottie smiled at me. Her myopic eyes beseeched forgiveness from me. They begged permission for her indulgence. And then she giggled and stooped to join her sisters.

I managed still to read. Quietly. For spite. I fulfilled the family obligation, alone, deserted by my mother's sisters, self-righteous before the crowds that mingled through the cemetery. And while I read, I thought of the story I could tell of the Kaplan sisters' play of fools. I planned to thank them for providing this grande finale after I finished the *Kaddish,* but I was haunted by Aunt Lottie's smile and could not take my mockery seriously.

So, I read to the last amen and then having finished I turned to look at them.

They did not realize I had completed the *Kaddish* or that it was time to tear up some grass and, in a gesture, end this visit. They were somewhere else. Three women in their fifties crawling over the unkempt grass, as oblivious as they were forty years ago when they made clover rings in Carondelet Park, innocent of the story I would tell. Happily, happily, they understood nothing and trusted everything.

With some coaxing, I gathered them up and brought them safely home. When I said good-bye to Aunt Bertha at her apartment, she promised she would find me a four leaf clover; and if not, well, she would try to find something else that would be just as good. "So, call me. Don't keep away. I've got a telephone, too, you know. Instead of calling Aunt Sissy next time, you can call me."

That was the last time we visited the cemeteries together. Shortly thereafter my father died and I moved to Boston. My trips to St. Louis did not coincide with Mother's Day or fall in the month before Rosh Hashanah when my family customarily made these visits. I kept the four leaf clover that Aunt Sissy had given me in my wallet, grey and rigid, until six years later when I laid it solemnly on a solitary plot, several rows behind my parents' gravesite. It was a freshly sodded, manicured grave. Everything was just as she would have wanted it. Aunt Bertha and Aunt Lottie must have brought the pot of plastic flowers that rested at the head of her grave. They never put flowers on my mother's grave, but I didn't mind; Aunt Sissy was the lady, beautiful and refined, and she loved pretty things. I remembered Aunt Lottie's letters to me describing Aunt Sissy's long battle with cancer and I tried to imagine the angelic expression she was said to have worn when she died.

When I left, instead of tearing some grass, I placed the flattened clover ceremonially on the center of her grave because the irony comforted me and because Aunt Sissy would have appreciated the sentiment. Otherwise, I did not know what else to do.

Henry Schvey
The Funeral

By the time it was my turn, the snow was ankle deep. I watched the row of men and women line up and take long, wood-handled shovels and sprinkle dirt down onto the lid of the coffin.

It was my turn now. I took the shovel and filled it with dirt. It was too heavy to move easily, so I sifted a bit off, then a bit more, until I could lift it easily over the hole in the ground. I closed my eyes and listened closely to the rain of earth spatter softly against the polished cherry wood. Cherry wood—the name made me think of Luden's cough drops. Even the shape was the same. I imagined I could taste and smell the medicinal, cherry-flavored lozenges as I heard the lacquered veneer of the coffin pelted by clods of earth.

It felt like a sin to cover such a beautiful carved thing as a cherry wood casket with dirt. I opened my eyes and saw a fat worm curl for warmth in the mound of dirt and snow.

A cold wind snapped against my cheeks and I saw Aunt Lila, dressed elegantly in black sable and coordinated black lace veil which set off her reddish hair, look towards me. Lila was my father's exact contemporary; they were first cousins and once very close. She was still a woman of elegance and beauty despite advancing years. Her flame-colored hair was now thinning and dyed a rather shocking shade of orange, yet in her eyes there was a sense of aristocratic bearing which subverted any possible mockery. She had lost her husband Morris five years ago now and was at this funeral with a slight, balding man clearly her social inferior. But so what? He was a wonderful companion to adorn these waning years. Last year they had traveled to the Greek Islands and the year before, to China. He was not Morris, not by any stretch of the imagination, but he was Abie: a good, honest man with the appetite of a twenty year old. She loved to watch him eat, kiss his bald spot and make his favorite foods—or rather, have Flora prepare them.

She was becoming more eccentric with each year and knew it. That was why Abie was such a joy. He brought her back to earth from Planet

Lila where it was all too comfortable to reside after Morris' heart attack. Abie was someone to travel with and care for and be just a little bit embarrassed by. He was not Morris and could never be. But he was a man. He never gained a pound no matter how much he ate, and he knew something about ordering wines and how to book a cruise. And he had just enough money so that the disparity in their wealth and upbringing was not entirely grotesque. Things could not have worked out better. "We help each other live," she told me when I last visited her. "I make him believe the little thingy between his legs is more than a small yellow piece of knotted string, and he phones and tells me to do my hair and get dressed days when I want to lie in bed all day with my face in the pillow and think of my poor Morris. God, I would pay to watch him eat." She then touched her wrist bone, protruding angrily through the skin, and caught my eye. I turned away.

The rabbi was a young man in his early thirties whose clean-shaven face seemed embarrassingly fresh and pink. He cleared his throat, bringing up a thick wad of phlegm which he then quickly swallowed. I reflected on our meeting in his study the previous evening, how my brother and sister-in-law had lavishly praised the dead man as a wonderful father and grandfather to their twin sons. How he had made them his special "bloody potion" of grenadine syrup mixed with orange and grape juice and how much the children looked forward to it on their holidays. Liars. Of course, they chose to omit how he literally forced them to drink it up, despite Gregory's fear he was drinking real blood, and how he called Jeffrey "a fairy" for refusing to taste it until he screamed in fear and rage. Their selective memories blotted out so much and were so foreign to my own that I could not speak when asked by Rabbi Jim ("Please call me Jim, not James") to give my own impressions.

My uncle interrupted with the story of his marriage twenty years before which Rabbi Hirschhorn had refused to allow in the temple because Mona was not Jewish. "I have not forgotten what you people did then, and I never will," he said. "What kind of synagogue refuses one of its own? Was it better to have me go elsewhere—to strangers?" He then stood up over the young rabbi in fierce rage. "How could you do this to me?"

"I'm sorry, sir," explained the rabbi, cheeks reddening even more and hacking up more phlegm and swallowing hard, "but you realize this happened a long time ago under Rabbi Hirschhorn's (of blessed memory) tenure here. I am only two years out of Hebrew Union and, of course I am pleased to tell you, our policies now are quite different in matters of marriage outside the faith."

"With all due respect, Rabbi, I don't give a rat's ass where you went to school, who kissed your prayer shawl when you were a baby or which *moyel* performed your circumcision. You follow? What I'm saying is that that bitch Mona would be eating borscht with me today in Miami instead of sitting with her lawyers plotting at which angle to slice off my balls if you people (and I say this with all due respect) hadn't fucked me over."

Here my uncle sat back down and lit an unfiltered Camel. "Mind if I smoke, Rabbi?"

Rabbi Jim chuckled nervously and waved at the NO SMOKING sign while handing my uncle a little blue clay dish with the Star of David to hold his ashes. "I think we can make an exception—under the circumstances," he said.

"Jesus—sorry, Rabbi. I didn't see it—honest to God. Well, in any case, as I was saying, I'm glad you've changed your policy about marrying outside the faith. But it's too little and too late as far as I am concerned." He then took a huge puff from his Camel, let the smoke seem to linger between his lips before sucking it in and inhaling through his nose and mouth. As he exhaled, a big cloud of smoke snaked itself around and through a stack of prayerbooks.

"Yes, sir. I understand your feelings exactly. But perhaps we could return to my sermon tomorrow. Since I never knew your brother I would like to be able to relate your own experiences of the deceased. What kind of man would you say he was...?"

I listened to the rhythmic sway of the words as he began the *kaddish:* "*Yis-ka-dah, vy-yis-ka-dah, she me rabah.*" Delivered by this boy, the holy magic of the prayer for the dead sounded like a play some children had concocted upstairs in the attic while their parents were asleep.

I remembered going upstairs into my secret room with two friends when I was nine or ten. We put on black clothes, white scarves (which served as prayer shawls), top hats and my father's wing-tipped shoes and chanted some magic incantation over our "coffin," the solemn rectangle of a box of Scrabble.

Gradually people began to leave. It was too cold to hang around. Even during the chanting of the *kaddish,* I saw people stamping their feet up and down to keep warm like old draught horses. It wasn't supposed to be funny, but it was, as they clomped time to the boy-rabbi's nasal drone and watched their warm breath freeze in the icy air.

I watched a thick-set Hasid I had never set eyes on before last night *daven* back and forth as he chanted prayers to himself. My father would be furious. For Christ's sake, he isn't even wearing a decent overcoat and the tips of his shoes are scuffed beyond recognition.

My daughter crept up beside me and slid her bare hand into my gloved one. We were still close to the grave and the mound of dirt beside it. Most of the mourners were now gone, and I spotted two skulking gravediggers wearing identical Riverside Chapel windbreakers and wool caps waiting to begin their work.

Instead of leaving with the others, my twelve year old clung to my hand with all her might. I felt her eyes burn toward me—though my head was slightly bowed and faced straight down. The pressure of her hand told me she needed to stay.

Minutes went by and all the other mourners had now gone back to their cars. Even my uncle and cousins were tucked away in warm stretch limos. Car motors were running and everyone was ready to depart, but no one dared leave; not until the dead man's son and his grandchild left the gravesite. I wanted desperately to go too, but the child's hand held me riveted to the spot.

I raised my head an instant—and saw one of the gravediggers scowling. We exchanged an embarrassed glance, and then I nodded to him as if to say, "Just a few minutes more, my friend. I know it's cold. It's cold for us both. But the child is grieving for the death of her grandfather. Surely just a few more minutes won't hurt."

But a few more minutes passed and nothing happened. She continued to squeeze my hand and refused to let either of us budge. I began to feel hot and feverish from the pressure. I wanted to tear my hand away from hers but could not. Instead, I turned my head and watched the gravedigger spit something yellow into the dirty snow.

Finally, realizing we would not be intimidated or leave any time soon, the two men exchanged looks and began to cover up the grave with mounds of earth. In a matter of seconds, the ritual shovelfuls of ceremonial earth from the immediate family were covered over with real dirt. I stood there not knowing why we had to wait. Only when the coffin was completely covered and the grave slowly filled to the level of the other burial plots did my daughter slowly relinquish her grip. She tossed the limp calle lily that hung from her hand onto the grave. Then she released me and turned away. I walked behind. As she led me back to the waiting limo, I felt strangely lightheaded. I could not have said so at the time, but somehow I knew the play of my childhood was over. My own daughter, a child with a white flower, had let the curtain slowly fall

Charles Schwartz
A Tale of Two Antique Dealers

So what do I have against Lefkowitz? Listen, we may both be antique dealers, but like they say, the same sun bleaches linen and blackens gypsies.

It was one morning about five years ago in Bettendorf's that Lefkowitz introduced himself to me. He looked to be in his early forties. He was balding and had a paunch. His eyes were large and worried, his skin yellowish and pockmarked. I didn't like the way he dressed. He wore a shiny suit and a raincoat that hung on him like wilted flowers. I never could understand why anybody would buy cheap clothes. I would rather buy something used of quality. Anyway, he seemed down on his luck, depressed.

I was sitting at the counter and we struck up a conversation. Lefkowitz told me he was new to the area and was looking for work. He said he had a wife who was ill.

"What about your parents?" I asked him.

"I'm an orphan."

"I'm sorry," I replied.

"May I ask what it is you do for a living?"

"You could say that I'm a businessman. I buy and I sell."

That piqued his interest, and soon I was telling him all about the two carat diamond ring that I bought at a flea market last summer for $125 and the star sapphire ring that I found last week when I bought a box of costume jewelry from an estate sale. I looked at my watch and realized I was running late. I tried to leave.

"Please take me with you," he begged. "I want to learn about, about buying and selling."

"No," I said. "That wouldn't be possible."

"Please, my wife is sick. I just want to be a good husband to her. I just want to be able to take care of her."

I knew what he meant. I remembered when I was first starting out. My father didn't want me to go into the business. He wanted me to do something else. But what? Buying and selling is all I know. Antiques is all

I know. Carpets, rings, watches, clocks, mirrors, candlesticks, statues, figurines, china, little boxes, earrings, bracelets, fountain pens, tarnished silver, faces from pocket watches, ticking, ticking, ticking, this is what goes through my head! So I went to Abe Goldberg. Abe had a pawn shop and he gave me a job. My father was angry. But Abe helped me out. Finally, after I dropped a typewriter on the head of the holdup guy as he bent over the safe, my father begged me to come and work for him. Soon I made enough money to buy the house next door to my parents'. And then I married Rose.

"Well, I don't know what you'll get out of it," I said, "but come on. I'm running late."

In the car, he picked up the newspaper where I'd circled the ads with a black pen. He was curious and wanted to know which areas of town the rich people lived in, and which items were the most popular on the local market.

"So let's say you see something good," I explained. "You open up the dresser drawer of some dead old society lady. And you see a Vasheron Constantine. But it's all dingy. The strap is broken. You want it. You can always sell it. It's exactly what you want. But you can't tell them that. You have to close the drawer and bite your tongue. If the relatives get wind of the fact that you want something, forget it. They won't even sell it to you. You have to make them think you're nuts. That you're very eccentric. Look around the house. Find something worthless. An old torn lampshade. Put your hands around it. Ask if you can put everything that you want in a box or on a table. A box is better. Keep moving. Find something else. Broken toasters, bald tires, old musty books. By now they're confused. Wander back to the bedroom. Pick up any piece of junk you see. An old alarm clock, a reading lamp, a quilt, open the drawer, grab the Vasheron. Throw it into the box.

Keep moving. Go into the kitchen. Ask the price on the kitchen set or even the oven. Set everything together. Ask for a glass of water. Say to them, "How much for everything?" They'll say, "you make me an offer." Tell them, "A hundred dollars." Keep a money clip ready with a hundred and fifteen. Reach in to your pocket and start counting. They'll say, "One-twenty-five." Count out the one-fifteen and look them in the eye. Say "Okay, one-ten." They'll take it .

Lefkowitz soaked up what I taught him like a stain. He thanked me a thousand times. That day I took him to three house sales. He stayed quiet and let me do my job. Afterward I let him accompany me while I sold a ring to a client.

This went on for several weeks. I grew to like the guy. We would meet in the mornings at Bettendorf's, and he would tag along. Soon he met all of my regular buyers. I lent him my reference books on jewelry and watches, although I cautioned him about diamonds. I explained that learning how to look at a diamond is an art that takes a lifetime to master.

"Diamonds are a funny thing," I said. "They're so portable and so valuable."

"I heard that Jews and diamonds go together," he said. "Because in the old days, when things got tough, people hid them on their person, and then they could take their wealth with them."

"I've heard that too. I've often wondered what treasures I've passed up at estate sales because the person who died took the secret to their grave."

"I guess every antique dealer must dream of buying some cheap piece of junk and finding some treasure hidden inside."

"Lots of people have dreamed of that," I said.

At one point I didn't see him for a few days. Then one morning I saw him in Bettendorf's and he was wearing a Hart, Schaeffer and Marx suit, just like mine. He had changed his hair style combing it back, the way I do. He even had a new pair of Bally shoes. That's what I wear. He was talking to one of my best clients, Jules Harman. I sat down and to my astonishment Lefkowitz was talking about a necklace he bought at a house sale.

"I remember that sale," I said. "I heard about the necklace. So you were the one to buy it? It has a diamond, right?"

"Yes," he said. He pulled out the necklace from his pocket and offered an eyeloop to Harman.

"Hum," said Harman. "Not bad. Here Harry, you take a look."

I took the necklace and eyeloop and I couldn't believe what I was seeing. It was a clear, slightly blue, well-cut stone. The facets were even, the refraction was good.

"What did it cost?" I said.

"Five hundred," said Lefkowitz.

"It's worth three thousand, or more. You were lucky this time." "Lucky, hell," said Harman. "Didn't Jake tell you? He used to work for Culbertson's in New York. He's a gem appraiser."

"I must have forgotten to mention it," said Jake.

"Well, I'd better be getting a move on," I said. I noticed the newspaper by Lefkowitz's chair. He had the classified ad section open and he had circled several ads.

"Well, see you all later," I said. "Good luck." Lefkowitz stopped calling after that and for the next couple of months I didn't see much of him except when I was coming or going from a sale. We would nod to each other and go on our way. When I would see him at Bettendorf's, we would sit at opposite ends of the room.

Then something happened. He switched into another gear, and all of a sudden, every time I went to a house, he had already cleaned it out. Soon all I heard from everybody in town was Lefkowitz this and Lefkowitz that. He was selling to all of my clients while my own business was declining.

"I don't know, Rose. Maybe I should retire. He's younger and more energetic."

"He's a *schmuck* and you know it," she said. "He pretended he didn't know anything and came in here and swindled you out of your business."

She was right. But what could I do? It was my own fault. Like they say, before you get married, make sure you know whom you're going to divorce.

Then he did something that broke the camel's back. People have to have some limits. Lefkowitz went too far. There was an accountant named Sam Wassermann who liked to collect the best of everything. When Sam died, antique dealers could talk about nothing else. Everybody wanted to find out what he had and to see if the widow wanted to part with any of her treasures. Like they say, a poor man's roast and a rich man's death are both smelled from far off. I waited a couple of weeks to give the widow a chance to sit shiva, and then one evening I called her up.

"Good evening, Estelle. This is Harry Goldstein. You remember me, don't you?"

"Of course I remember you. How have you been?"

"I was sad to hear about Sam. I want to express my deepest sympathies. Your husband was a kind and sensitive man. We'll all miss him."

"Thank you."

"The reason why I'm calling is I want to let you know that I buy and sell antiques and jewelry, and I have experience conducting estate sales if you ever need such a service."

"Why thank you. But I have already made arrangements with another man who was a close friend of Sam's."

"Whom might that be?" I asked, with a sense of foreboding.

"Jake Lefkowitz."

"Jake Lefkowitz? Jake Lefkowitz knew your Sam?"

"It was news to me too. But evidently Sam and Jake went back a long ways with one another. Jake was very upset when he heard that Sam had passed on."

"May I offer a suggestion? For a collection like your husband's, it may be better to have more than one dealer making appraisals."

"Why that seems like a good idea. There's just too much clutter. I'll tell you what, I've invited Jake over for brunch on Sunday. Why don't you come also? Perhaps we can all work together? There is so much junk here, and frankly, I just want to get rid of it because it reminds me of Sam. And then I get depressed."

"I understand completely. See you on Sunday."

For the next several days all I could think about was Lefkowitz and what a cad he was. To tell that poor widow that he and her husband went back for years. This time I wasn't going to be a patsy.

On Sunday morning, I pulled up to the house and before I could knock on the door, to my astonishment, the door opened and out marched Lefkowitz with a bronze bust. My heart dropped through my knees. "Good morning, Harry," he said with a self-assured grin. "What are you doing here?"

"I'm here to help Mrs. Wassermann liquidate her estate."

"Not in a thousand years," he said.

Just then Mrs. Wassermann showed up in the doorway.

"Harry, I'm glad you could make it. Jake is taking that statue to be melted down for scrap. Isn't that nice of him? He said the scrap will bring me twenty-five dollars."

Lefkowitz looked at me as if I were a fly that just flew up his nose. "Let me see that." I walked over to Lefkowitz's car and looked at the carefully wrapped bust in his trunk.

"Looks like Louis the XIV, " I whispered.

"Keep out of this, Goldstein."

"Twenty-five dollars?" I whispered. "This piece is worth at least three hundred."

"Listen," said Mrs. Wassermann, "while you boys get acquainted, I'll set the table. We can get started after we eat."

"Okay," I said. "We'll be there in five minutes."

Mrs. Wassermann went back into the house. Lefkowitz turned to me like a lunatic.

"What is this Goldstein? This is MY sale."

"Oh no it's not. It's Mrs. Wassermann's sale and she asked me to work with you."

"I won't forget this."

"That'll make two of us."

He fell silent for a moment and I could see the gears turning inside in head. "Let's be truthful with each other for once," said Lefkowitz.

"Truth," I said. "Like they say, truth is the biggest lie."

"Can't you forgive me? I was desperate to work."

"Maybe I'll forgive you—after I see how this sale turns out."

"Look. I've seen this collection. It's enormous. I'll make a deal with you. You can have the watch collection, the jewelry, the clocks, the paintings and the carpets. I'll take the rest."

"Which is?"

"Oh, just a few little things."

"Why are you suddenly being so generous?"

"Because I want us to make up and be friends again."

"We were never friends. You used me."

"I know. And I'm sorry. I was wrong. I didn't think you'd help me if you had known the truth."

"I won't argue that right now. Is this division you've come up with fair? Is it even?"

Asking Lefkowitz these questions was like asking my son if he smoked cigarettes after I threatened to kill him if he ever did. I knew he was lying, but I figured I could wait and catch him.

"It's more than fair, Harry."

"Okay, but if you've lied, the deal is off. I would rather lose out on everything here than see you steal it."

Mrs. Wassermann opened the door.

"Come inside boys, we can talk at the table."

"Coming, Stellie," he said.

"Stellie? ... By the way, why did you tell her that you were a friend of Sam's?"

"Did she tell you that?"

When I entered the house I was struck by the richness of the furnishings. Nothing but the best. We sat at an ornate round Italian table in the living room where the widow had prepared a spread fit for a king. Lox, pickled herring, fresh bagels, roast beef, corned beef, pastrami, half-done pickles, potato salad, cold borscht—in short, just about everything a person would dream of. Before I could turn around Lefkowitz had already piled his plate to the edges and was hunched over eating like a *hazer.*

"Take your time Jakie, " she said. "The food isn't running away."

"Jakie? By the way, JAKIE, has your WIFE been feeling better?"

"Oh my," chimed Mrs. Wassermann, "didn't Jake tell you? His beloved passed away last year."

I knew that was a lie because I'd seen her less than a month before at a garage sale. I kicked him under the table, and he moaned out, his mouth too full to scream.

"What is it, dear?" said Mrs. Wassermann, who was at least twice his age. She put her hand out to hold his.

"It's nothing," he said. "I just got a poppy seed caught in my throat."

"That's because you eat so fast. You're a hungry boy, aren't you?"

I couldn't believe what I was witnessing. My faith in humankind was being tested.

"So, Mrs. Wassermann," I said. "Please forgive me for bringing this up, but I never did hear what took Sam in the end."

"A stroke. He died in an instant. He was sitting here at this table, as a matter of fact, doing somebody's taxes. Something went wrong with his calculator. He started tapping on it and the next thing I knew he fell over on the floor. The doctor said he died instantly."

"I'm so sorry," I said. "Sam was a good man. I know he always did the books for the temple free of charge."

"Yes he did," she said with a tear in her eye. I reached out my hand to touch her shoulder.

"Thank you, thank you," she said, pushing away her plate which held an uneaten *knish*.

"It's so sad," said Lefkowitz as he reached over and took Mrs. Wasserman's *knish* from her plate. "You never quite know how lonely the world is until you lose your life long companion. But I'm so glad that we met, Stellie."

Her eyes widened in what I thought was a glimmer of recognition of Lefkowitz's phoniness. Even his mouth wasn't big enough to handle both condolence and *knish*. Both dribbled out. I couldn't take any more.

"Jake," I said, "How did it happen? I mean your wife . . ." Just then Lefkowitz spilled the borscht.

"Oh the table," said Mrs. Wassermann. "Let me get something to wipe that up right away."

"Sorry," said Lefkowitz. "Sometimes I'm a little *klutzy.*"

After she left the room Lefkowitz turned to me and said, "Enough of this, let's get down to business."

"Okay, I guess we can go around the house together and appraise each item and come to an agreement on prices."

"Now you're talkin' Harry. She doesn't have any idea what this stuff is worth."

"Listen you *goniff*, we're not going to steal from her. We're going to pay her a fair price."

"Of course we are," said Lefkowitz as he winked and punched my shoulder. Mrs. Wassermann cleaned up the mess and I started looking around the house. There were beautiful clocks in every room. On the mantle above the fireplace was a real prize, the statue of a woman with an outstretched finger. On her finger was a delicate green crystal sphere etched with a design like a map of the earth and the face of a clock. In the other rooms there were ships clocks, cuckoo clocks, clocks inside of paintings, and musical clocks. This was a real bonanza.

"What did I tell you?" snickered Lefkowitz.

For the next four hours Lefkowitz and I went around the house haggling over the prices to put on each item. When it came to the pieces I was buying he didn't have a problem being fair. When we were discussing a vase or lamp or set of silver candlesticks for him, he tried to chisel. In the end, he came around and agreed to pay the fair wholesale price—which only increased my suspicions.

"Well," he said. "That's seems to be the end of it."

I sat on the sofa and started to add up how much I would offer Mrs. Wassermann for the pieces I wanted. Mrs. Wassermann brought out macaroon cookies and tea. "Let me bring you Sam's calculator," she said to me. "I just bought a fresh battery for it. Would you put it inside?"

She took an old beat up leather briefcase out of the closet. "Here," she said, as she handed me the calculator and the battery.

"Listen boys," she said. "I've been thinking. I trust you both, of course... but I don't feel comfortable with the way we're doing this."

"How do you mean, Stellie?" said Lefkowitz. "This is the deal of a lifetime."

"Exactly," she said to Lefkowitz. "Sam's lifetime. I want to look at each of your appraisals. Then I want to have you bid for each item."

I looked over at Lefkowitz who seemed surprised to learn that Mrs. Wassermann wasn't as dumb as he thought she was. "Okay Stella," I said. "Here's my list. Do you have a Philips screwdriver?"

"For the calculator? I'll get you one."

While she was out of the room, Lefkowitz turned to me like Ivan the Terrible. "You put her up to this."

"I didn't, I promise. But I think it's a smart idea." Mrs. Wassermann came back and handed me the screwdriver.

"I should have said something earlier, but I just started thinking that as long as you're both here, well... why not get the best price I can for things? By the way Jakie, could you bring the bust back inside so Harry can bid on it?"

"But you sold that to me already! A deal is a deal."

"You haven't paid for it yet. Maybe Harry would pay more than the scrap price?"

"No," said Lefkowitz. "He can't buy it. You've already agreed to sell it to me."

"Look Jake," I said. "If you want it so bad, I'm sure we can work something out. Just do as the lady says and go get the bust."

Lefkowitz stood up and stomped out of the house like a spoiled child. I saw that buying that bust had become too important for him. All of a sudden I had an idea.

"Estelle, would you mind making some coffee?"

"Why sure, Harry. I'll be right back."

With both of them out of the way, I opened the back of the calculator. I took out a small scrap of paper out of my pocket and wrote a note: "Dear Estelle, If something should happen to me, look inside the bronze bust." Then I folded the paper and put it inside the calculator. Lefkowitz brought the bust inside and placed it on a table by the door.

"Jake," I said. "I'm afraid that I don't feel your bid of twenty-five dollars on that bust is enough."

Lefkowitz scowled.

"I'll have to examine it," I said. "Look," I said handing him the calculator, screwdriver and battery. "Could you do this? I have to use the bathroom."

I left the room and went into the bathroom. I was nervous. I combed my hair in the mirror. Was I still an honest man? What if Lefkowitz or even Mrs. Wassermann found out? I looked into my own eyes. What did I really want here? Was it to make money or to beat Lefkowitz? In all my years I'd never done anything like this. I felt dirty, yet gleeful. The bait was set and hopefully the fish would bite.

When I came back in the room Lefkowitz and Mrs. Wassermann were talking and sipping coffee. The mood in the room had changed.

"Harry," said Mrs. Wassermann. "Jake feels bad that I sold him the statue and now he thinks I'm trying to take it back."

"But you didn't pay for it, did you Jake?" I said with mock seriousness.

"He's been trying to get me to take a hundred dollars right now. He wants it so unless you want to pay more . . ."

"A hundred? I need to look at it more closely."

"Look Goldstein," he said with all the calm he could muster. "A deal is a deal. You're going to do fine here. We agreed that I would buy the statue."

"That deal is off. Estelle is the one running this show."

"Look, boys, don't argue. Harry ... maybe I'll take the hundred from Jake."

Jake was nodding his head and I figured that he had seen the note. The funny thing was, for some reason, I started believing that perhaps there WAS something in that bust.

"No, I'll pay two hundred."

Mrs. Wassermann gasped.

Lefkowitz's eyes shot poison arrows. "Three-fifty, " he said.

"You know, Jake," I said, "I really like this bust. I wouldn't mind keeping it for myself. Five hundred."

Just after I spoke I realized that Lefkowitz might catch on. Why would I pay five hundred for the bust when I knew that it wasn't worth more than three? I had to be careful.

"Come on, Harry," he said. We both know that this bust isn't worth that much."

"Well," said Mrs. Wassermann. "Jake, do you want to pay more? Or does the bust go to Harry?"

Lefkowitz was silent. He was making me crazy. Had he read the note? What if he hadn't? I'd be out five hundred bucks for the bust.

"I don't know," he said. "Can we wait a few minutes?"

"There's no rush," said Mrs. Wassermann. "We've got all night."

"Never mind," said Lefkowitz. "I want this statue. I will pay one thousand dollars."

"Jake Lefkowitz!" said Mrs. Wassermann. "If this statue is worth a thousand dollars, why did you try to buy it for twenty-five? I'm sorry Jake, but I really don't feel comfortable with this anymore. I think I'd better keep this statue and have it appraised by an uninterested party."

I nodded my head in agreement.

"No," said Lefkowitz. "Legally this statue is mine. You agreed to sell it to me. Until this dispute is resolved I will keep it in my possession."

"I feel sorry for you," she said. " I was willing to give you so much here. But you're a greedy *mumser.* I should have known when I saw you eat. If you take my statue, I'll call the police."

Lefkowitz and Mrs. Wassermann stood toe to toe. I thought she would punch him.

His face was as red as a baby boy after a *bris.*

"Listen ... friends ... enough, sit down. Jake, please let me speak to Estelle for a moment in the other room."

Lefkowitz nodded. Estelle and I walked into the kitchen. "Estelle, listen to me. Take his thousand dollars and give him the bust. It's not even worth three hundred."

"Then why does he want it so much? He's nobody's fool."

"In this case, he might be."

"He can have the bust, but then he leaves."

We walked back into the living room. Lefkowitz was sitting on the sofa holding the bust.

"One thousand dollars," said Mrs. Wassermann coldly.

"I've already written the check." He smiled like the Cheshire cat, handed her the check and left with the statue under his arm.

After we heard him drive away we looked at each other and she said, "Why do you think he wanted it so much?"

"I'm not sure. Have you seen the calculator?"

"It's over there, on the table. You still need to put the battery inside."

I saw the calculator and the screwdriver and the battery in the bubble pack.

"Estelle," I said. "Do you think you could make me another cup of coffee?"

"Of course. It'll just be a few minutes."

When she left the room I opened the back of the calculator. Thank God, the note was gone.

Howard Schwartz

The Book of Vessels

There shall not be found among
you any one that maketh his son
or his daughter to pass through
the fire, or that useth divination,
a soothsayer, enchanter, or a witch.

(Deut. 18:10)

Before Noah Talvi became a Sinologist, he had attended a Yeshivah in Jerusalem. For a while he had believed his destiny to be purely in the study of the Torah and the Talmud and the other sacred Jewish texts. But he had changed his path. He had left the Yeshivah for graduate school. He had studied under Richard Wilhelm in Berlin in the last years of his life and had let him become his master, as the head of the Yeshivah had once been. And like Wilhelm he had devoted himself to the mysteries of the *I Ching,* the 4000-year-old Chinese oracle.

Often Talvi would think to himself that the *I Ching* was in many ways like the Talmud. Both were commentaries on an earlier text. The *I Ching* was said to have evolved from an oracle read from the cracks of a tortoise shell burned in fire. Now it consisted of sixty-four oracles symbolic of all of the possibilities of being. There were many layers of commentary. The earliest meanings were attached to the six broken and unbroken lines, known as hexagrams, which make up each of the oracles. These early commentaries were amplified in the Confucian period, much as the Talmud, itself a commentary of sorts on the Torah, combined two texts, the Mishnah and the Gemara. In both cases there were strata of commentaries, like an archeological dig.

Without a doubt, Talvi's Yeshivah training had prepared him to be a fine scholar. Even the kinds of commentaries found in the Talmud were not dissimilar to those of the I Ching. Both sought to define and interpret life in this world; each drew upon the wisdom of the greatest sages; and each approached the subject in a methodical manner. And this was true despite the fact that the Talmud is, on the surface, the most disorganized of books, the compilation of the minutes of the debates of the rabbis, often shifting from one subject to another. In the *I Ching*, on the other hand, each oracle was highly focused on a specific phase in the cycle of creation. This cycle ended in the 63rd oracle, Completion, and began again in the 64th, Before Completion. And the commentaries were appended not only to the oracle as a whole, but to each of the individual lines that made it up.

More than once, as he meditated upon the rich commentaries of the *I Ching*, Talvi thought that Judaism lacked such a finely crafted system of divination. Impossible as it might seem, Talvi knew with certainty that the I Ching did indeed function as a true oracle. And he did not question this, but gratefully accepted it. Yet Judaism had explicitly rejected such an invaluable tool. For it was clearly written in the Bible about diviners that *because of these abominations the Lord thy God doth drive them out from before thee* (Deut. 18:12). Diviners were in the same category as witches, and the punishment for witches was clearly stated: *Thou shalt not suffer a witch to live* (Ex. 22:18). And this even though the high priests once read the future in the precious gems of their breast-plates known as Urim and Thummin.

In time this thought became something of an obsession. The truth was that Talvi was being called back to his Jewish roots, although he had not yet recognized this. He continued to imagine the effect of young Jews meditating on the lines of the Torah or Talmud the way those who contemplate the Chinese oracle do, knowing that their fate is written there, and trying to decipher the full implications of its meaning. Perhaps it was destined that he should decide to invent such a Jewish oracle, a Jewish *I Ching*.

When the notion of creating such a book of divination out of Jewish sources first occurred to him, Talvi quickly dismissed it. The reason was obvious: it wouldn't work. The mystery of why the *I Ching* served as a viable oracle had been obscured in the 4000 years since its creation. How it had been formed into such a perfect vessel could not really be understood at all. And no amount of scholarship could pierce the veil of this truth. How could one man form another such perfect vessel?

But one day the thought came to him that it is not the *I Ching* itself that serves as the oracle, but a benevolent spirit that animates it, which always makes its replies inevitable, and never arbitrary. This spirit used the oracle as a vessel through which to speak. All that this spirit required was a vessel. The more perfect the vessel, the more accurate the reply. That is why the *I Ching* worked: it was a perfect vessel.

At this point Talvi thought of the wonderful myth of the Ari, as Rabbi Isaac Luria was known, about the Shattering of the Vessels. According to this myth, at the time the world came into being, vessels filled with light emanated from the essence of the Holy One. For some reason—not even the Ari seemed to know why—the vessels shattered and scattered sparks of that primordial light all over the world. According to the Ari, this was the reason the Jewish people had been brought into being—to gather those scattered sparks wherever they had fallen. Finding one of these sparks was, for the Ari, the same as performing a good deed, or *mitzvah*. He called this part of his cosmology Gathering the Sparks. Each spark raised up from where it was hidden was a step towards restoring the shattered vessels. This notion of scattered sparks had caught the fancy of Jews everywhere, who finally saw a purpose in their wide dispersal around the world, as well as a goal towards which to strive, the restoration of the primordial world.

Now Talvi wondered if he might somehow create a vessel through which the spirit might speak to his fellow Jews, alerting them to every kind of danger, as the Chinese oracle was able to do. The notion drew him on, even though he always recognized that it was a mad project, or at least that it would be regarded as such in the eyes of the world. What did the Jews want with a book of divination? They had their books, and they had decided long ago what to do with diviners.

At first Talvi did his best to put these thoughts out of his mind. But having thought of the notion, Talvi's imagination proceeded without his permission to conceive ways the oracle might be brought into being. For example, the *I Ching* consists of sixty-four oracles, known as hexagrams. And in the Kabbalah, the texts of Jewish mysticism, there is frequent reference to the Thirty-two Paths. At first Talvi considered creating an oracle of thirty-two vessels, but then he considered the fact that the process of Ari's cosmology consists of two stages, the Shattering of the Vessels and the Gathering of the Sparks. If he retained the sixty-four oracles, he could divide half of them into oracles of the broken vessels, while the other half would constitute those in the process of being restored. This followed as well the basic assumption of the *I Ching*, that change is the primary law of the universe, and that there is a predictable pattern to this change. The meaning was obvious: if the oracle received was one of those of the broken vessels, the overall fate revealed a condition of unravelling, a world under the sway of the Fall; but if it fell into the second half, it revealed that the process of repair had begun, and the oracle would delineate how far it had progressed towards the restoration. This decision greatly pleased Talvi, because it enabled him both to remain true to the myth of the Ari and to the structure of the *I Ching*.

With this structure in mind, so similar to that he knew so well, Talvi began to create his oracle in earnest. One of his first major decisions was what to call it. It would not do to call it a Jewish *I Ching*. No, he would give it a title that echoed the Kabbalistic treatises that so abounded in the Middle Ages, all of which were called the Book of Something or Other. Talvi considered several titles: *The Book of Paths,* after the Thirty-two Paths; *The Book of Facing,* because whoever used it would be facing his innermost self; and *The Book of Vessels,* since the oracles would serve as a vessel through which the spirit might communicate, and because of the teachings of the Ari. It was this last title that he chose, in its Hebrew version, *Sefer ha-Kelim.*

Now that he had a book with a title and a structure, Talvi began to collect material that he might insert into the various oracles. He intended to model the book fully on the *I Ching*. He chose passages from the Bible as the primary judgments. These were modified and explained by passages from later texts, such as the other books of the Bible, the Talmud, the Midrash and the texts of Jewish mysticism. Soon Talvi found himself deeply involved in reading Jewish texts, selecting passages that might serve as the kind of commentaries required for an oracle.

As his work progressed, very slowly, Talvi began to consider the futility of creating a sacred book in a secular age. It might well be regarded as nothing more than one man's invention. A mere pastime. Who would have faith in it as an oracle? And Talvi was certain that without this faith, the oracle would not function. For the divine spirit only responds if its existence is recognized. It was at this time that the thought first occurred to him of presenting the book as if it had been a recently discovered ancient text.

Over the ages many others had come to this difficult pass. In the first few centuries after the books of the Bible were codified, many books were written in the biblical mold in the hope that they would be added to the sacred texts. But they were not. These books were classified as Pseudeipigrapha, and included The Book of Enoch, among others. Perhaps the most famous case of such a literary fraud was that of Moshe de Leon, who claimed in the 13th Century to have discovered a text written by the 3rd Century sage Simeon bar Yohai. It was known that Simeon had spent thirteen years in a cave, hiding from the Romans, who had condemned him to death. What had he done all that time? Moshe de Leon supplied the answer: he was writing *The Zohar*. Remarkably, the hoax was accepted as authentic, even though there were a great many suspicions at the time that Moshe de Leon was the true author of the text. Even his wife had confirmed these doubts, asserting that he had composed the manuscript himself. Nevertheless, in a few centuries *The Zohar* had become recognized as the central text of Jewish mysticism.

Talvi began to explore the history of divination within Judaism prior to its being forbidden and afterward. He found, to his surprise, that not only had the High Priests of the Temple used the stones of their breast-plates to divine, but divination was widely practiced by the people in many ways. Not only by the flight of birds and by singing, but also by fire, water, earth and air, by dreams, by lots, by the staff or wand, by oil and by cups. Yet no well-structured book of divination had been created, since the practice was forbidden by the rabbis, obeying the biblical injunction. It was carried on by the people, though, much as were many other superstitious practices.

The more Talvi thought over the matter, the more it became apparent to him that the only hope of the book's being accepted as a sacred text was to attribute it to another, of an earlier age. Since the book drew on texts through the 16th Century, Talvi decided to attribute it to the Ari, Rabbi Isaac Luria, himself. Talvi studied the teachings of the Ari and those of his disciples, and in time it became apparent that rather than attribute the book to the Ari, who left no writings of his own, it would be better to attribute it to the Ari's primary disciple, Hayim Vital. It was while studying the career of Hayim Vital that Talvi discovered the title of a lost book of his, and he could barely believe his eyes: it was called *Sefer ha-Kelim*.

In this discovery Talvi read the hand of fate. He did not imagine, or course, that his book was similar to that of Hayim Vital, but the fact that a book had existed with that title, by that author, and had been lost was perhaps too much of a coincidence. Talvi began to believe that in preparing his oracle for the world he was serving the intentions of the Divinity. It was at this point that he cast the *I Ching* and asked if his oracle was destined to be. The reply astounded him: "Ten pairs of tortoises cannot oppose it. All oracles—including those read from the shells of tortoises—are bound to concur in giving him favorable signs."

With this reply Talvi's resolve was confirmed. He would continue both in the creation of such a text, and in the effort to offer it to the world as the work of Hayim Vital. Thus, while he worked at a snail's pace in seeking out the sacred texts that would serve his oracle, at the same time he became a scholar of the school of the Ari and of his disciple, Hayim Vital, in particular. He held with his own hands the existing manuscripts written by Hayim Vital, and in the course of his readings he came across something that truly amazed him. For in one obscure kabbalistic text of the 17th Century it was noted that some claimed that the lost book, *Sefer ha-Kelim*, had been used as a book of divination. When Talvi first read this, a chill ran up and down him. And that was the first time he began to think that perhaps he was not inventing a book, as it had appeared, but rather restoring one that had disappeared, without any guidelines but his own intuition.

This discovery and its implications greatly affected Talvi. For one thing, it changed the emphasis of his wide research. From that time on he limited the texts from which he drew his sources to those mentioned in the writings of Hayim Vital or one of the other disciples of the Ari. Of course this in itself was a vast library, but it was also a highly focused one. And from the time this change in sources took place, a change also

occurred in the manner of his locating the proper passages for his oracle.
Now they seemed to leap out at him from the page. Soon he was able to
dispense with reading the whole text from beginning to end. Instead he
merely opened pages at random, selected in the same way a line to read,
and inevitably it was one that he required for his work. So it was that Talvi
came to think of himself as collaborating with a spirit, and in time this
spirit became a very specific one, none other than Hayim Vital himself.

At first it had appeared that Talvi's project was to take him many years.
He had estimated twenty. But all at once the pace of his creation quickened
far more than he had ever expected. The lines that leapt forth each fell into
the proper place. And Talvi found that he was working with an assurance
far greater than he had ever known.

In the third year since he had conceived his strange project, Noah Talvi
completed it. With trembling hands he cast the oracle for the first time, and
received for the reply one of the very first lines of Genesis: *And he looked
upon His creation, and He saw that it was good.* And then Talvi knew that he
had indeed served as a vessel, as he had hoped.

Now the remaining task that confronted Talvi was to present the text
as a long-lost manuscript. This was the most difficult part of all, because it
went against all of Talvi's well-developed scholarly instincts. He argued
with himself over this, and even raged. And in the end he concluded, as he
had at the first, that this was the only way the book would be acceptable
to the world at large. For Talvi believed that he had truly created, or
recreated, an oracle that could serve as well as the *I Ching* itself.

In his studies of the Ari and his circle, Talvi had learned that the center
for kabbalistic studies had moved in the next century from Safed to Padua
in Italy. Talvi had decided not to attempt to write a manuscript in the
handwriting of Hayim Vital, for that could too easily be shown to be a
forgery. Instead he planned to present a manuscript which would claim to
be a copy of Hayim Vital's, deriving from the 17th Century.

Once he had made his decision, Talvi worked with the same single-
minded determination that he had to create the oracle in the first place.
He was able to locate paper and inks dating from the 17th Century, and he
studied the handwriting of some of the minor kabbalists in the circle of

Luzzato. When he actually wrote the text, Talvi felt inspired as he had never felt before, and his hand moved as if the spirit of that obscure scribe had taken possession of him. In less than a month the copy had been made. Talvi even included several easily detectable errors, since even the best copyists inevitably let a few errors slip through. Then he traveled to Italy, taking the manuscript with him, and on his return he announced that he had purchased it there.

In the world of scholarship news does not travel very fast, except in rare instances. But the discovery of a text attributed to Hayim Vital that was intended as a book of divination was quite remarkable, and the discovery was announced and discussed not only in obscure scholarly journals, but even in the newspapers of the world that found room for such strange tales. After all, the practice of divination had clearly been forbidden to the Jews, and yet here was a manuscript that seemed to demonstrate that divination had indeed taken root among the people.

As might be expected, the scholarly debate over the validity of the book was heated. Those scholars who were certain that the injunction against divination had been obeyed by the rabbis wrote scathing attacks on its validity, while those scholars who had long suspected the kabbalists of having moved beyond the usual borders of mainstream Judaism claimed that they were not surprised, and tended to accept the authenticity of the book.

But it was not in the scholarly world, surprisingly, that the book had its greatest impact. In a short time it had been published by a small press in Jerusalem, and to the amazement of everyone, it went through half a dozen printings within weeks of publication. A brief article in *The Jerusalem Post* caught the eye of a visiting editor in Israel, and he quickly purchased the translation rights. Within a year the book had been published in English, French, and Spanish editions, and it soon became apparent that it was not being read as a scholarly discovery, but being used as an active oracle.

Noah Talvi, who viewed all this activity with considerable amazement, began to feel that he had restored to the world something that it had badly needed. But now that his work was complete he felt strangely empty, uninspired, and unwilling to undertake anything else. Although he received many invitations to speak on the manuscript he had discovered, and many requests for interviews, he rejected all of these, and added nothing to the ongoing debate.

The discussions among scholars are often intense, but they are rarely violent. Yet the debates about the authenticity of *The Book of Vessels,* as it was known in English, became most heated among the most religious Jews. By and large, these Jews angrily denounced the book as a forgery, since the penalty for diviners was clearly demarked in the Bible. Yet there was a small group of modern kabbalists among them who were able to recognize the logic of such a book among the disciples of the Ari. After all, the Ari had been able to divine mysteries from a flock of sparrows or in the trembling of leaves. Nothing escaped him—he understood every sign.

These kabbalists began to use *The Book of Vessels* as it was intended—as an oracle—much to the chagrin of the others. Attempts were made at excommunication of those using the book in this fashion, and several bookstores were broken into, and all copies of the book taken away.

The opponents of the book would have preferred, of course, to burn it. But that option was not available to them, as one of their most honored rabbis was quick to rule. After all, the book consisted entirely of texts taken from sacred books, and sacred books could never be burned. Instead, all the copies of the book that were collected were treated like worn out holy books and hidden away in a secret *Geniza.* This action, however, outraged those who had come to strongly believe in the power of the book, and led to the first raid by Jews on a *Geniza* in Jewish history, in which all of the stolen copies of the book were stolen back. In this fashion the battle raged on.

During this time Noah Talvi was very restless, for he had not expected the book to create such a divisive controversy. To see for himself that the antagonism against the book was as great as claimed in the newspapers, he attended a rally against the book in Mea Shaarim in Jerusalem. Standing at the back of the crowd along with several other curious onlookers, Talvi was suddenly recognized by one of the religious opponents of the book, who had seen his picture in a newspaper. He screamed his discovery to the others, and all at once, as hysteria descended on the crowd, Talvi suddenly realized that his life was in danger.

Only a few seconds later the first stone struck him sharply in the head, and he lost consciousness. It was followed by a myriad of others, for all of those present wanted to share the guilt for that murder, since they regarded it as simply obeying the Law of God. Talvi's murder was reported around the world, and for a short time was much discussed, but before long it was dismissed as a strange convulsion such as sometimes occurs among the most fervid believers and was soon forgotten. No one was ever brought to trial.

Seven years later, in Safed, a *Geniza* dating from the 16th Century was discovered beneath the foundation of one of the synagogues of the Ari that was being restored. A handful of new manuscripts were discovered, including two written by disciples of the Ari. Among them was the lost book *Sefer ha-Kelim* of Hayim Vital. To the amazement of the scholars who found and confirmed this, the manuscript, written in the hand of Hayim Vital himself, was identical, word for word, with that published by the late Noah Talvi, except for a very few errors that had crept into Talvi's copy.

Laya Firestone Seghi
Going to the Mikveh

Whatever other spiritual value may have been linked to her monthly immersion in the ritual bath, what Brenda enjoyed most about the *Mikveh* was the time to herself. Between raising a child, teaching, taking an evening course, and maintaining relationships with her husband, family and friends, not to mention all the other mundane activities from buying stamps to folding laundry, whenever she picked up the phone to make an appointment with Tzippy the bath attendant, she realized that once again, another month had gone by and she had not made any other time just for herself. To be alone. Why did it seem so impossible to arrange? After seeing the pattern repeat itself month after month, Brenda finally accepted her unkept promises to herself as inevitable, settling for the private time preparing for the ritual bath as her own guaranteed right. She could count on that time as regularly as she counted on her monthly period.

It was during that time alone with herself, as she brushed her teeth, carefully removed all traces of make-up, and cleaned beneath her nails, that she stopped to consider the thoughts that crossed her mind. Of course, she was aware of a steady stream of thoughts coming in and out of her mind at all times of the day or night, but only when she had this time alone could she actually stop to take note of them. As she removed her rings, her wedding band last of all, she often thought of the first moment it had been placed on her finger as she stood under the *chuppah,* aware of the many eyes upon her. That circle had bound her web of consciousness together with Jack's, but when she removed it, as she did every month at the *Mikveh,* it was as if her consciousness resumed its totality within itself.

That September she and Jack left Cleveland to explore England together. They had been looking forward to letting go of the layers of responsibilities they had gradually taken on over the years—obligations from their parents, their work, and their roles in the community. They had put money aside and now that Jack finally reached his Sabbatical year, they could afford to travel for at least six months without having to worry about finances. They planned to travel through Great Britain and as the weather got colder, they would head south to France, Spain and Italy. The thought of traveling in places where no one would know them seemed appealing to them both. Their two year old daughter Mindy would be the only one who knew who they were.

After their first night in a room in London, they took to the streets to explore. With Mindy swinging between them, they absorbed the oddities of English as a foreign culture—men in bowler hats, familiar words spoken "properly" as if in a parody of themselves, double-decker buses. They were eager to take it all in. In their first inquiries about finding a used car, they were directed to the street by the Australian Embassy where travelers gathered to buy and sell cars and vans. Although they hadn't planned on it, as soon as Brenda stepped into that particular used van, she realized it was perfectly designed for them. It had everything they needed to make it their own little home on wheels for the next few months. Behind the front seat, there were kitchen cabinets, a sink, a stove, a dining area with comfortable seats that converted to beds, and an upper deck with a safety panel that would be Mindy's crib. It even had curtains, plus an extra bonus of a tent that could be set up to extend off of the van's sliding doors for camping out. They decided to buy it immediately and soon they were ready to go.

The countryside was more beautiful than Brenda had ever imagined it could be. Singing with Mindy as they drove, they first visited Cambridge and then traveled north along the eastern coastline. Brenda was delighted with traveling through the landscape in autumn. The van gave them the ability to move with comfort, stopping whenever they wanted to look more closely at the castles or cathedrals, rock fences or cultivated gardens, the flowers, the factories, or just to walk the rugged coast. As she started counting the clean days following her period, four more to go, where would she be, three more days would it be York, Sheffield, or Gateshead, there was something reassuring about knowing that wherever she might be in this country, her time alone in the *Mikveh* would come.

As it happened, they pulled into the narrow streets of Gateshead about three thirty on a Tuesday afternoon. That would give them a few hours to shop for dinner, investigate where the Jewish part of town was so they could stock up on some kosher food, find the Mikveh and make an appointment. They stopped and got some meat and fresh vegetables they could stir-fry with rice for dinner. Then Brenda left Jack inside preparing dinner and playing with Mindy while she went out with a book in hand. It was the *Jewish Travel Guide*, a gift their rabbi had given them before their trip so that wherever they were they could find the local Jewish resources—synagogues, kosher butchers, ritual baths, and contact people for hospitality. Brenda looked for a telephone to call the *Mikveh*.

"Of course, my dear," the very British voice replied at the other end of the phone. "Someone will be here to attend to you at the *Mikveh*. Can you be here at seven o'clock?"

Brenda sighed with relief. It seemed that no matter where she and Jack had gone in England, even with Mindy bouncing along at their sides or on her Daddy's shoulders, they encountered an officious reserve. Everyone was polite, but no more than that. The courtesy seemed to serve almost as a barrier, as if to say, "this far and no further." But now, in this general atmosphere of cool British propriety, there was a pool of living waters into which she would descend. Rain water, gathered directly from the vast sky above. That reservoir of collected water would run into the ritual bath to create a sacred space for her and other Jewish women who sought it. In the privacy of the *Mikveh*, nature had been enclosed for their own sanctuary.

"I'll be there at seven," she replied. "And thank you. I'm so glad you're there."

When she walked up the steps to the building that housed the *Mikveh*, Brenda chuckled to herself. Who would know from the outside what goes on in here, she thought. The building was brick and plain-faced. Inside there was a corridor with a room off to one side where the attendant was seated. She was a large woman about sixty years old. Her hair was covered with a scarf pulled down on her forehead. She wore thick stockings, walking shoes, and a heavy cardigan over her dark, tweed skirt. Her style certainly seemed designed more for warmth and comfort than for fashion, but from the looks of her, beauty had never been even a consideration. Her mode was function, not style.

"Come, my dear. I'm Mrs. Ginzberg. We spoke on the telephone. I see you found us all right." Mrs. Ginzberg stood up and stepped forward to meet Brenda. "Let me show you where to put your coat." She waited as Brenda pulled herself out of her bright jade green jacket and then took it in her hands as if it were an unfamiliar flower she held before placing it in a vase. Leading Brenda into a small supply room, she hung the jacket on a coat rack. "What do you need to prepare yourself? We have all kinds of supplies—pumice stones, nail polish remover, toothpicks. Here, why don't you take this whole shoe box full and use whatever you need."

This was the only *Mikveh* Brenda had ever entered other than the one back home. The first time she went in Cleveland was the day before her wedding. During a brief orientation by Tzippy the bath attendant, she had been told that the laws of ritual purity were designed not only for physical and spiritual purification, but to enhance the love between a husband and wife. By limiting and regulating their sexual encounters, Tzippy told her, the relationship with her husband would constantly be renewed. It sounded somewhat idealistic to Brenda at the time, but she continued to go to the *Mikveh* monthly until she became pregnant, and then again after Mindy was born when her menstrual cycle resumed. Over time, in the abstinence during and following her menstruation, she gradually became aware of the difference between sexuality and intimacy in her relationship with Jack.

Brenda was curious about what things would be constant and what might vary from one *Mikveh* to another, just as she had been curious about the different customs in the various synagogues she had visited, even though the Hebrew liturgy was usually the same. At the other *Mikveh,* the supplies were much more limited. She had been given only soap and a towel. But detailed instructions about preparing one's body—washing thoroughly, removing jewelry, bandages and make-up, combing the hair to separate the strands—had been posted on the wall along with the Hebrew blessings printed below both in Hebrew and transliteration.

Mrs. Ginzberg led Brenda from the waiting room down a passageway to a private bath and dressing room. Two towels and a wash rag hung on the towel rack, their worn out nub a testimony to the many bodies that had already used them. "The second door leads directly out into the

Mikveh. Just ring the bell when you're ready and I'll meet you on the other side," she said, pointing to the brass bell on top of the toilet tank. "But take as long as you like. I'll be reading my book in the other room." Brenda thanked her and closed the door.

Ah, the silence. She turned the faucets to the tub on and watched the water force its way onto the porcelain tile. The steam rose. It was a silence she knew well. A silence of dampness, of fog. A rich silence in which the center of her own being resonated. As she watched the flow of the water gradually reaching its way to the back of the tub, she remembered the story that Tzippy, the attendant at the Cleveland *Mikveh,* had told her. One night after showing her to the dressing room, Tzippy grabbed her arm.

"Brenda, I have to talk to you. I have to talk to someone and you're the only one I can trust. I know you don't gossip; you've never said a word to me about anyone else."

Brenda had been taken by surprise. And then, sitting on the covered seat of the toilet, Brenda listened as Tzippy leaned against the vanity and poured out her story.

"She came here just like you or anybody else. Her name was unfamiliar, but so—I don't know everybody and maybe she was new in town. She came into this very room that you are using tonight. Can you believe me when I tell you that my husband has been seeing another woman and that now he sends her to the *Mikveh* to be attended by me?!"

Unsure of how to react, Brenda stalled by gathering more information. "How do you know?" she asked, an obvious question that untapped even more of Tzippy's torrent.

"How do I know? I'll tell you, Brenda. You won't believe it. I haven't told anyone. The woman, she says to me, 'Mrs. Cohen. I'm new at this. I want to make sure I do everything just the way I'm supposed to. This is my first time.' Then she hands me a piece of paper and says, 'I brought everything I need. It's all written down here. But would you go over it with me so that I do it right?'"

"Brenda, it was as if my heart jumped out into my hand. As soon as I looked at that paper. I'm telling you, it was Shmuel's handwriting, no question about it. I know that handwriting anywhere. It had a list of items to bring, everything from the toothpicks for under the nails to the large-toothed comb."

Brenda leaned over the side of the tub and felt the hot water, a bit too hot, and opened the cold faucet to cool the temperature down, as she remembered Tzippy's words spilling out all over.

"What could I do? I mean, she must have been completely innocent. She had no idea who I was. After all, this is the only *Mikveh* in town and he wanted her to go. It's him I wanted to kill, and her, I felt sorry for her, really sorry. She wanted to do right by him, just like I always wanted. What I didn't do for him! But did I please him?"

Brenda remembered wondering how long Tzippy's story would go on. She asked, "What did you do, Tzippy?" hoping it wasn't too obvious she was rushing the story forward.

Tzippy had continued to tell her story, oblivious to Brenda's prompting. "Well, I did with her what I would do with any young bride that comes to the *Mikveh* for the first time. I told her how to prepare herself, to make sure her hair was combed and separated, and I even watched as she dunked herself three times in the *Mikveh*. Each time I said, 'kosher,' but inside I was screaming, 'It's *treife,* it's *treife.* How could Shmuel do this to me behind my back?"

"And what did you say to him?" Brenda had asked.

"To him? To him I said, 'I gave you six children. I married you right out of the Yeshiva when the only two things you knew about were *G'mara* and basketball. And now you want to go and learn about women? You want to learn? Why didn't you come to me to teach you?' That's what I told him. I've been crying for a week; my eyes are like sponge balls. He calls my mother up and says, 'She's crying, what should I do to make her stop?' He actually says that. And my mother tells him, 'If you did something that hurt her, say you're sorry.' Oh Brenda, I don't even know why I'm telling you this."

Brenda looked at her, for the first time really. Tzippy actually wasn't bad looking. Her lips were thin but well formed, turning up ever so slightly at the corners as if she were about to smile, even though she wasn't. Brenda noticed the network of fine red lines in Tzippy's eyes and the puffiness of her lids. Because Tzippy had never called attention to herself in any way, Brenda had come to think of her as she did the cashier at the supermarket or the toll booth attendant—there to provide friendly service without making any personal demands. Now that she looked closer, Brenda saw Tzippy as more than just a *Mikveh* attendant. Her human quality was embodied in her pain. What good had all of her carefulness about the *Mikveh* done for her? Did it guarantee her husband's love and loyalty? No. Did it protect her from betrayal? No.

Brenda had answered Tzippy with some hopeful optimism. It wasn't simply to comfort her, but because she actually believed it.

"Maybe it was good that you are the attendant here," she had said, "because if you weren't, you wouldn't have found out what was happening. And now you have a chance to repair the damage. Maybe you and Shmuel were missing out on something you didn't even know about." Brenda saw a glazed look in Tzippy's eyes as if very, very deep down, some part of her knew the truth.

"Talk to him," she continued. "Make him understand that even if it's not actually forbidden in the Torah for a man to be with more than one woman, it's wrong. He must know that it's wrong. Even if he tells himself that since she's not married it's not really adultery, and that Abraham had a concubine, and Jacob had four wives, and on and on until he finally believes that it's OK for him too. And if he doesn't accept that he's doing something wrong, talk to the woman. You know she'll be back if they're together because Shmuel wouldn't want to sleep with her unless she went to the *Mikveh*."

Thousands of miles away, from one *Mikveh* to the other, Brenda followed her memory and her thoughts. Her tub had filled half way and Brenda began to undress. As she stepped in, she remembered the unsatisfactory ending to the story with Tzippy. That evening Tzippy had promised Brenda she would talk to Shmuel. Just because she had been hurt didn't mean she had to be destroyed. She could survive this.

But the next month, when Brenda called for her appointment and when she came, Tzippy acted as if nothing had happened.

"How are you?" Brenda had asked, and Tzippy responded flatly,

"Thank G-d," looking away in her usual servile manner.

Without a meeting of their eyes, Brenda couldn't think of any way to reopen their conversation of the previous month. Tzippy's inner world had been put off limits to Brenda and as she soaked in the tub months later, Brenda wondered what had developed between Tzippy and her husband. The night they had spoken together in the dressing room, Brenda had based her response to Tzippy on the belief that even the most negative conditions can be transformed. Perhaps she was naive, but Brenda believed that with pure intention, the disasters that people encounter can be transformed to blessings. She'd had that argument many times in college and mostly she was laughed at for her idea that problems come at a particular time and for a particular reason. "Right," her college roommate taunted. "And I suppose the people dying of starvation right now in Africa have the opportunity to become spiritually cleansed as they waste away."

Although she couldn't respond forcefully to all retorts, Brenda believed deeply that there was some meaningful order in the world. In this case she thought Tzippy's distress might open the way for her to reach a deeper understanding of her husband and a more fulfilled relationship. But Tzippy's business-as-usual manner suggested to Brenda that nothing at all had changed. Perhaps the other woman had continued to return to the *Mikveh* month after month, immersing herself for purity as Tzippy looked on with her eyes while looking away with her heart. Brenda still did not know whether Tzippy's domestic crisis had been resolved or just accepted. And she also wondered, usually when she had the peace of mind to do that in the *Mikveh,* whether her own knowledge of a secret wrong carried with it some obligation. She worried that question back and forth like a hangnail, pulled between silently honoring the secret and intervening somehow to help relieve a pain.

The tub was just what Brenda needed. She could feel the coldness of British manner being steamed out of her bones. As she leaned further back into the water, submerging herself up to her chin, she became aware of the subtle shifts of energy in her body. Gradually, with expanding awareness, her back adjusted itself ever so slightly and she felt the energy flow freely in alignment again. The bath before the ritual bath helped clear away

whatever got in the way of her natural attunement. She was coming back
to herself again.

That coming home to herself didn't have to happen in the *Mikveh*.
Brenda knew that theoretically it could happen anywhere. Whenever it
happened, wherever it happened, she noticed a quiet celebration bursting
forth inside. Awareness would move in, turning clouded confusion and
chaos to clarity. Suddenly, everything seemed exactly as it was meant to be.
No coincidences. No mistakes. And then she would perceive her own
actions, however insignificant on the surface, as infused with purpose. In
her routine state of mind, Brenda would think of her actions and
encounters as random. But during times of inner celebration, well then, of
course, whatever happened would seem to be just what was meant to be.

By the time Brenda rang the brass bell for Mrs. Ginzberg to attend to
her, the surface tension she had been living with for days was released. The
bathtub had softened her brittleness and opened her to relax. She stepped
down the steps as Mrs. Ginzberg looked on. She squatted as if to sit in the
water, but then lifted her feet from contact with the floor so that even the
souls of her feet were touched by water. The water rose above her neck,
nose and eyes until she could feel her freshly combed hair let loose in every
direction. She surrendered. Water entered her. And the water held her.

"Kosher," Mrs. Ginzberg intoned, seeing that Brenda was in total
contact with the water. Gravity had assumed a new relationship to her. She
had reentered the womb of life. She felt beyond gravity. Her rounded body,
knees rising toward her chest, might have looked to Mrs. Ginzberg like an
adult fetus. The water connected with every surface of Brenda's body, like
embryonic fluid, nurturing and containing her. Something even beyond
memory happened here. As she lowered herself all the way down, she let
herself merge with that life force.

After she came out, patted herself dry, put on fresh underwear and the
dress she had folded in her bag, Brenda's mind was free of thought. Her
entire being was alive, sensing the smooth rayon fabric of the print rubbing
against her skin, the comb squeaking through her hair, the dampness of her
skin. She left the bathroom and went to the supply room to pick up her
jade jacket when Mrs. Ginzberg came out of her room, book in hand, and

said, "Excuse me. Someone else using the *Mikveh* here tonight wanted to meet you."

Brenda was curious and followed Mrs. Ginzberg into the room in which she had been reading. A woman of medium build and dark brown eyes stood up. Her cheeks were flushed, shining as if they had just been polished, and the few locks of hair exposed from beneath her wig were still moist. "I'm Judy Kaplan," she said, stretching out her hand toward Brenda. "I do beg your pardon for being so forward, but I saw the van outside when I came in and thought perhaps we have a traveler visiting our *Mikveh*."

Brenda shook the woman's hand. "You were right. We *are* traveling. My husband is waiting outside with our daughter."

"I saw them on my way in tonight," Judy said. "Your daughter is precious. She was blowing bubbles and laughing as they floated away. Adorable. Now, I know it might be a bit awkward to explain to anyone how we met—after all, our coming to the *Mikveh* is such a private matter—but please, won't you and your husband and your little girl join us for dinner tonight?"

Brenda hesitated briefly, puzzled as to why this woman was so hospitable without having had any direct contact, and then not wanting to speak for Jack without asking him first. Judy saw Brenda's hesitation but didn't give her a chance to verbalize it. "Please," she insisted, kindly but firmly, "I would be so delighted if you would say yes."

Despite Brenda's initial doubt, Judy's determination had somehow persuaded her. "I don't see why not," Brenda answered and she noticed that Judy's rosy cheeks seemed to glow even brighter, as if to signal her approval. Then, realizing she would now have to see whether Jack wanted to go, Brenda added, "Of course, I'll have to see if it's OK with my husband."

As it turned out, Jack was receptive to the invitation. The vegetables he had cut could wait until their next cooked meal in the van. They found the house easily—it was just two blocks from the *Mikveh*. Introductions were made, Jack and Judy, Mindy, Judy's husband Henry, Brenda. When Henry turned to his wife Judy and asked, "And how did you happen to

meet them?" Judy smoothly evaded the question. Brightly turning to
Mindy and taking the small hand in her own, she led her to a corner of
the dining room where she began to show her the picture books, blocks,
and stuffed animals she had placed there for her. By the time she returned
and directed everyone to the table, the question was forgotten.

Brenda wondered about Judy and Henry's relationship. Tonight the
two of them would be sexually permitted to each other, just as she and Jack
were. How passionate were *they* after observing the required separation?
And then she wondered again about Tzippy in Cleveland. What had it
been like for her when she would come home from the *Mikveh* after
immersing herself, believing that by fulfilling her ritual obligations she was
actually enhancing her relationship with Shmuel? *Before* she knew about
the other woman? And what was it like for her afterward?

Brenda's curiosity was not satisfied at the table. The conversation was
almost as bland as the food—a variety of cold salads and fish. The only
pungent moment was when Judy said she liked to bring children to the
house whenever possible since she couldn't have children of her own.
Henry winced silently and looked at Mindy with detachment. Brenda
noticed how Judy continued to coax and tease Mindy throughout the
meal. Jack salted heavily. Henry inquired politely as to their travel itinerary.
As Jack explained that they were following the open road and had no
particular plan other than to see as much of the country as they could, Judy
momentarily turned her attention from Mindy and joined the
conversation. At once she became as single minded as she had been in the
Mikveh. "You absolutely must visit Cardiff. Your travels wouldn't be
complete without visiting there. It's on the southern coast of Wales, very
beautiful, rocky, fierce, tempestuous even."

Brenda wondered what Judy's actual experience of "tempestuous"
might be. She pictured Judy standing on a grey rock jutting out to the sea,
her pink cheeks the only spots of color on the dark, brooding seascape, the
wind blowing against her stiff wig. For Brenda the word evoked a whole
range or emotions that occasionally assaulted her. "Cardiff," she said to
Jack. "I've never even heard of it, have you?"

Jack pulled out a map of Great Britain from his jacket pocket. He was so good that way—making abstractions concrete with one gesture. "Well, let's see here," he said as he unfolded the map. "Southeast Wales, right there on the Bristol Channel. We can swing down there on our way back from Scotland. What do you say?"

Brenda trusted Jack's readiness to pick up and go without much of any plan. As different as she was from Jack, she felt they were linked by some unknown destiny. Inevitably, he was supposed to be exactly where he ended up whether he knew where he was going before he got there or not. That's how they had ended up together—after a seemingly "chance" encounter. His immediate recognition of her as an inevitable part of his future made all the intermediary steps from talking to dating to romance to marriage flow without any self-doubt or resistance. He just followed along, confident that every time he put one step down, the next step of his path would appear right before him. Now that Judy had placed Cardiff before them as a place they must visit, it was naturally incorporated into their loosely formed itinerary.

In Cardiff, before finding a place to stay, Brenda called the number in the *Jewish Travel Guide* for the *Mikveh*. Four weeks had passed since they left Judy and Henry in Gateshead. They had gone through Scotland, traveling farther and farther north until it seemed they had left civilization behind. The van had curved around one turn after another, each time revealing a panorama more majestic than the one before. The sheep seemed to multiply the further north they went. But the last dry days of fall were over. The moist chill in the air was hard to escape. More than a *Mikveh*, Brenda would have liked to find a sauna to dry her bones. She was ready to head south to France, Spain and Portugal. But according to her count since her period, she was due to immerse herself again on Saturday night.

After making an appointment for the *Mikveh*, Brenda called the kosher boarding home listed in the *Jewish Travel Guide*. A man answered the phone, his Polish accent mingled with a British one. It was agreed that they would come over later in the afternoon to make the arrangements. Meanwhile, they would have a chance to hike a bit along the coast. Waves were crashing against the rocks. The skies were grey. In between some craggy boulders,

Mindy spotted two white feathers which she held tightly during their walk.

When they got back to the van and began the street by street search for the boarding home address, they found that it was directly across from a large municipal hospital. Because the home was listed in the travel guide, Brenda and Jack were both surprised to walk into a living room that was in a state of disarray. But the elderly couple that met them made no apologies. Either they were oblivious to the unkempt surroundings or they were simply indifferent. Every surface in the room was covered. Brenda noticed endless knick-knacks, vases, nail polish, thermos bottles, old candies, various dishes, tablecloths in a corner, tea kettles and numerous old shoes on the floor. She was beginning to feel sick to her stomach as she saw dark hairs protruding from the old woman's chin.

"If you'd like a room, it comes with three meals, but don't expect us to make beds. We're too old for that now," the woman said in a thick Polish accent, the trace of a sneer on her face.

"That's all right," Jack said. "We can sleep in our van, we don't want to trouble you. We will just have our Shabbat meals here, if that's all right with you."

"Is anyone else staying here at the moment?" Brenda asked, looking for reassurance.

"Yes, there is one young woman, but she's across the street at the hospital. She's come down from Glasgow to be with her mother who is quite ill," the old man responded.

Even though the environment looked far from desirable, it was too late to plan an alternative. Brenda and Jack paid in advance for the Friday night meal and Saturday lunch.

"Dinner will be served at six thirty. We'll see you then," the old man said as they left.

As they walked back to their van, Brenda cursed to herself, wishing they had never come here. The weather, the boarding house, these old people—it was beginning to feel quite grim. Why Cardiff?

Perhaps going for a swim and showering before Shabbat might help change her mood. Jack was open. After some inquiry, they found a public natatorium with an Olympic size pool. Brenda's spirits rose as she and Mindy changed into their bathing suits in the dressing room, but as they came out into the pool area, she saw that the water looked brackish and grey. Mindy shivered in her towel and Brenda wondered whether even this was a good idea after all. The water was cold and uninviting. As she jumped in and felt the cold bite against her skin, Brenda sensed she was enduring an initiation of sorts. "Welcome to Cardiff," a mischievous voice mocked in her head. But the purpose of any initiation was beyond her grasp.

When they drove back to the boarding house, the sun was rounding its way down the western horizon. They had bundled Mindy up to protect her from the winds that were whipping about. Even as they walked the short distance from the hospital parking lot to the boarding house, they could feel the sting in the air. When they stepped back into the front hall and looked around, the living room seemed more cluttered than before, if possible, and worse: it was thickly coated with dust and grime. Brenda realized that the lights had been turned on since they had made arrangements for the two Sabbath meals.

Brenda asked where she could set her candles. The old woman moved a pile of mail to clear a space on the mantel. As six thirty approached, the appearance of the other boarding guest became the focus of Brenda's attention. She was becoming more and more uncomfortable, as if by some unknown force they were compelled to spend Shabbat in this unlikely place. Without Judy Kaplan's insistent prodding, they probably never would have happened upon Cardiff. They certainly would not have made it their resting stop. If only the guest would come already to help neutralize her sinking feeling.

"Has she come back from the hospital yet?" she inquired of the old woman.

The old woman squinted one eye and directed the other at Brenda.

"Hah," she cleared her throat and laughed at the same time. "She'll come whenever she comes. Maybe her mother needs her now. We'll begin dinner anyway. Let's go into the dining room."

The clear plastic cloth covering the white linen on the dining room table had been wiped too many times. A sticky residue made it opaque. At the sideboard, the candles that the old woman had lit earlier were already accumulating drippings along their sides, filling out like layered petticoats. Brenda stared at the blue-yellow flames, concentrating on the glow and trying to let all the other impressions of disorder melt away. The old man made the *Kiddush*, blessing the wine in familiar Hebrew words shaped by his peculiar Yiddish dialect, winking at Mindy before and after as if she were privy to his inner thoughts. A pitcher, bowl and towel had been set out by the candles and after washing hands, all were seated.

Brenda followed the old woman into the kitchen, offering to help bring in the meal. When she reached the kitchen door, she was sorry she'd gotten up. Dirty dishes from countless meals were piled high, pots and pans were set haphazardly on counter tops, food lay about in varying states of preparation and decay. Realizing that Brenda was standing behind her, the woman turned and glared, as if her secret were about to be revealed. "Stay out of the kitchen," she scolded, punctuating each word sharply. "I'll serve the meal myself."

Stunned, Brenda returned to the table. Jack gave her a quizzical look. They waited until the first course was brought in: boiled fish. The old woman went back into the kitchen. After tasting a forkful, Jack turned to Brenda and whispered, "Mine is frozen. Is yours?" Brenda couldn't eat what had been set before her. When the old woman came back, she learned over to them and said, "How do you like the fish? I made it fresh today."

They had just begun with their second course, when the guest appeared. She was a woman in her late twenties or early thirties, wearing a grey flannel skirt and cream colored sweater. Her face was ashen. She stepped into the dining room and all eyes turned to her, even those of Mindy, who suddenly became solemn.

"Mother died, not more than an hour ago," the young woman said. "I was with her for the past 36 hours, but now it's over." Her voice was flat and empty. She looked at the newer guests without curiosity, as if it were perfectly natural to share these initial moments of shock and grief with them. The old woman's eyes raced back and forth with no apparent object. Brenda wondered what could possibly be going through her mind.

Meanwhile, the old man stood up, slowly and calmly, and moved toward the empty chair at the table. He pulled it out for the guest.

"You must be hungry and exhausted now. Please, sit down with us and have something to eat. We will arrange to have your mother watched over, but now, just sit and eat."

With one slight movement of his head, he signaled his wife back to the kitchen to bring another plate. The young woman washed her hands at the basin and then seated herself, muttering a prayer quietly under her breath before biting into the bread. She seemed appreciative of the gentle direction offered by the old man.

"We knew her mother during the war," he said to Brenda and Jack as the young woman nibbled at her challah. "She and my wife were together in the same concentration camp in Poland. When we all ended up in England, we tried to leave those memories behind." For a moment, he seemed transported in reverie, but then he came back to the present and continued speaking, directing his words to the young woman. "We'll help you make the final arrangements. Don't worry. It will all be taken care of. Everything will be all right."

He began to explain the demographics of the Jewish community of Cardiff, emphasizing the fact that only a few older Jews remained in this part of town while the younger ones had moved across the channel. "So, you see," he said, directing his words to Jack more than to Brenda, "we all help each other out when there is a need. After Shabbat, I will call the Chevra Kadisha, the society for burying the dead, and they will call their people to watch before the funeral."

Jack understood the old man's hint and volunteered to help watch over the mother's body until Shabbat was over. The young woman thanked him and ate quietly, her fatigue evident in her slow and deliberate gestures. She had just entered a new status in life. She was now essentially on her own, without the benefit of a parent's concern. None of them were likely to open the subject of her grief at the table, but everyone felt its weight. Brenda had no appetite and ate nothing more than a piece of the fresh challah. Mindy continued to eat, under the watchful attention of her parents and the meal ended without further conversation.

After they walked out and crossed the street together, Jack stopped at the hospital and said good-bye. Brenda walked off with Mindy, hand in hand, toward the van. The wind had quieted down while they had been inside. The air was crisp. When Mindy and Brenda entered the van, it was warm from the small gas heater they had turned on before they left. As she sang Mindy to sleep and looked out the van window into the starry sky, Brenda wondered how on the great globe she happened to end up in this Cardiff parking lot on this particular November night. She dozed off cuddling close to Mindy's warmth. Then suddenly, she awoke, disoriented. She looked out into the sky again—it was filled with stars. How had they multiplied so? Just then she heard the cold clanking of the door handle turning as Jack slid the door open.

"I'm freezing," he said as he crouched to enter the van. "You've got to take it from here. She's down in the morgue. I told the attendant you'd follow me over. I was beginning to fall asleep there in the cold. It's unbelievably quiet."

Mindy heard the shuffling about as Jack took off his jacket and sat down on the bed to untie his shoes. The soft sucking rhythm meant she had found her thumb again and was sucking herself back to her dreams. Brenda reached for something, then slipped her hands into her pockets and walked out into the night.

A chair had been placed by the entrance to the hospital's morgue. That must be where Jack had been sitting. The attendant was filing papers in the corridor just outside. "So you're the wife he said was coming," he said cheerfully. "It's bloody cold in there. If you want a cup of hot coffee, just let me know and I can get it for you."

Brenda thanked him for the offer and entered the chilled room. There were large stainless steel vaults against one wall and three rolling stretchers lined up in the open space before them. Although the bodies were covered with sheets, the forms could be distinguished as male or female contours. Feet were exposed from under the sheets, a thin piece of twine and name tag tied onto the large toes for identification. Brenda looked first at the thin feet of the female form. The toes had been molded into each other over time and now retained their shape even without the pressure of shoes or gravity. The feet of the other bodies also had their unique features—calluses, bunions, yellowed nails. Brenda also noted the varying shades of blue. Blood no longer circulated in these bodies.

Brenda walked to the stretcher where the woman's feet were exposed. She picked up the tag and recognized the same family name as that of the young woman to whom they had been introduced that evening. Instinctively, as if to cover the nakedness, she pulled the sheet down over the toes. But then, without deliberating beforehand, she gently uncovered the face, and once seeing the deep ridges engraved in her cheeks, she continued, gradually, pulling the sheet back slowly to reveal the flattened breasts, the now smooth skin, and the chilling blue tattoo of concentration camp numbers, more noticeable than neon, across her forearm. The beauty of the immobile form, aged but dignified, was striking.

Brenda stood before the spent body as if before a holy offering. Only slowly did she replace the sheet and then quietly back away from the body. A slightly acrid smell in the room combined with a pervasive medicinal odor—was it chloroform?— and Brenda felt lightheaded, almost dizzy. Here she stood as if at the gate to another world. She pulled the seat closer from behind her and remained at the threshold, looking in.

The small book of Psalms she had slipped into her pocket before she had left the van now opened in her hands like a bird she may have sheltered there. She began to recite in a soft whisper. "*Amarai Ha'azinu*...Give ear to my words, O Lord, Consider my meditation..." The words passed through her lips like bubbles from a brook, "O Lord, in the morning shalt Thou hear my voice...for Thou art not a God that hath pleasure in wickedness; Evil shall not sojourn with Thee...lead me in Thy righteousness..."

She felt the words rippling around her, spreading further and further out until the entire room seemed permeated with a protective presence. The draped forms under the sheets were alive just hours ago and now she alone continued to breathe. She became aware of her breath as it filled her lungs and as she breathed out, she noticed how the exhalation flowed into the next rivulet of words: "I lay me down, and I sleep, I awake, for the Lord sustaineth me..." As the words continued to stream forth, only her lips moved, but she felt the divine presence expand as if sheltering her and all the bodies laying there under its wings. Her body became increasingly still and cold as her awareness focused only on that presence in the room.

Towards morning the old man appeared in the doorway and told her to get some rest. She slipped the book of Psalms back into her pocket and nodded to him as she left. A strange way to celebrate the Shabbat, she thought as she walked back to the van. The sun was just beginning to emerge, casting soft orange rays through the mist. She thought of the young woman's mother left behind in that room—growing colder and bluer—the sun's warmth would no longer reach her. What stories and memories would be buried with her? And what had Brenda carried with her from that last private encounter?

That night, as she left Jack and Mindy to go to the *Mikveh*, long after the sun had set, Brenda was still trying to absorb the multiple impressions of this strange Shabbat: the filthy boarding house, the inexplicable behavior of the old woman balanced by the kindness of the old man, the cold, still beauty of a woman whose body was finally at rest, awaiting interment. Removing her outer garments, Brenda began the mental preparations for immersion. Disparate thoughts and impressions surfaced and vied for attention. Once again, she considered how Tzippy, the bath attendant, could have resigned herself to her husband's betrayal. Then the grandeur of the Scottish landscape in autumn flashed before her mind's eye in dappled golden splendor. As she removed her undergarments and saw the contour of her exposed belly, never again to be as flat as before her pregnancy, she recaptured the sensual memory of fullness she experienced when Mindy was yet in her womb. The image of Judy Kaplan in Gateshead suddenly came to her with an ache. The fate of barrenness for a woman whose delight was in children. How endless were the sensations and feelings she continued to accumulate daily. She felt like a vessel, filled to capacity and spilling over.

As she stepped down into the *Mikveh,* Brenda felt she carried within her all the sensations she had ever experienced, all the stories she had been told, all the visual memories of the things she had witnessed. All of it— even that which had been forgotten and neglected—she contained in the vessel of her body. She lowered herself into the water, and as she submerged herself and felt the waters closing over her head, she imagined the confluence of her earthly experiences flowing together with the rainwater of the *Mikveh,* that reservoir of hope. She heard the word "Kosher" pronounced by the attendant above her. Her deepest prayer was that she could purify all that she contained within her. Then whatever was in need of healing could be healed. If she honored the vessel of her own body and if she were a worthy vessel, whatever she had witnessed or sensed—the suffering of childlessness and betrayal, of cruelty and of pain—all of it would be honored as she carried it within her and let it be held in the living waters of the *Mikveh.* "Kosher," she heard again. And again, she submerged. "Kosher."

Pamela Singer
The Real Revenge of Lilith

One thing people don't understand about Lilith is that she was lonely. There was all this talk about Adam's loneliness, but that was different. Adam was lonely without a woman; Lilith was lonely with Adam.

Part of the problem was that whole issue of naming things. Naturally there were a lot of things to name, which took a great deal of Adam's attention; but also Lilith became impatient with his inability to see the whole picture: she felt this was setting a dangerous pattern for future behavior of humans, as well as being annoying to her personally. For example, one time she sprained her ankle, which Adam didn't have a name for yet. (Yes, he also took it upon himself to name parts of beings.) So, he said to her, "You've hurt your ... um, your leg wrist..." and eventually told her that she had injured her "ankle"; but he never did ask *how* her ankle was *doing*.

Because Adam was unable to see connections between things, it baffled him when Lilith tried to help by coming up with names herself. For instance, when it came to naming the various kinds of dandelions (which of course *he* did not call dandelions) that would eventually relocate from a corner of the Garden to an island called Albion, later Great Britain, Lilith wanted to name the blooms after the other creatures she thought they resembled. What she called "colt's foot," "smooth hawk's beard," and "cat's ear," he gave names of six, seven and nine syllables. So, as a joke, she renamed her "goat's beard" an impressive sounding "Jack-go-to-bed-at-noon," referring to the flower's sun-closing habit. Adam missed the joke, muttering suspiciously, "Who on earth is Jack?"

Naturally Lilith won this battle. Hardly anyone knows the names Adam gave the flowers, but all of the common people use her everyday names. Partly this is because Lilith was a poet, another thing that Adam couldn't understand.

I know about Lilith's poetry, not just from hearing her flower names being used, but because she has often visited us. Adam would pretend not to listen to her recite, but then he'd find fault with things saying, " Well,

Lilith, that last bit sounds quite different from the rest, where it speeds up there." She would sigh and say, "Adam, dear, if the sound—or as you call it, the speed—changes in a poem, you know it's for a particular effect, which I'll be happy to explain to you."

Adam would shake his head and say, " The effect is it sounds like you made a mistake." Lilith, who has a very bad temper, would start to shout, "That's really rich, Mr. Artiste who wouldn't know poetic meter if a snake dropped it out of a tree onto your overly flat head!"

Adam's compulsive naming became part of even this particular feud. Stung by her disdain, he called her the Poetess next time she visited. "Poet, if anything," she snapped. "No," Adam said, shaking his head. "I'm not sure you're good enough to be a poet. Poetess." You can see why Lilith would get testy just at the sight of his head shaking or the sound of his voice, and she'd deliberately start reciting her poetry. Here is how one of her poems starts out:

Planets cold with sun stillborn
Swing distressed. No rhythmic spheres,
No frail music of new morn
Falls upon created ears.

From the shrouded silk cocoon
Nothing lovely will emerge.
Rising pale embarrassed moon
Shocked looks down on demi-urge.

I thought this expressed her feelings about leaving the Garden and the death of a vision of how her life was intended to unfold. Adam said all it showed is that Lilith is just plain twisted. Also he pointed out that, as a measure of her contrariness, she did after all leave the Garden voluntarily.

Even God had admitted that it was impossible for them to live together. One day God spoke to her as she was humming angrily about the Garden, and said, "Lilith, something has to be done about your constant bickering with Adam. It's depressing the angels."

"Oh, for heaven's sake," said Lilith. "I'll leave, just tell me how." Lilith liked the Garden well enough, but she knew that Adam truly loved it and besides, he kept finding new things to name, and would have been desolate to leave it himself. So God gave Lilith the Holy Name to invoke, which she saved for a dramatic escape the moment Adam got on her last nerve.

And so I came to live here, I, Eve, half-sister to Lilith. You may wonder how, if I know all these things about her and Adam, I can stay with him and indeed love him. The obvious and only answer is that I am able to see the divinity behind his human everydayness. This is a gift which God has crafted into my being, I am sure. Lilith herself was formed with qualities from rich organic material and eternal minerals (so foully distorted by later storytellers into "filth and sediment"), and after a while all that she could see in Adam was his unevolved nature. Of course, it didn't help that he reminded her repeatedly of her own primitive beginnings; but predictably he didn't see any connection between his superior view of her and her reflected growing contempt for him.

But still she visits us—or, should I say, me, since after all we are each other's only true peers and besides, I think she's fun to be around. Now Lilith is very far from being a perfect person: as I've said, she's bad-tempered, and she's opinionated and tends to repeat herself, and is insulting without meaning to be (heaven help you when she actually *tries* to be insulting). Worse than all this, as far as Adam is concerned, is that sometimes she brings a few of her children with her. "Those little demons," he calls them. Which is unfair, because they're not really any worse behaved than some of our own. The fact is that some of them don't look quite human—because, of course, they aren't. Apparently some incarnating spirits still haven't recognized the divine perfection of the human form and experiment with, shall we say, combinations. So these little mermaids, centaurs, satyrs and what-have-you tend to gravitate to Lilith: some are born to her, others find their way to her due to what they sense as a sympathy (or maybe just a lack of antipathy) to their situation. None of them live very long, anyway, probably because of the basic unnaturalness of their poor bodies.

When she's visiting, she likes to wander at night, talking to owls, which disturbs Adam. He doesn't care if she says it's too hot here during the day: God made the greater light for daytime and the lesser for night, he says; and while it's maybe appropriate for her to be attracted to the subordinate period, her owl screeching keeps him awake. "What does she see in the night?" he complained one time, and she responded with a wink, "Shadows reveal what the brightness of day obscures." He shook his head, shivering, and told me later, "I don't know what I ever saw in her. She gives me the creeps."

So, Lilith wanders the world. She is beautiful, she is free, and her reputation is doomed. All of the so-called dark things that men are frightened of in themselves, they will blame Lilith for; especially the things that happen in the night, to them and their children, when the spirit is farthest from the body.

But the final word, so to speak, is Lilith's. Some of Adam's many-times-great-grandsons will be poets, like their many-times-great-aunt. And while their brothers ascribe evil and cruelty, death and deceit to Lilith; while they falsely accuse her of many shameful things, the last word is nevertheless hers. For it is I, Eve, and my daughters who look after their daily lives and make it possible for them to create poetry. But it is Lilith, with all her myriad names, whom they are taught to fear, whom they long for, who reminds them of their first lost chance for wholeness; the Missing Beloved, the haughty goddess who chose to be alone, it is of Lilith whom they will write.

Morrie Warshawski
Moishe's Dream

It was the coldest winter ever. More snow than you could imagine. I kept rubbing my hands together, callus against callus, hugging myself, stamping my feet. Up and down in those thin leather shoes, like cardboard. I could feel the tiniest pebble on the ground. God help me if it rained—those shoes were like sponges! Not even the warmest fire in the grandest fireplace in Poland could dry them out.

I used to steal cigarettes just to get a little warm smoke into my lungs. We had these ugly little white worms called "paparoisen"—wrinkled paper stuffed with a few shreds of harsh tobacco that must have been the first cousin to a wild weed from the mountains.

My brother Moishe and I decided to make this sled. Not the kind you have today. This was a real sled, four feet long, made out of old boards we found in abandoned houses at night, the places drifters and drunks died. The runners, too, we made from wood. It creaked a little song when you pulled it over the snow. Such a beauty. Not one splinter, anywhere!

That sled saved our lives that winter. Moishe and I would roam the neighborhood and haul things for people. Anything. One morning an old ice box for the butcher. In the afternoon, sacks of flour. Evicted and moving from one dark hole to another? Here, throw your few *schmatas* on top of the sled. A large mahogany dresser? Don't worry, there's plenty of room. Grandma too? Why not! Here, Bubba, sit, relax, we're two strong young men, we'll pull you there in no time.

Remember, Moishe was a musician. Not just any musician. The best violinist in a hundred miles. No, the best in Poland. He had your hair, thick, black and curly. His hands were white and soft, like your check when you were a baby. For him to pull on a thick rough rope all day instead of stroking his violin.... Before that winter, maybe half a day in his whole life he worked at hard labor.

He played at the biggest balls, in all the nightclubs, and then until dawn at the taverns. In the morning, all twelve of us would have to tiptoe around the house. Don't wake Moishe! Shhh. Be Quiet. Get dressed outside. Don't raise the shade, the sun shouldn't meet his face until noon. Quiet! Quiet! Quiet! Quiet!

To tell you the truth, I hated him every morning! At noon, finally, he yawns awake. Next to his bed, his lover, the violin. For two hours they dance together. Only scales. Ya da da da de da dah. Ya de da de de de dah. High and low. Soft and loud. Around and around like a carousel, over and over up and down, his eyes closed and chin cupped on the violin like a soft boiled egg in its holder.

After lunch you can't imagine where the music took him. There in the little living room that was a bedroom and a dining room he had the whole world at the tips of his fingers – Vienna, Berlin, New York, Milan. The music went straight to your heart. He could make you cry, or laugh, or have you hopping around like a mad hen.

Moishe the dream master. He weaved a universe out of the thinnest threads of vibrating air. Even now I can't talk about it without feeling the hair on my neck tingle. When the Nazis killed him they took the rarest bird and strangled its song forever.

Anyway, it's so cold our fingers have forgotten why they came into this world. I'm puffing little clouds of smoke around them and asking their forgiveness when up walks this fur coat and cap. A fine Polish lady wrapped in black rabbit so thick only her flat pink nose peeks out.

It's getting late. The cabs are all taken. She's lost. The new chest of drawers has to get home before dark. Her daughter will be worried to death. Can our sled hold it all?

I can see the corners of neatly folded paper money—zlotys—tucked safely into her muff and I'm already spending them on baked potatoes and new gloves.

Moishe gives me a look like "I can live without this old bag and her heavy chest of drawers." But it's too late. I've already got her on board and we're off to grab the chest for her from Simcha the carpenter, and then into the woods. There, she points, take that path not far from where the road ends, follow the birches.

Moishe doesn't say a word the whole time. I can see how angry he is. The rope digs into his shoulder. His long, bony fingers are wrapped in old bed sheets. If he cracks one fingernail I'll never hear the end of it. But what of my own stubby fingers? I've promised them a new home of warm woolen gloves. They won't forgive me either unless we get this lady where she's going.

Finally we get there. Moishe looks like the living dead, but we make it. A nice little country house. The daughter opens the door. Such a plain piece of work for a face! I can see why the mother leaves her home.

We drag in the furniture from our sled and pull it next to her fireplace. Simcha's varnish comes to life. The chest shines like an apple. Even the daughter's crooked little face looks pretty in its reflection.

I put out my hand for the zlotys. The mother peels off a small wad from inside her muff and then adds a couple extra.

We've saved her life. We've done such a wonderful job. Can't we sit a bit and have a cup of tea to warm us up, it's such a long way back home through the woods.

Now it's me who wants to leave but I can see Moishe out of the corner of my eye staring at something, Please, God, I think, not the daughter. This brother of mine, this Moishe, God rest his soul, he had a very active bow in his pants too.

I follow his eyes to the wall. There, I can't believe it, hanging next to suspenders only a fat man could wear, peeking out from beneath a dark oily leather vest—the curves of Moishe's true mistress, a lovely old violin!

Do you mind, dear lady, if my brother looks at your violin? No, no, not at all, she says. In fact, she would love to have someone pick it up after all these years on the wall. No one has played it since her father died after the war.

She is pouring me a glass of dark tea with sugar cubes on the side. I've got a nervous eye on Moishe. He was always so unpredictable.

Moishe goes to the wall, gingerly peels the oily leather off the violin like a groom lifting the veil of his bride. He turns the thin neck around in his left hand and with the right runs his fingers across the strings lifting old rosin dust from around the sound holes. The next thing I know the bow is in his hand and he's squeezed the violin next to his shoulder and cheek.

Moishe slowly skates the horse hairs of the bow across the old catgut strings, tickling them back to life. The violin sings a little. I notice the daughter hiding in a corner on a stool, her hands in her lap and eyes on the floor.

Oh, I see your brother knows a little about music, says the old lady. Yes, I think, he knows a little. She pours more tea and Moishe begins to weave his dream.

It's a warm spring day. Just a wisp of a breeze in the air. The kind of day you find in one of those paintings in a book. Everyone is holding hands and there is no need to talk. The eyes have their own language.

The young ones are in the river splashing about in slow motion in a silent movie. Sparrows appear like a dark rug next to the clouds. Two of the young lovers call out to the children, but the cries catch in their throats like sharp knives. A large weeping willow shelters the lovers in a thick private curtain of leaves. Their shadows barely touch while they make love. It starts to snow.

Please, I think, Moishe, stop now and let's go. The old lady is already in tears. God knows what Moishe has done to her. And the daughter—she has squeezed her poor red palms into a small sweaty knot.

Moishe, I whisper, enough. It's dark. Leave these people alone. Let's go home already. I grab for his sleeve, but it's too late. His bow arm darts like an agitated bee in a swarm.

Now the snowstorm in his dream has thickened the air around the lovers. You can smell the foul, dense stench of too many old roses. The darkening sky is filled with layers of growls from every beast imaginable, lifting the lovers up into a twirling cobalt blue swirl held together by their fingers intertwined.

Moishe's delicate hands and the daughter's rough nails.

Their eyes close. The wind whips around them ripping their flesh into thin sheets from head to toe, like mother peeling potatoes, until nothing is left but a small speck of a new star in a twirling firmament

VI.
ESSAYS

Marc Bregman
The Four Who Entered Paradise: Evolution of a Talmudic Tale

Some stories seem to be inexhaustibly intriguing. In the vast expanse of rabbinic literature — sometimes referred to as "The Sea of the Talmud" — no story seems to have evoked more discussion and commentary than the famous story of the four sages: Ben Azzai, Ben Zoma, Elisha ben Abuyah, and Rabbi Akiba. For this enigmatic tale, preserved in several different versions in classical talmudic and early Jewish mystical literature, is clearly a key text for the study of Jewish mysticism in late antiquity (roughly from the end of the biblical period until about 500 C.E.). Not only has this mystical tale continued to elicit controversy among Jewish scholars throughout the Middle Ages and into modern times, but this provocative story has also inspired Jewish storytellers, who have told and retold this famous story and its related traditions, each in their own way, according to the genius of their imagination. The most recent, and perhaps the most expansive and imaginative, in this time-honored tradition of retelling is *The Four Who Entered Paradise* (Jason Aronson: 1995) by the well-known Jewish poet, writer and anthologist Howard Schwartz.

I have no intention of trying to resolve the many scholarly controversies concerning the original meaning of the core story and the complex debate over the historical development of its many variants and offshoots. My purpose is much more modest: to briefly chart for the reader some of the ways in which this enigmatic tale has evolved, from its earliest appearances in rabbinic tradition, through Jewish mystical texts, and on into modern times. However, as we shall see, the scholars' efforts at interpreting a text and the storytellers' seemingly different techniques of recounting a tale sometimes intersect in surprising ways.

Talmudic Versions of the Story of the Four Sages

Several versions of the story are found in Tannaitic tradition, that is to say, as part of the Oral Torah taught by the rabbis who lived in the period leading up to the compilation of the Mishnah in the first third of the third century. Three of these versions are found in three separate talmudic works as part of what David Halperin has called the "mystical collection." In each of these works this collection of traditions serves to explicate the term *merkavah*, "chariot" in Mishnah *Hagigah* 2:1, which places restrictions on the exposition of three potentially dangerous biblical passages: "One may not expound the Forbidden Sexual Relationships (found in Leviticus, chapters 18 and 20) with [as many as] three persons, nor the Work of Creation (Genesis, chapter 1) with [as many as] two, nor the [Work of the] Chariot (Ezekiel, chapter 1) with [even] one, unless he were wise and understands from his [own] knowledge."

In the context of the extensive discussion of the Mishnah it becomes clear that *merkavah* is more than simply a term for the divine chariot seen by the Prophet in the opening vision of the Book of Ezekiel, but a conceptual term or code word denoting the secret, mystical lore of ancient Judaism. In the course of the often highly allusive discussion of this concept, the story of the four sages is related:

[Tosefta]
Four entered *pardes*. Ben Azzai and Ben Zoma, Aher and Rabbi Akiba.

[Babylonian Talmud adds]
Rabbi Akiba said to them: When you arrive at the stones of pure marble, do not say: Water, Water! For it is said, *"The speaker of lies shall not endure before My eyes"* (Psalms 101:7).

[Tosefta]
One looked and died. One looked and was smitten. One looked and cut the shoots. And one ascended in peace and descended in peace. Ben Azzai looked and died; about him Scripture says, *"Precious in the eyes of the Lord is the death of His saints"* (Psalms 116:15). Ben Zoma looked and was stricken. About him Scripture says, "Have you found honey? Eat what is enough for you, etc." (Proverbs 25:16). Elisha [Aher] looked and cut the shoots; about him scripture says, "Do not let your mouth lead your flesh to sin, etc." (Ecclesiastes 5:5)

[Palestinian Talmud adds]
Who is Aher ["other"]? Elisha ben Avuyah, who used to kill the masters of Torah. And not only that, but he would go into the school-house and would see children sitting before the teacher and would say: What are these sitting and doing here?! This one's trade is builder, this one's trade is carpenter, this one's trade is hunter, this one's trade

is tailor. And when they heard this they would abandon [study] and leave [school]. About him [Aher/Elisha] scripture says, "Do not let your mouth lead your flesh to sin, etc."

[Tosefta]

R. Akiba ascended in peace and descended in peace; about him Scripture says, "Draw me, we will run after you, etc." (Song of Songs 1:4)

On the one hand, the similar wording of the basic story suggests that all the versions stem from a shared source that circulated, orally or in some rudimentary written form, as part of Tannaitic tradition. This basic story of the four sages seems represented in its simplest narrative form, among the texts that have come down to us, by the Tosefta version. In the other two versions, the basic story has been elaborated in different ways that may reflect the different editorial styles of these other works. In the Palestinian Talmud, several highly imaginative stories have been inserted, clearly by some later redactor of the text, to explain who Elisha is referred to by the derogatory alias Aher ("the Other"). In the Babylonian Talmud, Rabbi Akiba not only departs unscathed from the enigmatic adventure, but warns his three companions how they might avoid one of its primary dangers. Without going further into the complex question of how the different versions evolved, it is clear that even within classic talmudic literature the process of retelling and elaborating the story of the four sages had already begun.

The various interpretations of this highly elliptical and enigmatic tale turn on the various possible meanings of the word *pardes,* which the four sages are said to have entered. Two basic approaches have developed. The first approach interprets the word *pardes* according to its normal, well-attested meaning in both biblical and rabbinic Hebrew, as "orchard." According to this interpretation, the "orchard" is a metaphor for some kind of dangerous pursuit after knowledge, perhaps theosophical knowledge of God *(gnosis),* the goal of Gnosticism, one of the major religious-intellectual movements in late antiquity. Read this way, the story serves as a warning that only one in four learned seekers managed to survive this mental quest unharmed. The other basic approach interprets the word *pardes* as related to the Greek *paradeisos* meaning "paradise." Read this way, the beginning of the story tells us that the four sages attempted what is known as a "heavenly ascent." That is to say, Rabbi Akiba and his three companions engaged in something more than purely mental inquiry. Their enigmatic story tells of some sort of ecstatic, mystical adventure actually experienced by the four sages. The versions of the story found in the Tosefta and the Palestinian Talmud may be read as describing a purely intellectual quest. But whoever added Rabbi Akiba's warning to his three companions in the Babylonian Talmud clearly seems to have understood the story of the four sages as a legend of their having "entered paradise," that is, their attempt to make an ecstatic ascent to the heavenly realms and the dangers they encountered in this mystic adventure.

This reading of the story of the four sages as a "heavenly journey" is further developed in the ensuing discussion of the details of the story in the Babylonian Talmud. It is instructive to compare the "down-to-earth" explanation of why Elisha ben Abuyah was referred to by the derogatory alias *Aher* ("the Other") found in the editorial addition to the story in the Palestinian Talmud, with the "celestial" explanation of Elisha's sin found in the Babylonian Talmud *(Hagigah* 15a):

> Aher cut the shoots; about him Scripture says: "Do not let your mouth lead your flesh to sin, etc." (Ecclesiastes 5:5). What [did he see that led him to sin]? He saw that permission had been given to Metatron [one of the most important and puzzling angels] to sit and write down the merits of Israel. Aher said: It is taught that on high there is no sitting [out of respect for God]....Perhaps—Heaven forbid—there are two [divine] powers! They led Metatron out and flogged him with sixty fiery lashes [to show he was no more powerful than the other angels...but in return] permission was given to Metatron to erase the merits of Aher. A heavenly voice proclaimed: "Return, O backsliding children" (Jeremiah 3:14)—except for Aher.

In following the evolution of the story of the four sages, it is significant to note that in both the Talmuds, the sin of Elisha is "explained" using the storyteller's method of adding supplementary narrative material to the expanding initial tradition. The hermeneutic mode employed here and elsewhere could be characterized as telling a story to explain a story.

As we shall see, the Babylonian Talmud's interpretation of the core story as a tale of mystic ascent has been highly pervasive. This approach has been adopted not only by many interpreters, ancient and modern, but also by those who continued to retell the story from ancient times until now.

Hekhalot Literature

It is not surprising that the story of the four sages, understood as a key rabbinic legend of mystic ascent, should find expression in early Jewish mystical texts known collectively as the *Hekhalot* (or *Merkavah*) literature. As its name implies, this genre of literature deals largely with the "heavenly journeys" of various personalities through the celestial "palaces" *(hekhalot)* that are related to or are actually part of the "divine chariot" *(merkavah)*. One of these personalities is none other than Rabbi Akiba, who, according to one *Hekhalot* text, relates:

> Four we were who entered pardes. And these are they: Ben Azzai and Ben Zoma, Aher and I, Akiba. Ben Azzai looked and died; Ben Zoma looked and was smitten; Aher looked and cut the shoots. I ascended in peace and descended in peace. And how was it that I ascended in peace and descended in peace? Not because I am greater than my companions; but my deeds caused me [to succeed where my companions failed]—to fulfill what the sages taught in the Mishnah, "Your deeds will bring you near and your deeds will put you at a distance" (Mishnah Eduyot 5:7).

> Rabbi Akiba said: When I ascended on high I left a sign on the passageways to the heavenly firmament more than the passageways to my home. And when I arrived behind the celestial curtain (Pargod), the angels of destruction came and sought to push me away until the Holy One, blessed be He, said to them: My sons, leave this elder alone for he is worthy to gaze at my glory. About him it says, "Draw me, we will run after you, etc. [the King has brought me into his chambers]" (Song of Songs 1:4).

> Rabbi Akiba said: When I ascended on high, I heard a heavenly voice that came forth from under the Throne of Glory and speaking in the Aramaic language, in this language. What did it say in the Aramaic language, in this language? Before the Lord made Heaven and Earth He established...a passageway to go in and out; He established His immutable name...

The most consistent difference in this version is that here the story is recounted as a first-person narrative, told from the perspective of Rabbi Akiba who adds that it was his "deeds" that permitted him to ascend and descend in peace, in contrast to his less fortunate companions. These "deeds" are apparently related to his foresight in leaving some sort of "sign" during his ascent to the heavenly realms. The idea seems to be that Akiba marked his trail so that he would be able to remember the passageways (*mevo'ot*)—more than the passageways to his own home—leading through the heavenly firmament (*rakia*), that is, the various "palaces" (*hekhalot*). He alone reached the ultimate goal of the mystic ascent, to see beyond the celestial curtain (*Pargod*) and enter the actual presence of the Holy One. Like other *Merkavah* mystics, including even Moses, Rabbi Akiba encounters angelic opposition but is found worthy to gaze at God's glory and thus be saved by divine intervention. From the continuation of the passage, with the words that issue from under the Throne of Glory, it seems that Rabbi Akiba alone correctly understood that these divine passageways had been established not only for entering but also for leaving the heavenly realms. And so upon entering he had the foresight to leave a "sign" (*siman*). This sign, which Akiba left on the "passageway," seems to be related to God's "immutable Name," since both were established "before the Lord made Heaven and Earth." It may be that in this and similar *Hekhalot* passages, Rabbi Akiba's particular fame in talmudic literature, of being able to interpret "every jot and tittle" of the letters of scripture, is extended to a theurgic ability to make use of the letters of the Divine Name to return from the heavenly journey unscathed, where others failed.

Robert A. Cohn

The Shared Journey of Philip Roth and Woody Allen Re-visited: Back to Babylon From the Promised Land?

This essay is an update of one I wrote in 1991, and which appeared in the first issue of *The Sagarin Review.* That essay explored the remarkable similarities in the lives and work of the novelist Philip Roth and the filmmaker Woody Allen, based on my observations and reviews over two decades as editor-in-chief/publisher and book and film critic of the *St. Louis Jewish Light,* the weekly newspaper serving the Jewish community of St. Louis.

Because the books of Philip Roth and the films of Woody Allen which have been released in the years since that original 1991 essay add significant new layers to the works of both, I have been asked to update the piece as of 1997, shortly after the publication of Roth's latest novels, *Sabbath's Theater* and *American Pastoral;* the publication by Roth's ex-wife, Claire Bloom, of *Leaving a Doll's House,* a bitter memoir of their failed marriage; a similar tell-all memoir, *What Falls Away,* by Allen's ex-partner Mia Fawwow; and the release of Allen's newest films, *The Mighty Aphrodite* and *Everybody Says I Love You.*

Back in 1991, I pointed out that the writings of Roth and the films of Allen are strikingly similar in many ways, despite some significant differences. They are close in age and in many of their perspectives, and share an intensely Jewish background and consciousness that suffuses nearly all of their work. They have shared a complex journey from the Babylon of Diaspora ambivalence regarding their Jewishness and attitudes towards moral choices and sexuality in their early work, to an intermediate approach to the Promised Land of positive Jewish values applied to modern choices—and an abrupt shift back to their early moral confusion in their most recent works.

Among the many obvious similarities between Roth and Allen:

- Both were born on the East Coast to middle-class Jewish parents during the Depression.

- Both began their writing careers at an early age. Roth was only 26 when his first collection of stories, *Goodbye, Columbus,* was published. Allen was still in his teens when he began as a comedy writer for Sid Caesar's classic television variety program, *Your Show of Shows,* where he worked with such other comedy giants as Mel Brooks, Carl Reiner, and Neil Simon, a virtual Manhattan Project of comic talent.

- Both Roth and Allen have protagonists which seem to be modeled in many ways on themselves. Roth has many things in common with Gabe Wallach in When She Was Good; Neil Klugman in Goodbye, Columbus; Alexander Portnoy in Portnoy's Complaint; David Kepesh in The Breast; Peter Tarnopol in My Life as a Man; Nathan Zuckerman in Zuckerman Unbound, The Counterlife and American Pastoral; and with Mickey Sabbath in Sabbath's Theater. Allen has many similar traits to those of Allan Felix in Play it Again, Sam; Alvy Singer in Annie Hall; Isaac Davis in Manhattan; Sandy Bates in Stardust Memories; Cliff Stern in Crimes and Misdemeanors; Gabe Roth in Husbands and Wives and Lenny Weinrib in The Mighty Aphrodite.

- Both Roth and Allen have written extensively—almost obsessively— about relationships between Jewish men and their Jewish mothers and with Gentile lovers. In Roth's *Portnoy's Complaint,* the main character is trapped in a "Jewish joke," between his overbearing, almost castrating mother, Sophie Portnoy and his sexually fulfilling but intellectually stultifying Gentile lover he calls Monkey. In Allen's *Annie Hall,* the main character, Alvy Singer is caught between his disapproving Jewish mother and his All American Girl lover, Diane Keaton. In *Oedipus Wrecked,* Woody Allen's contribution to the trilogy *New York Stories,* Allen's character is watched over by his omnipresent Jewish mother who steps into a space and time warp to become a giant, hovering presence in the sky.

- Both Roth and Allen produced early work which was almost exclusively humorous and satirical. Their more recent works have dealt with more serious themes relating to both general and specifically Jewish issues.

Among Philip Roth's most significant recent books is *Patrimony,* a work of non-fiction detailing the author's true story of caring for his difficult but loving 86-year-old father during his final illness. In *Patrimony*, Roth confronts such issues as mortality, what it means to be a Jew in the Diaspora, parent-child issues and the struggle to become the *mensch* that his parents had urged him to become.

The publication in 1990 of Roth's *Patrimony* was preceded by a few months with the release of one of Woody Allen's most textured, complex and seriously Jewish films, *Crimes and Misdemeanors*. Although there are traces of the familiar Allen humor in his screenplay, *Crimes and Misdemeanors* is in no sense a comedy. The film, about a respected eye doctor who pays to have his unstable mistress murdered to save his marriage and career, explores such issues as why evil goes unpunished, why bad things happen to good people and whether or not there is an "all-seeing" God who will punish our misdeeds.

Both Roth and Allen seem torn between dealing with issues most familiar to them and closest to their own experience, and venturing into uncharted waters. Woody Allen's screen persona, most often the angst-ridden, urban Jewish intellectual *nebbish,* is his own version of Charlie Chaplin's endearing Little Tramp. Roth's fictional persona is often the angry young Jewish male rebelling against the stifling middle class values of his family, a kind of Lenny Bruce of the printed page. But in *Interiors,* a dark and convoluted film about a dysfunctional Gentile family, Allen openly emulates the great Swedish director Ingmar Bergman. And in some of Roth's novels, such as *The Ghost Writer,* Roth eliminates the ethnic coarseness from his prose and writes with the elegance of Henry James. Roth and Allen are most at home with Jewish themes, but every once in a while they venture into other realms as if to prove their refusal to be typecast.

In addition to the many similarities between Roth and Allen, there are a number of important differences:

Roth's work has been as a novelist, while Allen has been a writer, director and actor in films. While both novels and films require dedication and creative genius, they are very different modes of expression. A few of Roth's novels, notably *Goodbye Columbus, Portnoy's Complaint* and *The Ghost Writer,* have been made into films; Allen has written some short stories and an occasional essay for *The New Yorker* and other publications.

Allen's portrayal of himself as the pitiful, nervous Jewish *nebbish* who is insecure in his relationships with women, contrasts with Roth and his characters, who are conventionally handsome, and do not share Allen's lack of physical and social self-consciousness. The two men do share twin obsessions with sexual themes in their work and a desire for personal privacy.

Philip Milton Roth was born in Newark, New Jersey on May 19, 1933. He is the son of the late Herman Roth, a longtime executive with the Metropolitan Life Insurance Co., and Bess Finkel Roth, a devoted wife, mother and homemaker. In 1988, Roth published *The Facts,* an autobiography covering the first 35 years of his life. From that book, we learn that Roth had a happy and secure childhood and youth in suburban Newark, enjoying his high school career at Weequahic High School, which had a comfortable majority of Jewish students. Roth also describes fond memories of family summer outings with his parents, his older brother and their neighbors. Roth's family was intensely Jewish, although his parents abandoned the Orthodox Judaism of his grandparents and became Reform Jews.

In 1959, Roth published *Goodbye, Columbus,* his first of 23 books to date. *Goodbye Columbus* was a collection of short stories plus a title novella, which was later made into a successful film starring Richard Benjamin as Neil Klugman and Ali MacGraw as his girlfriend, Brenda Potemkin. Many of his stories dealt with middle-class Jewish behavior, apparently based on Roth's own experiences. This first book was generally well received and was favorably reviewed by the influential Jewish writer Irving Howe.

Goodbye, Columbus was followed by *Letting Go* in 1962 and *When She Was Good* in 1967—novels which dealt with mostly non-Jewish middle-class and middle-American values. Roth was to burst onto the best-seller list in 1969 with *Portnoy's Complaint,* a highly controversial novel about Alexander Portnoy, a "nice Jewish boy" who viciously ridicules his Jewish relatives and the values they represent. The novel was also controversial because of its frank descriptions of the private sexual activities of Alexander Portnoy, and because its mocking of Jewish behavior was so severe that many Jewish critics accused Roth—unfairly, I believe—of being a "self-hating" Jew.

In his book *Love, Sex, Death & the Meaning of Life: The Films of Woody Allen* (1981; revised in 1990), Foster Hirsch discusses the accusations against both Roth and Allen that they are self-hating:

"Many of the writers, particularly Roth and Allen, have been accused, in their satires of American Jewish folkways, of Jewish anti-Semitism. Ambitious, upwardly mobile Jews intent on making it in mainstream America, they have been charged with sacrificing their heritage. But in attempting to deny or take flight from Jewish tradition, artists like Roth and Allen, in fact, continue to be passionately engaged with it, conducting an ongoing dialogue with Jewishness as a state of mind and a way of life. Certainly there is ethnic hostility in their work, directed not only at Jews but even more fiercely at the dumb *goyim*."

Woody Allen more than Philip Roth seems to be attached to the notion that Gentiles, and especially Gentile women, are amusingly naive innocents who are placed on earth to dispel the clouds of neurosis under which Jews are condemned to dwell. In *Annie Hall,* Diane Keaton's well-scrubbed, alcohol-numbed, all-American family enjoying a placid dinner is contrasted in a famous split-screen sequence with Alvy Singer's *kvetching,* shouting, illness-obsessed Jewish family.

Through the main characters of two of his early books, Roth contrasts the middle-class, middle-American heritage of Lucy Nelson in *When She Was Good* to that of the protagonist of *Portnoy's Complaint:*

"Though not necessarily 'typical,' Alexander Portnoy and Lucy Nelson seem to me, in their extreme resentment and disappointment, like the legendary unhappy children out of two familiar American family myths," writes Roth in *Reading Myself and Others,* a 1975 collection of essays on his work. "In one book it is the Jewish son railing against the seductive mother, in the other the Gentile daughter railing against the alcoholic father (equally loved, hated and feared—the most unforgettable character *she* ever met). Of course, Lucy Nelson is seen to destroy herself within an entirely different fictional matrix, but that would result, among other reasons, from the enormous difference between the two environments that inspire their rage as well as their shared sense of loss and nostalgia."

Probably no two authors have more intensely explored the cultural differences between Jews and Gentiles as have Philip Roth and Woody Allen. They are simultaneously attracted to what Roth calls "those bland, blond exotics called *shicksas*," and repelled by what they perceive to be a barren landscape of white Protestant America.

In *The Facts,* Roth describes how the anti-Semitic comments directed at him at polite dinner parties while he lived for a time in London "made a Jew out of me in a matter of months." He could not wait to move back to New York City, where he kissed the television image of then New York Mayor Ed Koch for being a shrill, outspoken and unapologetic Jew.

In *Patrimony,* the grown-up "real-life" Philip Roth describes his appreciation of his father's detailed memory of his Jewish businesses in Newark, and recalls that a statement on discipline his father had made which made the adolescent Philip Roth fly into a rage, was accepted calmly by the adult Philip Roth. Far from being "self-hating," Roth's descriptions of his parents in *Patrimony* are affectionate. The nostalgia remains, but the rage is gone.

Roth's arrival at the edge of his Promised Land required a journey of almost two decades. Two years after *Portnoy's Complaint,* Roth published *Our Gang,* which was a biting satire on the Nixon Administration. This was followed in 1972 by *The Breast,* a satire of *Metamorphosis,* the novel by one of Roth's heroes, Franz Kafka, about a man who was metamorphosed into a cockroach. In *The Breast,* David Kepesh wakes up one morning to find himself transformed into a giant female breast—an image which was used in Woody Allen's film that same year based on Dr. David Reuben's book *Everything You Always Wanted to Know About Sex.*

Roth's slim, comical novel was followed in 1973 by *The Great American Novel,* which was based on a mythical American baseball season, and which anticipated W.P. Kinsella's *Field of Dreams* by a few years. All of Roth's writing about baseball is splendidly and lovingly crafted. He is a dyed-in-the-wool New York Mets fan, while Woody Allen supports the New York Knicks basketball team.

In 1974, Roth published *My Life as a Man,* a searing account of a

Jewish author's disastrous marriage to a Gentile woman, that apparently is largely autobiographical. Some critics consider this to have been Roth's best novel.

Roth's work began taking an even more serious turn in 1977 with the publication of *The Professor of Desire,* which dealt with the middle years of a college professor. In a reversal of the sexual hedonism of *Portnoy's Complaint,* the professor experiences an extended period of diminished interest in sex.

What followed for Roth was the publication of what is called his Zuckerman trilogy—books in which the protagonist, Nathan Zuckerman, shares many facts in common with the author. *The Ghost Writer* (1979) is about a young Jewish writer who spends a weekend with an older, established Jewish writer. The older writer has a failing marriage and a relationship with a young woman. The younger writer speculates that the young woman might be Anne Frank who miraculously survived the Holocaust, moved to America under an assumed name and kept her identity a secret so as not to destroy the lessons of her powerful diary. *The Ghost Writer* is one of Roth's most complex and interesting books and represents a venture into the more "serious" realm of Jewish fiction.

Roth also was deadly serious in his editorship of the *Writers From the Other Europe,* a series of novels by prominent Jewish and non-Jewish authors in Eastern Europe before the collapse of Communism. Thanks to Roth, the works of such important East European authors as Milan Kundera and Tadeusz Borowski were translated into English and enjoyed a wide audience of appreciative readers.

In *My Life as a Man* and in *The Anatomy Lesson, Zuckerman Unbound* and *The Counterlife,* Roth struggled with his fictional alter-ego, reliving through his fiction many of the crises in his personal and literary lives.

In 1988, Roth published *The Facts: A Novelist's Autobiography,* which covers the first thirty-five of his fifty-six years. In an introduction to *The Facts,* which is in the form of a "letter" to his most recent fictional protagonist, Nathan Zuckerman, he confesses that following a "nervous breakdown" related to the death of his mother, he felt compelled to render his experience "untransformed."

The Facts more or less confirmed what Roth for years was saying was of little or no importance: that many of the characters and events in his novels were based on actual or composite life experiences. Roth grew up on the literary tradition of the "New Criticism" espoused by Cleanth Brooks and Robert Penn Warren which holds that works of fiction or poems must stand alone as "organic units," and the biographical underpinnings of the author are totally beside the point. *The Facts* is an admission by Roth, bolstered in *Patrimony,* that the details of an author's life matter a great deal in understanding his creative output.

In 1991, Roth published a strange novel called *Deception,* which is about a writer named "Philip," whose notebook describing a love affair for a book in progress is discovered by his woman friend, who believes it must be based on fact. The author vehemently protests that the notebook is not true, but the lines between fact and fiction are blurred.

Allen Stewart Konigsberg, who later took the name Woody Allen, was born in Brooklyn on December 1, 1935, to middle-class Jewish parents, Martin and Nettie Konigsberg.

Roth's parents drifted away from traditional to a more Reform brand of Judaism, while Allen's household remained Orthodox. Allen himself became assimilated and basically non-religious, while Roth considers himself to be, in his own words, "not religious at all." Yet it is hard to imagine two writers who are more obsessed with Jewish issues and themes in their work than Roth and Allen.

While Roth began and remains primarily a novelist, Allen began in his teen years as a comedy writer and as a stand-up comedian. He eventually became, along with Mel Brooks, another Jewish comic genius, one of the two most successful directors of film comedy in America.

In 1966, Woody Allen wrote his first film, *What's Up, Tiger Lily?,* a rather broad comedy. This was followed by Allen's other "earlier, funnier work," including *Take the Money and Run; Bananas; Everything You Always Wanted to Know About Sex; Sleeper; Love and Death;* and *Play It Again, Sam.* Many of these films featured different incarnations of his famous urban, intellectual Jewish nebbish, who defeats his adversaries with wisecracks rather than his fists, a character who has become as familiar today as

Chaplin's "Little Tramp" was in the 1920s.

Allen's urban Jewish intellectual says he would "never join a club which would accept me as a member," and envies the suave approach to women of Humphrey Bogart's film persona.

Annie Hall (1977) was Allen's "bridge" film from the purely comic to the semi- or fully serious mode. While *Annie Hall* was indeed a very funny film, it was also a moving exploration of the complexity of male-female, Jewish-Gentile relationships.

Annie Hall was followed in 1978 by *Interiors,* a totally "serious" film which has been compared to the work of Ingmar Bergman, the Swedish director who is among Allen's heroes.

Philip Roth was inspired in his youth by the writings of Henry James, and his elegant prose is often compared to that of his hero. But while Roth was reared on Henry James and Allen worships Ingmar Bergman, each of them seems most authentic when dealing with Jewish themes.

After *Interiors,* Allen returned to more familiar territory with *Manhattan,* a more sober look at male-female, Jewish-Gentile relationships (in black and white) than *Annie Hall.* In *Radio Days* (1987), Allen takes a nostalgic and affectionate look back on his Jewish childhood in Brooklyn.

Allen has alternated between "serious" films like *Stardust Memories, Another Woman* and *September,* and lighter fare like *A Midsummer Night's Sex Comedy, The Purple Rose of Cairo* and *Alice.*

In *Crimes and Misdemeanors* (1989), Woody Allen presents a cast of characters, nearly all of whom are Jewish. They wrestle with such problems as whether God really sees evil in the world, or whether we can violate ethical principles without fear of divine retribution.

In the film, a prominent Jewish eye doctor has a woman he has been having an affair with murdered so as to prevent her from wrecking his marriage and career. In a key sequence, the eye doctor returns to the Brooklyn home of his childhood and vividly recalls his late father's stern warnings that God sees all of our actions and that He will hold us accountable for them. The eye doctor seems at first to get away with murder, while one of his patients, a morally upright rabbi who is going blind apparently is unfairly made to suffer. *Crimes and Misdemeanors* is anything but a "funny" movie.

Just as Woody Allen embraces serious Jewish concerns in *Crimes and Misdemeanors*, Philip Roth in *Patrimony* struggles valiantly with his eighty-six-year-old father to sort out the meaning of Jewish life in America.

In *Patrimony*, Roth confronts life and death issues in the most literal sense. He faces up to the fact that both he and his father had drifted away from Jewish traditions, but neither could escape from their strong sense of Jewishness. Roth wonders why his father abandoned his grandfather's *tefillin* in the locker room of the YMHA. He later must decide whether his worldly "work-a-day" father should be buried in a business suit or in the traditional Jewish burial shroud.

Many of the attitudes and habits of the father that had provoked rage and ridicule in the young Alexander Portnoy-like Philip Roth, stirred feelings of affection and respect in the more mature novelist.

In their most recent work, Roth and Allen continue to struggle with the complex issues of love, lust, sex, death and the meaning of life. Even after all of these years, both Roth and Allen seem still to be suffering from what Alexander Portnoy's famous psychiatrist, Dr. Otto Spielvogel defined as "Portnoy's Complaint"—"A disorder in which strongly-felt ethical and altruistic impulses are perpetually warring with extreme sexual longings." Roth also jokingly called it "Putting the Id back in the Yid," allowing Jews to surrender to their sexual longings, which for centuries had been rigidly suppressed by Jewish legal injunctions against masturbation, immodesty, adultery and marriage to Gentiles.

In real life, both Allen and Roth could be called unlucky in love. Allen was married briefly to the actress Louise Lasser, who divorced him as she launched her own successful television career. The major love of his life, Diane Keaton (his co-star in *Annie Hall*), with whom he did his best work, dumped him. And his long-term significant other, actress Mia Farrow, angrily ended their relationship after Allen became romantically involved with Farrow's 21-year-old adoptive daughter, Soon-Yi Previn. Roth's first marriage, to Margaret Martinson Williams, the divorced mother of two children whom he had met at the University of Chicago, was a disaster which ended when she died in a 1968 automobile accident while they were in the process of a bitter divorce.

Roth's second marriage—to the British Jewish actress Claire Bloom—was to last longer than his first, but ultimately also ended in disaster and divorce. Recently, Claire Bloom published *Leaving a Doll's House*, a bitter memoir of her 18-year relationship with the author she describes as "brilliant, hilarious, and very, very cruel." In her book, Bloom details what she calls her "long, complex, rich, but ultimately tortured relationship" with Roth. The Roth she describes is alternately loving and cruel, using his literary brilliance and rapier-like wit to make Bloom's position in arguments "appear futile and humiliating."

Bloom remembers that almost from the first, Roth's behavior contained "warning signals" that their relationship would ultimately fail: deep and irrepressible rage...anger at being trapped in marriage; fear of giving up autonomy; and a profound distrust of the sexual power of women," the latter being yet another shared obsession with Woody Allen. Bloom even accuses Roth of having made unwelcome advances to Rahael Hallawell, the best friend of Bloom's daughter, Anna, her daughter by her previous marriage to the actor Rod Steiger. Bloom said that Hallawell was "practically a daughter" to her.

In an interview with Bloom titled "Marrying Portnoy" in *New York* magazine, Peter J. Smith quotes Rafael Navarro as recalling Roth's reaction to Woody Allen's affair with Soon-Yi Previn: "Philip always abhorred Woody Allen because of the sentimentality and vulgarity. The thing about Philip is that he has exquisite taste because he always knows when he is being vulgar. When [the affair with Soon-Yi Previn] came out, he was so full of contempt, full of thunder—'How disgusting,' et cetera..." Could it be that Roth "abhors" Woody Allen because Allen is just a "vulgar, tasteless" version of himself?

Just as the actress Claire Bloom chronicles her traumatic relationship with Philip Rother in her memoir *Leaving a Doll's House*, so does Mia Farrow describe her harrowing relationship with Woody Allen, and his seduction of her adopted daughter Soon-Yi Previn, in *What Falls Away*. The two memoirs cover remarkably similar ground.

The "nymphet" obsession that inspired Vladimir Nabokov to write his acclaimed Lolita seems less becoming in the lives and works of Roth and Allen.

In *Husbands and Wives,* Allen's first film after his breakup with Farrow, he portrays Gabe Roth, (a conscious homage to his literary alter-ego?) an English professor who becomes infatuated with Rain, a beautiful and brilliant 21-year-old student, stunningly portrayed by Juliette Lewis. In the film, Gabe Roth shows greater restraint than his real-life counterpart and turns down Rain's invitation that they have an affair.

In *Manhattan Murder Mystery,* Roth is reunited with his former lover Diane Keaton (who stepped in after Mia Farrow left Allen). *Manhattan Murder Mystery* re-visits Allen's earlier comic roots, and his on-screen relationship with Keaton is credible and affecting.

In 1996, Allen wrote, directed and starred in *The Mighty Aphrodite,* in which he portrays Lenny Weinrib, an old-style romantic New York sports writer. Trapped in a stable, but stagnating marriage to Amanda (Helena Bonham Carter), Lenny becomes obsessed with finding the birth mother of their adoptive child. The birth mother turns out to be Linda (Mira Sorvino, in an Oscar-winning performance), a classic whore-madonna: a prostitute and porno film star who is incredibly sweet and without guile. While the movie contains numerous funny lines and situations, there is also a faintly sad quality about Woody Allen's character and his desperate lusting after the much-younger co-star, especially when juxtaposed with his real-life involvement with Soon Yi Previn. The Mighty Aphrodite derives its title from the Greek goddess of love and features a Greek chorus led by the actor F. Murray Abraham.

Allen's 1997 film, *Everybody Says I Love You,* a quirky musical, is a detour back to his "earlier, funnier" period, although the film does not eual his best work in comedy.

In Roth's 1996 novel, *Sabbath's Theater,* the protagonist is Mickey Sabbath, a bitter, sex and death-obsessed puppeteer, whose career is ending due to severe arthritis. He and his alcoholic second wife, Roseanna, whom he hates, but upon whom he financially depends, have moved to a small New England village called Madamaska Falls. Mickey is fired from his drama teaching job at a local college in the aftermath of a scandal involving an affair with a student. He had been having a 13-year-long affair with Drenka Balich, the Croation-born wife of the local innkeeper. Drenka, whom Roth as Sabbath describes as resembling, "at her heaviest ... those clay figurines molded circa 2000 B.C., fat little dolls with big breasts and big thighs unearthed all the way from Europe down to Asia Minor and worshipped under a dozen different names as the great mother of the gods." Both Mickey Sabbath and Drenka Balich are addicted to repeated sexual encounters, which are vividly described in *Sabbath's Theater* in explicit language that might make Alexander Portnoy blush.

Like Lenny Weinrib, Mickey Sabbath expresses a fascination with prostitutes and ancient, non-Jewish cultures. Sabbath confesses that "whores played a leading role in my life. Always felt at home with whores," just as Lenny Weinrib, bored with his increasingly unavailable wife, finds comfort in the arms of the prostitute birth mother of his adoptive child.

Roth's and Allen's fixation on pagan, Egyptian, Greek and Roman mythology, symbols and culture was shared by their one-time intellectual mentor, Sigmund Freud, who kept clay figurines of Egyptian, Greek and Roman gods on the desk of his study, and who wrote a book claiming that Moses was really Egyptian and not a Hebrew. In *Operation Shylock*, Roth's main character meets an impostor posing as himself, who calls himself a "Diasporist," as opposed to a Zionist, an apt adjective for the sensibilities of Roth and Allen. Toward the end of *Sabbath's Theater*, when the nearly suicidal Mickey Sabbath has an emotional encounter with Fish, an Alzheimer's-afflicted cousin of his father, the old man moves him with his comment, "Isn't that remarkable?" when Sabbath tells him his parents had sent him to see Fish.

Sabbath reflects, "Remarkable. Yes, that's the word for it. It was all remarkable. Goodbye, remarkable. Egypt and Greece goodbye, and goodbye, Rome!"

Is Mickey Sabbath, who has spent much of his adult life desecrating not only the Sabbath but nearly every tenet of Jewish morality, at last coming to his senses and rejecting the temptations of the whores of Babylon, the Fleshpots of Egypt, the Hellenism of Greece and the fleeting glory that was Rome? In *Husbands and Wives*, did Woody Allen's character

Gabe Roth refuse to accept his student's invitation to a first kiss to affirm a higher plane of morality than he achieved in his off-screen "real life?" Is Roth still Alexander Portnoy whose altruistic impulses are overpowered by his lust and his "profound distrust in the sexual power of women" as described by Claire Bloom?

Roth's most recent novel, *American Pastoral,* explores the insights Roth gains by probing the life of a high school classmate, Seymour Levov, nicknamed the "Swede," an idealized "Gentile-looking," Jewish athlete, whose real life turns out to have been even more troubled than that of the angst-ridden Zuckerman.

Roth and Allen continue to demonstrate their skills as writers of effective satire and social commentary. But increasingly, both in their lives and work, they are grappling with more profound and serious issues about love, sex, death, the meaning of life—and the eternal and internal battle between the *Yetzer HaTov,* the impulse to do good and the *Yetzer HaRa,* the impulse to do evil, the Jewish way of describing *Portnoy's Complaint* and the dilemma of Philip Roth, Woody Allen and their diverse characters.

Every year or so, almost without fail for nearly 25 years, there has been a new Philip Roth novel and a new Woody Allen film to entertain and enrich our lives. It took the Children of Israel forty years in the wilderness of Sinai before they reached their Promised Land. How long will it be before Woody Allen's Greek chorus and Philip Roth's wailing protagonist can truly say: "Egypt and Greece, goodbye, and goodbye, Rome?" How long will it be before these two brilliant and talented men embrace the Jewish values they once mocked and each learn to be the *mensch* their loving Jewish parents wanted them to be?

Walter Ehrlich

The Jewish Community of St. Louis: the First Hundred Years, 1807-1907

By 1907, St. Louis and its Jewish citizenry both had made significant advances. When Joseph Philipson settled there in 1807, St. Louis was still a bustling and roisterous frontier town of fewer than 1,500 people, mostly French-Creole in origin or emigrants from Virginia and Kentucky. One hundred years later St. Louis ranked as the fourth largest city in the United States, its population exceeding 600,000. People whose ancestry was German, Irish, Polish, Italian, African and Jewish comprised the majority of the population. Jews alone numbered more than 40,000, approximately six percent of the total. St. Louis had developed into one of the country's major industrial and commercial centers, and Jewish merchants and businessmen had become an integral part of that scene. Jews also had held important political and civic positions.

Major changes had taken place also within the Jewish community. If 1907 marked the one hundredth anniversary of the first permanent Jewish resident in the city, few if any realized it at the time. Far from being concerned about their local roots, St. Louis Jewry at the turn of the century focused on more pressing contemporary problems: how to attain and solidify economic and social stability in its non-Jewish American surroundings; how to assist the increasing flow of eastern European immigrants in acclimating to their-new environment; and how to achieve Jewish continuity—despite internal differences over what constituted Judaism—so that future generations would be able to nourish and perpetuate their faith.

Nevertheless, St. Louis Jewry had crossed important thresholds. Except for Chicago, Jews numbered more in St. Louis by the turn of the century than in any other Midwestern city. Reflecting immigration patterns elsewhere in the country, those Jews who came to St. Louis during most of the 19th century were overwhelmingly German Jews from central and western Europe. Poor though they were—as was wont with most immigrants from any land—they brought with them the skills of the craftsman and the merchant, and they grew here in those economic areas. Many became the small neighborhood merchants so necessary to the growth of any city; some grew into the giants exemplified by Rice-Stix, Famous-Barr and Stix, Baer and Fuller. Jewish entrepreneurs predominated among the Washington Avenue manufacturers of all kinds of clothing apparel, their products reaching diverse markets all over the world.

Equally important, Jews participated fully in virtually every phase of St. Louis community life. Of course they aided co-religionists, especially those afflicted by the bloody Russian anti-Semitic pogroms. But they joined also with the larger St. Louis community in helping victims of the frightful 1906 San Francisco earthquake. In the press, from the pulpit, and at the ballot box, the Jewish community strongly endorsed and supported the 1906 St. Louis bond issue to build a municipal free bridge across the Mississippi, to enhance the city hospital, and to improve city court, fire and police department facilities and streets and sewers. By 1907 St. Louis Jewry's voice and actions clearly had contributed toward the city's progress.

In addition, much had transpired within the Jewish community itself. The original *minyan,* congregation, burial association and benevolent society—those institutions which almost universally have marked the existence of a Jewish community—had expanded perceptibly and dramatically. From the standpoint of religion, St. Louis Jewry reflected what other German Jews had done in America. To break away from what they viewed as repressive characteristics of European life, many sought to distance themselves from religious practices which they felt contributed toward that denigration. Between that and the pervasive urge to "Americanize," St. Louis German Jews followed several different paths. Some assimilated and abandoned their Judaism completely, not unlike what countless numbers of Jews had done for centuries before. Most, however, retained their Judaism, but led lives which placed very little emphasis on religion. Except for life-cycle events such as a *bris* or a wedding or a burial, their existence was very secular. For them being part of the Jewish community reflected itself in cultural or fraternal or philanthropic activities, through participation in a B'nai B'rith or a YMHA or a Jewish charitable institution. Finally, those who overtly maintained their Jewish religious beliefs fell into two groups. The smallest retained traditional orthodoxy and founded several *shuls,* only one of which, B'nai Amoona, survived. Most, however, found the new Reform Judaism more to their liking. United Hebrew and B'nai El, originally Orthodox, became Reform, and Shaare Emeth and Temple Israel came along later. By 1907, those five congregations that emerged within German Jewry ranked as the leading religious institutions in the Jewish community.

Equally significant with those economic and religious achievements were the many philanthropic and cultural organizations which enhanced Jewish community cohesiveness. Leading the way, perhaps, was the evolution of cooperative philanthropy which ultimately led to the Charitable and Educational Union and the Jewish Federation. Institutions such as the Home for the Aged and Infirm Israelites, the Hebrew Free and Industrial School, the YMHA, the Alliance and the Jewish Hospital, though plagued by developmental and growth pains, stood as monuments of prideful Jewish community achievement. So, too, the many men's and women's charitable, philanthropic and mutual aid organizations which reached out to help all needy Jews and, indeed, many non-Jews as well. Young people found stimulating cultural and social outlets in a variety of literary and musical societies. The Jewish press, exemplified by the *Voice* and the more recent *Modern View,* acted as another bonding agency by communicating Jewish awareness to all St. Louis Jewry.

By the beginning of the twentieth century, then, German Jewry had, in a sense, attained its goal. It had been able to maintain its own Jewish identity, and at the same time had become part of the overall St. Louis community. Jews contributed to and participated in virtually every phase of St. Louis life, and, except for rare instances of overt anti-Semitism, felt very comfortable in their Midwestern environment. Although many still associated with German *vereins* and similar German cultural organizations, they considered themselves to be fully American, albeit with German ancestry and resultant German affinities. But their most comforting sensibility was the confidence that as Jews they had found a secure home in America.

Yet a pervasive and gnawing concern remained. In the late 1870s and increasingly after the 1880s, a new element entered St. Louis Jewry: refugees from oppressive life in eastern Europe. Slavic rather than Germanic in tradition, Orthodox rather than Reform in religious outlook, culturally and linguistically more attuned to the eastern European *shtetl* and ghetto than to the more liberalized lifestyle of western Europe, the new wave of Jewish immigrant personified an unmistakably different kind of Jew. More than that, though, this new immigration represented the very type of religious and cultural life-style from which the German Jews had distanced themselves. Indeed, many now comfortably established in their new American environment viewed the newcomers as a distinct threat, fearful that their "backward" ways might actually undermine the status German Jews had finally achieved. Many actually questioned helping the Russian *schnorrers*. Yet the strong Judaic concept of *tzedakah* prevailed. Philanthropic efforts by German Jewry unquestionably helped many eastern Europeans escape from terrorist anti-Semitic depredations. Comparable efforts helped those refugees when they came to St. Louis, through support and assistance in such basic needs as clothing, housing, medical care and employment. Institutions such as the Alliance and the Hebrew Free School—and, of course, the St. Louis public schools—educated many and paved the way for productive employment. The new immigrants responded phenomenally, as they, too, acclimated to the new American environment.

Despite that successful acclimatization, though, the newer immigrants remained different from the older German element in two significant ways. Overwhelmingly the German Jews had embraced Reform Judaism; eastern European Jews virulently rejected Reform and sought to transplant their orthodoxy to their new St. Louis environment. Furthermore, where German Jews had readily and willingly acculturated in lifestyle to fit into their non-Jewish environment, the eastern Europeans strove to retain as much as possible of their eastern European culture and way of life. True, they did "Americanize," but primarily where absolutely necessary for physical survival. In the process, too, eastern European Jewry conscientiously and diligently established its own community requisites—*minyanim,* synagogues, cemeteries and benevolent institutions, making sure they satisfied Orthodox standards.

The result was that in a very short time two separate Jewish communities resided in St. Louis, the German/Reform community and the eastern European/Orthodox community. Despite cooperation and amity in some areas and ventures, bitter and acrimonious differences emerged in others; none was more divisive than the issue of *kashrut*. As long as the German/Reform element predominated numerically and financially, its philosophies and ways prevailed. But as the newer immigration grew in both numbers and financial abilities, some sort of showdown loomed as inevitable. That conflict pervaded the creation of the Jewish Hospital, in which the German/Reform element had its way. The opposite occurred in the establishment of the Orthodox Old Folks Home on North Grand and Blair. Indeed, those and other developments in the first few years of the twentieth century foreshadowed the growing need to resolve the serious divisiveness between the two St. Louis Jewish communities.

The year 1907, then, represents a historical watershed in St. Louis Jewish history. It was the one hundredth anniversary—the centennial year—of the arrival in St. Louis of the first identifiable Jew to settle there permanently. It was the time one could look back upon a century of considerable progress. It was the time also one could look ahead to the next century with more than a modicum of anxious and exciting anticipation. Would the Jews of St. Louis remain in two separate communities? Could they afford to? Was reconciliation of their deep differences even possible? How would existing institutions and forces affect the future? What new forces, either internal or external, would affect St. Louis Jewry? Could the second hundred years be as productive as the first hundred years? Only time would tell.

Pinchas Giller
The Deluge Continues

The classical Jewish mystics knew that there had been a Flood; the question was whether or not it had ever ended. Indeed, according to the mystical classic, the Zohar, the world never escaped the maelstrom of the Flood, which serves as a metaphor for the dilemmas of contemporary society and the existential plight of humankind. The spiritual elect, the saving remnant of Judaism, besieged by forces of internal corruption and external persecution, have taken refuge in the ark, which is tossed about on the turbulent sea. The ark represents the true Judaism—its inner, mystical core. At the Flood's recession, the remnant of true believers will emerge into the messianic age.

This allegory encompasses the images of the raven and the dove. In the original account, of course, the raven perishes in the sea, while the dove returns to the ark to signal the eventual passage of the elect to safety. The dove—*yonah* in Hebrew—is a multifaceted, numinous image in classical Jewish lore. It represents the exiled *shekhinah,* the incarnate presence of God in the world, who seeks a resting place, with Jerusalem as her eventual nest. The word *yonah* is also the Hebrew name of the willful prophet Jonah, whose cry to God from the depths is associated, by the Zohar, with the dove's mission in the Flood, for both Jonah and the dove are agents of redemption.

According to the Zohar, the raven and the dove symbolize two movements in Judaism. The movement represented by the raven has failed in its mission, pulled down by the overwhelming demands of existence in an alienating community, like the raven that flies off to perish in the waters.

The failure of the raven, the corrupted Judaism, leaves the dove to reveal the redemptive process.

Read this way, the symbols and metaphors of the story provide a rationale for the social upheavals and arbitrary tragedies of Jewish history. Those events are the deluge through which the elect must pass. Similarly, the Flood also served as symbol for the drama of the Day of Atonement. Repentance is the agency of redemption, saving the adherent from annihilation, as signaled by the image of the prophet Jonah, who is the dove, redeemed from the roiling depths. The wide use of the Flood in the later Zoharic work, *Tikkunei ha-Zohar,* caused that work to be identified liturgically with the season of penitence from the beginning of the month of Elul through the Day of Atonement. Many editions of *Tikkunei ha-Zohar* are divided so as to guide the pious reader through a recitation of the whole work during that 40-day period.

These interpretations present the Flood as a recurring myth of renewal. There is a redemptive aspect in both the personal and the national understandings of the Flood. If the Flood represents the searing processes of repentance, or *teshuvah,* then the dove represents the deliverance provided by morality and the Torah. If the Flood is a social upheaval, then the true doctrines of Judaism are symbolized by the dove. In each situation, however, the raven represents a blind alley or misguided choice that can only lead to oblivion.

In considering these choices anew, at the onset of a new year, we are called upon to consider which is the true, viable Jewish path and which is the illusion, which is the dove and which is the raven?

Desolation

Like characters in a musical, Biblical figures are apt to step outside the narrative and break into song. So Hannah does, in exultation upon the birth of Samuel (I Samuel 2:1-10), or Jonah when he expresses faith from the fish's belly (Jonah 2:3-10).

In the Biblical "musical," the song is called a prayer and is presented in the familiar style of a psalm. But these extemporaneous prayers have only a vague connection, in their content, to the events of the narrative. Perhaps Hannah and Jonah spontaneously began to recite popular prayers of their day.

In the Book of Psalms, on the other hand, what otherwise might appear to be general prayers are linked to crises in the life of the psalmist, such as "A Victory Song of David, when he fled before Saul in the cave" (Psalm 57), "A Psalm of David, when he was fleeing before Absalom his son" (Psalm 3), or "A Hymn of David, when Nathan the prophet came to him, after he had been with Bathsheba" (Psalm 51). Expressive poetic prayer, Biblical spirituality teaches us here, is often situational. It is based on a character's existential condition, what he or she is going through at the time.

When Moses steps forward to begin his parting song in the Torah portion of *Ha'azinu,* he knows that he is going to die, and has come to remonstrate with the people of Israel, in a last surge of Deuteronomic moral rage. Primordial figures—the elders and officers of the people, the very heavens and earth—are his witnesses (Deuteronomy 31:29), "for I know that after my death, you will become degenerate, straying from the path which I have commanded you." The whole Book of Deuteronomy is his farewell oration; the final song is a testament to the inevitability of human inadequacy. Moses is literally singing for his life, denying, through images of eternity, his impending death.

The song portrays God as a rock, nurturing yet unyielding (32:4, 18, 30, 31). God is the father-creator (32:6) who finds the people of Israel as desert orphans (32:10) and nurtures them with an eagle's feral obsession (32:11). As the triumphant master of nature (32:13), God draws enormous fecundity from the arid, unforgiving land, "suckling [Israel) with honey from the rock, oil from flint," raising fat, complacent, bovine children (32:14).

Israel's response is to turn to the degeneracy of paganism and the occult (32:17). The song expresses classical prophetic astonishment at the emptiness of pagan belief, calling its object a "non-god." God's response is to afflict Israel with a "non-people" (32:21) and then, when Israel is wholly decimated, to exclaim "I, I am He, there is no god besides Me, I kill and I bring to life, I wound and I heal." This truth is expressed in an orgy of blood and vengeance, the triumph of God's "flashing sword" (32:41), and "arrows drunk with blood" (32:42).

A hairdresser in Berkeley once told me that the Biblical God often seemed like an alcoholic parent. It was painful to hear, because I knew she had been reading closely. Certainly God's response to the song itself is brutal: "Go up onto Mount Nebo ... and die on that mountain ... for you dishonored me, and did not sanctify me . . . from afar you will see the land where you will not go" (32:49-50). Moses' silent acceptance of this judgment is the mute perversity of the codependent.

As prophecy, the song in *Ha'azinu* is as personal as the anguished cries of Jeremiah, an expression of Moses' dispossession. The song is altogether relevant to Moses' condition. As God will bring rough justice to Israel, so Moses must pay for his transgression. He will die orphaned and alone, hounded by the memory of his own inadequacy and unacceptability, doomed to the alienation of exile, with the terrible knowledge that it is his own fault.

Rabbi Zvi Magence
Generosity

We read in the Torah that Abraham called in his faithful servant, and made him swear to do what he asked of him. The request was: "Go unto my country, and to my kindred, and take a wife for my son." The servant, who was surely Eliezer, faithfully swore to fulfill Abraham's wish. He came to the place which Abraham had told him to go to. However, a strange thing happened once he came there. Instead of going to the house of Abraham's family, he went to the well. Moreover, the servant made an unusual wish: He would go up to one of the young girls, and ask her for a drink of water. If she would say: "Drink, and I will give thy camels drink also," then she would be the one whom Isaac should marry.

Of course Eliezer wanted to test the kindness and generosity of the woman who would deserve Isaac for her husband. Nevertheless it was a very unusual and even strange wish. The Rabbis say his wish was wrong, since he had been told exactly where to go, and instead of going to the well, he should have gone there. Yet the Almighty helped him—his wish was fulfilled, and the girl was Rebecca of Abraham's family.

In order to understand the strange wish and consequent events, we have to know more about Abraham and his servant, Eliezer. The Rabbis tell us that Eliezer had a daughter, and that he naturally wished to see her married to the Master's son. He proposed this match to Abraham, but Abraham turned it down. He said: "Your daughter is not the right person to build the future nation of Israel." Eliezer suspected that Abraham was not as liberal as he preached. He had said that all men are equal, that they are God's children, and should serve Him. Those were nice slogans, but in practice, he suspected, Abraham did not live by these ideals. Otherwise why should he object to the proposed marriage?

Eliezer's daughter, who had been raised in Abraham's house, had absorbed his generosity. She would welcome a stranger, give him a drink of water, and food. She might be busy, yet she would take the time to help a man in need. What more did Abraham expect? Therefore Eliezer made this strange wish. His daughter would say: "Here is my pail, there is the water, stranger, help yourself. I will wait for you, although I may be late for my dinner." This in itself is an act of kindness. However, if the girl would say: "I will do it, not withstanding the fact that others are stronger, and are more accustomed to this work." Then she would be the right person to marry Isaac. She would build a generous nation. So it was that in this way Eliezer came to recognize that Rebecca was truly the one destined for Isaac, and any anger he may have held towards Abraham for refusing his daughter vanished.

Generosity and kindness are the cornerstones upon which Judaism is built. We exist by these qualities, and because of them. Even when there are others more affluent, and even if it may be easier for them to help, we say: "I will help." We consider helping people in need a privilege and a duty. The Jewish nation was established upon this foundation, and we continue upon the path our forefathers revealed to us.

Marc Saperstein

The Simpleton's Prayer:
Transformations of a Motif in Hebrew Literature

The Simpleton's Prayer, which is criticized by a representative of the religious establishment and then validated by a higher authority, is a recurrent theme in the literatures of many nations. It may be viewed from different perspectives: as a folkloristic motif,[1] as a religious doctrine proclaiming the value of simple sincerity in God's sight, or as an expression of a challenge to established norms that make knowledge and conformance with standardized procedures paramount for the service of the Almighty. Relatively little attention has been paid to the literary contexts in which this theme appears. Several well-known Hebrew tales built upon this motif have been lumped together, as if they were a single story with minor variations, but a careful reading reveals that each incarnation of the common motif is actually an independent literary unit, with an identity and meaning of its own.

The first story is from *Sefer Hasidim,* that unique compendium of the aspirations and superstitions of medieval German Pietism:

> Whatever a person can do in the nature of a *mitzvah,* he should do, and whatever he is incapable of doing, he should *think* of doing.
>
> Once upon a time, there was a man who worked as a shepherd. He did not know how to pray. Every day he used to say, "Master of the universe, You know very well that if You had animals and gave them to me to watch, though I receive a fee for watching the animals of everyone else, I would watch Yours for nothing, because I love You." The man was a Jew. Once a great Jewish scholar came his way and found the shepherd praying in this manner. He said to him, "Fool, do not pray like that."
>
> The shepherd asked, "How should I pray?"
>
> The scholar taught him the order of blessings, the reading of the *shema,* and the eighteen benedictions, on condition that he would never again say what he used to say.
>
> After the scholar went away, the shepherd forgot all that he had been taught, so that he could not pray at all. He was afraid to say what he used to say, because the *tzaddik* had forbidden him to do so.
>
> One night, the scholar had a dream in which he was told, "If you do not

go and tell him that he should say what he used to say before you came to him, great evil will befall you, for you have robbed Me of someone from the world to come." Immediately he went and asked the shepherd, "What are you praying?"

He answered, "Nothing, for I have forgotten what you taught me, and you commanded me not to say, 'If He had animals. ... .'"

The scholar replied, "This is what I dreamed: say what you used to say."

Here there was neither learning nor good deeds, but he intended to do good, and God considered it as if he had done something great, for "the Merciful One desires the heart." Therefore, a person should think good thoughts about the Holy One, blessed be He.[2]

The story is set in a doctrinal framework, but it may be analyzed independently, without reference to the moral drawn. The shepherd is presented as an uneducated man who does not know the words of the fixed liturgy. Infused with a love of God, he expresses this love through his own ritual, a liturgy that he himself created and utters every day. From the perspective of the scholar, the problem with the shepherd is not that he holds an anthropomorphic view of God, but rather that he fails to fulfill the *mitzvah* of prayer. There is nothing intrinsically wrong with the shepherd's words, which express a willingness to serve without reward through a hypothetical situation familiar to him.

The scholar who is by no means portrayed as a man of arrogance, condescension, or cruelty, is disturbed because the shepherd says these words in place of the proper liturgy. He, therefore, does more than criticize; he acts constructively, teaching the illiterate shepherd all that is necessary for the fulfillment of the *mitzvah,* an educational task presumably requiring patience and perseverance. He then leaves the scene, assuming that the shepherd is capable of fulfilling the commandment properly. Even the condition that he imposes is understandable. Once the shepherd learned the liturgy, he is obligated to make the effort necessary to pray with the proper words. If the option of returning to the familiar formula were to remain, the shepherd might be tempted to revert to his accustomed manner because it is easier. The scholar agrees, therefore, to teach him, only with the proviso that the shepherd's own liturgy be permanently abandoned.

The behavior of the scholar is reasonable and responsible. If the shepherd had, indeed, prayed regularly in the words that he had learned, the dream conveying divine displeasure would never have occurred. The scholar errs, not in his attempt to teach, but in his assumption that the effects of what he has taught would be permanent. He takes it for granted that, given a minimal education, everyone can achieve the same standard of religious observance. He does not respond to the man as he is: a shepherd unaccustomed to sustained intellectual effort and isolated from the reinforcement of other worshippers, incapable of persisting in the new discipline that he has been taught, yet sufficiently respectful of the scholar to observe scrupulously the prohibition imposed upon him. Therefore the scholar unwittingly causes harm, directly to the shepherd and indirectly to God Himself, because the shepherd no longer prays at all. Fortunately, the damage can be undone.

It has been noted that the thrust of this story seems to conflict with the German Pietists' insistence that the standard text of the liturgy must be guarded against even the minutest change.[3] Yet there is no necessary contradiction. The story never challenges the traditional liturgy. Nowhere is it implied that the shepherd's formulation is in any way preferable to the standardized prayer. It is said to be preferable only to nothing at all, which is certainly not an anti-establishment doctrine. The words of the shepherd are obviously inappropriate for a scholar or a *hasid*. They still do not fulfill the *mitzvah* of prayer. But they are adequate for the shepherd, sufficient to make him eligible for the "world to come."

The second story is set against a totally different background: the return to Judaism of *conversos* who had grown up as Christians without any Jewish education.

> It happened in the days of the Ari, of blessed memory. One of the *conversos,* who came from Portugal to the holy city of Safed in the upper Galilee, heard the rabbi of one of the holy congregations there give a sermon about the showbread that was offered in the sanctuary every Sabbath. Apparently, the rabbi sighed during his sermon and said in sorrow, "And now, because of our many sins, we have nothing designated for sacred use, which would enable the divine emanation to fall upon that which is not so designated."

The *converso,* who heard this, went home and, in the naivetÈ of his heart, commanded his wife that no matter what the circumstances, she should prepare for him every Friday two loaves of bread (from flour) sifted thirteen times, that it should be kneaded in purity, given the very best treatment, and baked well in the home oven, for he wanted to bring it as an offering before the Lord's altar. "Perhaps God will consider us, and accept them, and eat this offering." His wife did just as he said. Every Friday he would bring the two loaves of bread before the altar, entreat God to accept them with good will and eat them, and pray that they be pleasing and enjoyable to Him. He would say things of this kind persistently, like a son who importunes his father. Then he would leave the loaves and go on his way

The sexton used to come and take the two loaves of bread without investigating their source. He would eat and rejoice in them, as one does at harvest-time. At the hour for evening prayer, that God-fearing man (the *converso*) would run to the synagogue. Not finding the loaves there, he would rejoice exuberantly. He would then go and say to his wife, "All praise and thanks to God, for He has not despised the lowliness of the poor. He has already received the bread and eaten it hot. For His Name's sake, do not be negligent in making them; take great care. . ." He continued in this manner for a long time.

It happened one Friday that the rabbi whose sermon had led the man to bring the loaves was standing in the synagogue on the *bimah,* practicing the sermon that he was to give on the following day. The *converso* came with the loaves, approached the altar as usual, and began to utter his supplications in the accustomed manner. So deeply was he engrossed in exuberant joy as he brought his gift that he did not notice the rabbi standing on the *bimah.* The rabbi grew silent; he saw and heard everything that the man did. He then became extremely angry, called him over and rebuked him, saying, "You fool! Does *our* God eat and drink? Obviously the sexton is taking the bread, and you think that it is God who takes it. It is a great sin to attribute any corporeality to God, who has no likeness of a body and is incorporeal." He continued to berate the man until the sexton came, in his accustomed manner, to take the loaves, When the rabbi saw him, he called out, "Thank this man for the two loaves that you came to take; he is the one who has brought them every Friday to the synagogue." The sexton thanked him, without embarrassment.

When the man heard this, he began to weep. He besought the rabbi to forgive him for having misunderstood the sermon. He had thought that he was performing a *mitzvah,* whereas, according to the rabbi, he was actually transgressing. While this was happening, a special emissary from the Ari came to the rabbi and said to him in the name of that godly sage, "Go home, and set your household in order, for tomorrow, at the time you intended to deliver your sermon, you will die! The proclamation has already been made about this."

The rabbi was aghast at this dire message. He went to the Ari to inquire what was his sin. The Ari replied, "I have heard that it is because you have spoiled the pleasure which was God's. For from the day of the destruction, He had no pleasure comparable to that when this *converso,* in the naivetÈ of his heart, would bring two loaves of bread and offer them before His altar." The rabbi went and set his household affairs in order. On the Sabbath day, at the time when he was to have begun preaching, he passed into eternity.[4]

Structurally, this story is similar to the one found in *Sefer Hasidim.* The *converso* corresponds to the shepherd, the rabbi to the scholar. The Ari plays a role analogous to the dream, as a channel of divine communication. While one purpose of the story is to tell of Rabbi Luria's miraculous knowledge, from a literary point of view there would be no essential difference if he were replaced by a voice from heaven. Yet, despite the similarities of structure and theme, this is a very different story from the first; it is more complex, more disturbing, more suffused with pathos.

The naive misunderstanding of the sermon[5] makes the relationship between rabbi and *converso* significantly more intricate than that between the scholar and the shepherd of *Sefer Hasidim,* for the rabbi is indirectly responsible for the act that he later seeks to halt. Having been raised as a Christian in Portugal, the *converso* takes the rabbi's discussion of the showbread literally. In the belief that God actually eats the bread, he resolves to do something about the cessation of the sacrificial offerings by fulfilling the Biblical injunction himself. This, of course, perverts the rabbi's intention. But the "misunderstanding" turns out to be correct on a higher level, for the Ari describes the *converso's* oblation as bringing God greater pleasure than any He has experienced since the suspension of the Temple cult.

The cast of characters is expanded by the addition of two minor personalities, the *converso's* wife and the sexton; both are needed for the plot, but they are little more than props. In contrast, the *converso* and the rabbi emerge from these few lines as believable and real. At issue is not a sin of omission, as in the case of the shepherd, but a sin of commission: a grossly anthropomorphic view of God, leading to actions that could be interpreted as idolatrous. From the perspective of the religious establishment, what the *converso* does is far more opprobrious than the shepherd's "prayer." And, yet, even before the final vindication, we see that he is depicted with approval. He is said to be "God-fearing," he acts without duplicity or ulterior motive and, in the naivetÈ or innocence of his heart, he experiences "exuberant joy" in his service. The dissonance between the scandalous act and the narrator's sympathy for the purity of the *converso's* intention and inner religious state creates a powerful tension at the heart of the story.

The rabbi is actually quite different from his analogue in *Sefer Hasidim*. It is not that he is a bad man. He feels deeply the imperfections of Jewish life in exile, even while living in the land of Israel, and he is conscientious about preparing his sermon. But he acts in a manner that is totally destructive. Unlike the scholar, he does not offer to teach the ignorant man. He insults him, humiliates him, lectures at him in anger. He even alludes disparagingly to the *converso's* Christian background as the cause of his error—"*our* God does not eat and drink"—despite a long tradition prohibiting this type of affront. Nevertheless, the severity of the ending comes as something of a shock. Herein lies the greatest difference between the two stories. Instead of a warning with instructions to rectify the wrong that he has done, the rabbi hears that his fate has been sealed inexorably, as a punishment for his action. This follows from the inner logic of the story. What the rabbi has done cannot be undone. The shepherd can return to his original profession of love for God, but once the *converso* has learned that the sexton has been taking his loaves, he can never return to his innocent devotion. The rabbi has irrevocably destroyed something precious to God, and his punishment for this fatal error is as ineluctable as the denouement of a Greek tragedy.[6]

The third variation on the theme is probably the best known:

A certain villager used to pray on the Days of Awe in the House of Prayer of the Baal Shem Tov. He had a son whose wit was dull and who could not read even the letters in the prayer book, much less recite a holy word. His father never brought him along to the city, because the boy was completely ignorant. But when the boy became Bar Mitzvah, his father took him with him to the city on Yom Kippur, so as to be able to watch him and keep him from eating out of simple ignorance on the holy fast day.

Now the boy had a little flute on which he used to play all the time when he sat in the field tending his flock. He took the flute with him from home and put it in his coat, and his father did not know about it. The boy sat in the House of Prayer all Yom Kippur without praying, because he did not know how. During the *Musaf* Prayer he said to his father, "Father, I want to play my flute." His father became terrified, and spoke sharply to the boy. The boy had to restrain himself.

During the Afternoon Prayer the boy repeated again, "Father, let me play on my flute." Again the father spoke sharply to his son, and warned him not to dare do any such thing. But he could not take the flute away from his son, because of the prohibition against unnecessary handling *(mukzeh)* on Yom Kippur.

After the Afternoon Prayer, the boy said again, "Please let me play on my flute." Seeing that the boy wanted so much to play on his flute, his father said to him: "Where is the flute?" The child pointed to the pocket of his coat. The father took the child's pocket and held it in his hand, to keep the boy from taking out the flute and playing on it. Holding the pocket with the flute in this way, the man stood and prayed the Closing Prayer. In the middle of the prayer, the boy forced the flute out of his pocket and blew a blast so loud that all who heard it were taken aback. When the Baal Shem Tov (who was the Reader) heard the sound, he shortened his prayer.

After the prayer the Baal Shem Tov said, "With the sound of his flute this child lifted up all the prayers and eased my burden. For this child does not know anything, but, by dint of his seeing and hearing the prayer of Israel all of this holy day, the prayer's holy spark kindled an actual fire in him. One who knows how can clothe that sacred flame with the words of prayer before God. But this one knew nothing, and he could find no means of quenching his thirst except by blowing upon the whistle. When his father prevented him, the flame of his longing burned ever more strongly, until it nearly consumed his soul. The power of this craving impelled him to blow from the true depth of his heart, without any constraint, purely for God. 'The Merciful One desires the heart,' and the pure breath of the boy's lips was very acceptable to Him. In this way, he lifted all our prayers."[7]

The boy is obviously paralleled to the shepherd and the *converso* in the preceding stories. His intellectual limitations are emphasized not only in his inability to master the letters of the Hebrew alphabet, but, also, in the fact that, though he is thirteen, constant supervision is required to keep him from eating on the Day of Atonement. The transformation of the itinerant scholar and the rabbi–preacher into the father of the simpleton adds a new twist to the story. He represents, not the established leadership, but the ingrained sensibilities of the Jewish community. More important, it is not the insensitivity of an outsider, but the anguished concern of a loving parent that is examined.

The reader may infer the father's patient attempts to teach his son the rudimentary Hebrew necessary for public worship, and his disappointment at the futility of these efforts; he may sense how much it would have meant to the father to be able to share the experience of Yom Kippur in the Baal Shem Tov's synagogue, and empathize with the sad loneliness of having to leave the child behind "because he was completely ignorant." That year, it would undoubtedly have been easier for the father to have left his son at home. He risks embarrassment and distraction for the boy's sake, in order to keep him from sinning by eating on the great fast. Presumably, the boy could have taken the whistle and blown it before his father knew what was happening, but he respectfully asks permission, thereby creating a conflict that intensifies as the closing hour draws near. With the son's ever more urgent pleading, the father's response escalates, from surprised dismay, to exasperated anger, to desperate action. In order to guard his son from what he believes would be a grave sin, he himself risks transgressing, by holding the boy's pocket closed over the forbidden flute.

When the shrill tone pierces the prayers of the faithful, the tension concealed in the conflict between father and son becomes overt. The reaction of the worshippers is not described in detail; their amazement is noted and their hostility can be assumed. The focus of tension lies in the awaited reaction of the Baal Shem Tov, who acts in an unusual manner, shortening the climactic prayers of the concluding service. Like the divine communication through the dream and like the Ari, the Baal Shem Tov represents the ultimate source of authority. But his function is different: it is neither to reprimand and instruct nor to proclaim punishment, but, rather, to justify and explain. There is little, if any, criticism of the father. We have, instead, an elucidation of what has happened, based on a knowledge that penetrates through external appearances to the very core.

As in the case of the shepherd's tale, the value of simple and sincere spontaneity in one unable to learn the words of the fixed liturgy is emphasized. But two new elements make this a more radical story than the other one. First, the action validated by the Baal Shem Tov involves an infringement of the halakhic prohibition against holding and sounding a musical instrument on Yom Kippur. And, second, here there is an explicit comparison between the idiosyncratic expression of the simpleton and the normative prayer of the ordinary Jew, with the normative prayer found wanting. The boy's outburst is superior to the traditional worship of the others and, in seeking to frustrate his son, the father is inadvertently harming the entire congregation. All three stories make the point that the fire of devotion in the ignorant makes their chosen means of expression acceptable and pleasing to God. Here, alone, we find the concomitant teaching: that without the fire of devotion, the words of the fixed liturgy may be far less acceptable than the notes of a flute.

The Hasidic story points toward a parallel in a classic of modern Hebrew literature, "Faivke's Judgment Day," by Isaac Dov Berkowitz. Here, too, a Jew from an outlying village brings his son to the city to pray in the synagogue on Yom Kippur; here, too, the boy is unable to participate in the service because of his complete lack of knowledge. Both father and son are subjected to humiliation and torment by the local Jews. Matis, the father, is able to shrug it off; Faivke, bewildered, becomes angry and defiant. The climactic moment comes in the afternoon:

> Soon the prayers began again. After a thunderous bang on the table, the silent prayer began. Afterwards the young cantor chanted away with a now faltering voice and waning strength. It seemed as if the whole thing had become burdensome; he was now merely completing his obligations and putting the interests of the majority before his own. For a moment Matis the smith, standing near the window, forgot where he was; he forgot about the open prayer book, and stared out at the tops of the trees aglow in the setting sun. Then something happened that startled the worshippers. Matis dropped his head on to the windowsill, hid his face in the prayer book, and wept bitterly. Everyone turned towards him. Some burst out laughing. The words that the cantor had just chanted should, in no way, have evoked tears. Why should anyone weep at the

words "Michael praises on the right" in the late afternoon service? Laughing and joking, several young boys and some men came up to Matis. The innkeeper's son-in-law tugged at his *tallit*.

"Mister, you made a mistake, no one cries at this place!"

Matis controlled his tears and did not reply: he did not even acknowledge the man's presence. The red-headed, bird-faced lad with the freckles also leaped into the fray and pulled at Matis' *tallit*:

"Mister, we don't cry here!"

Faivke (the son of the smith) looked in confusion first at his father and then at the crowd. He leaped up impetuously and glued his piercing, black eyes on the red-head's face:

"You, you ... may wolves devour you!"

Boisterous laughter exploded in the room and in the confusion that followed someone yelled out, "Brat! In a holy place?" One of the worshippers responded with, "Ha, ha, the lad from Starodubov must be a fullfledged *goy*."

Later, on the way home, after a fight with his tormentors that leaves him battered, Faivke confronts his father in anguished confusion:

Faivke was silent and continued staring at his father with feverish eyes. Then he blurted out, "What about you. . . what happened to you? ... Why did you cry? Tell me, why did you cry there?"

"I didn't really cry, you silly boy," said Matis. "I didn't cry at all. It's only that today is Yom Kippur ... and mother is at home all alone ... waiting for us.. . . Get up, Faivke, let's go home! Mother'll put a bandage on your head."

"No!" Faivke persisted, "tell me, why did you cry? Why did you cry, when they were all laughing? You shouldn't cry when they laugh. You cried and they laughed... we ought to knock their teeth out, slap their faces, bite them, bite them... bite them all. May wolves devour them ... !"[8]

While Matis the smith is not depicted as an ignorant man incapable of reading the prayerbook, his spontaneous sobs, interrupting the worship toward the end of Yom Kippur, are obviously analogous to the boy's blast on his flute. Matis' expression of genuine religious sentiment is all the more poignant in its stark contrast with the mechanical performance of the cantor and the irreverent behavior of the other worshippers, who sanctimoniously invoke the holiness of the time and the place while showing themselves oblivious to the holy.[9] One waits for a vindication of Matis, if not before the derisive local worshippers, then at least before his bewildered son.

But there is no voice from heaven, no messenger from the Ari, no explanation from the Baal Shem Tov. No higher authority intercedes to set things right by vindicating the sobs of the blacksmith. Matis continues to appear embarrassed and foolish. And Faivke, his son, who had risen to his father's defense, ultimately vents his confusion against the man who sobbed while the others laughed. Unable to comprehend either the traditional society, with its perversion of religion, or a father too deeply rooted in this society to stand up for himself, Faivke tries to fight back and is destroyed, a victim not only of Jews without compassion, but of a Judgment Day without a judge. It is the anticipation of divine intervention, produced by the literary background, that makes God's silence appear as tacit approval of the hypocritical and heartless Jewish townsmen. The framework in which the ultimate Power intercedes on behalf of the powerless is forever shattered.

It has been argued that modern Hebrew literature can be defined by its secular stance, entailing a revolutionary repudiation of the traditional world-view that is based on faith in the reality of God and the inherent sanctity of all experience.[10] While overly simplistic, failing to account either for secular components in medieval literature or for religious dimensions in certain modern writings, this criterion is exemplified in the tales that have been analyzed here. Yet the first three stories should not merely be grouped together in contrast with the last. To subsume them under a motif number in a folklore index is to overlook the nuances that give each one its distinctive literary power.

---

[1] See, for example, Dov Noy, *"Tefillat ha-Tamim Moridah Geshamim,"* Mahanayim, 51 (1960):34–45, especially p. 36, n. 11.

[2] Sefer Hasidim, ed. Wistinetzki (Frankfurt am Main, 1924), p. 6, translated by the author. For a discussion of parallel treatments of this theme in Christian and Moslem literature and related motifs in the aggadah, see Bernard Heller's *Gott Wunscht das Herz,"* HUCA, 4 (1927), especially pp. 368–79.

[3] See Joseph Dan, *Ha-Sippur ha-Ivri Biyemei ha-Beinayim,* p. 180. Dan's suggestion that the story was included in Sefer Hasidim by editors who did not understand its "antinomian conclusions" is not warranted by our analysis.

[4]*Mishnat Hakhamim,* quoted in Simha Asaf, "*Anusei Sefarad u-Portugal be-Sifrut ha-Teshuvot,*" *Zion,* 5 (1933): 25-26, translated by the author; cf. M.J. Bin Gurion, *Mimekor Yisrael: Classical Jewish Folktales* (Bloomington, Indiana, 1976). II, pp. 524-26. The showbread discussed in the sermon is mentioned several times in the Pentateuch; see especially Leviticus 24:5-9. The *converso* confuses this with the "two loaves" that were to be offered in relation to the holiday of Shavuot (Leviticus 23.17). The thirteen siftings apply to neither the showbread nor the two loaves, but to the *omer; see Mishnah Menahot* 6.7.

[5]The misunderstanding leading to comic results and the "literal fool" are well-known folkloristic motifs. If the shepherd in *Sefer Hasidim* had heard the scholar speak about the "flocks of the Lord" and drawn his own conclusions, there would have been a parallel.

[6]Another underlying theme of this story may be its hostility toward the philosophical approach to Judaism. The rabbi, in emphasizing the absolute incorporeality of God and the sin of attributing any physical properties to Him, articulates a doctrine central to the Jewish philosophers. Maimonides, who insisted that one who prays to a God envisioned corporeally, no matter how well-intentioned he may be, is guilty of idolatry, worshipping not the true God but a creation of the imagination, would certainly not have been pleased with this story. In contrast, the narrator represents a position similar to that of R. Joseph Yabetz, who maintained that a simple Jewish woman who conceives of God as corporeal but believes in Him, loves Him, and keeps His commandments, is far superior to the philosopher with all his lofty conceptions (*Or ha-Hayyim,* p. 32b). This view is ultimately ratified by the Ari.

[7]*Emunat Zaddikim* (Tel Aviv, 1965), P. 12, translated in *Days of Awe* by S.Y. Agnon, (New York, 1965), pp. 268-70; the final paragraph has been modified by the author in accordance with the Hebrew text. This story should not be confused with the technical teachings of the Hasidim concerning prayer, on which see Louis Jacobs, *Hasidic Prayer* (New York, 1973), and especially pp. 34-35.

[8]"Faivke's Judgment Day," translated by Avraham Holtz in *Isaac Dov Berkowitz: Voice of the Uprooted* (London, 1973), pp. 187-88, 191. The nature of this passage as a transformation of the motif we have been discussing has been pointed out in a fine study of this study by Gershon Shaked, *Al Arba'ah Sippurim* (Jerusalem, 1963), p. 21.

[9]There is trenchant irony in the narrator's question, "Why should anyone weep at the words 'Michael praises on the right' in the late afternoon service?" The *piyut* continues, "Gabriel acclaims on the left saying, 'There is none like God in Heaven! Who is like Thy people Israel on earth?'" The unworthiness of the Jews in this synagogue and the consequent emptiness of these words might, indeed, move a sensitive soul to tears.

[10]See, for example, Baruch Kurzweil, *Sifruteinu ha-Hadashah: Hermshekh a Mahaprekhah?* (Jerusalem, 1958), p. 16 and *passim.*

Howard Schwartz
Spirit Possession in Judaism

Most students of Jewish folklore and mysticism are familiar with the concept of the *dybbuk,* in which the soul of one who has died takes possession of one of the living, and must be exorcised. S. Ansky's famous drama *The Dybbuk* portrays such a possession, and the third act of the play is based on an actual rabbinic exorcism ceremony. This is a negative form of possession, but there is also a little known form of spirit possession in Judaism in which the soul of an ancestor or a master enters the soul of a living person in order to comfort or instruct them. This form of metempsychosis is known as an *ibbur,* which literally means "impregnation." The presence of an *ibbur* was regarded as an exceptional blessing by Jewish mystics, especially those of Safed in the 16th century, while the same mystics strove greatly to exorcise *dybbuks* from those who were possessed by them.

Just as there are tales in which the possession of a *dybbuk* is portrayed, so too are there tales about possession by an *ibbur.* However, there are far more *dybbuk* tales, as such possession was often the explanation for madness, and the exorcism served as the cure, one that often worked. These *dybbuk* tales, virtually all of which are presented as true accounts, always follow the same pattern. An evil spirit, pursued by avenging angels, enters into various objects and beings, such as a rock, a flower, a dog, a cow, or a person. The person begins to behave strangely, with the spirit speaking in a voice of its own. A rabbi is called in, who determines that a *dybbuk* has taken possession of them. The rabbi then compels the *dybbuk* to recount the story of his sin and the history of his soul after death, until it took possession of that person. Then the rabbi exorcises the *dybbuk* and it is forced to depart.

In one famous tale from the 16th century, "The Widow of Safed," a *dybbuk* takes possession of a widow because she does not believe that the waters of the Red Sea truly parted. Rabbi Isaac Luria, known as the Ari, sends his disciple, Rabbi Hayim Vital, to exorcise the *dybbuk.* Hayim Vital questions the *dybbuk,* extracts its story, and exorcises it. Later it is discovered that the text inside the *mezzuzah* on the doorpost of the widow's house was flawed and therefore ineffective. Thus it was her failure of belief and the loss of the protective powers of the *mezzuzah* that opened her to the danger of possession by the *dybbuk*.

Considering that possession by a *dybbuk* is so closely linked to evil and madness, it is remarkable to discover a Jewish form of spirit possession that is regarded as positive. Yet that is indeed the case, as demonstrated by the tales about possession by an *ibbur*. Unlike that of a *dybbuk*, however, this kind of possession is temporary, and is linked to a sacred object, such as a holy book or to phylacteries known as *tefillin*. Whenever the living sage opens that book or puts on the *tefillin*, the spirit of the *ibbur* fuses with his own.

In one such tale, "A Kiss from the Master," a rich man was invited to join the sages of Safed on Lag Ba'omer at the shrine of Rabbi Shimon bar Yohai in Meron. It was there that Rabbi Shimon bar Yohai was said to have written the Zohar, the primary text of the Kabbalah (even though modern scholarship tells us that he did not). The sages and their guest sat in a circle near the grave, and one by one read passages from the Zohar, as was their custom, and interpreted them. But when the guest received the book, he could not read the Aramaic in which it was written. And he was deeply ashamed.

After they had finished reading, everyone but the rich man returned to their tents. But he remained in the shrine, weeping bitterly for his lack of knowledge, until at last he fell asleep. And no sooner did he sleep than he dreamed that Rabbi Shimon bar Yohai appeared to him in a dream and he comforted him, and before he departed he kissed him on the mouth. And that is when the rich man woke up.

From the moment he opened his eyes, the rich man felt as if a new spirit was within him. He picked up the book of the Zohar and opened it to the first page. There he found, much to his amazement, that he could now read the Hebrew letters. Not only that, but the true meaning of every letter rose up in his vision, for the spirit of Rabbi Shimon had fused with his soul. In this way his eyes were opened to the hidden meanings of the Torah and its mysteries were revealed to him.

Later the others returned to the shrine, and they began to discuss a difficult passage in the Zohar, which none of them could understand. Then the rich man spoke and explained that passage to them as if it were elementary, and their eyes were opened to its true meaning. Even more, they were amazed at his wisdom, for they knew he could not even read the language, and yet what he said could only come from a master of the Torah. Then the sages demanded that the rich man explain how this transformation had taken place, and he revealed his dream about Shimon bar Yohai. And when the sages heard this dream, they understood that a miracle had occurred, and that the rich man had been possessed by the *ibbur* of Shimon bar Yohai.

After that the rich man found that all he had to do to call forth the soul of Rabbi Shimon was to open the book of the Zohar. And then he would be able to understand the mysteries of the Zohar as if they were elementary. And in the days that followed, the sages invited him to remain in Safed, and made him the head of the kabbalists of the city, for they knew that he spoke with the wisdom of Shimon bar Yohai.

Note that the possession by the spirit of Rabbi Shimon bar Yohai only takes place when the man opens the Zohar, the book so closely identified with Shimon bar Yohai. And the possession only lasts as long as the book is open. But during that time the spirit of Shimon bar Yohai fuses with his own. This tale was collected orally in the city of Safed in modern day Israel, demonstrating that even to this day the tradition about the ibbur is still recounted there.

Likewise, other *ibbur* tales portray this temporary kind of possession, such as the famous tale of "The *Tefillin* of the Or Hayim." Here Rabbi Hayim ben Attar, known as the Or Hayim after the title of his most famous book, told his wife on his deathbed that after he died a man would come from another city and seek to purchase his *tefillin* (phylacteries). The rabbi encouraged her to sell them for a high price, and to warn the man that he must never allow himself to become distracted when he wore them.

All took place as the Or Hayim had said, and when the man tried on the *tefillin* he was suddenly filled with a deep sense of holiness. And when he prayed, he did so with a fervor he had never known, and his prayers ascended on high. This lasted as long as he wore the *tefillin,* but when he took them off, the holy spirit departed.

One day, while he was wearing the *tefillin,* the man was distracted by one of his servants about a business matter. And when he returned to his prayers, the holy spirit was gone—for good. Finally he took the *tefillin* to a scribe, who opened the wooden box of the *tefillin* and found that the parchment inside it was blank, for the letters had flown, along with the soul of the Or Hayim.

As this tale makes abundantly clear, the presence of an *ibbur* was regarded as a great blessing, and unlike possession by a *dybbuk,* there was no attempt to exorcise the *ibbur.* How did the concept of the *ibbur* originate? It may have developed from a well-known tradition about the Sabbath which is found in the Talmud, dating back to the 5th century, in which every Jew is said to receive an extra soul (*Neshamah Yeterah*) on the Sabbath. This is a holy soul, that remains with a person throughout the Sabbath, and only departs after the performing of the ritual of Havdalah, which closes the Sabbath. Among the Hasidim, it was customary to delay this closing ceremony of the Sabbath for as long as possible, in order to hold on to this extra soul. This extra soul is closely linked with the figure of the *Shekhinah,* the Divine Presence, who is also identified as the Sabbath Queen, who is also said to be present during every Sabbath. It seems likely that the extra soul is the manifestation of the Sabbath Queen, as experienced in each person. This is also a kind of spirit possession, a precursor of the *ibbur.*

There is still another form of spirit possession found in Jewish lore which comes even closer to the concept of the *ibbur.* This refers to the strange case of Rabbi Joseph Karo, who lived in the city of Safed in the 16th century. Rabbi Karo was the author of the *Shulhan Aruch,* the Code of Jewish Law. Even to this day, this book is the ultimate reference for decisions about matters of ritual and law. Yet, remarkably enough for one with such a finely tuned legal mind, Joseph Karo was a mystic who wrote a book recounting his possession by a spirit when he studied the Mishnah, the core text of the Talmud. He identified this spirit as a *maggid,* a heavenly teacher. On several occasions others were present when this spirit of the Mishnah spoke through him. On such occasions Rabbi Karo seemed to go into a trance, and the spirit spoke in his place, in a voice of its own. The spirit remained as long as he continued to study the Mishnah, then departed. Rabbi Karo regarded this spirit as his heavenly guide, and recorded its pronouncements. Again, this kind of possession, while not that of the spirit of a human being, is very closely linked to the concept of the *ibbur.*

There are also *ibbur* tales told among the Hasidim of Eastern Europe. One of the most intriguing concerns a Hasidic rabbi, Zevi Hirsch of Zhiadchov, who was said to have been possessed by the *ibbur* of Rabbi Isaac Luria of Safed, one of the greatest mystical rabbis, who lived in the 16th century. How this took place is recounted in the tale of "The Soul of the Ari:"

One winter morning Reb Zevi rose very early, when it was still very dark outside. Although no candles in the house had been lit, still a light pervaded the rooms as if it were day. Curious to know the source of this light, Reb Zevi searched until he found that it was coming from a little cupboard. There he found a precious stone as large as an egg which glowed with a bright light from within. Reb Zevi realized that the value of that stone could not be calculated, and he hid it away.

Then he fasted from the end of one Sabbath until the beginning of the next so that heaven might inform him of what it was. And in a dream he was told that this stone had been a gift for him from heaven. If he chose to keep it, he and all of his descendants would be very wealthy. But if he chose not to keep it, then the soul of the holy Ari would become fused with his own.

Now Reb Zevi did not desire wealth, and the choice was not difficult for him to make. He asked in a dream question how he should return the precious stone, and he was told to fling it up toward heaven. This he did, and fiery sparks flew from it until nothing more could be seen.

Later one of Reb Zevi's students, who slept in the room next to his, heard a voice speaking to his master during the night. He knew that no one else was with Reb Zevi, so he rose and washed his hands and stood beside the wall and listened. The voice that spoke was interpreting a passage of the Zohar, casting great light on its mysteries. The student was filled with wonder, but he dared not ask the rabbi about it.

During the next Sabbath, Reb Zevi began to expound on a passage from the Zohar, and the student recognized the teachings of the mysterious voice he had heard. And when Reb Zevi finished, he said: "This is what I learned from the very mouth of the Ari." Then the student knew whose voice he had heard that night.

As this tale makes abundantly clear, possession by an *ibbur* of a great master, such as the Ari, was even considered more precious than great wealth, and was one of the ultimate blessings that heaven could bestow on a living sage. What this unusual kind of spirit possession provided was a greater knowledge of the mystical meaning of Torah. For only with the assistance of the spirit of a great sage could a living sage penetrate the hidden light of the Torah, which was concealed from everyone else.

Thus we find an unusual dual tradition of spirit possession in Judaism where possession by an evil spirit, a *dybbuk,* required exorcism, and, at the same time, possession by the spirit of a departed sage, an *ibbur,* was regarded as the greatest possible blessing.

Rabbi Susan Talve
Creating New Jewish Rituals

My first talk as a new rabbi in St. Louis presented a challenge to new parents: If you are planning to welcome your new sons into the Covenant with a big celebration, relatives from out of town, and lots of food, we must find a way to welcome your new daughters with equal enthusiasm. Traditionally, the *Brit Milah,* or ritual circumcision for newborn boys, is celebrated on the eighth day of life with the love and care that this miracle deserves. The usual way of welcoming newborn girls is at 30 days with a quiet naming at the synagogue with or without the presence of the child or the mother. After my talk, a soon-to-be mother took on the challenge. "Boy or girl, on the eighth day we will make a great celebration with relatives from out of town, and lots of food! But what ritual will replace the circumcision?" Not too long after a healthy girl was born. We gathered at the grandparents home and with great celebration welcomed this new Jewish soul destined to help bring the Messiah into the Covenant of our people with prayer, with blessings and with a ritual washing of her hands and feet, dedicating them to holy service.

I have repeated the "Brit *Rechitzah,*" the ritual washing, to welcome both baby girls and boys into the covenant for the past 13 years in St. Louis many, many times. We recall the way that Abraham welcomed the visitors into his tent with washing, we feel the connectedness to the well of Miriam that miraculously fed our physical and spiritual thirst in the wilderness and we celebrate the "*mayim chaim,*" the living waters of the *mikveh* that give new life and fill the life-giving womb. I always recall that first time when the grandmother of this beautiful child held her for a blessing and said, "I hope that this ritual means that you will be able to accomplish anything you want in your life and that you will not have to be twice as good or fight twice as hard because you are a woman." We were all touched deeply, knowing that her blessing came out of her experience and her desire to see that her granddaughter would benefit from the struggles of her life. Then her grandfather took her in his arms and gave her a blessing that changed the world a little that day. He said, "Shayna, I was going to tell you to stay home and be a good girl…but I guess it's too late. Be the best that you can be and I'll be there to help."

Many of the rituals I am called to help create appear to be new rituals, but rituals that work, those that heal and transform and guide us from one place to another, are never really new, even if we have never done them before. I know, for instance, that there must always have been women who, when they felt life move within them for the first time, did something to mark that remarkable moment in their lives with some kind of ritual as we do now. We do know that there was a time when fathers made feasts for their wives at the weaning of, at least, their sons because Genesis tells us that Abraham made a great feast at the time of Isaac's weaning.

Today, we understand that there must be ritual mourning for a miscarriage, an abortion or a child who dies too young to have been named. While the Bat Mitzvah celebration has encouraged young women to feel good about their Jewish selves, more private menstruation rituals that we have created help them to overcome the shame that is often attached to bleeding and teach them to value these precious bodies that may one day give life. Using the *mikveh* for festive celebrations of the changes in a woman's body, rather than the more quiet usual use has given birth to new-old rituals for the bride, for women with hysterectomies and women experiencing natural menopause.

Any ritual is an opportunity for transformation. To participate in a ritual you must be willing to be transformed in some way. That inner willingness is what makes the ritual come alive and have power. Like the "wise child" of the Passover Haggadah who knows that it is about her or him, if you understand that it is about you, you will benefit. If you aren't willing to be changed by the ritual, don't go through motions, for they will remain empty. If you are lucky, in spite of yourself, the energy of the ritual will drag you along and you may find yourself transformed or healed or with more peace or wisdom in your life. But usually, as the prophet Isaiah warns, empty rituals will not help and might even hurt.

Ritual affirms the value of any transition in our lives. When we celebrate the changes and challenges of our lives together as community, we create strong bonds of intimacy and trust that generate new culture.

When we undergo a change uncelebrated and unmarked, that transition is devalued and rendered invisible. Giving thirteen-year-old people a chance to experience humility, a struggle with the presence of God in their lives, and a great success at this critical moment is an example of the great wisdom of our ritual tradition. If we do it right, that one experience can serve as the roots and the wings that will get them through the most challenging years of their lives with a meaningful success to hold onto when they begin to lose themselves.

Jewish tradition is filled with these rituals. From the moment we receive Torah, we commit ourselves to lives of doing and then knowing. We light the Shabbat candles and then experience the transformation of ordinary to sacred time. We observe the ritual of the Passover seder and each one of us is transformed into the slave freed from Egypt, crossing the sea.

A while ago I led an unveiling for a child who died just before he was two. It was exactly one year after his death. We gathered at the cemetery, read psalms to remind us that others had passed through this valley and survived, cried together, said the words of the *kaddish* and placed small stones on the new gravestone to tell others that this child would never be forgotten. His parents told close family and friends that though the year was over, their mourning continued. I reminded them that it would never be over, but that our tradition teaches that this was a time to step onto the bridge of their own recovery. The year is marked because they had completed a year of firsts and though those dates would come again, it would not be exactly the same. Jewish ritual understands mourning. The 7 days, 30 days, 11 months or a year all mark the human experience of mourning and if we follow the prescription they work to heal the broken heart of loss. We stand up to the human instinct for denial and gently nudge the mourners to do the work we must do to heal, with *kaddish,* with *yahrzeit,* and with community.

Rituals work when they are associated with critical moments of life. Rituals of passage, like birth, the passing on of a name, puberty, marriage, death have possibilities of transformation built into them. Other rituals mark the passage of time and invite us to give them historical meaning; to anchor them like the Sabbath, the fall new year, the winter miracles of Hanukkah, the spring hopefulness of Pesach and the summer mourning of Tisha b'Av. Just as there can be no Pesach without first having Purim, there can be no new year without the summer mourning.

Still, other rituals are born from human experience plus human creativity and *chutzpah* like, the "*Shinui ha shem,*" the changing of a name of someone who is about to die to fool the angel of death. With these rituals we put ourselves in arms greater than our own and hope to tap into the energy flow of the universe. When we experience something greater than ourselves we are challenged to reach higher and to do our part to bring the world closer to *tikkun:* to the kind of repair that will bring peace. May it come soon.

Glossary

All of the following terms are in Hebrew unless otherwise noted.

Adonai the name of God that is used most often in prayer to substitute for the four-letter Name known as the Tetragrammaton.

Aggadah (pl. Aggadot) the body of Jewish legends; specifically, those found in the Talmud and Midrash.

Aher lit. "the Other." The name given to the talmudic sage Elisha ben **Abuyah** after he became an apostate.

Altekaker (Yiddish) a crotchety, fussy old man.

Amidah the prayers also known as *Shmoneh Esreh* or the Eighteen Benedictions, which are found in all daily, Sabbath and holiday services. This prayer is recited while standing.

Avinu Malkeinu a high holiday prayer.

Babushka (Russian) a head scarf.

Balebosteh (Yiddish) a "super" head of a household or housewife.

Baruch ha-Shem lit. "Bless the Name." A phrase of thanksgiving.

Bashert preordained, inevitable.

Bench lecht (Yiddish) to recite the blessing over Sabbath or holiday candles.

Beth Din a rabbinical court.

Bimah the podium from which prayers are offered.

Bracha lit. blessing.

Brit (bris) lit. covenant. The circumcision given to every male Jewish child on the eighth day after birth. The complete term is *brit milah,* or "covenant of the circumcision."

Bubbe (Yiddish) grandmother.

Bubbe meisa (Yiddish) an old wives' tale.

Challah bread baked for the Sabbath or holidays which is often braided.

Chaver (pl. chaverim) friend.

Chuppah Jewish wedding canopy.

Chutzpa (Yiddish) brazen nerve.

Conversos (Spanish) Jews who converted to Christianity under duress during the Inquisition.

Daven (Yiddish) to pray.

Dreck (Yiddish) trash or cheap or worthless things.

Dreidl a four-sided top used for a Hanukkah game.

D'var Torah lit. "word of Torah." A concise lesson in Torah, interpreting a portion of the Bible or other sacred text.

Dybbuk the soul of one who has died that enters the body of one who is living and remains until exorcised.

Elohim God.

Erev lit. "evening." The eve on which Jewish celebrations begin.

Etrog the citron, one of the four species of plants carried and symbolically shaken as part of the Sukkot celebration.

Gehenna the place where the souls of the wicked are punished and purified; the equivalent of hell in Jewish legend.

Geniza lit. "hidden, stored away." A storage place for sacred books and religious articles.

Get a bill of divorcement.

Gilgul someone with a reincarnated soul.

Goniff (Yiddish) thief.

Goy (pl. goyim) (Yiddish) a non-Jewish person.

Gribinas (Yiddish) crisp, fried pieces of poultry fat or skin after rendering.

Halakhah the code of Jewish religious law, which also includes ethical, civil and criminal matters.

Hanukkah festival celebrated for eight days to commemorate the successful struggle of the Jews led by Judah Maccabee and the rededication of the Holy Temple in Jerusalem.

Hasid (pl. Hasidim) lit. "a pious one." A follower of Hasidism, a Jewish sect founded by the Baal Shem Tov. Hasidim are usually associated with a religious leader, known as a "rebbe," as disciples.

Havdalah lit. "to distinguish" or "to separate." The ceremony performed at the end of the Sabbath, denoting the separation of the Sabbath from the rest of the week that follows.

Hazer (Yiddish) a person who behaves like a pig, a glutton.

Hazzan a cantor.

Hekhalot lit. "palaces." Refers to the visions of the Jewish mystics of the palaces of heaven.

Ibbur the spirit of a dead sage that fuses with a living person and strengthens his faith and wisdom. A positive kind of possession, the opposite of possession by a *dybbuk*.

Kaddish an ancient prayer, written in Aramaic, sanctifying the name of God, which is recited by mourners as a prayer for the dead.

Kashrut pertaining to kosher preparation and foods.

Kibitz (Yiddish) to joke or fool around.

Kippah (pl. kippot) skullcaps worn by religious Jews.

Klezmer (Yiddish) an informal group of musicians who play traditional and folk music.

Klutzy (Yiddish) clumsy.

Knish (Yiddish) a little dumpling with various fillings.

Kugel a traditional Jewish noodle pudding.

Lamed Vav Tzaddikim the thirty-six Just men who, according to legend, exist in every generation. By their merit, the world is sustained.

Landsleit (sing. landsman) (Yiddish) people who come from the same home town in Europe.

L'chaim lit. "to life." A traditional Jewish toast at joyous occasions.

Lilith Adam's first wife, according to Jewish legend, who went on to become the Queen of Demons.

Lulav a palm branch used in the Sukkot festival.

Maariv the evening prayer.

Maggid an itinerant storytelling rabbi.

Malach ha-Moves the Angel of Death.

Mensch (Yiddish) an upright, honorable and decent person.

Merkavah lit. "chariot."

Messhuge (Yiddish) crazy.

Mezuzzah lit. "doorpost." A small case containing a piece of parchment upon which is written a prayer. This oblong case is affixed to the right doorpost of a Jew's home in accordance with the biblical injunction.

Midrash a manner of analyzing biblical text through stories or homilies.

Mikveh the ritual bath.

Mincha the afternoon prayer.

Minyan the quorum of ten males over the age of thirteen that is required for any congregational service.

Mitzvah (pl. mitzvot) a divine commandment. There are 613 *mitzvot* listed in the Torah. The term has also come to mean a good deed.

Moyel (Yiddish) a ritual circumciser

Mumser (Yiddish) bastard.

Musaf additional service on Sabbath and festivals.

Nebbish (Yiddish) an inept person.

Neshamah a soul.

Nilah lit. "closing." The last of the five prayers recited on Yom Kippur.

Nosh (Yiddish) a snack.

Nu (Yiddish) so or well.

Olam Habah lit. "the world to come."

Parasha the weekly portion of the Torah that is read aloud during Sabbath (and festival) services.

Pardes lit. "orchard;" also a root term for Paradise.

Pargod lit. "curtain." In Jewish mysticism it refers to the curtain that is said to hang before the Throne of Glory in Paradise, which separates God from the angels.

Payess (Yiddish) earlocks.

Pesach the holiday of Passover.

Pidyon ha ben lit. "redemption of the son," a biblical ceremony of the redemption of the mother's firstborn son so he will not be required to devote his life to Temple service.

Rosh Hashanah the Jewish New Year.

Schmaltz (Yiddish) the renderings of an animal, such as chicken fat.

Schmatas (Yiddish) rags or old clothes.

Schnorrer (Yiddish) a person who begs or wheedles.

Schvartze (Yiddish) a black person.

Seder lit. "order," the ceremony, including the meal, that takes place in the home on the first two nights of Passover.

Shabbat the Sabbath.

Shacharit the morning prayer.

Shaitel a wig worn by married Orthodox Jewish women.

Shalom lit. "peace," a greeting, hello.

Shalom Aleichem a greeting, lit. "peace be unto you."

Shammas the caretaker of the synagogue.

Shekhinah lit. "to dwell." The Divine Presence, usually identified as a feminine aspect of the Divinity, which evolved into an independent mythic figure in the kabbalistic period.

Shema the central prayer of Judaism: *Shema Yisroel, Adonai Elohanu, Adonai Ehad*--Hear O Israel, the Lord our God, the Lord is One. It is based on Deuteronomy 6:4-9.

Shiur the time between the Mincha and Maariv services, often utilized as a study session.

Shiva the seven days of mourning following the burial.

Shlak (Yiddish) a cheaply made article.

Shloshim the thirty day mourning period for a close relative.

Shmachel (Yiddish) a smile.

Shmooz (Yiddish) chat or talk.

Shtetl (Yiddish) a small rural village inhabited almost exclusively by Jews.

Shuk a marketplace.

Shul (Yiddish) a synagogue.

Siddur a prayer book.

Sufganiot doughnuts eaten during Hanukkah.

Sukkot the festival commemorating the completion of the harvest.

Tallis (tallit) a prayer shawl.

Teffillin phylacteries worn by men over the age of thirteen during the morning prayers (except on the Sabbath).

Tekhelet a blue dye that Jews were enjoined to use to color a thread in the fringes of the *tallis* (Num. 15:37-38).

Teshuvah lit. "return," repentance.

Tikkun lit. "repair," restoration or redemption.

Tzaddik an unusually righteous and spiritually pure person.

Tzedakah charity or righteousness.

Tzitzit the fringes attached to the four corners of the *tallis*.

Tzuris (Yiddish) troubles or woes.

Vereins (German) a German social organization.

Yahrzeit (Yiddish) anniversary of the death of a close relative.

Yenne Velt (Yiddish) lit. "the Other World," the realm of angels, spirits and demons.

Yeshivah school for talmudic and rabbinic studies.

Yizkor memorial prayer for close relatives.

Yom HaShoah the day of Holocaust remembrance.

Yom Kippur the most solemn day of the Jewish religious year, the Day of Atonement.

Yonah dove.

Zunne (Yiddish) son.

Notes on the Contributors

Diann Joy Bank is a home-grown professional storyteller in Missouri. She has produced a young children's story tape, "Stories to Grow On."

Rabbi James M. Bennett is currently the rabbi at Temple Beth El in Charlotte, North Carolina. He previously served a rabbi at Congregation Shaare Emeth in St. Louis. He has published several articles in the field of Jewish education.

Gloria Shur Bilchik, a native of Cleveland, Ohio, is a St. Louis based feature writer, editor and business owner.

Rabbi Tsvi Blanchard is a former St. Louisan who is currently a member of the CLAL organization in New York. His stories have been published in the anthologies *Imperial Messages* and *Gates to the New City.*

Marc Bregman, originally of Clayton, is a professor of Midrash at Hebrew Union College in Jerusalem. Some of his stories have been published under the pseudonym of Moshe ben Yitzhak HaPardesan in the anthology *Gates to the New City.* He contributed the Introduction and Commentary to *The Four Who Entered Paradise* by Howard Schwartz.

Irving H. Breslauer served in the United States Air Force for 30 years from World War II through the Vietnam War. In addition to numerous American military decorations, he received awards from the Polish Home Army, the Republic of Vietnam and from Queen Juliana of the Netherlands. His work has been published in *Playboy, The Retired Officer Magazine,* NATO's *Fifteen Nations Magazine, Stars and Stripes,* the *St. Louis Post-Dispatch* and the *St. Louis Jewish Light.*

Louis Daniel Brodsky, a native St. Louisan, is the author of numerous volumes of poetry, the most recent entitled, *Paper Whites for Lady Jane.* He has also coedited eight scholarly books on Nobel laureate William Faulkner and authored a biography, *William Faulkner, Life Glimpses.*

Michael Castro is a professor at Lindenwood College. He is the author of several books of poems, including *Ghost Hiways & Other Homes, Cracks, The Kokopilau Cycle, US and of Interpreting the Indian: Twentieth Century Poets and the Native American*. A selection of his poems are included in *One Hundred Years of Sephardic-American Writings*, edited by Diana Matzah.

Amy Cohen, a freelance writer, earned a B.A. in English Literature from the University of Michigan.

Ira Cohen is a poet, photographer and performance artist. He has made several avant-garde films, including *Paradise Now,* a documentary on the Kumbh Mehla, India's periodic convention of holy men and women. His poems can be heard in a variety of musical settings on the *Sub Rosa* CD, *The Poetry of Ira Cohen,* and collected in several books, most recently in *On Feet of Gold*.

Rabbi Helen T. Cohn is a former St. Louisan who is currently the associate rabbi at Temple Emmanu-el in San Francisco. She holds degrees from Berkeley, Brandeis and Hebrew Union College, where she was ordained.

Robert A. Cohn is the Editor-in-Chief/Publisher of the *St. Louis Jewish Light*. He is president of the Press Club of Metropolitan St. Louis and of the International Jewish Media Association, which is a world-wide organization of Jewish publications and journalists. He is widely known for his lectures on Jewish cinema and has received national awards for his film reviews.

Lorraine Eason works as an editor and teacher. She is a teacher at Shaare Emeth religious school in St. Louis. She is slowly completing her Master's degree in English at Southern Illinois University at Edwardsville.

Walter Ehrlich is professor emeritus of history at the University of Missouri-St. Louis. He is the author of several books. His essay, "The Jewish Community of St. Louis: The First Hundred Years, 1807-1907," is reprinted from *Zion in the Valley: The Jewish Community of St. Louis, 1807-1907, Volume*

I by Walter Ehrlich, by permission of the Univeristy of Missouri Press, copyright 1997 by the Curators of the University of Missouri.

Janet B. Eigner both practices psychology and writes. She reviews dance for national and St. Louis magazines and public radio. Her poetry has been published in *Blue Mesa Review, Hawaii Review* and *The Reconstructionist*. She has written a book of poems about 20 years of backpacking in the Grand Canyon.

Larry Eigner was born in 1927 in Swampscott, Massachusetts and died in 1996. He had cerebral palsy as a result of a birth injury. Nevertheless he managed to sustain a poetry career for more than fifty years. He was included in Donald Allen's famous anthology *The New American Poetry* in 1960. His books include *From the Sustaining Air, On my Eyes, Another Time in Fragments, Select*ed *Poems* and *Things Stirring Together or Far Away.*

Stanley Elkin was the Merle Kling Professor of Modern Letters at Washington University. He won the 1983 National Book Critics Circle Award for fiction, and received fellowships and awards from the Guggenheim and Rockefeller foundations. He was the author of numerous books including *George Mills, The Rabbi of Lud, The Franchiser* and *Pieces of Soap.* He died in 1995. *"Criers and Kibitzers, Kibitzers and Criers"* is copyright (c) 1961 by Stanley Elkin. Reprinted by permission of Georges Borchardt, Inc. for the author. All rights reserved.

Ben Feldman is a native St. Louisan. He is a businessman and freelance writer whose work has been published in the *Poet's Choice.*

Donald Finkel was Poet-in-Residence at Washington University for many years until his recent retirement. He has published a dozen books of poems, including the recent *Selected Shorter Poems.* He has been the recipient of a Guggenheim Fellowship and a grant from the National Endowment for the Arts. In 1974 he received the Theodore Roethke Memorial Award for his book-length poem, *Adequate Earth.* In 1980 he received the Morton Dauwent Zabel Award from the Academy and Institute of Arts and Letters for *Endurance and Going Under.*

Rabbi Miriam Tirzah Firestone, a former St. Louisan, is a psychotherapist and rabbi in Boulder, Colorado. She is currently completeing her autobiography to be published by Victory Press.

Shelly R. Fredman has worked as an editor at the *St. Louis Jewish Light* and has studied creative writing at Washington University. The story "Love Like Coriander" is based on the incident reported in "Between Two Worlds," in the Life Stories section of this anthology.

Rachel Friedlander was born, raised and educated in and around St. Louis. She currently works for a nonprofit organization in Philadelphia, Pennsylvania. She still introduces herself to people as a native Midwesterner.

Robert Friedman has written over 200 book reviews for the *St. Louis Post Dispatch.* He has conducted seminars and lectured on the principles of play writing and served as president of the Missouri Association of Playwrights from 1982-87. He is currently completing a handbook for playwrights.

Allison Funk is a professor of English at Southern Illinois University at Edwardsville. She is the author of two books of poems, *Living at the Epicenter* and *Forms of Conversion.*

Diane Garden grew up in St. Louis and is currently living in Mobile, Alabama where she teaches in a gifted program. Her work has appeared in *Jewish Spectator, Present Africaine, MidAmerica* and other magazines.

Pinhas Giller is a professor of Jewish Studies at Washington University, where he specializes in kabbalistic studies. His book on the *Zohar, The Enlightened Will Shine,* was recently published. He is presently completing a book on reading the Zohar.

Gloria Rudman Goldblatt is a freelance writer and collector of family history and folklore. She has published articles on art and antiques. She is currently working on a biography of Ada Clare, a nineteenth century writer, actress and feminist.

Naama Goldstein spent her childhood in Israel. She graduated from Washington University in St. Louis and is currently in a Master of Fine Arts program at Emerson College in Boston, Massachusetts. "The Follower" is her first published piece.

Rabbi James Stone Goodman is rabbi of Congregation Neve Shalom. He is also director of SLICHA, The St. Louis Information Committee and Hotline on Addiction. He is a musician, founding and leading two ensembles: Zambra Mediterranean Jam and Zig-a-Zuck Klezmer Orchestra.

Felicia Graber is a retired teacher of French and German language. Her Holocaust memoirs were published in *Too Young to Remember* by Julie Heifetz. She has lived in St. Louis since 1972.

Julie Heifetz–Klueh is a writer and therapist. She is the author of three books, *Jordie's Present, Oral History and the Holocaust* and *Too Young to Remember;* three plays, *Just Talk to Me, Sarah's Songs,* and *Home Signs;* and the libretto for an oratorio, *Song of Sparrows.* Her poems have been published in many journals including *Agada* and *Lilith.* The memoir "The Blue Parakeet" is based on a recorded account from a Holocaust survivor.

Gene Holtzman, currently a businessman, has taught literature and has published several short stories and essays on contemporary fiction.

Betty Harris Ibur is the author of six children including the author Jane Ellen Ibur. Her work appears in numerous grandchildren.

Jane Ellen Ibur teaches creative writing throughout the St. Louis area, including a course at the Adult Correctional Facility in St. Louis County to juvenile males for which she received a World of Difference Award from the Anti-Defamation League in 1993. Her work has appeared in many literary journals and anthologies. She is the co-host of a literary talk show, "Literature for the Halibut," on KDHX.

Rabbi Robert P. Jacobs is the Executive Vice President of the St. Louis Rabbinical Association and was the founder and director of the B'nai B'rith

Hillel at Washington University for 30 years. He edited *Religions in St. Louis* for the Interfaith Clergy Council.

Malka Z. Kornblatt, a former St. Louisan, is currently the director of The House of Learning in Boca Raton, Florida.

Staci D. Kramer is a graduate of Washington University and also studied at Hebrew University. She currently lives in University City, Missouri and is a journalist who writes for numerous national and regional publications.

Rachel Kubie was born in St. Louis in 1968. She has edited literary magazines and published in small journals and in the anthology *Imperial Messages: One Hundred Modern Parables.* She has recently completed an MFA in Creative Writing from Johns Hopkins University.

Cissy Lacks is a well-known teacher and photographer living in St. Louis. She has a Ph.D. in American Studies and a master's degree in Broadcast and Film. She is presently working on a film about Rabbi Susan Talve.

Lynn E. Levin is a former St. Louisan who now lives in Bucks County, Pennsylvania. Her poes have appeared in Jewish and literary journals including *The New Laurel Review, Potato Eyes, Midstream* and *Jewish Spectator.* "The Bath" originally appeared in the Spring, 1993 issue of *The Reconstructionist.*

Rabbi Bernard Lipnick served as rabbi of B'nai Amoona Congregation for 40 years and is presently rabbi emeritus. He is currently living in Idyllwild, California.

Irving Litvag is a lifelong St. Louisan whose published writings include two non-fiction books, *Singer in the Shadows* and *The Master of Sunnybank,* as well as magazine and newspaper articles, plays and radio dramas.

Susan Litwack was born in St. Louis and presently lives in New York City, where she teaches. Her first book of poems, *Inscape,* was published in 1976. She has published poems in many journals, including *Tikkun, Zone and Southern Poetry Review.* Her poems also appear in the anthology *Voices Within the Ark.*

Edward M. Londe writes stories on Jewish themes, many of them based on his dreams. He has previously published fiction in the *St. Louis Jewish Light*.

Rabbi Maurice Lyons is the author of *Encyclopedia of Biblical Humor* and *A Brief Primer of the Yiddish Language*.

Rabbi Zvi Magence studied in the great yeshivahs of Europe and was a student of Rav Kook in Israel. He was a great talmudic scholar and the author of numerous books and articles both in the theoretical as well as the applied areas of Halakah, Jewish law. His great passion was the Land of Israel, and he wrote his magnum opus entitled, *Magen Zvi, the Shied of Zvi,* which was dedicated to the law of the Land of Israel. He was a congregational rabbi for many years at Beth Midrash Hagadol.

Jerred Metz is a former St. Louisan who lives in Pittsburgh. He is the author of three books of poetry, *Speak Like Rain, The Temperate Voluptuary,* and *Angels in the House.* He has also edited *Drinking the Dipper Dry* and a book about Halley's Comet.

Bert Minkin was a professional storyteller and free-lance writer. He had a master's degree in rhetoric from the University of California at Berkely and taught storytelling and creative writing at the Conservatory and School for the Arts in University City. He was a frequent contributor to *The Sagarin Review.* He died at the age of 45 in 1996.

Marcia Moskowitz, a native New Yorker, has been a resident of St. Louis for 17 years. She teaches English at Parkway West High School.

Howard Nemerov was a prize winning poet who taught at Washington University. His *Collected Poems,* published in 1977, won the National Book Award and Pulitzer Prize in 1978. He also served two terms as Poet Laureate of the United States. He died in 1991.

Sherry K. Park was educated at Lindenwood College, the University of Chicago and the University of Missouri-St. Louis. She lives with her two daughters in Webster Groves, Missouri.

Vicki E. Pickle is currently working as a freelance writer, a substitute teacher and for Temple Shaare Emeth in a writing/publicity position. She also does volunteer work with young people in many subject areas, including creative writing.

Seymour V. Pollack was born in raised in Brooklyn in a neighborhood were signs in the local post office were printed in English as well as Yiddish. In 1966 he joined the faculty of Washington University as assistant professor of computer science. He became an associate professor in 1968, professor in 1977 and professor emeritus in 1995. He has authored or co-authored eighteen textbooks.

Rachel Popelka is a senior at Horton Watkins High School in Ladue. She plans to attend Washington University in the fall of 1995. Some of her poetry has won local competitions sponsored by the St. Louis Art Museum, the St. Louis Poetry Center and the Wednesday Club.

Miriam Raskin, who writes poems, fiction and essays, is the administrator of Central Reform Congregation in St. Louis.

Barbara Raznick is a storyteller and the director of the Saul Brodsky Jewish Community Library in St. Louis.

Dana Robbins Regenbogen writes poetry and has worked as a Special Education teacher.

Lilia Rissman is a student at Clayton High School in St. Louis.

Michele Klevens Ritterman is a native St. Louisan. She is currently a clinical psychologist in private practice in Oakland, CA. She is the author of two books: Using Hypnosis in Family Therapy and Hope Under Siege.

Daphna Rodin has lived in St. Louis most of her life. She is a librarian by profession, and has served as Director of the Poetry Center in St. Louis. Her poems have been published in numerous journals.

Bronia Rosen was born in Lodz, Poland. She came to the United States in 1956 and settled in St. Louis. She is a prolific author of poetry and short stories.

Lisa Rosen, a graduate of University City High School, attended California State University, Long Beach where she earned an M.A. in Criminal Justice. She currently lives in Seal Beach, California. She has been published in various small poetry magazines.

Marylou Ruhe is a Holocaust survivor who spent her youth in the Lodz ghetto, Auschwitz, Bergen-Belsen, the Salzwedel munitions factory. After four years in a displaced persons camp, she arrived in St. Louis in 1949. Some of her work has been published in the *St. Louis Post Dispatch* and the *St. Louis Jewish Light.*

Karen Beth Sachs is a student at Ladue Horton Watkins High School. She attended the Alexander Muss High School in Israel, and has published her writing in the *St. Louis Jewish Light* and *Crescendo.*

Rabbi James L. Sagarin is the rabbi at Temple Menorah in Chicago. He was previously the Director of Continuing Education at the Central Agency for Jewish Education in St. Louis and a professor at Washington University. He has published two books, *Hebrew Noun Patterns* and *Oseh Shalom,* and has had articles in numerous journals including Hebrew Studies, *Chicago Jewish Star* and *Chicago News-Star.*

Marc Saperstein served for eleven years as Gloria M. Goldstein Professor of Jewish History and Thought at Washington University. He is currently Charles E. Smith Professor of History at George Washing University. His books include *Decoding the Rabbis, Jewish Preaching 1200-1800: An Anthology* and *Your Voice Like a Ram's Horn: Themes and Texts in Traditional Jewish Preaching.* He has twice received the National Jewish Book Award.

Jane Schapiro was born in St. Louis and currently lives in Annandale, Virginia. She has taught physical education and adult creative writing workshops.

Hal Schmerer, originally from Miami, has lived in St. Louis for over twelve years. He devloped a strong interest in Jewish learning and writing the the Florence Melton Adult Mini-School program.

Beverly Schneider, a graduate of University City High School, is a psychoanalyst and writer living in New York City.

Andrew Schreiber is a student at Clayton High School and is an editor for the yearbook. His poem was written for a class assignment to write about someone who made a difference in his life. The subject of his piece, Esther Klevens, was his Hebrew tutor.

Steven Schreiner is a professor of English at the University of Missouri-St. Louis. He has published poems in many journals, including Missouri Review, Denver Quarterly and Prairie Schooner. He is the author of two books of poems, Imposing Presence and Too Soon To Leave.

Joan Schultz, a native St. Louisan, is a writer, poet, artist, photographer and musician. She shares her enthusiasm for her art through lectures, seminars and private piano lessons.

Henry Schvey is the chairman of the Performing Arts Department at Washington University. He directed a highly praised production of S. Ansky's drama *The Dybbuk* in 1996. He is currently writing a novel about the joys and perils of trying to grow up in New York City in the 1950's and 1960's.

Charles Schwartz is a native St. Louisan who currently lives in New York City and works for New York University. He has studied creative writing at the University of Oregon and has published his stories in various journals and in the anthology *Imperial Messages: One Hundred Modern Parables.*

Howard Schwartz is a professor of English at the University of Missouri-St. Louis. He has edited three anthologies, *Imperial Messages, Gates to the New City* and *Voices Within the Ark,* as well as four collections of Jewish folktales, *Elijah's Violin, Miriam's Tambourine, Lilith's Cave* and *Gabriel's Palace.* He has also published three books of poems, *Vessels, Gathering the Sparks,* and *Sleepwalking Beneath the Stars,* and several books of fiction, including *The Captive Soul of the Messiah, Adam's Soul* and *The Four Who Entered Paradise.* His book *Next Year in Jerusalem: 3000 Years of Jewish Stories* won the National Jewish Book Award and the Aesop Prize of the American Folklore Society in 1996.

Maury L. Schwartz worked as a Director of Education for many years in congregations in Omaha, Kansas City and Miami Beach. He presently works as a psychotherapist in Chicago.

Shira Schwartz is a senior at Ladue Horton Watkins High School. She attended high school in Israel in the spring of 1996. She plans to attend Oberlin College in the fall of 1997. Her poems have appeared in *The St. Louis Jewish Light* and *Crescendo.*

Tsila Schwartz is a native of Jerusalem who now makes her home in St. Louis. She is a Jewish folk artist who specializes in Ketubot (Jewish wedding contracts) and other Jewish texts. She has also illustrated the book *Rooms of the Soul,* and her calligraphy appears in the book *Elijah's Violin.*

Laya Firestone Seghi is a native St. Louisan who now lives in Miami Beach and works as a psychotherapist. She has served as Poetry Editor of The Reconstructionist and her poems and stories have been published in many magazines and in the anthologies Voices Within the Ark and Gates to the New City. She has also translated the poems of the Hebrew poets Sholomo Vinner and Gabriel Preil.

Barbara Langsam Shuman is a writer, public relations practitioner and a columnist with the *Ladue News.* She was formerly an associate editor with the *St. Louis Jewish Light.* She is currently writing children's books.

Jean Simon is the author of a collection of poems, *Pretending to Be Back,* and her poems have been published in *Break Word with the World.* She is currently living in Israel.

Pamela Singer has lived in St. Louis for eleven years. She studied fiction writing at the University of Iowa International Writers' Workshop and poetry writing at Trinity College in Wales. Her poem, The Real Revenge of Lilith, published in the first edition of *The Sagarin Review* is being included in an anthology of Lilith poetry and fiction.

Jason Sommer is a professor at Fontbonne College, where he teaches poetry writing. He has published his poems in many journals, including *The New Republic, Ploughshares* and *Chicago Review.* His books of poems include *Lifting the Stone* and *Other People's Troubles,* published by University of Chicago Press.

Rabbi Lane Steinger is the head of the midwest UAHC office in St. Louis. He was the senior rabbi at Temple Emmanuel in Detroit for 25 years.

Judith Saul Stix has published poetry, essays and biography. Her book, *Bessie Lowenhaupt from Life: a Very Personal Portrait* appeared in 1995. In addition to poetry, she has published biographical and genealogical articles. Her work has appeared in *The Webster Review* and *Avotaynu*.

Daniel Suffian works in the computer field in St. Louis. This is his first published work.

Phil Sultz taught in the Art Department at Webster University in St. Louis for many years. He is an accomplished painter and writer. He currently lives in Dennysville, Maine.

Wendy Surinsky is a native St. Louisan who is currently studying film-making at Temple University in Philadelphia. She has previously made two short feature films, one of which won third prize in a national film contest.

Rabbi Susan Talve is the rabbi of Central Reform Congregation. Her work has been published in *The Tribe of Dina*.

Michah Turner was born and raised in Utah before moving to St. Louis eighteen years ago. He works in the insurance industry.

Constance Urdang was born in New York City. A graduate of Smith College (cum laude) and athe University of Iowa Writers' Workshop, she moved to St. Louis in 1960 with her husband, poet Donald Finkel. Urdang's nine volumes of poetry and fiction won her, among other honors, the Carleton Centennial Award for Prose, a National Endowment for the Arts fellowshiip, the Delmore Schwartz Memorial Poetry Award and the Oscar Williams and Gene Derwood Award. She died in 1996.

Shlomo Vinner is a native of Jerusalem who teaches mathematics and science education at the Hebrew University. He speant a year teaching at the University of Missouri-St. Louis in 1975-76. He has received the ACUM Prize and the award of the Jerusalem Foundation for Literature for his poetry. Two of his books of poetry, *For a Few Hours Only* and *Jerusalem As She Is,* have been translated into English.

Morrie Warshawski is a writer and consultant who is a regular contributor to the *St. Louis Jewish Light.* He has also published articles in many journals including the *Los Angeles Times Syndicate, Philadelphia Inquirer* and *St. Louis Post Dispatch.*

Jane O. Wayne's first book of poems, Looking Both Ways, won the Devins Award for poetry in 1985. Her work has appeared in many journals, including *American Scholar, Poetry and Ploughshares.* She recently published *A Strange Heart,* a book of poems.